# COMMENTARY
## 2024–2025
### VOLUME 117

The lessons in this commentary are based on the International Uniform Sunday School Lesson Outlines, copyright ©2023, Division of Christian Education, the National Council of the Churches of Christ in the U.S.A., and is used with permission.

Entered according to Act of Congress in the Office of Librarian of Congress in the year 1903 at Washington, DC, by R. H. Boyd, D.D., LL.D.

R. H. Boyd, D.D., LL.D., Founder (1896–1922)

H. A. Boyd, D.D. (1922–1959) • T. B. Boyd Jr., D.D. (1959–1979) • T. B. Boyd III, D.D. (1979–2017)

LaDonna Boyd, EdD
President/CEO (2017–Present)

**LaDonna Boyd, EdD**
*President/CEO*

**EDITORIAL STAFF**
Rev. Olivia M. Cloud, M.R.E.
*Associate Editor*

Monique Gooch, B.A.; Brittany Batson, B.A.; Carla Davis, B.A.

**Rev. Nicole Tolliver • Dr. Angela Davis**
**Dr. Barry Johnson • Dr. Nika Davis**
*Writers*

**Jasmine Cole**
*Cover Design*

For Customer Service
and Toll–Free Ordering, Call
1–877–4RHBOYD (474–2693)
Monday–Friday
8 a.m.–5 p.m. Central Time or
Fax Toll–Free (800) 615–1815.

www.rhboyd.com

6717 Centennial Blvd.• Nashville, Tennessee 37209–1017

## A WORD FROM THE PUBLISHER

To Our Readers,

Welcome to the 2024–2025 edition of *Boyd's Commentary for the Sunday School*.

We humbly present for your consideration the latest edition of *Boyd's Commentary for the Sunday School*, our most scholarly and in-depth resource for use by pastors, deacons, Sunday school teachers, and laypersons. The 2024–2025 edition is packed with cogent, penetrating Scriptural exposition and theological analysis. Christian educators—whether in the pulpit or the classroom—who endeavor to explain the Word to their students will find *Boyd's Commentary* an invaluable resource. Laypersons who simply want to develop a closer relationship with God are sure to gain great insights as well.

R.H. Boyd is committed to engaging highly qualified scholars to develop the material you are about to study. Not only do our writers possess the appropriate academic credentials, but they also are men and women who bring essential and practical ministry experience to their expository writings. In conjunction with them, our highly skilled and conscientious editorial staff has worked to ensure the reliability and readability of every lesson. Truly, this is a labor of love for our entire staff—from developmental stage to printing to shipping to your door.

We pray God's blessings upon each of you in your faith journey.

Onward,

*[signature]*

LaDonna Boyd, EdD
Fifth–generation President/CEO

## A WORD FROM THE ASSO. EDITOR

Greetings!

It is with great pleasure that we release the 2024–2025 edition of *Boyd's Commentary for the Sunday School*. Now in its 117th year, *Boyd's Commentary* has an enduring reputation for providing sound biblical commentary that reveals the truth of God's Word and enhances the value of that Word in addressing the contemporary and timeless issues of human existence. Each lesson in this commentary seeks to strike a balance between delving into the biblical text while emphasizing practical applications to apply these teachings of Scripture to everyday life. Throughout this commentary, the writers and editors give attention to the myriad ways the Bible informs the social and ethical challenges that characterize the complex national and international environment in which we live.

Designed with the needs of busy pastors, church leaders, Sunday school teachers, and lay Bible students in mind, *Boyd's Commentary* allows readers to probe beyond a surface reading of the biblical text to venture into the many wonders of exegetical and theological insight. This commentary is an holistic resource for both sermon and class preparation. It is our hope, that this year's commentary will do much good for you and for the Kingdom of God.

May your ministry be blessed by the Lord as you seek His face and lead others in that quest.

Yours in Christ,

*[signature]*

Rev. Olivia M. Cloud, MRE
Associate Editor, R.H. Boyd

# NOTES FROM THE EDITOR

The layout of the *2024–2025 Boyd's Commentary* has been formatted for easy use in the classroom. In keeping with our rich history of publishing quality Christian literature, we include the Unifying Principle as a feature to enhance your study while using our commentary. Listed below is an explanation of each feature and the intended use of each.

**Lesson Setting:** Gives the basic time line and place for the events in the lesson.

**Lesson Outline:** Provides the topics used in the exposition of the lesson.

**Unifying Principle:** States the main idea for the lesson across age groups. This feature allows the teacher to understand exactly what each lesson is about.

**Introduction:** Gives the thesis and any background information that will be useful in the study of the lesson.

**Exposition:** Provides the exegetical study done by the writer, breaking down the text for discussion.

**The Lesson Applied:** Provides possible life applications of the biblical text for today's learners.

**Let's Talk About It:** Highlights ideas from the text in a question–and–answer format.

**Home Daily Devotional Readings:** Located at the end of each lesson, the topics are designed to lead into the following lesson.

# KNOW YOUR WRITERS

## Rev. Nicole Tolliver

Nikki Harris Tolliver is a native of Cleveland, Ohio currently residing in Nashville. A graduate of Fisk University, she earned her Master of Theological Studies degree with emphasis in Black Church Studies from Vanderbilt University Divinity School. She has previously served in full time ministry as a youth pastor and later as pastor of assimilation. Currently, Nikki works as an Operations Associate for Faith Matters Network and serves as director of student success at American Baptist College in Nashville and an associate minister at the historic Jefferson Street Baptist Church.

## Dr. Angela Miller

Dr. Angela Miller earned her Doctor of Education degree in Educational Leadership. Throughout her career in higher education, Dr. Miller has served in various leadership positions at public and private universities. She is also the founder of Purpose Ministries, providing sound biblical teaching and mentorship to help others grow in their personal relationship with Christ.

## Dr. Barry Johnson

Dr. Barry C. Johnson, Sr. resides in Louisville, Kentucky. He earned the Bachelor of Music Composition and the Master of Music Composition degrees from the University of Louisville, and a Doctor of Musical Arts degree from the University of Kentucky. In addition, Dr. Johnson earned Master of Divinity and Doctor of Ministry degrees from The Southern Baptist Theological Seminary in Louisville. Dr. Johnson serves as a tenured associate professor of music composition and theory in the Division of Fine Arts at Kentucky State University in Frankfort. In addition, Dr. Johnson serves as pastor of Evergreen Baptist Church in Lawrenceburg.

## Dr. Nika Davis

Dr. Nika Davis is pastor of the Second Missionary Baptist church in Waco, Texas where the church has implemented numerous ministries that serve the community. He holds a Doctor of Ministry degree from Houston Graduate School of Theology, a Master of Divinity degree from Southwestern Theological Seminary, Ft. Worth, Texas, and a Master of Arts degree in history. For 12 years Dr. Davis was a public school educator and during that time received the honor of Teacher of the Year at Lufkin High School. He is author of The Beauty of the Christian Faith. He and his wife Beverly are parents to three children.

# 2024–2025 LESSON OVERVIEW
## *Worship: Altars, Songs, and Sacrifices*

The lessons of the fall, spring, and summer quarters offer an intertestamental study of both personal and communal elements that characterize faithful worship. Over the course of God's salvation history we see shifts and changes in how God invites people to worship, from altars and sacrifices to songs and prayers. Nevertheless, from Genesis to Revelation what remains constant is our focus on one Lord and God whom alone we worship and serve and in whom alone we put our trust. The lessons consider biblical practices of self-offering as indicative of the character of true worship and sacrifice in every age.

**Fall:** *Worship in the Covenant Community*—These lessons are a study of worship practices offered as a grateful response to the covenantal relationship God initiates, first with Abraham, and later with the people of Israel. The patterns of worship reflect the gamut of community life, from praising God's goodness and mercy to calling on God for help in times of crisis.

**Spring:** *Costly Sacrifice*— The theme of worship, sacrifices, and offerings runs through the Scriptures. Understanding the Old Covenant sacrifices and offerings is essential to understanding the New Testament's view of Christ's sacrifice.

**Summer:** *Sacred Altars and Holy Gifts*— The lessons of this quarter are a study of worship practices offered as a grateful response to the covenantal relationship God initiates, first with Abraham, and later with the people of Israel. The patterns of worship reflect the gamut of community life, from praising God's goodness and mercy to calling on God for help in times of crisis.

**Winter:** *God's Kingdom Come.* The winter quarter turns the learners' gaze from worship as a human response to God toward a focus on the One who is worshiped. *A King Forever and Ever* explores the broad sweep of biblical teaching about God's reign as it relates to Jesus as the earthly exhibition of the divine Kingdom. This quarter explores the broad sweep of biblical teaching about God's reign and connects to Jesus as the earthly exhibition of the divine Kingdom.

• • • • • • • • • • • • • • • • • • • • • • • • •

## Boyd's Commentary for the Sunday School (2024–2025)

Copyright © 2024 by R.H. Boyd
6717 Centennial Blvd., Nashville, TN 37209–1017

KJV, the (KJV) *The KJV* is in the public domain.

Scriptures taken from the Holy Bible, *New International Version*. Copyright © 1984 by International Bible Society. Used by permission of Zondervan Publishing House. All rights reserved worldwide. The NIV and *New International Version* trademarks are registered in the United States Patent and Trademark Office by International Bible Society. Use of either trademark requires the permission of the International Bible Society.

Scriptures taken from the *NRSVue* of the Bible © 1989 by the Division of Christian Education of the National Council of Churches of Christ in the United States of America. Used by permission. All rights reserved.

Scripture quotations are from The *Holy Bible, English Standard Version*® (ESV®), copyright © 2001 by Crossway, a publishing ministry of Good News Publishers. Used by permission. All rights reserved.

All rights reserved. This book may not be reproduced in part or in whole in any form or by any means without prior written permission from the publisher.

*Printed in the United States of America.*

The publisher, R.H. Boyd Publishing Corporation, bears no responsibility or liability for any claim, demand, action, or proceeding related to its content, including but not limited to claims of plagiarism, copyright infringement, defamation, obscenity, or the violation of the rights of privacy, publicity, or any other right of any person or party, and makes no warranties regarding the content.

# PREFACE

The *2024–2025 Boyd's Commentary* has been formatted and written with you in mind. This format is to help you further your preparation and study of Sunday school lessons over the next 12 months.

We have presented parallel Scripture lesson passages using the *New Revised Standard Version Updated Edition* alongside the timeless and revered *King James Version*. This allows you to have a clear and contemporary approach to the Scripture passages each week. These versions are reliable and reputable. They will bless you as you rightly divide the word of truth (2 Tim. 2:15, KJV).

The abbreviations used throughout the commentary are as follows:

    KJV — King James Version
    NIV — New International Version
    NKJV — New King James Version
    NLT — New Living Translation
    NRSVue — New Revised Standard Version Updated Edition
    RSV — Revised Standard Version
    TLB — The Living Bible
    NEB — New English Bible
    JB — Jerusalem Bible
    ESV — English Standard Version

**To the Pastor:** Our hope is that this commentary will provide context and insight for your sermons. Also, we hope this commentary will serve as a preparatory aid for the message of God.

**To the Bible Teacher:** This commentary also has you in mind. You can use it as a ready reference to the background of the text and difficult terms that are used in the Bible. To be sure, this commentary will provide your lesson study with the historical context that will enable you to interpret the text for your students more effectively.

**To the Layperson:** This resource is for anyone who wants to get a glimpse at the glory of God. This commentary seeks to highlight and lift the workings of God with His people and to make God's history with humanity ever present.

We hope and pray God will bless and keep you as you diligently study His mighty and majestic Word. Remain ever steadfast to our one eternal God. Keep the faith, and pray always.

# CONTENTS

## 1ST QUARTER

### UNIT THEME: LEADERS SET WORSHIP EXAMPLE

LESSON 1    SEPTEMBER 1—**Abram Builds an Altar at Mamre**
Topic: Marking Transitions (Genesis 13:8–18).............................. 12

LESSON 2    SEPTEMBER 8—**Solomon Dedicates the Temple**
Topic: Our House Is a Very Fine House
(1 Kings 8:22–24, 37–39, 46, 48–50) ...................... 18

LESSON 3    SEPTEMBER 15—**Hezekiah's Prayer**
Topic: Is It Inevitable? (2 Kings 19:14–20, 29–31) ....................... 24

LESSON 4    SEPTEMBER 22—**Josiah Celebrates Passover**
Topic: Claiming the Treasures of the Past
(2 Chronicles 35:1–6, 16–19)........................................30

LESSON 5    SEPTEMBER 29—**Moses and Miriam Lead the People in Praise**
Topic: Time to Party! (Exodus 15:1–3, 11–13, 17–18, 20–21) ....... 36

### UNIT THEME: SONGS OF THE OLD TESTAMENT

LESSON 6    OCTOBER 6—**Prayers of Repentance and Confession**
Topic: Regret and Remorse (Psalm 51:1–4,10–12, 15–17)............ 42

LESSON 7    OCTOBER 13—**A Plea for Deliverance**
Topic: We're in a Tight Spot (Psalm 22:1–11) ............................... 47

LESSON 8    OCTOBER 20—**Praise for Deliverance**
Topic: Dinner Time! (Isaiah 25:1–10)............................................ 52

LESSON 9    OCTOBER 27—**Trust in God Alone**
Topic: Let the Silence Speak (Psalm 62:1–12) ............................. 58

### UNIT THEME: PSALMS OF THANKSGIVING AND PRAISE

LESSON 10    NOVEMBER 3—**Confidence in God's Shepherding**
Topic: When the Road Is Long (Psalm 23) .................................. 64

LESSON 11    NOVEMBER 10—**Songs of Praise**
Topic: Who Can You Trust? (Psalms 146; 150)............................ 70

LESSON 12    NOVEMBER 17—**A Song of Thanksgiving**
Topic: A Gratitude Attitude (Psalm 100)...................................... 76

LESSON 13    NOVEMBER 24—**God's Promised Presence**
Topic: Wonderful, Marvelous! (Psalm 139:1–12).......................... 82

# CONTENTS

## 2ND QUARTER

### UNIT THEME: JESUS, THE HEIR OF DAVID

**LESSON 1** DECEMBER 1—**The Ancestry of King David**
Topic: A Noble Family Tree (Ruth 4:9–17; Luke 3:23, 31–32)....... 89

**LESSON 2** DECEMBER 8—**God's Promise to David**
Topic: A Very Fine House (2 Samuel 7:4–17) ................. 95

**LESSON 3** DECEMBER 15—**The Prophet Who Prepares the Way**
Topic: Get Ready! (Luke 1:67–80) ................................ 101

**LESSON 4** DECEMBER 22—**Born in the City of David**
Topic: Breaking News! (Luke 2:1–16) ........................... 107

**LESSON 5** DECEMBER 29—**The Merciful Son of David**
Topic: A Miracle in Jericho (Luke 18:35–43) ................. 113

### UNIT THEME: OUR GOD REIGNS

**LESSON 6** JANUARY 5—**The Lord Is King**
Topic: In Times of Trouble (Psalm 10:12–18) ................ 119

**LESSON 7** JANUARY 12—**The Lord Is Robed in Majesty**
Topic: The Majesty of a King's Reign (Psalm 93) ........... 125

**LESSON 8** JANUARY 19—**The Lord's Throne Is Established**
Topic: Don't Forget! (Psalm 103:1–14) ......................... 130

**LESSON 9** JANUARY 26—**My God, the King**
Topic: Doesn't Anything Last Anymore? (Psalm 145:1, 10–21) 136

### UNIT THEME: LIFE IN GOD'S KINGDOM

**LESSON 10** FEBRUARY 2—**Praying for Relief**
Topic: Too Much Debt (Matthew 6:5–15) ..................... 142

**LESSON 11** FEBRUARY 9—**Resistance to the Kingdom**
Topic: Stand Up (Matthew 11:7–15, 20–24) .................. 148

**LESSON 12** FEBRUARY 16—**The First Will Be Last**
Topic: What More Do I Have to Do? (Matthew 19:16–30) ........ 154

**LESSON 13** FEBRUARY 23—**Kingdom Life**
Topic: Don't Be a Goat (Matthew 25:31–46) .................. 160

# CONTENTS

## 3RD QUARTER

### UNIT THEME: TABERNACLE, SACRIFICES, AND ATONEMENT

**LESSON 1** MARCH 2—**A Kingdom of Priests, a Holy Nation**
Topic: Bound by Love (Exodus 19:1–14) .................................... 167

**LESSON 2** MARCH 9—**Pitching a Tent**
Topic: A Space for God (Exodus 25:1–9; 26:1, 31–37) ................ 173

**LESSON 3** MARCH 16—**The Ordination of Priests**
Topic: Preparation for Service (Exodus 29:1–9, 35–37) ............. 179

**LESSON 4** MARCH 23—**Offering a Sweet Aroma to God**
Topic: Up in Smoke (Leviticus 1:3–17) ..................................... 185

**LESSON 5** MARCH 30—**The Day of Atonement**
Topic: What a Day! (Leviticus 16:11–19) ................................... 190

### UNIT THEME: CHRIST'S ALL-SUFFICIENT SACRIFICE

**LESSON 6** APRIL 6—**Christ's Once-for-All Sacrifice**
Topic: It Only Takes One (Hebrews 9:23–10:4, 11–14, 19–25) ..... 196

**LESSON 7** APRIL 13—**Christ the Atoning Sacrifice**
Topic: All You Need Is Love (1 John 2:1–6; 4:9–17) .................... 202

**LESSON 8** APRIL 20—**Christ Dies and Rises to New Life**
Topic: They Couldn't Keep Him Down
(Matthew 27:39–40, 45–54; 28:1–10) ................................ 208

**LESSON 9** APRIL 27—**The Lamb Is Worthy**
Topic: Sing a New Song (Revelation 5:1–10) ............................ 214

### UNIT THEME: SPECIAL OFFERINGS AND THE SANCTUARY

**LESSON 10** MAY 4—**David's Sacrifice**
Topic: It'll Cost You Everything (1 Chronicles 21:14–30) .......... 220

**LESSON 11** MAY 11—**Solomon Dedicates the Temple**
Topic: A Grand Opening (2 Chronicles 7:1–7, 11) ..................... 226

**LESSON 12** MAY 18—**Worship Is Restored after Exiles Return**
Topic: Mourning the Past or Celebrating the Future?
(Ezra 3:1–6, 10–13) ......................................................... 232

**LESSON 13** MAY 25—**A Covenant Renewal**
Topic: Here We Go Again! (Nehemiah 10:28–39) ...................... 238

# CONTENTS

## 4TH QUARTER

### UNIT THEME: THE GENESIS OF ALTARS AND SACRIFICES

LESSON 1   JUNE 1—**Cain and Abel Offer Sacrifices**
Topic: Gift–Giving that Matters (Genesis 4:1–15) ...................... 245

LESSON 2   JUNE 8—**Noah Builds an Altar**
Topic: The Rainbow Promise (Genesis 8:13–22; 9:11–13) .......... 250

LESSON 3   JUNE 15—**Abraham Makes an Offering**
Topic: The Value of a Life (Genesis 22:1–14) .............................. 257

LESSON 4   JUNE 22—**Isaac Calls on the Name of the Lord**
Topic: Digging Your Own Well (Genesis 26:24–33) .................... 262

LESSON 5   JUNE 29—**Jacob Sets Up a Sacred Pillar**
Topic: Jacob Marks God's Faithfulness (Genesis 28:10–22) ....... 267

### UNIT THEME: JESUS AND THE TEMPLE

LESSON 6   JULY 6—**The Boy Jesus in the Temple**
Topic: Home Alone (Luke 2:41–52) ............................................. 273

LESSON 7   JULY 13—**Lord of the Sabbath**
Topic: A Question of Authority (Matthew 12:1–8) ..................... 278

lesson 8   July 20—**Cleansing the Temple**
Topic: Bake Sales Gone Bad! (John 2:13–25) ............................. 284

LESSON 9   JULY 27—**Jesus Predicts the Temple's Destruction**
Topic: The Harder They Fall (Matthew 24:1–14) ........................ 290

### UNIT THEME: CHRISTIANS AND SACRIFICE

LESSON 10   AUGUST 3—**Believers (the Church) as God's Temple**
Topic: Construction Zone (1 Corinthians 3:10–23) .................... 296

LESSON 11   AUGUST 10—**Our Bodies Belong to God**
Topic: How to Be Happy (1 Corinthians 6:12–20) ...................... 301

LESSON 12   AUGUST 17—**Jews and Gentiles Form One Temple**
Topic: Finding Peace in a Conflicted World (Eph. 2:11–22) ....... 306

LESSON 13   AUGUST 24—**Sacrifices of Praise and Good Works**
Topic: All We Need Is Love (Hebrews 13:9–21) .......................... 311

LESSON 14   AUGUST 31—**Living Stones in a Spiritual Temple**
Topic: Building from the Ground Up (1 Peter 2:1–12) ............... 316

# First Quarter

*September*

*October*

*November*

Lesson material is based on International Sunday School Lessons and International Bible Lessons for Christian Teaching, copyrighted by the International Council of Religious Education, and is used by its permission.

LESSON I

SEPTEMBER 1, 2024

# ABRAM BUILDS AN ALTAR AT MAMRE

ADULT TOPIC:
MARKING TRANSITIONS

BACKGROUND SCRIPTURE: GENESIS 12–13
LESSON PASSAGE: GENESIS 13:8–18

## GENESIS 13:8–18

### KJV

AND Abram said unto Lot, Let there be no strife, I pray thee, between me and thee, and between my herdmen and thy herdmen; for we be brethren.
9 Is not the whole land before thee? separate thyself, I pray thee, from me: if thou wilt take the left hand, then I will go to the right; or if thou depart to the right hand, then I will go to the left.
10 And Lot lifted up his eyes, and beheld all the plain of Jordan, that it was well watered every where, before the Lord destroyed Sodom and Gomorrah, even as the garden of the Lord, like the land of Egypt, as thou comest unto Zoar.
11 Then Lot chose him all the plain of Jordan; and Lot journeyed east: and they separated themselves the one from the other.
12 Abram dwelled in the land of Canaan, and Lot dwelled in the cities of the plain, and pitched his tent toward Sodom.
13 But the men of Sodom were wicked and sinners before the Lord exceedingly.
14 And the Lord said unto Abram, after that Lot was separated from him, Lift up now thine eyes, and look from the place where thou art northward, and southward, and eastward, and westward:
15 For all the land which thou seest, to thee will I give it, and to thy seed for ever.
16 And I will make thy seed as the dust of the earth: so that if a man can number the dust of the earth, then shall thy seed also be numbered.
17 Arise, walk through the land in the length

### NRSVue

THEN Abram said to Lot, "Let there be no strife between you and me and between your herders and my herders, for we are kindred.
9 Is not the whole land before you? Separate yourself from me. If you take the left hand, then I will go to the right, or if you take the right hand, then I will go to the left."
10 Lot looked about him and saw that the plain of the Jordan was well watered everywhere like the garden of the Lord, like the land of Egypt, in the direction of Zoar; this was before the Lord destroyed Sodom and Gomorrah.
11 So Lot chose for himself all the plain of the Jordan, and Lot journeyed eastward, and they separated from each other.
12 Abram settled in the land of Canaan, while Lot settled among the cities of the plain and moved his tent as far as Sodom.
13 Now the people of Sodom were wicked, great sinners against the Lord.
14 The Lord said to Abram, after Lot had separated from him, "Raise your eyes now, and look from the place where you are, northward and southward and eastward and westward,
15 for all the land that you see I will give to you and to your offspring forever.
16 I will make your offspring like the dust of the earth, so that if one can count the dust of the earth, your offspring also can be counted.
17 Rise up, walk through the length and the

**MAIN THOUGHT:** So Abram moved his tent, and came and settled by the oaks of Mamre, which are at Hebron; and there he built an altar to the LORD. (Genesis 13:18, NRSVue)

## GENESIS 13:8–18

### KJV

of it and in the breadth of it; for I will give it unto thee.

18 Then Abram removed his tent, and came and dwelt in the plain of Mamre, which is in Hebron, and built there an altar unto the Lord.

### NRSVue

breadth of the land, for I will give it to you."

18 So Abram moved his tent and came and settled by the oaks of Mamre, which are at Hebron, and there he built an altar to the Lord.

## LESSON SETTING

**Time:** 2100 — 1850 BCE

**Place:** Canaan

## LESSON OUTLINE

I. Kinship and Conflict
(Genesis 13:8–10)

II. Choice and Consequence
(Genesis 13:11–18)

## UNIFYING PRINCIPLE

Throughout life, threshold opportunities arise that determine our future. How do we honor such opportunities with solemnity and gratefulness? Abram built altars to mark those occasions in which God called him to greater faithfulness.

## INTRODUCTION

The passage takes place in the land of Canaan, specifically in the area around Bethel (Genesis 13:3,6). This region, located in modern-day Central Israel, was inhabited by Canaanite and Perizzite tribes at the time (Genesis 13:7). While the exact location within Canaan is not specified, the text mentions landmarks such as the Jordan Valley and the oaks of Mamre at Hebron, providing some general geographical context.

Genesis 13 is the first story in the trilogy of Abram and Lot. Abram is Lot's uncle, the brother of Lot's father, Haran (11:27).

A central theme of Genesis 13 concerns choices—the very different choices made by two men. We read about them here precisely because these are the sort of choices that human beings have continued to make ever since, and the sort of choices you must make in one way or another virtually every day of your life.

Both Abraham and Lot had been in Egypt, as Genesis 13:1 reminds us. Lot had known of Abram's clever plan to save his skin at the risk of his wife's virtue. And Lot had seen how that plan had gone wrong. Lot also had seen God intervene to save His covenant with Abraham. He had heard the rebuke (or at least had heard of the rebuke) God addressed to Abram and witnessed the shame that was Abram's penalty for his faithlessness, his cowardice, and his setting too much store by this world.

This lesson passage, Genesis 13:8–18, presents a pivotal moment in the Abrahamic narrative, where a seemingly minor dispute between Abram and Lot foreshadows a dramatic divergence in their destinies. This seemingly simple passage, packed with theological and historical significance, has been the subject of much scholarly debate and interpretation. The lesson aims to delve deeper into the text, exploring its literary nuances, theological implications, and historical context, offering a fresh perspective on this enduring story.

# EXPOSITION

## I. KINSHIP AND CONFLICT (GENESIS 13: 8–10)

At the heart of the passage lies a conflict, not of enemies, but rather, of family members. Abram was the paternal uncle of Lot. He appeals to Lot to attempt a peaceful resolution to their conflict (v. 8). While the Bible does not explicitly state the reason for the conflict between Abram and Lot in Genesis 13:8–18 several factors could have contributed to their family conflict.

Both Abram and Lot had grown wealthy in livestock and needed ample space for their livestock to graze. The text mentions, "the land was not able to bear them, that they might dwell together" (Genesis 13:6), which suggests there was an intense competition between Lot and Abram's herdsmen for resources, potentially leading to tensions.

The narrative opens with Abram and Lot dwelling together in the land of Canaan, their combined households having grown prosperous in livestock. However, this shared prosperity breeds tension: "The land was not able to bear them, that they might dwell together; for their possessions were great, and they could not dwell together" (Genesis 13:6). This statement, while seemingly straightforward, resonates with multiple layers of meaning. The land's inability to sustain both households suggests not merely physical limitations but also a burgeoning conflict. Using the plural "possessions" hints at competition for resources, potentially leading to disputes between their herdsmen.

As the elder statesman and sage in their relationship, Abram takes initiative because he values peace and unity. Recognizing the potential for discord, Abram takes the initiative. His words, "Let there be no strife, I pray thee, between me and thee, and between my herdsmen and thy herdsmen; for we are brethren" (Genesis 13:8), reveal a man of peace and diplomacy. He prioritizes harmony over dominance, appealing to their shared kinship as a means to resolve the conflict. This proactive approach starkly contrasts Lot's later actions, who choose self–interest over familial unity. We can learn much from Abram about choosing peace, harmony, and love over materialism and possessions. Like Abram, we must not allow inheritances, insurance beneficiary checks, and minor petty misunderstandings to break up families.

Abram's rhetorical question in verse 9, "is not the whole land before you?", might seem disingenuous since Canaanites already possessed the majority of the land. But the question is a reflection of Abram's belief and confidence in God's promise. Abram was confident in God's covenant to him, and though it had not come to pass in totality, he operated as it had in good faith. Christians should do the same. God has made every believer a promise, and though it may not have all come to pass, yet believers should have so much trust in God that they live their lives reflective of God's promise. Abram spoke with anticipation as if the land were already his to divvy up to whomever he chose. Lot makes his choice, and Abram accepts what Lot rejects.

Lot makes his choice, and verse 10 displays the irony that the lush green land that Lot chooses will later be destroyed by fire (Genesis 19:12–29). The land Lot chose was beautiful. The vegetation was likened to the "garden of the Lord." The land was like Egypt: well watered, seemingly rich in resources and attractive. The beauty of the land distracted Lot and made him oblivious to wickedness and evil that was in the land. Verse 10 serves as a foreboding of the tragic turn of events and for Lot and the catastrophic events to come.

Beyond the theological implications, the passage offers fascinating literary and historical nuances. The motif of land division, echoed in the later story of Isaac and Jacob, suggests a common theme of conflict and choice within the Abrahamic lineage. Additionally, the mention of the Canaanites and Perizzites in the land introduces a historical context, highlighting the challenges faced by nomadic groups in securing resources and negotiating with established communities.

## II. CHOICE AND CONSEQUENCE (GENESIS 13:11–18)

Abram's offer initiates a unique resolution: "Is not the whole land before thee? Choose for thyself: if thou wilt go to the left, I will go to the right; or if thou wilt go to the right, I will go to the left" (Genesis 13:9). This seemingly magnanimous gesture carries deeper implications. It highlights Abram's faith in God's promise—regardless of Lot's choice, Abram will remain faithful to the divine covenant.

In contrast, Lot's choice of the Jordan plain, described as "well watered, like the garden of the Lord" (Genesis 13:10), resonates with the allure of immediate gratification. This lushness, however, foreshadows moral decay, hinting at the consequences of prioritizing earthly prosperity over spiritual alignment.

The two land choices are contrasts: Lot lived outside of Canaan whereas Abram lived within Canaan. Lot lives among the cities, and Abram lives in the land. The geographical entities by themselves convey the message of judgment, for the cities Sodom and Gomorrah became proverbial types for societal evil and divine destruction. The infamy of the male populace marked them forever as "wicked" and "great sinners."

The story of Sodom's destruction (chap. 19) echoes the flood account, indicating that Sodom and Gomorrah's sins deserved the same catastrophic response from God. Specific mention of Sodom's sin as against the Lord only adds to the dire prospects of the cities' future. Identifying Sodom's populace as "sinners" calls for the reader by implication to identify the righteous, who must be Abram's group, including Lot. It is the polarization between sinners and the righteous that motivates Abram's worries over the righteous in Sodom (18:23–25).

Verses 15–17 highlight that the Lord gave the land to Abram and his descendants forever and will multiply his descendants. God will give Abram perpetual provisions by granting him and his descendants land forever (v. 15). God will multiply his descendants, his seed, so much that they will be innumerable like the dust of the earth (v. 16). God makes Abram a promise to give him land and a sizable prolific offspring. Then God tells Abram to go and walk the land as a sign of ownership (v. 17).

This took an enormous amount of faith. The land was still occupied by the Canaanites, Abram and his nephew have just split up, and his wife Sarai is barren. The circumstances in Abram's life indicate that this promise is not possible. Yet God makes him this enormous promise and Abram choses to believe and act on the promise. A lesson can be learned from Abram's choice to believe, trust and wait on God even though he could not see how the promise could come into fruition. Christians also have promises that God has made, and many times they do not seem reasonable and that they defy human possibilities, but it is God's job to fulfill the promise and the believer's job to believe, trust and obey. Abram's response to God and God's promise is to take up residence at Hebron and build an altar to worship Him (v.18). Abram was immediately compliant and trusted that God would do what God said He would do. Abram knew that God made the promise so it was God's bill to pay and God is fully capable of settling His bill. Instead of worrying and doubting Abram built an altar and worshiped. Perhaps the next time you are in the middle of God-given transition and the situation is out of your hands, instead of trying to interfere, just worship.

Following the separation, God renews his covenant with Abram, reiterating the promise of the land to him and his descendants forever (Genesis 13:14–15). This divine assurance stands in stark contrast to Lot's uncertain future in Sodom. While Abram remains tethered to God's promise, Lot's choice leads him down a path of moral decay and eventual destruction.

## The Lesson Applied

The story of Abram and Lot offers valuable insights and principles that can be applied to contemporary life, particularly in the areas of conflict resolution, humility, the pursuit of peace, and faith. Additionally, their story raises timeless questions about the balance between personal ambition and familial unity and the consequences of prioritizing material gain over spiritual values and family and interpersonal relationships.

Abram models behavior that we would do well to emulate. First, he chose to separate and go to areas that would allow each man to grow his enterprise. In so doing, Abram would to preserve a relationship that was meaningful to him. Abram and Lot chose to separate to avoid further conflict over material things. This principle should apply to modern relationships as well. Greed and selfishness often result in conflict among family members, who often seek redress through the legal system. It is a sad sight to witness parents in court against children or lifelong friends at odds over money or possessions.

The second behavior Abram modeled was to communicate openly and honestly about the matter of contention. Abram initiated a conversation with Lot to address the issue directly. Perhaps being the elder, Abram found it easier to initiate open dialogue rather than to sulk or fume privately in resentment and/or anger.

Honesty and openness allow the conflicted parties to express their concerns, understand each other's perspectives, and work their way to finding mutually acceptable solutions.

Finally, Abram sought compromise and reconciliation. Again, family members and friends may go years without speaking because of a disagreement, making no effort toward resolution in the interim.

Abram, being sure of God's promise, gave Lot first choice of the land, demonstrating humility and a willingness to compromise. Amid conflicts, parties involved should be prepared to negotiate and find solutions to meet the needs of all involved.

Abram prayed for God's blessing on both himself and Lot, demonstrating his desire for peace and prosperity for all. This passage continues to inspire scholarly debate thousands of years later, with interpretations ranging from psychological explorations of family dynamics to feminist critiques of gender roles.

Genesis 13:8–18 recounts the story of Abraham and his nephew Lot as they faced a conflict over land and possessions. Abraham, known for his generosity and faith, made a remarkable decision that showcased his faith and his character.

## LET'S TALK ABOUT IT

In this passage, Abraham and Lot are in a dispute due to their increasing wealth and the scarcity of land to accommodate their possessions.

1. **What does Abram's act of selflessness reveal about his character? How does it affirm his faith in God?**

Abram's act of allowing Lot to choose first reveals important aspects of his character and his faith in God. Abram, being the elder, easily could have chosen the best land for himself. However, he willingly gave Lot first choice. By doing so, Abram shows his faith in God's ability to provide for him. He trusts that God will guide him to the right place, even if it means choosing what's leftover. Abram's actions prioritize peace over possessions. He understands that conflict over land could lead to strife and division. Abram's actions suggests a long-term vision. He recognizes that conflict over land could hinder the growth of his family and his relationship with God. He prioritizes the future well-being of his descendants over short-term gain.

Abram's selflessness is a reflection of his trust in God's provision. His trust moves him to sacrifice his own desires for the advancement of God's will.

## GET SOCIAL

Share your views and tag us @rhboydco. Use #rhboydco.

@rhboydco

## HOME DAILY DEVOTIONAL READINGS
### SEPTEMBER 2–8, 2024

| MONDAY | TUESDAY | WEDNESDAY | THURSDAY | FRIDAY | SATURDAY | SUNDAY |
|---|---|---|---|---|---|---|
| Sighs Too Deep for Words | God Hears Our Cry for Help | Celebrate with Rejoicing, Thanksgiving, Singing | Bring Your Requests Before God | Lord, Teach Us to Pray | God the Promise Keeper | Hear Our Plea and Grant Compassion |
| Romans 8:18–28 | Psalm 34:11–22 | Nehemiah 12:27–30, 44–47 | 2 Chronicles 7:12–22 | Luke 11:1–13 | 1 Kings 8:22–24, 27–30, 37–43 | 1 Kings 8:44–53 |

LESSON II  
SEPTEMBER 8, 2024

# SOLOMON DEDICATES THE TEMPLE

ADULT TOPIC:  
OUR HOUSE IS A VERY FINE HOUSE

BACKGROUND SCRIPTURE: 1 KINGS 8:22–53  
LESSON PASSAGE: 1 KINGS 8:22–24, 37–39, 46, 48–50

## 1 KINGS 8:22–24, 37–39, 46, 48–50

### KJV

AND Solomon stood before the altar of the Lord in the presence of all the congregation of Israel, and spread forth his hands toward heaven:

23 And he said, Lord God of Israel, there is no God like thee, in heaven above, or on earth beneath, who keepest covenant and mercy with thy servants that walk before thee with all their heart:

24 Who hast kept with thy servant David my father that thou promisedst him: thou spakest also with thy mouth, and hast fulfilled it with thine hand, as it is this day.

• • • • • •

37 If there be in the land famine, if there be pestilence, blasting, mildew, locust, or if there be caterpiller; if their enemy besiege them in the land of their cities; whatsoever plague, whatsoever sickness there be;

38 What prayer and supplication soever be made by any man, or by all thy people Israel, which shall know every man the plague of his own heart, and spread forth his hands toward this house:

39 Then hear thou in heaven thy dwelling place, and forgive, and do, and give to every man according to his ways, whose heart thou knowest; (for thou, even thou only, knowest the hearts of all the children of men;)

• • • • • •

46 If they sin against thee, (for there is no man that sinneth not,) and thou be angry with them,

### NRSVue

THEN Solomon stood before the altar of the Lord in the presence of the whole assembly of Israel and spread out his hands to heaven.

23 He said, "O Lord, God of Israel, there is no God like you in heaven above or on earth beneath, keeping covenant and steadfast love with your servants who walk before you with all their heart,

24 the covenant that you kept for your servant my father David as you declared to him; you promised with your mouth and have this day fulfilled with your hand.

• • • • • •

37 "If there is famine in the land, if there is plague, blight, mildew, locust, or caterpillar; if their enemy besieges them in any of their cities; whatever suffering, whatever sickness there is;

38 whatever prayer, whatever plea there is from any individual or from all your people Israel, all knowing the suffering of their own hearts so that they stretch out their hands toward this house;

39 then hear in heaven your dwelling place, forgive, act, and render to all whose hearts you know—according to all their ways, for only you know the human heart—

• • • • • •

46 "If they sin against you—for there is no one who does not sin—and you are angry with them and give them to an enemy, so that they

**MAIN THOUGHT:** "Whatever prayer, whatever plea there is from any individual or from all your people Israel, all knowing the afflictions of their own hearts so that they stretch out their hands toward this house; then hear in heaven your dwelling place." (1 Kings 8:38–39 NRSVue)

# 1 Kings 8:22–24, 37–39, 46, 48–50

| KJV | NRSVue |
|---|---|
| and deliver them to the enemy, so that they carry them away captives unto the land of the enemy, far or near; | are carried away captive to the land of the enemy, far off or near, |
| • • • • • • | • • • • • • |
| 48 And so return unto thee with all their heart, and with all their soul, in the land of their enemies, which led them away captive, and pray unto thee toward their land, which thou gavest unto their fathers, the city which thou hast chosen, and the house which I have built for thy name: | 48 if they repent with all their heart and soul in the land of their enemies who took them captive and pray to you toward their land that you gave to their ancestors, the city that you have chosen, and the house that I have built for your name, |
| 49 Then hear thou their prayer and their supplication in heaven thy dwelling place, and maintain their cause, | 49 then hear in heaven your dwelling place their prayer and their plea, maintain their cause, |
| 50 And forgive thy people that have sinned against thee, and all their transgressions wherein they have transgressed against thee, | 50 and forgive your people who have sinned against you and all their transgressions that they have committed against you, |

## LESSON SETTING

**Time:** 967 BCE.
**Place:** Jerusalem, Israel

## LESSON OUTLINE

I. Solomon's Prayer
  (1 Kings 8:22-24)
II. Wrestling with Justice
  and Mercy
  (1 Kings 8: 37–39; 46)
III. Chosenness
  (1 Kings 8:48–50)

## UNIFYING PRINCIPLE

Great events cause people to anticipate a better future. How can we keep a proper perspective during and after such events? At the worship–dedication of the Temple, Solomon called on God to hear and heed the Israelites' future prayers.

## INTRODUCTION

This is estimated based on various chronological systems used for the Ancient Near East. Some scholars might offer slightly different dates, but the general consensus places the dedication of Solomon's Temple around this time. The text describes the events inside the newly built Solomon's Temple, situated on the Temple Mount in Jerusalem.

The book of 1 Kings provides a rich narrative of the reign of King Solomon and the construction of the magnificent temple in Jerusalem. Within this context, 1 Kings 8:22–24, 37–39, 46, and 48–50 presents a significant theological passage. This scholarly commentary aims to explore the textual, historical, and theological dimensions of these verses, shedding light on their implications for Israel's understanding of God's presence, covenant, and the nature of prayer.

These select verses from 1 Kings 8 offer a glimpse into the rich theological tapestry woven into the narrative of Solomon's

Temple dedication. The text unveils a God who is both transcendent and immanent, just and merciful, inclusive and yet choosing a particular people. The temple itself becomes a microcosm, a physical manifestation of this multifaceted theology, a point of contact between heaven and earth, a symbol of both divine judgment and enduring covenant love. Understanding these theological nuances deepens our appreciation for the enduring significance of this pivotal event in Israelite history.

## EXPOSITION

### I. SOLOMON'S PRAYER (1 KINGS 8:22–24)

The construction of the Temple was a significant event in Israel's history. It symbolized the establishment of a central place of worship and the culmination of God's covenant with the people. The dedication of the temple served as a pivotal moment, marking the transfer of the Ark of the Covenant from the tabernacle to its permanent dwelling.

Standing before the altar, Solomon raises his hands in supplication, his words echoing through the hallowed halls of the newly built temple. He begins by invoking the omnipresence of God, stating that "even the heavens, the highest heavens, cannot contain you" (8:22). This grand opening gesture establishes a crucial theological tension: the transcendent vastness of God juxtaposed with his immanence, his intimate dwelling within the earthly temple. Solomon recognizes that God is transcendent and immanent. Solomon's prayer acknowledges the paradoxical nature of God's presence. While recognizing that no physical structure can contain God fully, the temple serves as a symbolic dwelling place where God's presence can be experienced. This tension between transcendence and immanence highlights the mystery and greatness of God.

Further amplifying this duality, Solomon pleads with God to remember his covenant with his father David, his servant's unwavering faith, and the promise of an enduring dynasty (8:23–24). This invocation connects the temple to the Davidic covenant, suggesting that it serves not just a place for worship but also as a symbol of divine loyalty and continuity.

The theological significance of this passage lies in its portrayal of the temple as a sacred space where God's presence would dwell among His people. Solomon's prayer acknowledges God's transcendence, but also affirms His immanence by recognizing that God will hear and answer the prayers offered in the temple. Solomon's prayer acknowledges the paradoxical nature of God's presence. He recognizes that no physical structure can truly contain the fullness of the Almighty. In verse 27, Solomon exclaims, "But will God indeed dwell on the earth? Behold, heaven and the highest heaven cannot contain you; how much less this house that I have built!" This declaration emphasizes God's transcendence, His infinite nature that cannot be confined by human construction. The temple is not intended to limit or restrict God but rather to provide a focal point for His people to encounter His presence.

However, Solomon's prayer also affirms God's immanence, His willingness to dwell among His people. In verse 29, Solomon asks that God's eyes be open "night and day toward this house, the place of which you have said, 'My name shall be there.'" The Temple becomes a symbolic dwelling place for God's name, a sacred space where His presence can be encountered and experienced. This tension between transcendence and immanence highlights the mystery and greatness of God, who is both infinitely beyond and intimately near to His people.

## II. Wrestling with Justice and Mercy (1 Kings 8:37–39; 46)

The text takes a somber turn as Solomon acknowledges the possibility of Israel's transgressions. He paints a bleak picture of famine, pestilence, and military defeat, consequences for disobeying the Lord's commandments (8:37). This vivid depiction highlights the covenantal principle of reciprocity: blessings for obedience, but curses for disobedience.

Yet, even in the midst of potential calamity, Solomon offers a path to restoration. He pleads with God to hear their prayers for forgiveness and extend compassion when they inevitably stumble (8:38–39). This compassionate plea underscores another facet of Israelite theology: God's unwavering love and willingness to forgive repentant people. The passage stresses the importance of repentance, confession, and seeking God's forgiveness. It reminds the people of their responsibility to turn from sin and seek reconciliation with God. It also reveals God's willingness to restore and bless those who genuinely repent and seek forgiveness.

The passage stresses the importance of repentance, confession, and seeking God's forgiveness. It reminds the people of their responsibility to turn from sin and seek reconciliation with God. It also reveals God's willingness to restore and bless those who genuinely repent and seek forgiveness.

In verse 46 Solomon shifts his focus from the newly consecrated temple to the people, declaring that it represents a sacred space bridging the gap between heaven and earth. He states, "If they sin against you... and turn away from your wrath and return to you with repentance and supplication… hear in heaven your dwelling place and forgive… their sin" (8:46). This statement imbues the temple with immense significance. It becomes a conduit for communication, channeling human prayers upward and drawing down divine forgiveness.

Verse 46 underscores the universality of human sinfulness, acknowledging that no one is exempt from sin. Solomon prays for forgiveness and restoration when the people turn their hearts back to God, recognizing that they will stumble and face the consequences of their actions. The passage emphasizes the central role of repentance and forgiveness in Israel's relationship with God. Solomon understands that sin can lead to drought, famine, and other hardships. He highlights the importance of confession, repentance, and seeking God's forgiveness as the means to restore the covenant relationship with the Lord.

## III. Chosenness (1 Kings 8:48–50)

The final verses under consideration reveal a fascinating tension within Israelite theology. While acknowledging the possibility of foreigners seeking the Almighty's blessings within the temple (8:48), Solomon simultaneously emphasizes Israel's chosen status. He prays that

God will "hear the prayer of the foreigner who comes from a faraway land, for the sake of your name" (8:48). This openness to outsiders suggests a universal aspect of Yahweh's character, his willingness to hear anyone who seeks him.

However, Solomon simultaneously affirms Israel's unique position as God's chosen people. He states, "for you chose them to be your inheritance out of all the peoples of the earth" (8:50). This tension between universalism and chosenness has been a point of theological debate throughout history, highlighting the complex relationship between Israel's particularity and its role in God's broader plan for humanity. Solomon's petition for God's continued presence and blessing upon the temple recognizes that the temple is a dwelling place for God's name and prays for God's attentive ear to the supplications offered in the temple. Solomon appeals to God's covenant with David, expressing confidence in the fulfillment of God's promises.

Furthermore, Solomon's appeal to God's covenant with David reflects the continuity and faithfulness of God's promises throughout Israel's history. The temple is seen as the fulfillment of God's pledge to establish David's dynasty forever, providing a sense of hope and assurance for the future of the nation. Solomon's appeal to God's covenant with David underscores the significance of God's faithfulness to His promises. It reinforces the idea that God's covenant extends beyond generations, providing hope and assurance for the future. The temple becomes a visible sign of God's enduring commitment to His people. The temple itself becomes a visible sign of God's faithfulness to His covenant.

Its construction and dedication represent the fulfillment of God's promise to dwell among His people and establish a place for His name. The temple serves as a tangible reminder of God's steadfast love and His commitment to maintaining a relationship with His people.

## THE LESSON APPLIED

The verses of 1 Kings 8:22–24, 37–39, 46, and 48–50 offer profound insights into Israel's understanding of God's presence, covenant, and the significance of prayer. The passage highlights the tension between God's transcendence and immanence, emphasizing the centrality of repentance and forgiveness in the covenant relationship. Furthermore, it underscores God's faithfulness to His promises and the temple as a sacred space for communion with the divine. In studying these verses, one gains a deeper appreciation for the theological richness embedded within the narrative of Solomon's prayer of dedication. These verses serve as a reminder of the profound truths and principles that continue to resonate with believers today, inviting us to reflect on our own relationship with God, our need for repentance and forgiveness, and the power of prayer as a means of communication with the Divine.

In the Church today, we need, like Solomon and the Israelites, a way to look back and forward at the same time. We need to see that the great events that we celebrate today are a continuation of God's great story. We can both celebrate the particularity of our circumstances and acknowledge that the same God who worked in the midst of the Biblical stories is still manifesting His greatness and glory in our times, as well. As we move forward with hope, we, like Solomon, must cover our lives, works, and communities in prayer. God is for us, but not only for us; God's goodness extends to all people.

## Let's Talk About It

Solomon's prayer is a powerful example of humility, repentance, and faith in God. His petition covers a wide range of concerns and reflects the belief that God is merciful and forgiving, and that He desires to bless His people.

**In a society that often emphasizes individual achievement, what does Solomon's prayer for God to turn the hearts of the people back to Him teach us about true success?**

Solomon's prayer is not about his own success or the glory he has achieved. It's about the well-being of the entire nation. He prays for God's blessings on the people, their crops, their livestock, and their land. He prays for their prosperity and protection. This underscores that true success is not about individual gain but about the collective flourishing of the community. Solomon acknowledges that all success ultimately comes from God. Individual effort is important but insufficient without God's blessing. True success is not simply about hard work but also about recognizing and relying on God's grace. Solomon's prayer emphasizes the importance of a right relationship with God. He prays for God's forgiveness, for the people's hearts to be turned back to Him, and for their commitment to His laws. True success includes internal transformation and a deep connection to God. Solomon prays for generations to come, recognizing that true success is not a sprint but a marathon. He understands that a thriving community is built on strong foundations of faith and character, not just temporary achievements. In our society, where individual achievement is often celebrated above all else, Solomon's prayer offers a refreshing perspective, reminding us that true success is not about climbing a ladder of achievement, but rather about building a community of love and faith, where God's people thrive and God is honored.

## Get Social

Share your views and tag us @rhboydco. Use #rhboydco.

@rhboydco

## Home Daily Devotional Readings
### September 9–15, 2024

| Monday | Tuesday | Wednesday | Thursday | Friday | Saturday | Sunday |
|---|---|---|---|---|---|---|
| We Are More than Conquerors through Christ | Do Not Lose Heart | God Protects Me | The Lord Hears the Needy | God Will Strengthen and Guard You | A Humble Prayer for Help | God Is a Powerful Defender |
| Romans 8:29–39 | 2 Corinthians 4:8–18 | Psalm 69:1–15 | Psalm 69:16–21, 29–36 | 2 Thessalonians 3:1–5 | 2 Kings 19:14–19 | 2 Kings 19:20–31 |

LESSON III                                      SEPTEMBER 15, 2024

# HEZEKIAH'S PRAYER

ADULT TOPIC:                          BACKGROUND SCRIPTURE: 2 KINGS 19:1–34
IS IT INEVITABLE?                     LESSON PASSAGE: 2 KINGS 19:14–20, 29–31

## 2 KINGS 19:14–20, 29–31

### KJV

AND Hezekiah received the letter of the hand of the messengers, and read it: and Hezekiah went up into the house of the Lord, and spread it before the Lord.
15 And Hezekiah prayed before the Lord, and said, O Lord God of Israel, which dwellest between the cherubims, thou art the God, even thou alone, of all the kingdoms of the earth; thou hast made heaven and earth.
16 Lord, bow down thine ear, and hear: open, Lord, thine eyes, and see: and hear the words of Sennacherib, which hath sent him to reproach the living God.
17 Of a truth, Lord, the kings of Assyria have destroyed the nations and their lands,
18 And have cast their gods into the fire: for they were no gods, but the work of men's hands, wood and stone: therefore they have destroyed them.
19 Now therefore, O Lord our God, I beseech thee, save thou us out of his hand, that all the kingdoms of the earth may know that thou art the Lord God, even thou only.
20 Then Isaiah the son of Amoz sent to Hezekiah, saying, Thus saith the Lord God of Israel, That which thou hast prayed to me against Sennacherib king of Assyria I have heard.

• • • • • •

29 And this shall be a sign unto thee, Ye shall eat this year such things as grow of themselves, and in the second year that which springeth of the same; and in the third year sow ye, and

### NRSVue

HEZEKIAH received the letter from the hand of the messengers and read it; then Hezekiah went up to the house of the Lord and spread it before the Lord.
15 And Hezekiah prayed before the Lord and said, "O Lord the God of Israel, who are enthroned above the cherubim, you are God, you alone, of all the kingdoms of the earth; you have made heaven and earth.
16 Incline your ear, O Lord, and hear; open your eyes, O Lord, and see; hear the words of Sennacherib, which he has sent to mock the living God.
17 Truly, O Lord, the kings of Assyria have laid waste the nations and their lands
18 and have hurled their gods into the fire, though they were no gods but the work of human hands—wood and stone—and so they were destroyed.
19 So now, O Lord our God, save us, I pray you, from his hand, so that all the kingdoms of the earth may know that you, O Lord, are God alone."
20 Then Isaiah son of Amoz sent to Hezekiah, saying, "Thus says the Lord, the God of Israel: I have heard your prayer to me about King Sennacherib of Assyria.

• • • • • •

29 "And this shall be the sign for you: This year you shall eat what grows of itself and in the second year what springs from that; then in the third year sow, reap, plant vineyards, and

**MAIN THOUGHT:** "So now, O LORD our God, save us, I pray you, from his hand, so that all the kingdoms of the earth may know that you, O LORD, are God alone." (2 Kings 19:19 NRSVue)

## 2 KINGS 19:14–20, 29–31

| KJV | NRSVue |
|---|---|
| reap, and plant vineyards, and eat the fruits thereof.<br>30 And the remnant that is escaped of the house of Judah shall yet again take root downward, and bear fruit upward.<br>31 For out of Jerusalem shall go forth a remnant, and they that escape out of mount Zion: the zeal of the Lord of hosts shall do this. | eat their fruit.<br>30 The surviving remnant of the house of Judah shall again take root downward and bear fruit upward,<br>31 for from Jerusalem a remnant shall go out and from Mount Zion a band of survivors. The zeal of the Lord of hosts will do this. |

## LESSON SETTING

**Time:** Between the 6th and 4th centuries BCE

**Place:** Judah

## LESSON OUTLINE

I. Hezekiah's Prayer: A Powerful Demonstration of Faith (2 Kings 19:14–19)

II. Divine Pronouncement and Hezekiah's Illness: Paradox and Trust (2 Kings 19:20, 29–31)

III. Signs and Deliverance: Divine Intervention and Divine Presence (2 Kings 19:29–31)

## UNIFYING PRINCIPLE

Disaster seems inevitable when a chain of events points to an inescapable outcome. What can people do when all seems lost? In a time of crisis, Hezekiah turned to worshipful prayer and was heard.

## INTRODUCTION

Most scholars agree that the Book of Kings, including 2 Kings 19, was compiled and edited sometime between the 6th and 4th centuries BCE. The events recounted in 2 Kings 19, the siege of Jerusalem by Sennacherib, occurred in 701 BCE. Therefore, verses 14–20 and 29–31 were likely written sometime after 701 BCE but before the final compilation of the Book of Kings.

Place: Given the focus on Hezekiah, king of Judah, and the events surrounding the siege of Jerusalem, it's highly likely that the verses were composed in Judah, possibly even within the city itself. Later exilic or post-exilic editors may have incorporated and reinterpreted earlier traditions relating to Hezekiah and the Assyrian threat.

While the exact time and place of composition for 2 Kings 19:14–20, 29–31 remain debatable, we can estimate that it was likely written sometime between the late 8th and early 4th centuries BCE, most likely in Judah/Jerusalem.

Second Kings 19:14–20, 29–31 presents a pivotal moment in the reign of King Hezekiah of Judah, as he faces the imminent threat of the mighty Assyrian army led by Sennacherib. This passage captures Hezekiah's desperate plea to God for deliverance and the subsequent divine intervention. The narrative raises important theological questions regarding the relationship between human agency and divine sovereignty, and it offers valuable insights into the nature of faith and trust in God.

The events recounted in 2 Kings 19:14–20, 29–31 occurred during the late 8th century BCE when the Assyrian Empire exerted its dominance over the Near East. Hezekiah's reign (715–686 BCE) marked a period of political tension as Assyria sought to expand its territory and exert control over the smaller kingdoms in the region. Sennacherib's invasion of Judah was part of this larger Assyrian campaign, which aimed to quell any resistance and secure the empire's hegemony.

2 Kings 19:14–20, 29–31 offers a compelling narrative of faith, divine intervention, and deliverance in the face of overwhelming threat. The passage depicts King Hezekiah's response to the blasphemous taunts and military might of the Assyrian king Sennacherib, showcasing both the fragility of human existence and the power of faith in a transcendent God. This commentary will delve into the literary nuances, theological implications, and historical context of these verses, aiming to illuminate their enduring significance for religious thought and human experience.

## EXPOSITION

### I. HEZEKIAH'S PRAYER: A POWERFUL DEMONSTRATION OF FAITH (2 KINGS 19:14–19)

The narrative opens with Hezekiah's reaction to Sennacherib's provocative and threatening letter. Faced with the Assyrian king's boastful claims of invincibility and mockery of the Israelite God, Hezekiah chooses prayer as his weapon. This monarch recognizes that some battles cannot be fought on the battlefield; they must be fought on the knees of the beleiver. Hezekiah wisely ascends to the Temple, lays the ominous letter before God, and engages in a poignant supplication. This act of seeking divine assistance in the face of imminent danger reflects a profound trust in God's power and sovereignty. It can be difficult for powerful people to humble themselves. Hezekiah understood the limitations of his power. Going immediately to the temple to pray, Hezekiah demonstrates his recognition of God's sovereignty and his decision to seek divine counsel and protection. Hezekiah's prayer demonstrates his deep faith and trust in God's ability to save his people.

Hezekiah's prayer itself is a masterpiece of theological articulation. He addresses God as the "enthroned between the cherubim," a potent image symbolizing God's absolute dominion over the universe. He acknowledges God's role as the creator of heaven and earth, showcasing a deep understanding of God's cosmic power. Further, Hezekiah carefully contrasts the omnipotent Yahweh with the false gods of the Assyrians, who are mere "wood and stone, fashioned by human hands." This act of theological distinction serves to bolster Hezekiah's appeal for intervention, emphasizing the unique and unassailable power of the Israelite God.

Hezekiah's prayer after receiving the letter is a reminder of the power of faith and prayer in times of crisis, trouble and uncertainty. Hezekiah's act of taking the letter before God and seeking divine intervention exemplifies the importance of turning to God in times of trouble. The text is a reminder that God is attentive to the prayers of His people and is willing to intervene on their behalf.

## II. Divine Pronouncement and Hezekiah's Illness: Paradox and Trust (2 Kings 19:20, 29–31)

The pronouncement of Hezekiah's illness in 2 Kings 19:20 is indeed perplexing and open to interpretation. While the text doesn't explicitly name the nature of his illness, it offers some clues and raises questions about the nature of his illness. The text is unspecified regarding his illness. The text simply states that Hezekiah was "gravely ill and near death." This lack of detail leaves room for various interpretations and adds to the dramatic tension of the text. Some scholars suggest that the illness might be symbolic, representing the spiritual or political vulnerability of Judah during the Assyrian siege. Other scholars argue for a literal interpretation, pointing to possible diagnoses based on historical context and ancient medical knowledge. Some potential illness possibilities include an abscess, boils, or a severe infection.

However, Hezekiah's immediate response to prayer is not deliverance but a seemingly contradictory pronouncement from the prophet Isaiah. God, through Isaiah, declares that Hezekiah will die and not recover from his illness. This stark message initially appears discordant with Hezekiah's fervent prayer for deliverance. Hezekiah could have questioned God's divine response but instead he leaned further into his faith and acknowledged the limits of human understanding.

The pronouncement of the illness serves as a crucial test of Hezekiah's faith. Despite receiving news of his impending death, he demonstrates unwavering trust in God through fervent prayer. He believed that the illness and subsequent reversal might be seen as part of a larger divine plan, challenging human expectations and showcasing God's ultimate sovereignty. Notably, Isaiah 38 offers a parallel account of Hezekiah's illness, adding details about a boil or ulcer causing the near–death experience. This adds a layer of ambiguity, as it's unclear if the illness in 2 Kings and Isaiah refer to the same event or represent different literary traditions. Assyrian records don't mention Hezekiah's illness, focusing instead on the overall campaign and eventual withdrawal from Judah. This lack of external confirmation challenges efforts to pinpoint the exact nature of the illness. Despite receiving news of his impending death, Hezekiah's response is not despair but renewed prayer. He turns his face to the wall, a gesture suggestive of deep sorrow and supplication, and pleads with God, citing his faithful walk and obedience. This act demonstrates an unwavering trust in God's ultimate plan, even when it diverges from human expectations.

## III. Signs and Deliverance: Divine Intervention and Divine Presence (2 Kings 19:29–31)

Finally, God provides Hezekiah with a sign – a promise of healing and renewed prosperity despite the Assyrian threat. This response through a sign resonates with biblical tradition, recalling episodes like Abraham's covenant with God (Gen 15:17–21) and Moses' encounter with the burning bush (Ex 3:1–4). The sign was a year of self–sufficiency followed by two years of gradual rebuilding which offered reassurance and a clear timeline for God's intervention.

The deliverance from the Assyrian threat, recounted in the subsequent chapters of 2 Kings, further underlines the significance of Hezekiah's faith. The Assyrians' sudden withdrawal remains unexplained, prompting interpretations that ascribe the victory to divine intervention. This reading aligns with Hezekiah's concluding statement, acknowledging God's role in protecting Jerusalem and declaring God's supremacy over all nations.

The passage underscores the sovereignty of God. Despite the might of the Assyrian army, God asserts His authority over the affairs of nations and demonstrates His ability to protect and deliver His people. The assurance of divine protection serves as a source of hope and encouragement for believers facing overwhelming challenges.

Furthermore, the passage reveals God's commitment to His covenant promises. The mention of David, the beloved king of Israel, highlights the role of God's covenant with David's descendants in preserving and safeguarding Jerusalem. God's intervention against the Assyrians serves as a testament to His faithfulness and His commitment to fulfill His promises regardless of the threat or enemy.

## THE LESSON APPLIED

Applying the lessons from 2 Kings 19:14–20, 29–31 to current times involves drawing insights from the passage's themes of faith, prayer, and God's sovereignty. Here are some practical ways to apply these lessons in your life:

Cultivate a strong prayer life: Just as Hezekiah turned to God in prayer during a time of crisis, we can follow his example by developing a consistent and intentional prayer life. Prayer is a powerful tool that allows us to communicate with God, express our concerns, seek guidance, and find strength in difficult situations. Set aside dedicated time each day to engage in prayer, both individually and collectively with other believers.

Trust in God's sovereignty: In times of uncertainty and challenges, it is important to remember that God is sovereign over all circumstances. Recognize that God is in control, even when things seem overwhelming. Trust in His wisdom and His ability to work all things together for good. This trust allows us to find peace and assurance, knowing that God is faithful and will provide for our needs.

Seek guidance from God's Word: Just as Hezekiah sought counsel from the prophet Isaiah, we too should turn to God's Word for guidance and direction. The Bible is a source of wisdom and truth, providing principles and teachings that can guide our decisions and actions. Regularly engage in studying and meditating on Scripture, allowing its truths to shape your thinking and actions.

Develop a strong faith: The passage highlights the power of faith in God's ability to intervene and deliver His people. Cultivate a deep and unwavering faith in God, even in the midst of challenging circumstances. Remember past instances where God has been faithful and trust that He will continue to be faithful in the future. Strengthen your faith through regular engagement in spiritual disciplines, such as worship, fellowship, and studying God's Word.

Find hope in God's promises: Just as God reassured Hezekiah of His protection and deliverance, we can find hope in the promises of God. The Bible is filled with promises of God's provision, guidance, and faithfulness. Meditate on these promises and allow them to instill hope and confidence in your heart. Remember that God is faithful to His Word and will fulfill His promises in His perfect timing

Support and encourage others: Hezekiah's prayer and God's intervention not only affected him but also had an impact on the entire nation of Judah. Similarly, as believers, we have the opportunity to support and encourage others in their faith journey. Be a source of encouragement, hope, and prayer for those around you. Offer words of comfort, lend a helping hand, and share the hope found in Christ.

By applying these lessons from 2 Kings 19:14–20, 29–31, you can deepen your faith, find strength in challenging times, and experience the peace and assurance that come from trusting in God's sovereignty and faithfulness.

## Let's Talk About It

The narrative offers an account of King Hezekiah's prayer for deliverance and God's subsequent intervention.

**Have you ever desperately needed help? Did you pray about it? How was that experience for you? What are barriers that get in the way of a vibrant prayer life for you?**

This passage highlights the interplay between human agency and divine sovereignty. Ultimately, this passage serves as a reminder of God's faithfulness and His willingness to deliver His people in times of distress. Hezekiah confessed his limitations and put his trust in God's ability to deliver them. He specifically addresses the threat and pleaded for God's intervention with clear and earnest language.

Hezekiah drew strength from God's past faithfulness and promises, and so can we. We serve a God of proven power. Remembering God's promises and relying on His faithfulness gives us strength to endure difficult times.

## Get Social

Share your views and tag us @rhboydco. Use #rhboydco.

**@rhboydco**

LESSON IV  
SEPTEMBER 22, 2024

# JOSIAH CELEBRATES PASSOVER

ADULT TOPIC: BACKGROUND SCRIPTURE: 2 KINGS 22–23; 2 CHRONICLES 34:1–35:19
CLAIMING THE TREASURES OF THE PAST   LESSON PASSAGE: 2 CHRONICLES 35:1–6, 16–19

## 2 CHRONICLES 35:1–6, 16–19

### KJV

MOREOVER Josiah kept a passover unto the Lord in Jerusalem: and they killed the passover on the fourteenth day of the first month.
2 And he set the priests in their charges, and encouraged them to the service of the house of the Lord,
3 And said unto the Levites that taught all Israel, which were holy unto the Lord, Put the holy ark in the house which Solomon the son of David king of Israel did build; it shall not be a burden upon your shoulders: serve now the Lord your God, and his people Israel,
4 And prepare yourselves by the houses of your fathers, after your courses, according to the writing of David king of Israel, and according to the writing of Solomon his son.
5 And stand in the holy place according to the divisions of the families of the fathers of your brethren the people, and after the division of the families of the Levites.
6 So kill the passover, and sanctify yourselves, and prepare your brethren, that they may do according to the word of the Lord by the hand of Moses.

• • • • • •

16 So all the service of the Lord was prepared the same day, to keep the passover, and to offer burnt offerings upon the altar of the Lord, according to the commandment of king Josiah.
17 And the children of Israel that were present kept the passover at that time, and the feast of unleavened bread seven days.
18 And there was no passover like to that kept in Israel from the days of Samuel the prophet;

### NRSVue

JOSIAH kept a Passover to the Lord in Jerusalem; they slaughtered the Passover lamb on the fourteenth day of the first month.
2 He appointed the priests to their offices and encouraged them in the service of the house of the Lord.
3 He said to the Levites who taught all Israel and who were holy to the Lord, "Put the holy ark in the house that Solomon son of David, king of Israel, built; you need no longer carry it on your shoulders. Now serve the Lord your God and his people Israel.
4 Make preparations by your ancestral houses by your divisions, following the written directions of King David of Israel and the written directions of his son Solomon.
5 Take position in the holy place according to the groupings of the ancestral houses of your kindred the people, and let there be Levites for each division of an ancestral house.
6 Slaughter the Passover lamb, sanctify yourselves, and on behalf of your kindred make preparations, acting according to the word of the Lord by Moses."

• • • • • •

16 So all the service of the Lord was prepared that day, to keep the Passover and to offer burnt offerings on the altar of the Lord, according to the command of King Josiah.
17 The people of Israel who were present kept the Passover at that time and the Festival of Unleavened Bread seven days.
18 No Passover like it had been kept in Israel since the days of the prophet Samuel; none of

**MAIN THOUGHT:** Josiah kept a passover to the LORD in Jerusalem; they slaughtered the passover lamb on the fourteenth day of the first month. (2 Chronicles 35:1, NRSVue)

## 2 Chronicles 35:1–6, 16–19

### KJV
neither did all the kings of Israel keep such a passover as Josiah kept, and the priests, and the Levites, and all Judah and Israel that were present, and the inhabitants of Jerusalem.
19 In the eighteenth year of the reign of Josiah was this passover kept.

### NRSVue
the kings of Israel had kept such a Passover as was kept by Josiah, by the priests and the Levites, by all Judah and Israel who were present, and by the inhabitants of Jerusalem.
19 In the eighteenth year of the reign of Josiah, this Passover was kept.

## LESSON SETTING

**Time:** Eighteenth year of King Josiah's reign (approx. 621 BCE)

**Place:** Jerusalem, Judah

## LESSON OUTLINE

I. **The Passover Celebration Instructions**
(2 Chronicles 35:1–6)

II. **Reinstatement of the Passover Observance**
(2 Chronicles 35:16–19)

## UNIFYING PRINCIPLE

Promises and commitments can become neglected over time as their importance is forgotten and otherwise not communicated. One generation may not pass on the values and commitments of the next. Alternatively, a new generation may need to reflect and appropriate for themselves the commitment of the last one. Yet some commitments, like God's commandments, must stand the test of time. How can we keep our commitments, which, in turn, honor God and our communities? These are the questions that King Josiah must face, charged with leadership under challenging circumstances.

## INTRODUCTION

The book of 2 Chronicles provides a comprehensive account of the history of the kings of Judah, with an emphasis on the religious reforms and the centrality of the temple in Jerusalem. 2 Chronicles 35:1–6, 16–19 recounts the story of Josiah's Passover celebration, highlighting the king's commitment to restoring proper worship in the land, directed exclusively to YHWH. These actions are what designates Josiah as a "good" king in the mind of the discerning historical writers. This commentary aims to explore the historical, religious, and theological dimensions of this passage, shedding light on its significance and relevance for both ancient and contemporary readers.

To fully grasp the significance of Josiah's Passover celebration, it is essential to understand the historical context as well as the broader social and political situation.. Josiah reigned as king of Judah from approximately 640–609 BCE, during a period of political turmoil and spiritual decline. The nation had experienced a series of unfaithful kings who led the people astray, promoting idol worship and neglecting the house of God. It was against this backdrop that Josiah ascended to the throne at the tender age of eight, determined to bring about religious reforms and restore the worship of God. King Josiah ascended the throne in 640 BCE at a tumultuous time for Judah. The Assyrian empire, once dominant, was waning, creating a power vacuum exploited by rival powers like Egypt and Babylon. Internally, Judah grappled with religious syncretism and idolatry, a stark departure from the Deuteronomic law outlined in the recently discovered scroll (2 Chronicles 34:14–18). Josiah's pivotal role in reviving this law and enacting widespread religious reform becomes the backdrop for the grand Passover celebration described in 2 Chronicles 35.

2 Chronicles 35:1–6, 16–19 narrates the monumental Passover celebration orchestrated by King Josiah of Judah. This event, unlike any other described in the Hebrew Bible, holds immense historical and theological significance, demanding in–depth analysis beyond a cursory reading. This commentary will delve into the passage, exploring its context, ritual specifics, and multifaceted implications for understanding Josiah's reign, Judean religious reform, and the broader themes of covenant and renewal within the biblical narrative.

## EXPOSITION

### I. THE PASSOVER CELEBRATION INSTRUCTIONS (2 CHRONICLES 35:1–6)

The text opens with King Josiah making preparations to observe the Passover. The passage portrays Josiah as an exemplary king, devoted to Yahweh and prioritizing religious reform. His unwavering dedication to the Deuteronomic law serves as a model for future generations of Judean monarchs. While the Chronicler provides the exact date of the Passover in verse one, they contrast with the delayed observance of the Passover in the days of Hezekiah (30:2–3). Josiah celebrates a great Passover feast, just as Hezekiah had following his reforms. The Chronicler emphasizes that Josiah follows the procedures from the Torah, celebrating at the proper time and place (35:1), unlike the delay of Hezekiah.

The Chronicler aims to present Josiah's Passover as a model celebration. In 2 Chronicles 35:1–6, we read of Josiah's preparations for the Passover. The passage highlights Josiah's commitment to the Law of Moses and his desire to renew the covenant between God and His people.

Before the feast Josiah gives special instructions and charge to the Levites. Josiah sends out a call to the Levites, instructing them to sanctify themselves and the temple, and to prepare for the sacred feast. He reminds the Levites that they are no longer responsible for the physical portage of the Ark and the tabernacle: the temple is in place and the Ark will now reside in it. Their new task is to serve in worship in the liturgy of the temple (35:3).

The Levites would now be responsible for teaching all of Israel. They were also charged with preparing families according to the directions King David of Israel. Josiah's instructions (2 Chronicles 35:4–6) explicitly reference "the instructions written by David king of Israel and by his son Solomon," which scholars generally link to the recently discovered book of the law, most likely the core of Deuteronomy. This meticulous adherence marks a conscious choice to return to the pure worship prescribed by God, purging foreign practices and syncretic elements.

Finally, Josiah directs the Levites to be responsible for killing the Passover lamb. A sect of Levities was given responsibility for each of the ancestral houses. The passage meticulously lays out the roles of priests and Levites in slaughtering, distributing, and preparing the sacrificial lambs (2 Chronicles 35:5–15).

Because the Passover celebration was a mandated ritual according to Mosaic Law (Exodus 12), it required participants to be ritually pure. Josiah's emphasis on purity ensured that the celebration adhered to the prescribed regulations. Ritualistic purity symbolized holiness and separation from impurity. By observing these rituals, the people acknowledged their unworthiness before God and sought His cleansing and forgiveness.

## II. REINSTATEMENT OF THE PASSOVER OBSERVANCE (2 CHRONICLES 35:16–19)

These verses provide a glimpse into the importance of ritual and religious observance in ancient Israel. Josiah's Passover celebration was a model of faithfulness and obedience, and it served as a catalyst for national renewal and spiritual revival. The passage reminds us of the significance of worship, unity, and adherence to God's commands in the life of a nation and its people. Josiah's determination confirms that no people be drawn so far from God that they cannot be restored.

Josiah's Passover celebration conveys several theological themes. First, it demonstrates the importance of proper worship and obedience to God's commands. Josiah's commitment to the Law and his efforts to restore the Temple reflect his understanding that true worship requires fidelity to God's revealed will. Secondly, the passage underscores the centrality of the Temple and its role as the focal point of Israelite worship. Josiah's reforms aimed to reinstate the Temple as the center of religious life and to ensure the purity of the worship offered there.

Moreover, Josiah's Passover celebration serves as a reminder of the consequences of spiritual neglect and the restoration possible through sincere repentance. The neglect of the Passover for an extended period had resulted in a loss of religious identity and a departure from the Lord's covenant. However, Josiah's reforms and the subsequent celebration of the Passover marked a return to the Lord and a renewal of the covenant relationship. The grand scale and unprecedented nature of the event have led some scholars to see it as foreshadowing the eschatological gathering and future restoration of Israel. Josiah's Passover is evidence that God can and will restore what has been neglected, misused, and forgotten. God can take what is broken and repair it, making it whole.

The Chronicler compares Josiah's Passover to Samuel, "No passover like it had been kept in Israel since the days of the prophet Samuel" (35:18). Throughout the text the writer has paralleled Josiah to Hezekiah. However, Hezekiah's Passover had many irregularities while Josiah's is presented as a celebration that mirrored perfection. The reference to Samuel plays a part in the structure of the entire Chronicler's history. The three great feast in the Chronicler's history—Hezekiah's Passover, the Festival of Booths, and Josiah's Passover—look progressively further into Israel's traditions. The Chronicler retrieves the traditions of ancient Israel as a foundation for the present.

## THE LESSON APPLIED

The story of Josiah's Passover celebration in 2 Chronicles 35:1–6, 16–19 offers valuable lessons that individuals can apply to their own lives. Following are a few practical ways to apply teachings gleaned from this passage.

*Commitment to God's Word:* Like Josiah, we should prioritize the study and application of God's Word. Regularly reading and meditating on Scripture helps us understand God's will and align our lives with His commands. By immersing ourselves in the truth of Scripture, we can cultivate a deeper relationship with God and make decisions that honor Him.

*Pursuit of Worship:* Just as Josiah sought to restore proper worship in the land, we should prioritize worship in our lives. This involves not only attending church services, but also engaging in personal devotion, worship, and prayer. By giving God the reverence and adoration He deserves, we can experience a deeper connection with Him and find spiritual renewal.

*Repentance and Restoration:* Josiah's Passover celebration was a result of his recognition of the nation's spiritual decline and his commitment to repentance and restoration. Similarly, we should regularly examine our hearts and confess any sins or areas of spiritual neglect. Through repentance, we can experience God's forgiveness and restoration, allowing Him to work in our lives and bring positive change.

Yet restoration is not only about bringing individuals' hearts to God, but also, gathering the entire people. Even as people needed to examine their own consciences and repent, this act of contrition was collectively shared. Josiah's celebration of Passover meant that everyone was again celebrating the feast together. We can imagine that fissures in the community were closed as everyone joined in celebration. Therefore, in our own communities, we can initiate repentance in the hope that our hearts will draw closer to God as well as the hearts of everyone around us. Our communities can be rejoined as one body.

*Adaptability*: Josiah celebrated Passover in the tradition of his forebears, but at the same time, some things changed. The situation of Josiah, as a king of Judah, was different than that of the Hebrews who celebrated the first Passover while still slaves in Egypt. The Levites were no longer responsible for carrying the Ark around, as the temple housed it, but instead, served in temple liturgy. Even as Josiah honored and followed tradition, he also kept up with what God was doing in the world today.

*Generosity:* Josiah's example of contributing generously to the Passover demonstrates the importance of sacrificial giving. As believers, we are called to be generous with our resources, time, and talents, supporting the work of God's Kingdom and meeting the needs of others. By cultivating a spirit of generosity, we reflect God's character and participate in His redemptive work in the world.

Incorporating these principles into our lives can lead to spiritual growth, a stronger connection with God, and a positive impact on those around us. By following Josiah's example of commitment, worship, repentance, generosity, faithfulness, and intentional leadership, we can live our faith in a way that honors God and brings about transformation in our lives and communities.

## LET'S TALK ABOUT IT

Josiah shows us how tradition and change sometimes go hand-in-hand. Even as we follow tradition, we also need to be dynamic with the times.

**How can we apply the principles of commitment, worship, repentance, generosity, faithfulness, and intentional leadership from Josiah's story to our own lives?**

King Josiah's story offers an inspiring profile in courage and an example of how to live a life that is truly pleasing to God. Josiah led by example, inspiring others to follow God. We can use our gifts and influence to make a difference in the lives of others, speaking truth in love and standing for what is right. His commitment to reform and his dedication to leading the nation back to God can inspire us to live with greater intentionality and faithfulness. The young king displayed an unwavering commitment to God's will. He wasn't swayed by the pressures of his time or the resistance he faced. We can do this in our own lives by shaping our values and priorities according to the Word of God. Ask yourself: Am I living in accordance with God's Word? Am I allowing my worship to be held hostage by traditions that are no longer relevant?

Josiah's commitment to restoring the Temple and promoting worship shows the importance of prioritizing God in our lives. We can apply this through devoting time for prayer and Bible study and putting what we learn into practice. Part of their Passover experience included leading the nation in a period of repentance, acknowledging their sins and seeking God's forgiveness. We can apply this to our own lives by asking the Holy Spirit to reveal areas where we need to turn away from sin and seek God's forgiveness. Josiah used his resources to rebuild the temple and support the priests and Levites. How are you using your time, talents, and resources to bless and affirm others?

### GET SOCIAL

Share your views and tag us @rhboydco and use #rhboydco.

**@rhboydco**

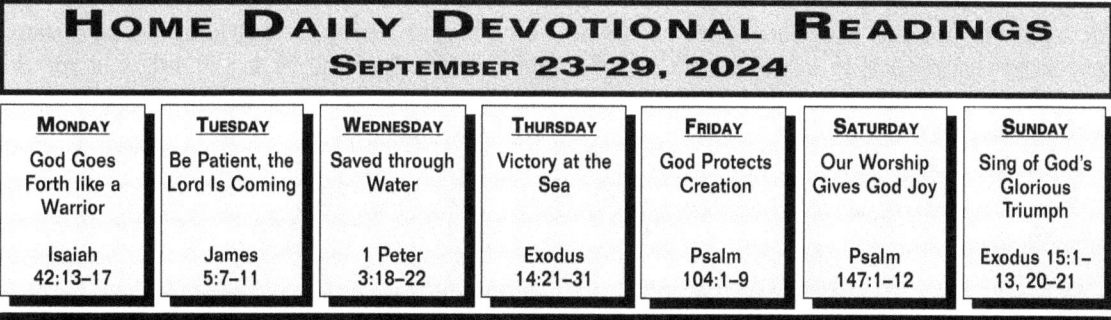

LESSON V

SEPTEMBER 29, 2024

# MOSES AND MIRIAM LEAD THE PEOPLE IN PRAISE

ADULT TOPIC:
TIME TO PARTY!

BACKGROUND SCRIPTURE: EXODUS 14:21–31; 15:1–21
LESSON PASSAGE: EXODUS 15:1–3, 11–13, 17–18, 20–21

## EXODUS 15:1–3, 11–13, 17–18, 20–21

### KJV

THEN sang Moses and the children of Israel this song unto the Lord, and spake, saying, I will sing unto the Lord, for he hath triumphed gloriously: the horse and his rider hath he thrown into the sea.
2 The Lord is my strength and song, and he is become my salvation: he is my God, and I will prepare him an habitation; my father's God, and I will exalt him.
3 The Lord is a man of war: the Lord is his name.

• • • • • •

11 Who is like unto thee, O Lord, among the gods? who is like thee, glorious in holiness, fearful in praises, doing wonders?
12 Thou stretchedst out thy right hand, the earth swallowed them.
13 Thou in thy mercy hast led forth the people which thou hast redeemed: thou hast guided them in thy strength unto thy holy habitation.

• • • • • •

17 Thou shalt bring them in, and plant them in the mountain of thine inheritance, in the place, O Lord, which thou hast made for thee to dwell in, in the Sanctuary, O Lord, which thy hands have established.
18 The Lord shall reign for ever and ever.

• • • • • •

20 And Miriam the prophetess, the sister of Aaron, took a timbrel in her hand; and all the women went out after her with timbrels and with dances.

### NRSVue

THEN Moses and the Israelites sang this song to the Lord: "I will sing to the Lord, for he has triumphed gloriously; horse and rider he has thrown into the sea.
2 The Lord is my strength and my might, and he has become my salvation;
this is my God, and I will praise him; my father's God, and I will exalt him.
3 The Lord is a warrior; the Lord is his name.

• • • • • •

11 Who is like you, O Lord, among the gods? Who is like you, majestic in holiness, awesome in splendor, doing wonders?
12 You stretched out your right hand; the earth swallowed them.
13 In your steadfast love you led the people whom you redeemed; you guided them by your strength to your holy abode.

• • • • • •

17 You brought them in and planted them on the mountain of your own possession, the place, O Lord, that you made your abode, the sanctuary, O Lord, that your hands have established.
18 The Lord will reign forever and ever."

• • • • • •

20 Then the prophet Miriam, Aaron's sister, took a tambourine in her hand, and all the women went out after her with tambourines and with dancing.

**MAIN THOUGHT:** The prophet Miriam, Aaron's sister, took a tambourine in her hand; and all the women went out after her with tambourines and with dancing. Exodus 15:20, NRSVue)

# Exodus 15:1–3, 11–13, 17–18, 20–21

| KJV | NRSVue |
|---|---|
| 21 And Miriam answered them, Sing ye to the Lord, for he hath triumphed gloriously; the horse and his rider hath he thrown into the sea. | 21 And Miriam sang to them: "Sing to the Lord, for he has triumphed gloriously; horse and rider he has thrown into the sea." |

## LESSON SETTING

**Time: 13th Century BCE (POSSIBLY)**

**Place: Depatable**

## LESSON OUTLINE

I. Moses's Song Part I
(Exodus 15:1–3)

II. Moses's Song Part III
(Exodus 15:11–13)

III. Moses's Song Part V
(Exodus 15:17–18)

IV. Miriam's Song
(Exodus 15:20–21)

## UNIFYING PRINCIPLE

People enjoy finding opportunities to celebrate. Celebration can also affirm the power of God to deliver and redeem His people. By celebrating, we affirm not only our own strengths, but also, God's power in our lives. Moses and Miriam led the people with praises in song for God's victory in the lives of the Israelites. In what ways can we celebrate the victories in our lives?

## INTRODUCTION

The events described in Exodus 15:1–3, 11–13, 17–18, and 20–21, including the crossing of the Sea of Reeds and the subsequent Song of Moses and Miriam, are believed to have taken place around the 13th century BCE by those who read this event as history rather than an ancestral liberation story. The specific location of the crossing of the Red Sea remains a subject of debate and speculation among scholars.

According to the biblical account, the Israelites, led by Moses, left Egypt after experiencing a series of ten plagues. They crossed the Red Sea on dry ground while being pursued by the Egyptian army. After the Israelites safely crossed, the sea closed back over the pursuing Egyptians, drowning them. This event marked the Israelites' liberation from Egyptian slavery and is considered a pivotal moment in their history.

The passage in Exodus 15:1–3, 11–13, 17–18, 20–21, known as the "Song of Moses and Miriam," are triumphant hymns celebrating the Israelites' miraculous deliverance from Egyptian slavery through the parting of the Red Sea. These verses capture a pivotal moment in the biblical narrative, depicting the Israelites' joyful response after their deliverance from Egypt and the crossing of the Red Sea. This commentary delves into the historical, literary, theological, and cultural dimensions of the text, shedding light on its significance within the broader context of the Exodus story and its enduring relevance for believers today.

The Songs of Moses and Miriam follow the miraculous events of the Exodus, including the ten plagues, the Passover, and the crossing of the Red Sea. The Israelites, now liberated from bondage, respond with a song of praise and thanksgiving. Upon their miraculous rescue from the Egyptian army, now drowned, Moses and the Israelites sing a hymn to God's power, known as the Song of the Sea (Exodus 15:1–18). When they have finished, Miriam—now identified as a prophetess—takes a timbrel, and, along with the other Israelite women, dances and plays while singing the same hymn that Moses had just sung: "Sing to the Lord, for he has triumphed gloriously; horse and rider he has hurled into the sea!" (Exodus 15:21). The Song of Moses and Miriam is a multifaceted masterpiece embedded within the Exodus narrative. It celebrates divine power, employs evocative language, and offers theological insights that reverberate throughout the Bible.

## EXPOSITION

### I. Moses's Song Part I (Exodus 15:1–3)

The Song of Moses conveys several significant theological themes. Firstly, it exalts the divine attributes of Yahweh, the God of Israel. Moses's song is an immediate expression of praise and response for what the Israelites had just experienced (v. 1). The song begins with a personal intent to praise God. Moses uses mostly the noun Yahweh throughout the song because Yahweh was a way to specify the only true God in the polytheistic world. The song then begins to speak to why Yahweh is highly exalted and above other gods. Moses's song points to Yahweh's power, protection and provision during the plagues and the Red Sea experience.

Moses shifts from collective praise to personal conviction. He claims Yahweh as his "strength," "song," and "salvation," establishing a deep bond of faith and gratitude. This verse also reflects the intergenerational nature of the covenant, connecting Moses to his ancestors. "The Lord is my strength and my song" (v. 2) joins together two metaphors that convey the truths that human strength is no match for challenges of life. After all, humans can not defeat Satan or evil within their own abilities.

Moses' song looks back at what God has done. It celebrates God as the victor over Pharaoh. Its theme characterizes Yahweh as a warrior (v. 3). For many, this central affirmation at the heart of Israel's story of salvation confirms the image of the Old Testament God which is a God of war, wrath, and violence. However, this song is not in praise of war–crazed God but a hymnic praise of God's victory over evil. This unusual depiction of Yahweh as a "man of war" underscores his unmatched power and dominance over enemy forces. It's not just a battle victory; it's a divine demonstration of strength that solidifies Yahweh's position as the Israelites' protector. It also acknowledges Yahweh's willingness to fight for and defend His people against their enemies. Israel was a small nation and would have to fight against other nations and they would have to fight often going forward. Before they could reach Mount Sinai they would have to fight the Amalekits at Rephidim (17:18–16). Within their own strength they would not have been able to win they were outmatched and the odds were against them. It was essential for them to understand that God would be their warrior who would lead them into battle and who would defend them and ensure they are victorious in battle. So it was important for Moses and Israel to recognize before battles that God would be the only ally needed and have confidence in God's ability to defend them.

## II. Moses's Song Part III (Exodus 15:11–13)

In this stanza of the song Moses is the focus. Moses, filled with awe at Yahweh's majesty, poses a series of rhetorical questions (v.11). No other deity can compare to his "holiness," "splendor," or ability to perform "wonders." This poetic outburst emphasizes Yahweh's uniqueness and reinforces his supremacy over all other gods. Moses highlights Yahweh's uniqueness. Moses sings that God has no equal. Some scholars argue that the mention of gods is not a suggestion on polytheism. Instead it is suggested that the plural gods are in reference to various powers, authorities and angels. The song suggests that Yahweh is infinitely superior to all beings, including angels and pagan gods. Moses and Israel sang that no one on earth, in heaven, hell or any other place is like God.

This vivid image portrays Yahweh's direct involvement in the Israelites' deliverance. His outstretched hand signifies his power, while the act of the earth swallowing the Egyptians emphasizes the awe-inspiring nature of the miracle. "With your steadfast love you have led the people you redeemed; with your strength you have guided them to your holy dwelling (v. 13)." This verse shifts from victory to Yahweh's motivations. He is driven by "steadfast love" and "strength" in redeeming and guiding his people. This glimpse into his character offers a deeper understanding of his actions beyond mere power or triumph.

## III. Moses's Song Part V (Exodus 15:17–18)

Moses looks beyond the immediate escape, envisioning a future where the Israelites will be planted on Yahweh's "mountain of inheritance." This foreshadows their arrival in the land of Canaan, further solidifying the covenant relationship and Yahweh's role as their king. The song concludes with a resounding declaration of Yahweh's eternal reign. This echoes throughout the Old Testament, solidifying his position as the one true God and offering hope for future deliverance from any oppressor.

## IV. Miriam's Song (Exodus 15:20–21)

In taking up the Song of the Sea, Miriam does more than simply echo Moses. She provides space for the Israelite women, so often subsumed into the Israelite community, to have their own moment of celebration. In the entire Torah (the first five books of the Hebrew Bible), this is indeed the only place where the Israelite women act as a separate body. It may be no coincidence that this is the time and place, or that it is Miriam who steps forward. The drowning of the Pharaoh and the Egyptians in the waters of the Sea of Reeds echoes and reverses Pharaoh's decree to drown the Israelite boys in the Nile. The women who saved Moses as a baby have now seen their brave choices pay off in the final elimination of the Egyptians. And who better than Miriam to lead them in celebrating their accomplishments?

In a powerful expression of female agency, Miriam takes center stage. Playing the tambourine and leading the women in dance, she actively participates in the celebration, breaking away from the traditionally male–dominated narrative. Miriam echoes Moses' opening verse, uniting the women's voices with the men's in a chorus of jubilant praise. This reinforces the collective nature of the experience and celebrates.

## THE LESSON APPLIED

The Song of Moses in Exodus 15:1–3, 11–13, 17–18, and 20–21 carries practical applications that can be relevant to believers today. Here are a few ways in which the lessons from this passage can be applied practically:

*Expressing Gratitude and Praise:* The Song of Moses serves as a powerful example of expressing gratitude and praise to God for His deliverance and faithfulness. Similarly, believers can cultivate a lifestyle of gratitude and praise, recognizing God's work in their lives and expressing thanksgiving for His provision, guidance, and protection.

*Trusting in God's Power and Providence:* The Israelites' experience of crossing the Red Sea demonstrates the power and providence of God. The passage encourages believers to trust in God's sovereignty and His ability to overcome seemingly insurmountable challenges. It reminds them that God is in control, even in the face of adversity or impossible situations, and that they can rely on His guidance and provision.

*Dependence on God:* The Song of Moses highlights the contrast between human weakness and God's strength. It serves as a reminder that our strength alone is insufficient, but through dependence on God, we can find true deliverance and victory. Practically, this means acknowledging our limitations, surrendering our self–reliance, and seeking God's guidance and empowerment in all aspects of life.

*Embracing God"s Faithfulness:* The faithfulness of God is a central theme in the Song of Moses. It is a reminder that God remains faithful to His promises and His people throughout history. This encourages believers to have confidence in God's faithfulness in their own lives, even in times of uncertainty or difficulty. It invites them to reflect on God's past faithfulness, which can strengthen their faith and provide hope for the future.

*Worship and Celebration:* The Song of Moses is a song of worship and celebration, and it has inspired countless songs throughout history. Believers can learn from this example by engaging in heartfelt worship, both individually and corporately, as a means of expressing their love, adoration, and gratitude towards God. Worship can be a source of encouragement, joy, and spiritual renewal in the lives of believers.

*Remembering God's Deliverance:* The Song of Moses was composed as a remembrance of God's deliverance from Egypt. Similarly, believers can benefit from regularly reflecting on God's faithfulness and deliverance in their own lives. This practice helps to cultivate a spirit of gratitude, strengthens faith, and provides encouragement during challenging times.

In summary, the practical applications of the Song of Moses include expressing gratitude and praise, trusting in God's power and providence, cultivating dependence on God, embracing His faithfulness, engaging in worship and celebration, and remembering God's deliverance. These lessons can guide believers in their daily lives, fostering a deeper relationship with God and a greater appreciation for His work in their lives.

## LET'S TALK ABOUT IT

The prophet Miriam took up her tambourine and the Israelites sang a new song, a new identity. Not as defenseless and oppressed slaves, but as a defended, protected, beloved people of God whose lives held new possibilities.

**The Israelites are spared through God's deliverance at the Sea of Reeds, but many Egyptians die. While Israelite women celebrate, Egyptian women must grieve. How do you reconcile this difficult text? Can a Bible story mean deliverance for some and oppression for others?**

The Bible presents a God who is both just and merciful. The death of the Egyptians, while tragic, can be understood within the context of God's righteous judgment against oppression. The Egyptians had enslaved the Israelites for centuries, and their cruelty was well-documented. God, as the ultimate judge, was exercising his authority to deliver his people and bring justice to the situation. This event is not about human control but rather about God's power and sovereignty. He is ultimately in control, and even though we may not understand the full reasoning behind His actions, we can trust that He acts righteously and with purpose. The Red Sea event is part of a larger story of God's redemption and deliverance. The Israelites were freed from slavery and given a chance to start anew. This act of deliverance is a foundational event in the Bible, setting the stage for God's covenant with His people.

## GET SOCIAL

Share your views and tag us @rhboydco. Use #rhboydco.

@rhboydco

## HOME DAILY DEVOTIONAL READINGS
### SEPTEMBER 30–OCTOBER 6, 2024

| MONDAY | TUESDAY | WEDNESDAY | THURSDAY | FRIDAY | SATURDAY | SUNDAY |
| --- | --- | --- | --- | --- | --- | --- |
| Do Not Persist in Sin | Godly Grief Leads to Repentance | The Righteous and the Wicked | Sin's Deadly Spiral | God, Restore Us | Follow Christ | Create in Me a Clean Heart |
| Hebrews 10:26–35 | 2 Corinthians 7:5–11 | Proverbs 28:4–18 | 2 Samuel 11:1–5, 14–24 | Lamentations 5:1–3, 15–22 | John 21:15–19 | Psalm 51:1–13, 16–17 |

LESSON VI                                                       OCTOBER 6, 2024

# PRAYERS OF REPENTANCE AND CONFESSION

ADULT TOPIC:                    BACKGROUND SCRIPTURE: PSALM 51; 2 SAMUEL 11
REGRET AND REMORSE                      LESSON PASSAGE: PSALM 51:1–4,10–12, 15–17

## PSALM 51:1–4,10–12, 15–17

### KJV

HAVE mercy upon me, O God, according to thy lovingkindness: according unto the multitude of thy tender mercies blot out my transgressions.
2 Wash me throughly from mine iniquity, and cleanse me from my sin.
3 For I acknowledge my transgressions: and my sin is ever before me.
4 Against thee, thee only, have I sinned, and done this evil in thy sight: that thou mightest be justified when thou speakest, and be clear when thou judgest.

• • • • • •

10 Create in me a clean heart, O God; and renew a right spirit within me.
11 Cast me not away from thy presence; and take not thy holy spirit from me.
12 Restore unto me the joy of thy salvation; and uphold me with thy free spirit.

• • • • • •

15 O Lord, open thou my lips; and my mouth shall shew forth thy praise.
16 For thou desirest not sacrifice; else would I give it: thou delightest not in burnt offering.

17 The sacrifices of God are a broken spirit: a broken and a contrite heart, O God, thou wilt not despise.

### NRSVue

HAVE mercy on me, O God, according to your steadfast love; according to your abundant mercy, blot out my transgressions.
2 Wash me thoroughly from my iniquity, and cleanse me from my sin.
3 For I know my transgressions, and my sin is ever before me.
4 Against you, you alone, have I sinned and done what is evil in your sight,
so that you are justified in your sentence and blameless when you pass judgment.

• • • • • •

10 Create in me a clean heart, O God, and put a new and right spirit within me.
11 Do not cast me away from your presence, and do not take your holy spirit from me.
12 Restore to me the joy of your salvation, and sustain in me a willing spirit.

• • • • • •

15 O Lord, open my lips, and my mouth will declare your praise.
16 For you have no delight in sacrifice; if I were to give a burnt offering, you would not be pleased.
17 The sacrifice acceptable to God is a broken spirit; a broken and contrite heart, O God, you will not despise.

---

**LESSON SETTING**
   Time: Around the 10th century BCE
   Place: Jerusalem

**LESSON OUTLINE**
   I. Request for Forgiveness
      (Psalm 51:1–4)

**MAIN THOUGHT:** Create in me a clean heart, O God, and put a new and right spirit within me. (Psalm 51:10, NRSVue)

II. Inner Renewal
(Psalm 51:10–12)

III. The Offering of a Contrite Heart
(Psalm 51:15–17)

## UNIFYING PRINCIPLE

It is challenging for people to acknowledge that they have hurt others. When we have wronged others, how do we make amends for our actions and words? When David's sinful actions caused harm to others, he repented and found forgiveness in the Lord.

## INTRODUCTION

The events described in Psalm 51, including the composition of the prayer, take place within the historical context of ancient Israel. According to the superscription of the psalm, it is attributed to King David. The precise time and place of its composition can be inferred from the narrative accounts in the Hebrew Bible. The narrative indicates that David's transgressions occurred during his reign as king of Israel, which is estimated to have taken place around the 10th century BCE.

The location of these events is primarily within the city of Jerusalem, the capital of the kingdom of Israel during David's reign. However, it is important to note that the composition of the psalm itself is likely not limited to a specific physical location, but rather emerges from the personal and spiritual journey of David as he comes to terms with his sins and seeks forgiveness from God. Jerusalem is the most likely location, considering David's residence and the events surrounding Bathsheba.

Psalm 51 is one of the most well-known and beloved psalms in the Hebrew Bible. It is a penitential psalm, a prayer of confession and repentance spoken by a grevious person who has sinned against God. The psalm is traditionally attributed to King David, and it is thought to have been written after his rape of Bathsheba and the subsequent murder of her husband Uriah (2 Samuel 11–12).

The verses chosen for this explanation, Psalm 51:1–4, 10–12, 15–17, are some of the most powerful and moving in the entire psalm. They capture the depth of the psalmist's sin and his desperate need for God's forgiveness. To understand the depth of David's penitential prayer, it is crucial to grasp the historical context in which it was composed. David, a man after God's own heart, had fallen into grave sin, leading to severe consequences for his personal life and his reign as king. His encounter with the prophet Nathan and the subsequent exposure of his sins brought him face to face with the devastating consequences of his actions. Psalm 51 thus emerges from a place of brokenness and deep spiritual introspection, seeking God's mercy, forgiveness, and restoration.

## EXPOSITION

### I. REQUEST FOR FORGIVENESS (PSALM 51:1–4)

The psalm is a prayer made by David after the prophet Nathan had confronted him about his sinful rape of Bathsheba (2 Samuel 11–12). In the opening verses, King David implores God's mercy and forgiveness, recognizing his transgressions. The use of vivid metaphors, such as "blot out my transgressions" and "wash me thoroughly from my iniquity," underscores the depth and severity of his sins. David appeals to God's steadfast love and abundant mercy as the sole source of cleansing and restoration. His plea is rooted in the conviction that God alone can purify and redeem him, highlighting the centrality of divine grace in the process of repentance. Psalm 51 is a prayer for help. The prayer is written from a person in trouble. The prayer is not an indictment against other people and God but recognition that the indictment is for self.

The psalm begins with a plea for God's mercy. Mercy is used here as the language of a person who has no claim for the favor they request. The plea appeals to God's steadfast love and abundant mercy (v.1). The prayer is not merely an expression of human remorse or preoccupation with failure and guilt; it looks beyond himself to God and lays hold on the marvelous possibilities of God's grace. Confession of sin is already on the way to justification because it is first of all a response to grace. It is the act in which humanity acknowledges what it is before God and how amazing and wonderful God is for us. Humans sin and God is loving and gracious.

The psalmist goes on to ask God to wash away his iniquity and cleanse him from his sin (v. 2). He recognizes that his sin is not just an external act, but that it has stained his very soul. He longs to be made clean and pure again. The psalmist knows that he has sinned and that he deserves punishment. He has raped another man's wife and impregnated her. If that was not enough he tried to through an elaborate scheme to falsely place paternity on Bathseba's husband Uriah. When his plan falls through he has Uriah placed on the front line of the battle to be killed ultimately. King David is confronted by the prophet and upon the confrontation he realizes that he has sinned and deserves to be punished. But he also knows that God is merciful and that he is willing to forgive those who repent. The psalmist asks God to blot out his transgressions, to erase them from the record as if they had never happened.

Christians know that their life is judged by God and therefore confess their sins knowing God is faithful and just to forgive. In verse three David is remorseful, not only because of his act of sin but also because of the consequences of his sin. He also understands the meaning and reality of sin. The psalmist confesses that his sin is ultimately against God. He has not just sinned against himself or against another person, but he has sinned against the one who created him and who loves him. This confession is an important part of the repentance process, as it allows the psalmist to take full responsibility for his actions.

## II. INNER RENEWAL (PSALM 51:10–12)

David's prayer then turns to a plea for inner transformation. Using the word "create," the psalmist asks for something that God alone can do; but it can also refer to a process that only God can sustain. He acknowledges the need for a renewed heart, asking God to create in him a clean heart and a steadfast spirit. The psalmist recognizes that true repentance involves not only the forgiveness of sins but also the restoration of a right relationship with God. The confession of sin seeks renewal as forgiveness. The psalm leads the penitent to seek both justification and sanctification. The prayer's central theme is in verse 10: "Create a clean heart for me, O

God, and renew a steadfast spirit within me." He recognizes that his sin has corrupted him and that he needs God's help to be made anew. The prayer seeks a clean heart and renewed spirit. What is unclean is inimical to God. A clean heart would be a mind open and oriented to God. A steadfast spirit would be a mind and will fixed toward God.

The psalmist longs to experience the joy of God's salvation again. He asks God to restore this joy to him and to uphold him with a willing spirit. A willing spirit is a spirit that is obedient to God's will. The psalmist wants to be a person who is fully committed to following God. While the prayer for steadfastness was obviously fitting, after a great fall from grace, the earnest plea for a willing spirit may strike us as less relevant. But upon reflection, such a spirit is God's own antidote to temptation.

## III. THE OFFERING OF A CONTRITE HEART (PSALM 51:15–17)

The enormity of his sin continues to horrify David. Nowhere in this psalm is he concerned to escape the material consequences of his sins: it is the guilt of them that burdens him. He longs to worship freely, gratefully again; and he believes that by the grace of God he will (v.15). This heartfelt plea moves from confession to praise. The psalmist promises to praise God if he is forgiven. He knows that the only way he can truly repay God for his forgiveness is to live a life that glorifies him. The final section of the selected verses focuses on the offering of a contrite heart. David declares that God does not desire mere external sacrifices but a broken spirit and a contrite heart. He recognizes that true worship flows from a heart that is genuinely remorseful and humble before God. David's words highlight the importance of genuine repentance and the need to align one's inner disposition with external acts of worship. It emphasizes the significance of true humility and surrender as essential aspects of the repentance process.

The psalmist understands that God does not require sacrifices or burnt offerings. What God truly desires is a broken and contrite heart (Psalm 51:17). The psalmist ends with a powerful declaration of his faith. He knows that God will not despise a broken and contrite heart. He is confident that God will forgive him and restore him to fellowship with him. Psalm 51:1–4, 10–12, and 15–17 encapsulate the essence of David's penitential prayer, offering a profound reflection on the nature, process, and implications of repentance. The selected verses demonstrate David's heartfelt contrition, his profound awareness of the need for God's forgiveness, and his desire for inner transformation.

## THE LESSON APPLIED

Applying the lessons from Psalm 51 to one's life involves a personal and introspective journey of repentance, forgiveness, and spiritual growth. Here are a few ways believers can apply the lessons from David's psalm to their own lives:

*Acknowledge and confess one's shortcomings:* Like King David, it's important to honestly acknowledge and confess one's sins or areas of weakness. This requires introspection, humility, and a willingness to confront the truth about oneself.

*Seek forgiveness and restoration:* Just as David pleaded for God's forgiveness, individuals can seek forgiveness from those they have wronged and from God. This involves genuine remorse, expressing sincere apologies, and making amends where possible. It also means seeking God's forgiveness through prayer and cultivating a restored relationship with Him.

*Embrace inner transformation:* David's prayer emphasizes the need for a renewed heart and a steadfast spirit. It involves surrendering one's desires, attitudes, and behaviors to God, allowing Him to transform and shape one's character. This may involve cultivating virtues such as humility, compassion, and self–discipline.

*Extend forgiveness to others:* Just as God has forgiven us and continues to do so, we should forgive one another.

*Embrace the transformative power of grace:* Psalm 51 reminds individuals of the boundless nature of God's grace. Applying this lesson involves embracing the belief that no sin is beyond redemption and that God's forgiveness is available to all who sincerely seek it. It also means extending grace to oneself, recognizing that personal growth is a lifelong journey that involves learning from mistakes and embracing the opportunity for transformation.

Applying the truths from Psalm 51 to our lives requires self–reflection, humility, a sincere desire for forgiveness, and an openness to personal transformation. It involves cultivating a contrite heart, seeking God's forgiveness and embracing reconciliation with others, and embracing the life-changing power of God's grace.

## Let's Talk About It

Psalm 51 is a powerful and moving psalm of repentance. It teaches us that no matter how great our sin, God is always willing to forgive us if we repent and turn to him in faith.

1. **The psalm also teaches us that. "Have you ever reflected on the power of repentance and forgiveness?**

Psalm 51, a profound penitential prayer attributed to King David, explores the depths of remorse, the plea for restoration, and the transformative nature of genuine repentance. It is a fascinating journey for Bible students to delve into the historical context, literary structure, and theological themes of this ancient but moving prayer.

### Get Social

Share your views and tag us @rhboydco. Use #rhboydco.

@rhboydco

## Home Daily Devotional Readings
### October 7–13, 2024

| Monday | Tuesday | Wednesday | Thursday | Friday | Saturday | Sunday |
|---|---|---|---|---|---|---|
| Set Free from Bondage | Our God Is Able to Deliver | Our God Is Unstoppable | A Cry for Help in Distress | Have Mercy on Me! | God Delivers Us from Our Distress | Deliver My Soul, O God |
| Luke 13:10–17 | Daniel 3:8–18 | Daniel 3:19–27 | Matthew 8:5–17 | Mark 10:46–52 | Psalm 107:23–32 | Psalm 22:1–11, 19–22 |

LESSON VII                                                    OCTOBER 13, 2024

# A Plea for Deliverance

ADULT TOPIC:                                    BACKGROUND SCRIPTURE: PSALM 22; DANIEL 3
WE'RE IN A TIGHT SPOT                                          LESSON PASSAGE: PSALM 22:1–11

## Psalm 22:1–11

### KJV

MY God, my God, why hast thou forsaken me? why art thou so far from helping me, and from the words of my roaring?
2 O my God, I cry in the day time, but thou hearest not; and in the night season, and am not silent.
3 But thou art holy, O thou that inhabitest the praises of Israel.
4 Our fathers trusted in thee: they trusted, and thou didst deliver them.
5 They cried unto thee, and were delivered: they trusted in thee, and were not confounded.
6 But I am a worm, and no man; a reproach of men, and despised of the people.
7 All they that see me laugh me to scorn: they shoot out the lip, they shake the head, saying,
8 He trusted on the Lord that he would deliver him: let him deliver him, seeing he delighted in him.
9 But thou art he that took me out of the womb: thou didst make me hope when I was upon my mother's breasts.
10 I was cast upon thee from the womb: thou art my God from my mother's belly.
11 Be not far from me; for trouble is near; for there is none to help.

### NRSVue

MY God, my God, why have you forsaken me? Why are you so far from helping me, from the words of my groaning?
2 O my God, I cry by day, but you do not answer; and by night but find no rest.

3 Yet you are holy, enthroned on the praises of Israel.
4 In you our ancestors trusted; they trusted, and you delivered them.
5 To you they cried and were saved; in you they trusted and were not put to shame.
6 But I am a worm and not human, scorned by others and despised by the people.
7 All who see me mock me; they sneer at me; they shake their heads;
8 "Commit your cause to the Lord; let him deliver— let him rescue the one in whom he delights!"
9 Yet it was you who took me from the womb; you kept me safe on my mother's breast.

10 On you I was cast from my birth, and since my mother bore me you have been my God.
11 Do not be far from me, for trouble is near, and there is no one to help.

---

**LESSON SETTING**

Time: Post–Exilic Era
(after 538 BCE)

Place: Unknown

**LESSON OUTLINE**
I. Feeling Abandoned
   (Psalm 22:1–2)
II. Faith of the Ancestors
   (Psalm 22:3–5)
III. Facing Others Attacks
   (Psalm 22:6–11)

**MAIN THOUGHT:** My God, my God, why have you forsaken me? Why are you so far from helping me, from the words of my groaning? (Psalm 22:1, NRSVue)

## Unifying Principle

People may feel desperate or alone amid tragic circumstances. What can calm their feelings? Calling on God for help gives a sense of release and bolsters hope for divine rescue.

## Introduction

Unfortunately, pinpointing the precise time and location of Psalm 22:1-11's composition remains a matter of scholarly debate. There are several competing lines of evidence, offering different possibilities:
- Some scholars associate the psalm's style and themes with the Psalter's first book, traditionally attributed to King David. Historical events from David's life, such as his persecution by Saul, could offer parallels to the psalmist's suffering.
- Other scholars point to linguistic features and allusions to later historical events, suggesting the psalm might have been written during or after the Babylonian exile. This context could explain themes of suffering and divine abandonment experienced by the returning Jewish community.
- The lack of definitive historical markers within the psalm itself makes precise dating and location challenging. Some scholars argue for a composite authorship, with different sections added over time, further complicating the question of origin.

Ultimately, while a definitive answer remains elusive, recognizing the various proposed contexts enriches our understanding of the psalm's potential interpretations. The themes of suffering, faith, and hope resonate across eras and locations, regardless of the specific circumstances surrounding its creation.

Psalm 22 is a psalm of lament traditionally ascribed to King David. The first eleven verses of this psalm, in particular, paint a vivid picture of anguish and desperation. This lesson aims to delve into the various dimensions of Psalm 22:1-11, shedding light on its historical context, literary structure, and theological implications.

To grasp the full import of Psalm 22:1-11, it is crucial to consider the historical backdrop against which it was composed. David, the purported author, experienced numerous trials and tribulations throughout his life, including persecution by King Saul and his own son Absalom's rebellion. These personal and political challenges likely influenced the emotive tone and content of the psalm.

Psalm 22:1-11 exhibits a chiastic structure, with the opening and closing verses sharing similar themes. The psalm begins with a cry of abandonment, shifts to a description of suffering and mockery, and concludes with a plea for deliverance. This carefully crafted structure contributes to the psalm's overall impact and serves to emphasize the psalmist's plea for divine intervention.

## Exposition

### I. Feeling Abandoned (Psalm 22:1-2)

Psalm 22:1-11 stands as a stark and poignant expression of human suffering, a raw cry of anguish directed towards the heavens. Within its eleven verses, the psalmist grapples with profound questions of faith, abandonment, and the very nature of God's presence in the face of unimaginable pain.

The psalm launches with a gut-wrenching plea, "My God, my God, why have you forsaken me?" (Psalm 22:1). This opening line, repeated in the Gospel accounts of Jesus' crucifixion (Mark 15:34, Matthew 27:46) where Jesus repeats these words, resonates with the universality of human suffering. Centuries before Jesus quoted these words from the cross, someone in mortal pain cried out, "My God, my God, why have you forsaken me?" This question transcends specific contexts and speaks to the deep existential concerns that arise in the face of pain and isolation. The psalmist opens with a cry toward their God. Referring to God as "my God" suggest a level of closeness and intimacy based upon personal prior experiences.

For many the sense of abandonment is the primary reason why they might lose faith in God. He seems too often like an absent deity. Too often, when we cry out in need or pain, we receive nothing but silence and absence. It embarrasses us, it angers us, and it casts the shadow of doubt over many people's already tenuous faith. The remarkable thing is that the Bible itself is not reticent on the subject. One can find those doubts and struggles with God's absence all over the Bible. Of course, almost every Psalm of lament, like this one, expresses the pain of God's absence, but beyond that it appears throughout Scripture.

There's Job, where God seems absent to the suffering Job, while we get to look behind the curtain to see something of what God is up to, and it's not very nice. There's Isaiah 45:15, where, right in the middle of a series of staggering promises, the prophet admits, almost as an aside, "Truly you are a God who has been hiding himself." It's a major theme in the prophet Habakkuk: How long, Lord, must I call for help, but you do not listen? Or cry out to you, "Violence!" but you do not save? Why do you make me look at injustice? Why do you tolerate wrongdoing? Destruction and violence are before me; there is strife, and conflict abounds. (1: 1–2)

Imagine the pain of feeling abandoned by a loved one. The psalmist's statements about God are confessions of faith and confidence in God. The psalmist questions God by asking why. The cry "My God" shows that the Forsaken One truly did have a relationship with God. He was a victim of the cruelty of humanity, but the cry and the complaint is to God. Second, the repetition of the plea shows the intensity of the agony. For many this questioning is viewed as sacrilegious and disrespectful, but the psalmist knows that the Almighty is powerful, loving, kind and big enough to handle big questions. The questioning is not a lapse of faith or broken relationship but a cry of awareness and a cry of trust. The psalmist was so dependent on God's presence that he was keenly aware of the seemingly lack thereof. The psalmist is so familiar with God's presence that the lack of presence feels abandoned and like a withdrawal.

## II. FAITH OF THE ANCESTORS (PSALM 22:3–5)

The psalmist remembered God and His greatness, even when immersed in suffering. He did not curse or blaspheme God, and he knew that his present agony did not change God's holiness "You are holy,"

"Enthroned in the praises of Israel" (v.3). The present crisis that the psalmist was facing had filled him with doubt and confusion, yet he would not allow doubts as to the holiness or greatness of God. Whatever he did not know in his present situation, he did know that God was holy. The psalmist shifted his focus away from his circumstance and recalled God's holiness.

David also remembered how God had answered and delivered many times before. Strangely, this would add measures of both comfort and despair: comfort, knowing that he cried to the same God who had delivered before and who could deliver again; despair, knowing that the God who had delivered before now seemed so distant and silent. David called upon his memory of God's faithfulness to his ancestors brings both contentment and despondency. He knew God was able based upon God's previous performances in the lives of his ancestors but was angst by the possibility of God being unwilling to help him.

## III. Facing Others' Attacks (Psalm 22:6–11)

The intensity of the conflict made David feel not only ignored, but insignificant. God seems to help other people, but seems to give no help to worms. The low standing he had in his own eyes and in the eyes of others simply added to his agony. He felt himself to be comparable to a helpless, powerless, down–trodden worm, passive while crushed, and unnoticed and despised by those who trod upon him. David, the psalmist's misery is exasperated at those who mocked and misunderstood his agony. People used David's misery to question his relationship with God. It was as if they said, "It seemed that he trusted in the LORD, but we all know that the LORD rescues those who trust in Him. It seemed that he delighted in God, but that must be false because he is not delivered." Still today people interpret suffering and misery as an absence of relationship with God.

"Let Him deliver Him, since He delights in Him (v.8)" reveals the frequent ignorance and cruelty of those who oppose God and His people. These words claim to see no deliverance, when deliverance would indeed come soon. The phrase also questions the delight of God in the Forsaken One, when God did and does truly delight in that one. Despite his suffering, David stays steadfast in his faith and hope in God.

In verse eleven David makes another plea. The plea for help is again eloquently and persuasively stated. God seems far away; but trouble is near – and there is none to help, so God must intervene. He shows his reliance on God.

## The Lesson Applied

Psalm 22 remains a powerful and relevant text for readers today. Its unflinching portrayal of human suffering resonates with anyone who has experienced pain, loss, or existential doubt. The psalm's oscillation between despair and hope offers a mirror to our own internal struggles, reminding us that even in the darkest moments, faith can offer a glimmer of light.

Often, church congregations can become very uncomfortable or defensive when people start asking "why" to God. Some people can even experience alienation from their beloved church family when they ask questions like this, appearing to question the Almighty. The psalmist invites us to embrace the questioning. The fact that these questions are embedded in Scripture reminds us of their validity. When we, or others in our congregation, experience hardship, Scripture invites us not to shush questions and anguish, but rather to embrace them.

Following the Bible's example of healthy lament, we can voice our pain in the confidence that God hears us. This is a sign of faith, not its opposite—a point emphasized by the fact that Jesus himself quotes, "My God, my God, why have you forsaken me?" on the cross.

## LET'S TALK ABOUT IT

In Psalm 22:1–11, we witness the psalmist's raw expression of anguish and their unwavering trust in God amidst suffering. As you consider the lesson, reflect on the following prompts and share your insights:

1. **How do you personally relate to the psalmist's cry of abandonment in verse 1? Have there been moments in your life when you felt distant from or abandoned by God? How did you navigate through those challenging times?**

   The psalmist uses vivid imagery to depict their suffering and humiliation in verses 6–8.

2. **Can you think of any instances in your life when you felt similarly vulnerable or experienced scorn? How did you find strength and hope in those moments?**

   Despite the psalmist's anguish, they maintain a steadfast trust in God's faithfulness throughout the passage.

3. **How do you cultivate trust in God during times of adversity? What practices or perspectives help you hold onto faith when faced with difficulties**

   In verses 9–11, the psalmist recalls God's faithfulness to their ancestors.

4. **Are there instances from your own life or from history where you have witnessed God's faithfulness? How do these experiences shape your trust in Him during challenging times?**

   Sharing God's "track record" in your life can strengthen and encourage you when facing difficulties and can encourage others to maintain their faith.

## GET SOCIAL

Share your views and tag us @rhboydco. Use #rhboydco.

@rhboydco

## HOME DAILY DEVOTIONAL READINGS
### OCTOBER 14–20, 2024

| MONDAY | TUESDAY | WEDNESDAY | THURSDAY | FRIDAY | SATURDAY | SUNDAY |
| --- | --- | --- | --- | --- | --- | --- |
| Redemption through Christ's Blood | Praise God for New Birth | May Your God Deliver You | God Shut the Lions' Mouths | Deborah's Song of Deliverance | Praising God with a Loud Voice | God's Victory Feast |
| Ephesians 1:3–14 | 1 Peter 1:3–12 | Daniel 6:10–17 | Daniel 6:18–28 | Judges 5:1–5, 12–22 | Luke 17:11–18 | Isaiah 25:1–10 |

# LESSON VIII

OCTOBER 20, 2024

# PRAISE FOR DELIVERANCE

ADULT TOPIC:
DINNER TIME!

BACKGROUND SCRIPTURE: ISAIAH 25; DANIEL 6:10–28
LESSON PASSAGE: ISAIAH 25:1–10

## ISAIAH 25:1–10

### KJV

O LORD, thou art my God; I will exalt thee, I will praise thy name; for thou hast done wonderful things; thy counsels of old are faithfulness and truth.
2 For thou hast made of a city an heap; of a defenced city a ruin: a palace of strangers to be no city; it shall never be built.
3 Therefore shall the strong people glorify thee, the city of the terrible nations shall fear thee.
4 For thou hast been a strength to the poor, a strength to the needy in his distress, a refuge from the storm, a shadow from the heat, when the blast of the terrible ones is as a storm against the wall.
5 Thou shalt bring down the noise of strangers, as the heat in a dry place; even the heat with the shadow of a cloud: the branch of the terrible ones shall be brought low.
6 And in this mountain shall the Lord of hosts make unto all people a feast of fat things, a feast of wines on the lees, of fat things full of marrow, of wines on the lees well refined.
7 And he will destroy in this mountain the face of the covering cast over all people, and the vail that is spread over all nations.
8 He will swallow up death in victory; and the Lord God will wipe away tears from off all faces; and the rebuke of his people shall he take away from off all the earth: for the Lord hath spoken it.
9 And it shall be said in that day, Lo, this is our God; we have waited for him, and he will save

### NRSVue

O LORD, you are my God; I will exalt you; I will praise your name, for you have done wonderful things, plans formed of old, faithful and sure.
2 For you have made the city a heap, the fortified city a ruin; the palace of foreigners is a city no more; it will never be rebuilt.
3 Therefore strong peoples will glorify you; cities of ruthless nations will fear you.
4 For you have been a refuge to the poor, a refuge to the needy in their distress, a shelter from the rainstorm and a shade from the heat. When the blast of the ruthless was like a winter rainstorm,
5 the noise of foreigners like heat in a dry place, you subdued the heat with the shade of clouds; the song of the ruthless was stilled.
6 On this mountain the Lord of hosts will make for all peoples a feast of rich food, a feast of well-aged wines, of rich food filled with marrow, of well-aged wines strained clear.
7 And he will destroy on this mountain the shroud that is cast over all peoples, the covering that is spread over all nations;
8 he will swallow up death forever. Then the Lord God will wipe away the tears from all faces, and the disgrace of his people he will take away from all the earth, for the Lord has spoken.
9 It will be said on that day, "See, this is our God; we have waited for him, so that he might save us. This is the Lord for whom we have

**MAIN THOUGHT:** On this mountain the LORD of hosts will make for all peoples a feast of rich food, a feast of well-aged wines, of rich food filled with marrow, of well-aged wines strained clear. (Isaiah 25:6, NRSVue)

# Isaiah 25:1–10

## KJV

us: this is the Lord; we have waited for him, we will be glad and rejoice in his salvation.
10 For in this mountain shall the hand of the Lord rest, and Moab shall be trodden down under him, even as straw is trodden down for the dunghill.

## NRSVue

waited; let us be glad and rejoice in his salvation."
10 For the hand of the Lord will rest on this mountain. The Moabites shall be trodden down in their place as straw is trodden down in the manure.

## LESSON SETTING

**Time:** 8th Century BCE or Post-exilic Setting (6th Century BCE)

**Place:** Jerusalem

## LESSON OUTLINE

I. **A Song of Thanksgiving** (Isaiah 25:1–5)

II. **God's Feast** (Isaiah 25:6–8)

III. **A Song of Praise for God's Deliverance** (Isaiah 25:9–10)

## UNIFYING PRINCIPLE

People seek refuge during the stormy trials of life. Who can encourage and support us in our distress? God's promises and faithfulness can assure us that we will endure until the storm passes. Just as the the prophet Isaiah can affirm faith in God in the midst of tumult, contemporary readers are asked to remember the promises of God actualized in their own times.

## INTRODUCTION

The dating and specific historical context of Isaiah 25:1–10 remain debated among scholars. Some place it within the Assyrian period (8th century BCE), while others suggest a post-exilic setting (6th century BCE). Regardless of the precise time frame, the passage likely addresses the anxieties and hopes of a community facing significant challenges, whether external threats or internal struggles. The promise of divine deliverance and ultimate vindication offered solace and encouragement in the midst of hardship.

Isaiah 25:1–10 is a profound passage in the Book of Isaiah that presents a vivid prophetic vision of divine salvation and restoration. This commentary aims to explore the rich theological themes embedded within these verses, highlighting their significance in the context of Israel's history and their relevance for believers today. The Book of Isaiah is renowned for its prophetic messages of judgment, hope, and restoration. Isaiah 25:1–10 stands as a remarkable passage within this book, offering a poetic depiction of Yahweh's sovereignty, faithfulness, and ultimate victory over Israel's enemies. This commentary endeavors to unpack the theological nuances and interpretive challenges present in this passage, shedding light on its implications for ancient Israel and contemporary readers alike. Isaiah 25:1–10 stands as a vibrant tapestry of praise and judgment, woven together by the thread of divine deliverance. The prophet, in a powerful crescendo of pronouncements, extols the Lord's faithfulness and might, while simultaneously pronouncing doom upon the oppressive and arrogant.

The passage in Isaiah 25:1–10 aligns with the overall message of the book of Isaiah in several ways. It contributes to the broader themes and motifs found throughout the book, reinforcing key theological concepts and prophetic visions that run consistently from beginning to end. The book of Isaiah repeatedly emphasizes the sovereignty of God over all nations and events. Isaiah 25:1–10 echoes this theme by extolling Yahweh as the powerful and faithful God who has full control over history. The passage underscores God's ability to bring down powerful nations and establish His reign, highlighting His ultimate authority and dominion.

Throughout the book of Isaiah, there are messianic prophecies that point to a future figure, often referred to as the "Servant of the Lord" or the "Anointed One," who will bring salvation and establish God's Kingdom. Isaiah 25:1–10 participates in this messianic vision by describing a future time of divine salvation, where death is swallowed up, tears are wiped away, and a lavish banquet is prepared. This eschatological hope is consistent with other messianic promises in Isaiah, contributing to the anticipation of the coming Messiah.

Isaiah frequently emphasizes that God's redemptive plan extends beyond the borders of Israel to encompass all nations. Isaiah 25:1–10 echoes this theme by proclaiming that all peoples will be invited to the grand feast prepared by God. The passage highlights God's desire to draw all nations to Himself, foreshadowing the New Testament concept of the inclusion of the Gentiles into the people of God through faith in Christ. Thus, the theme of the universality of God's love is present in both the Old and New Testaments.

Overall, Isaiah 25:1–10 aligns with the broader message of the book of Isaiah by emphasizing God's sovereignty, the themes of judgment and deliverance, the anticipation of the Messiah, and the inclusiveness of God's salvation. It contributes to the overarching narrative of God's redemptive plan for His people and the ultimate establishment of His Kingdom.

## EXPOSITION

### I. A SONG OF THANKSGIVING (ISAIAH 25:1–5)

The passage begins with the writer addressing God and professing their relationship of devotion and commitment. The writer's confession of "my God' is a statement of commitment to a personal relationship with God. The writer boldly expresses his appreciation to the Almighty for grace, faithfulness and relationship.

In the following verses the writer provides the reasons for praising and thanking God. The first reason for praise is because of God's faithfulness in effectuating marvelous deeds (v. 1). The writer recognizes God's incredible power on behalf of God's people. The writer recalls God's mighty acts of deliverance and salvation throughout history. It highlights God's faithfulness and His ability to fulfill His plans, which were established long ago. This verse sets the tone for the passage, expressing the prophet's deep reverence and gratitude towards God. The writer's words of thanks are words of assurance to all who heard in

Judah. It is believed that at the time Judah was being attacked by Assyria, the people of Judah could be assured that God's plans for them were permanent and the future would be fine because they were predestined. Given the strenuous geopolitical circumstances that God's people were facing at the time, this pronouncement is all the more extraordinary. Contemporary believers can have the same confidence. God is faithful and no enemy, circumstance, or evil will interfere with God's plan, power, will and purpose for His people.

The second reason for thanksgiving can be found in verse 2. The writer goes into detail about God's previous deeds for His people. God's people are called upon to remember what God has already done for all of them and understand that the same deeds of power can take place in the present time. Here, Isaiah reflects on God's judgment upon the enemies of Israel. The "city" and the "fortified city" represent the strongholds of Israel's adversaries. The destruction of these cities symbolizes God's power to overthrow the enemies of His people. The phrase "it will never be rebuilt" emphasizes the finality of this judgment and suggests that the enemy's power will be permanently eradicated.

In this verse, the writer of Isaiah predicts the response of the nations witnessing God's deliverance. The phrase "strong peoples" refers to the powerful nations that had oppressed Israel. The prophet foresees that their encounter with God's mighty acts will lead them to acknowledge His greatness and give Him glory. Additionally, the "cities of ruthless nations" will experience fear in the presence of God's power, recognizing the futility of opposing Him. The writer states that these ruthless nations will come to praise God because God will radically convert and transform those ungodly and oppressive people.

Additionally the writer identifies another reason for thanking God because of His protection for the oppressed and poor (v.4). He writes that in their time of weakness and persecution, God will mercifully become a refuge and protect those who could not protect themselves. God will subdue the oppressors and protect His people. Certainly, African Americans can identify with God's protection for the oppressed and poor. God has protected African Americans through systematic economic oppression and racial oppression and that is reason to praise God.

This verse also highlights the compassionate nature of God. It portrays Him as a refuge and defender of the marginalized and vulnerable, such as the poor and the needy. The imagery of a "shelter from the storm" and "shade from the heat" conveys the idea of God's protection and provision in times of trouble. The mention of the "ruthless" emphasizes the destructive power of human oppression, which is likened to a storm battering against a wall. However, God's strength and care serve as a secure refuge for those who seek Him.

Verse five continues the theme of God's protection and deliverance. The metaphor of heat in a dry place conveys the discomfort and oppression inflicted by foreign powers. However, God's intervention is likened to a cloud providing cool shade, calming the noise and song of the ruthless. This imagery suggests that God's presence and intervention bring relief and silence to one's enemies, signifying their defeat and subjugation. What comfort to know that our enemies have no power over our God, and by extension, no power over us!

## II. A Song of Praise for God's Deliverance (Isaiah 25:6–8)

The scene now changes from singing praises to a banquet God will prepare for His people. The banquet is a joyful celebration for all of God's people not just a few chosen but for Hebrews, Gentiles and all of God's children. The mountain symbolizes a place of divine presence and authority. The feast described here is not limited to Israel but is open to "all peoples." It signifies God's inclusive salvation and His desire to extend His blessings to all nations. The imagery of rich and abundant food and wine portrays the abundance of divine blessings and joy that will be experienced in this messianic age.

In addition to the blessings of food for all people in the Kingdom, God will swallow up death forever, wipe away all tears and remove disgrace. This verse proclaims God's ultimate triumph over death and His promise to bring comfort and restoration to His people. The phrase "swallow up death forever" signifies the defeat of death and the assurance of eternal life in God's presence. While the text is unclear about how God will accomplish these miraculous acts the focus is not on how but communicating that God will do it and this will happen. God is almighty and death will no longer have power over His people.

The wiping away of tears and the removal of reproach suggest the complete restoration of joy and dignity for God's people. This verse provides hope and reassurance in the face of adversity and suffering, assuring the readers that God's promises will be fulfilled because He has spoken.

The tears referenced are not just tears of sadness but tears of oppression, sickness, pain, disappointment, rejection, financial trouble, loss, racism, sexism, classism, ageism, homophobia and all other ills of the world. God will wipe these evils out and God's people will no longer have to endure the pain of these.

## III. God's Feast (Isaiah 25:9–10)

The prophet envisions a future time when the people of God will joyfully acknowledge and celebrate His salvation. The phrase "on that day" refers to the eschatological fulfillment of God's redemptive plan. The repetition of "we have waited for him" emphasizes the patient expectation and trust of the faithful. The verse encourages believers to rejoice and find gladness in the salvation that God brings, recognizing Him as the source of their deliverance.

Verse nine contains a response of trust in God. The writer says that the people from all over the earth will gather on the mountain and sing and declare their trust in God. People will come from all over the globe and form a community of believers. This community will sing about its relationship with God broadly proclaiming the Almighty to be "their God." Their God has rescued them alone not with any human assistance it was through and by God alone. All credit is given and directed to God. This faith community has two things in common: they have previously placed their trust in God.

Trust is an act of hopeful waiting. God will reward those who hopefully wait upon

Him. Secondly, they now rejoice over what God has done. They rejoice because God's plan has been accomplished and they are the recipients of God's love, grace, protection and provision.

The reason why the people are able to sing and rejoice is because they see God's power His hand continuously resting on Mount Zion. God's unchanging hand represents God's continued guidance and power over His people. God would be with them forever. What a wonderful reason to sing, knowing that God will guide and protect His people. Isaiah 25:1–10 stands as a testament to God's faithfulness, justice, and love. By engaging with this text we gain a deeper appreciation for its enduring message of hope and transformation. As we grapple with the challenges of our day, this passage reminds us that God remains active in history, offering deliverance to the oppressed and calling all people.

## The Lesson Applied

Isaiah 25:1–10 presents a prophetic vision of divine salvation, encompassing themes of praise, judgment, restoration, and hope. The passage expresses the prophet's deep reverence for God, celebrates His faithfulness, and proclaims His ultimate victory over Israel's enemies. It offers a glimpse into the inclusive and universal scope of God's salvation, pointing towards a future messianic age characterized by joy, restoration, and the defeat of death. This passage continues to inspire believers today, reminding them of God's sovereignty, His promise of deliverance, and the hope that we have in His salvation.

## Let's Talk About It

1. Reflecting on Isaiah 25:1–10, how does this passage inspire hope and reassurance in the face of challenges and difficulties?
2. How does the depiction of God's sovereignty, His deliverance, and the promise of a future banquet of joy and restoration speak to your own faith journey?
3. In what ways can we find encouragement and find practical application in our lives from the themes presented in this passage?

## Get Social

Share your views and tag us @rhboydco. Use #rhboydco.

@rhboydco

LESSON IX                                                    OCTOBER 27, 2024

# TRUST IN GOD ALONE

**ADULT TOPIC:**  
LET THE SILENCE SPEAK

**BACKGROUND SCRIPTURE:** PSALM 62  
**LESSON PASSAGE:** PSALM 62:1–12

## PSALM 62:1–12

### KJV

TRULY my soul waiteth upon God: from him cometh my salvation.
2 He only is my rock and my salvation; he is my defence; I shall not be greatly moved.
3 How long will ye imagine mischief against a man? ye shall be slain all of you: as a bowing wall shall ye be, and as a tottering fence.
4 They only consult to cast him down from his excellency: they delight in lies: they bless with their mouth, but they curse inwardly. Selah.

5 My soul, wait thou only upon God; for my expectation is from him.
6 He only is my rock and my salvation: he is my defence; I shall not be moved.
7 In God is my salvation and my glory: the rock of my strength, and my refuge, is in God.
8 Trust in him at all times; ye people, pour out your heart before him: God is a refuge for us. Selah.
9 Surely men of low degree are vanity, and men of high degree are a lie: to be laid in the balance, they are altogether lighter than vanity.

10 Trust not in oppression, and become not vain in robbery: if riches increase, set not your heart upon them.
11 God hath spoken once; twice have I heard this; that power belongeth unto God.

12 Also unto thee, O Lord, belongeth mercy: for thou renderest to every man according to his work.

### NRSVue

FOR God alone my soul waits in silence; from him comes my salvation.
2 He alone is my rock and my salvation, my fortress; I shall never be shaken.
3 How long will you assail a person, will you batter your victim, all of you, as you would a leaning wall, a tottering fence?
4 Their only plan is to bring down a person of prominence. They take pleasure in falsehood; they bless with their mouths, but inwardly they curse. Selah

5 For God alone my soul waits in silence, for my hope is from him.
6 He alone is my rock and my salvation, my fortress; I shall not be shaken.
7 On God rests my deliverance and my honor; my mighty rock, my refuge is in God.
8 Trust in him at all times, O people; pour out your heart before him; God is a refuge for us. Selah
9 Those of low estate are but a breath; those of high estate are a delusion;
in the balances they go up; they are together lighter than a breath.
10 Put no confidence in extortion, and set no vain hopes on robbery; if riches increase, do not set your heart on them.
11 Once God has spoken; twice have I heard this:
that power belongs to God,
12    and steadfast love belongs to you, O Lord. For you repay to all according to their work.

**MAIN THOUGHT:** For God alone my soul waits in silence, for my hope is from him. (Psalm 62:5, NRSVue)

**LESSON SETTING**
Time: Possibly Between the 10th and 9th century BCE

Place: Possibly Israel/Judah

**LESSON OUTLINE**

 I. Stillness in Stress
    (Psalm 62: 1–4)

 II. Security in God Alone
     (Psalm 62:5–8)

 III. Security Is Found Only in
      God (Psalm 62:9–12)

## UNIFYING PRINCIPLE

There are times when the fast pace of life keeps us in a frenzy. Where can we find solitude and calm? In stillness and quiet, the psalmist finds God's salvation, hope, refuge, and deliverance.

## INTRODUCTION

To fully appreciate the richness of Psalm 62, it is essential to understand its historical and literary context. Scholars attribute its composition to King David, a figure renowned for his intimate relationship with God amidst triumphs and trials. The psalm is classified as an individual lament, expressing personal distress and seeking divine intervention. Its lyrical structure, marked by parallelism and repetition, reinforces its poetic beauty and emotional impact.

Psalm 62 holds a potent mix of personal conviction, theological depth, and practical wisdom invites careful exploration. It stands as a testament to the enduring human longing for security and refuge in the midst of life's uncertainties. It resonates with readers across generations by articulating a profound trust in God that transcends the challenges of our daily existence.

In a world marked by volatility and uncertainty, Psalm 62 offers a timeless message of hope and guidance. The psalmist's unwavering trust in God amidst hardship demonstrates the transformative power of faith in navigating life's challenges. The call to prioritize love for God and trust in divine justice resonates in contemporary struggles for social justice and ethical living.

Moreover, the psalm's literary artistry—the vivid imagery, the powerful metaphors, and the rhythmic repetition—makes its message readily relatable and impactful in the human experience. His poetic words become more than theological discourse; it transforms into a song of resilience, a testimony of one who has walked with the Lord, a whispered prayer in the face of doubt, and a clarion call for righteous action.

## EXPOSITION

### I. STILLNESS IN STRESS (PSALM 62:1–4)

David begins by emphasizing his dependence upon God and God solely. However difficult or dangerous David declares that he is dependent and relying on God. The phrase "Truly my soul finds rest in God" expresses a deep sense of inner peace and security that comes from knowing and relying on God. The psalmist acknowledges that true salvation, both in this life and the next, comes solely from God. This verse sets the tone for the entire psalm, emphasizing the psalmist's unwavering confidence in God as the ultimate source of refuge and deliverance. David is making a bold declaration.

While some have translated this verse to mean silence it is not meant to be a verbal silence. Instead it is an inner stillness. This inner stillness is one that comes from completely relinquishing fears, insecurities and anxieties to God as a sign of trust.

The psalmist confidently boasts of God and the security that God provides (v.2). He declares that he will not be shaken. Here, the psalmist continues to extol the unwavering faithfulness of God. By using metaphors such as "rock," "salvation," and "fortress," the psalmist emphasizes God's unchanging strength and security. God is his refuge. When David speaks of salvation here he is not referencing salvation in the same sense of Christians; remember this generations before Jesus' earthly birth. Instead salvation is meant to express the security of deliverance from trouble and or enemies. The psalmist's declaration, "I will never be shaken," reflects a steadfast confidence in God's ability to provide unwavering protection and stability. David is confident even amidst potential confusion and conflict.

The psalmist expresses the distress and opposition they are facing (.v3). The psalmist uses vivid imagery to describe their adversaries as assaulting and attempting to throw them down. The metaphors of a leaning wall and a tottering fence convey vulnerability and weakness in the face of opposition. This verse highlights the contrast between the psalmist's trust in God's unshakable strength and the temporal nature of human power. Emphasizing the fragility of human opposition compared to God's strength. David describes hostility in a social setting and directly addresses his enemies. David was facing external pressure from his enemies. These unfair attacks seemed to last excessive lengths of time which is why he uses the phrase "how long." These lengthy attacks were excessively unbalanced, reminiscent of bullying, because the strong are attacking one man who is very vulnerable.

The psalmist describes the malicious intentions and deceptive nature of their adversaries. The enemies seek to undermine the psalmist's position and take pleasure in spreading falsehoods. The psalmist recognizes the hypocrisy of their adversaries, who outwardly bless with their words but inwardly curse with their hearts. The enemies have contrasting actions and thoughts revealing their moral bankruptcy. This verse serves as a reminder of the fallen nature of humanity and the duplicity that can exist within relationships and social structures. The psalmist's adversaries behavior highlights the possibility of deception and hypocrisy of enemies. Which underlines the dangers of misplaced trust in humanity. Christians should be ever mindful not to misplace their trust but to always trust solely like David in God.

## II. Security in God Alone (Psalm 62: 5–8)

Verses five and six repeat David's opening but there are some subtle differences. David urges on himself the silence which he stated in verse one. Secondly, he substitutes hope for salvation. David confesses his expectation in God. He finds rest in the silence and with God. Amidst the turmoil caused by their adversaries, the psalmist reaffirms their hope in God as the ultimate source of comfort and assurance. This verse emphasizes the psalmist's deliberate choice to turn to God for solace and to anchor their hope in Him.

Similar to verse 2, the psalmist repeats the affirmations of God's unchanging nature and steadfast protection in verse 6. By reiterating these declarations, the psalmist reinforces their resolute trust in God's reliability and their conviction that they will not be shaken, despite the challenges they face. What an amazing self assurance; that the psalmist will not be moved regardless of what may come his way. The psalmist words here are similar to the African American hymn lyrics:

> Oh I, shall not, I shall not be moved
> I shall not, I shall not be moved
> Just like a tree planted by the water
> I shall not be moved
> "I Shall Not Be Moved" (Public Domain)

Based upon his personal experiences of God's protection David encourages the people to trust in God continually. David is making a universal call to trust, thus expanding the message of trust beyond his own personal experiences. As king of Israel David is responsible for leading God's people. David urges the people to trust God. Not only are they to trust God but to be vulnerable with God (v.8). They are to pour out their hearts before God. Pouring out one's heart is to express one's true self before God. Once the people were secure in God as their rock then the vulnerability and freedom to expose themselves would be the natural next step. David urges the people to exercise vulnerability and openness with God. Sharing burdens with God strengthens dependence. As Christians we too should exercise this type of dependence and trust in God. Pour out your heart to God and trust God with your hurt, dreams, aspirations and healing.

The psalmist acknowledges their complete dependence on God for salvation and honor. They recognize that their worth and security come from God alone. By referring to God as their mighty rock and refuge, the psalmist emphasizes their unwavering confidence in God's ability to provide both physical and spiritual protection. David's conclusion that God is a refuge for us reemphasizes the thesis of verse seven. God is our rock and is a hiding place. When our souls have been poured out before God, we are the most vulnerable. God rewards our vulnerability by embarrassing us with His love and grace.

The psalmist extends a call to trust in God to all people. This verse serves as an invitation for individuals to wholeheartedly place their trust in God, regardless of their circumstances. The psalmist encourages the pouring out of hearts before God, emphasizing the importance of honest and intimate communication with Him. The psalmist declares God as the refuge for all, underscoring the universal nature of God's provision and care.

## III. Security Is Found Only in God (Psalm 62: 9–12)

Here David reflects on the transitoriness of humanity (v.9). The phrases "men of low degree" and "men of high degree" could represent the polarities of the lowborn or highborn of humanity or just simply a representation of humanity. Either way he says these people are but a vapor, a breath, and a lie. They are empty and when placed on God's scale there is nothing there. Our true substance is spiritual and is found in our relationship with God. This is what puts weight on the scale. There is a fleeting nature of human power and status with the enduring nature of God. The psalmist asserts that both the lowborn and highborn, when compared to God, are insignificant and transient. This verse serves as a reminder that worldly accomplishments and social hierarchies hold no eternal value. Often we place so much weight in amassing earthly accomplishments and possessions but David says these have no weight only a consistent reliance and trust in God will give you the weight.

The psalmist warns against placing trust in ill-gotten gains and material possessions. They caution against the pursuit of wealth and the temptation to find security in material abundance. Note the psalmist is not against gaining material abundance but scolds those who find security and place their trust in those things. This verse emphasizes the futility of placing ultimate value in earthly possessions and highlights the importance of prioritizing spiritual riches and trusting in God rather than in material wealth. Oppressing or robbing others to receive material possessions is not lasting. They will not bring security in fact they will bring a greater sense of insecurity. Only a life and heart dedicated to God will bring that type of security. Those who oppress others are only planting seeds of their own destruction. David's warnings are not just for ancient Israel but also for modern day believers as well.

David is now bring this psalm to a close with a witness and prayer. God has spoken again to him directly (v. 11). This is the reward of waiting before God in silence. If you want to hear from God again perhaps wait patiently in silence. Our living God uses words, visions, dreams, messengers, angelic visitations to speak to us this one of the ways that differentiates God from other gods.

David heard from God that "power belongs to God." In this verse, the psalmist reflects on the divine revelation they have received. The psalmist states that God has spoken, emphasizing the authority and truthfulness of God's words. The phrase "Power belongs to you, God" underscores God's sovereignty and ultimate dominion over all things. This verse reaffirms the psalmist's trust in God's unlimited power and serves as a reminder of God's unwavering control in the midst of uncertain circumstances.

The psalmist acknowledges two fundamental aspects of God's character: His unfailing love and His righteous judgment (v.12). The psalmist affirms that God's love is steadfast and unwavering. Additionally, they acknowledge that God is the ultimate judge, rewarding individuals based on their actions. Lastly, the psalmist lets us know that we can count on God's justice: "you reward everyone according to what they have done. (vs.12)" God is the ultimate judge and He rewards those who trust in Him.

## THE LESSON APPLIED

Psalm 62 is a powerful expression of unwavering trust in God amidst life's trials. Through its verses, the psalmist proclaims their confidence in God as their rock, salvation, and fortress. They contrast the transient nature of human power with the enduring strength and sovereignty of God. The psalmist encourages all people to trust in God, pour out their hearts before Him, and find refuge in His unwavering love. Ultimately, Psalm 62 serves as a timeless reminder that our ultimate security and hope are found in God alone. True security lies not in fleeting solutions or earthly power, but in the unwavering trust and love for the eternal God. As the closing verse declares, "In God alone is my salvation and my glory; my strong rock, my refuge is in God" (verse 8). This message endures, offering a timeless fortress of faith in the face of life's ever–shifting landscapes.

## Let's Talk About It

Psalm 62 emphasizes the importance of placing our trust in God amid life's challenges and uncertainties. Reflecting on this psalm, engage in a conversation about the significance of trusting in God and how it can impact our lives and our faith walk. In this psalm, the writer contrasts the transient nature of human power and wealth with the enduring strength and sovereignty of God. Waiting on God is a recurring theme in the psalm. What does it mean to "Wait on the Lord and be of good courage"?

**How can we avoid placing our trust in temporal things and instead anchor ourselves in God's unwavering nature?**

Psalm 62 beautifully paints a picture, juxtaposing the dangers of relying on temporal things against the security found in anchoring our trust in God alone. Consider where you truly place your trust. Then ask yourself whether what you trust in has the capacity to provide lasting security and fulfillment.

The things of this world are constantly changing. They fade, break, disappoint, and ultimately cannot fulfill our deepest needs. James 4:14 asks, "For what is your life? It is even a vapor that appears for a little time and then vanishes away." Verse 8 says, "Trust in him at all times." This level of trust comes through intentional time spent in prayer, Bible study, and seeking to know God more deeply through His Word and His presence in our lives.

## Get Social

Share your views and tag us @rhboydco. Use #rhboydco.

@rhboydco

## Home Daily Devotional Readings
### October 28–November 3, 2024

| Monday | Tuesday | Wednesday | Thursday | Friday | Saturday | Sunday |
|---|---|---|---|---|---|---|
| Sheep without a Shepherd | God Opposes Unfit Leaders | God Will Appoint a Shepherd | The Good Shepherd Defends the Flock | The Good Shepherd Gives His Life | The Lamb Will Be Their Shepherd | The Lord Is My Shepherd |
| Ezekiel 34:1–6 | Ezekiel 34:7–16 | Ezekiel 34:17–31 | John 10:1–10 | John 10:11–18 | Revelation 7:1–4, 9–17 | Psalm 23 |

LESSON X                                        NOVEMBER 3, 2024

# CONFIDENCE IN GOD'S SHEPHERDING

ADULT TOPIC:                            BACKGROUND SCRIPTURE: PSALM 23; JOHN 10:11–14
WHEN THE ROAD IS LONG                                      LESSON PASSAGE: PSALM 23

## PSALM 23

### KJV

THE Lord is my shepherd; I shall not want.
2 He maketh me to lie down in green pastures: he leadeth me beside the still waters.
3 He restoreth my soul: he leadeth me in the paths of righteousness for his name's sake.
4 Yea, though I walk through the valley of the shadow of death, I will fear no evil: for thou art with me; thy rod and thy staff they comfort me.

5 Thou preparest a table before me in the presence of mine enemies: thou anointest my head with oil; my cup runneth over.
6 Surely goodness and mercy shall follow me all the days of my life: and I will dwell in the house of the Lord for ever.

### NRSVue

THE Lord is my shepherd; I shall not want.
2 He makes me lie down in green pastures; he leads me beside still waters;[a]
3 he restores my soul. He leads me in right paths for his name's sake.
4 Even though I walk through the darkest valley, I fear no evil,
for you are with me; your rod and your staff, they comfort me.
5 You prepare a table before me in the presence of my enemies;
you anoint my head with oil; my cup overflows.
6 Surely goodness and mercy shall follow me all the days of my life, and I shall dwell in the house of the Lord my whole life long.

---

## LESSON SETTING

**Time:** Between the 10th and 9th century BCE

**Place:** United Kingdom

## LESSON OUTLINE

I. The Shepherd's Provision
   (Psalm 23 1–3)

II. God's Protection
   (Psalm 23:4–6)

## UNIFYING PRINCIPLE

People seek out trustworthy guidance and direction in all of life's experiences. How do we find assurance that we are on a good path? The psalmist asserts that the Lord leads us just as a good shepherd leads and tends the sheep, and in John's Gospel Jesus identifies himself as a true shepherd.

## INTRODUCTION

The exact circumstances and location in which David wrote Psalm 23 are not explicitly mentioned in the biblical text.

---

**MAIN THOUGHT:** Surely goodness and mercy shall follow me all the days of my life, and I shall dwell in the house of the LORD my whole life long. (Psalm 23:6, NRSVue)

However, tradition and scholarly speculation provide some insights.

The biblical accounts do not specify a specific incident or event that inspired Psalm 23. Instead, it is regarded as a general expression of David's trust in God's care and guidance throughout his life.

Overall, while we do not have definitive historical evidence regarding the specific time and place of its composition, Psalm 23 reflects David's personal experiences and his deep faith in God as his shepherd.

Psalm 23, a lyrical masterpiece of just six verses, has resonated with religious communities for millennia. Perhaps one of the most popular and well known psalms in the Bible. Its simple yet profound imagery of God as a shepherd and the psalmist as his sheep continues to offer solace and strength in times of uncertainty and fear.

To gain a deeper understanding of Psalm 23, it is crucial to consider its historical backdrop. Traditionally attributed to King David, this psalm reflects the experiences and emotions of a shepherd-turned-king. Psalm 23 is a masterful composition that employs various literary devices to convey its message effectively. The psalm is structured in a symmetrical manner, with three verses describing the shepherd's care and three verses expressing the psalmist's response of trust and gratitude. Furthermore, the use of metaphors, such as the shepherd/sheep dynamic, green pastures, and still waters, evokes a sense of peace and security. By delving into the rich symbolism and imagery employed, this commentary seeks to illuminate the enduring relevance and significance of Psalm 23 in the lives of believers.

# EXPOSITION

## I. THE SHEPHERD'S PROVISION (PSALM 23 1–3)

Psalm 23 is an exposition of proper dependency on the Lord as the great shepherd and how he cares for His sheep. King David is credited as the author of the psalm because of his previous vocation as a shepherd (1 Samuel 16:11). Since David is well acquainted with how to care for sheep, he is able to gracefully and powerfully to use this metaphor as a mirror to his relationship with God.

In the opening verse David makes a powerful declaration. He writes the Lord is "my shepherd" (v.1). Yes, God is the God of Israel, the God of the Bible, the God of Abraham, Issac and Jacob, the God of the tribes of Judah but is not just corporate. God is also a personal God. In this opening verse, the psalmist declares a profound truth: the covenant God of Israel is his personal shepherd. This metaphorical language draws upon the imagery of a shepherd caring for his flock, emphasizing the intimate relationship between God and His people both as a flock and individually. David doesn't use that image to convey the idea that God has humbled himself. We might suppose that, since shepherds were among the lowest classes in ancient Hebrew society. No, David plucked this image from ancient Near Eastern courts, where kings were often spoken of as shepherds who guided and protected their people. David himself had been a shepherd and now he was a King. Here he confesses with deep humility and trust that Yahweh was his shepherd. From that confession comes his and our comfort. Whatever else we say about this beloved Psalm, we must be sure to point out the centrality of that article of faith. It is Yahweh, my Shepherd, who does all the things about which Psalm 23 speaks.

This is not the only time God is called a shepherd. In Psalm 80:1 God is addressed: "Give ear, O Shepherd of Israel, You who lead Joseph like a flock." Israel's kings are also called shepherds. After denouncing the unfaithful shepherds of His people, God promises, "I will set up shepherds over them who will feed them; and they shall fear no more, nor be dismayed, nor shall they be lacking" (Jer. 23:4; cf. Ezek. 34:2). And Jesus identifies Himself as the "good shepherd," the Messianic King (John 10:11). His goodness is in His giving His life for the sheep.

For David to call God "shepherd" is to acknowledge God as his King, his Savior, the One who meets all of his needs. Verse 1 concludes with the direct inference from confessing the Lord as his shepherd: "I shall not want." Every need will be met by the guiding, providing hand of God. By proclaiming that he shall not want, the psalmist affirms his trust in God's provision and guidance, acknowledging that the Lord will meet all his needs. David acknowledges God's provision and care in his life, and because God is his shepherd he has no wants. God provides each of His children with all they will need.

How then will this happen? First, the shepherd allows His sheep rest: "He makes me to lie down in green pastures." In our frantic life God desires our rest. The Sabbath was instituted, in part, to guarantee this. God rested on the seventh day after creating all things in heaven and earth (Genesis 2:2) and if God rested certainly humanity should as well. The place of rest is "green pastures." The green pastures symbolize abundant provision, nourishment, and rest. The Hebrew word used here means "fresh shoots" or fresh grass. God does not intend this rest to be because of age or sickness. God desires to give rest in the lush and soft grass of life. Contemporary society is filled with so much hustle, and people are overly consumed with compulsions and achieving goals that some feel guilty for resting. Rest is essential to being in God's presence and discipleship. It is through rest that our imaginations are recharged, we feel God's hand upon us, and we hear from the Almighty.

Secondly, the Lord leads the sheep. The psalmist uses the imagery of still waters to represent tranquility and refreshment. It would be challenging for a sheep to drink from raging waters and raise the chances of the sheep being lost in the current. A good shepherd will only allow the sheep to drink from still water. The shepherd provides the sheep with rest, food and water. God provides what the sheep needs. The shepherd leads the sheep to rest, food and water. In a world where people fight to get ahead, Christians can be assured that there is no need to worry. God will lead you to everything you need. Together, these images convey the idea of God's gentle leading and His desire to bring His people to a place of peace and fulfillment. This verse highlights God's role as the loving provider and caretaker of His flock.

Next David says "He restores my soul" (v.3). The Lord not only takes care of our physical needs but also cares that our soul is refreshed. Life can trouble our souls. Watching the nightly news, reading the latest headlines, and witnessing oppression can weaken the soul. David says that God will restore your soul when the enemy has tried your soul. In this verse, the psalmist acknowledges the restorative work of the shepherd in his life. The term "soul" refers to the inner being or the whole person, emphasizing the holistic nature of God's care. The shepherd not only provides physical replenishment but also offers spiritual renewal. By leading the psalmist in paths of righteousness, God guides him in the ways that honor His name, demonstrating His faithfulness and righteousness.

God promises to meet our needs and to guide our lives. When we offer our bodies to Him in worship, He transforms our minds and guides us in His will, that which is "good, acceptable, and perfect" (Rom. 12:2). Thus David continues: "He leads me in the paths of righteousness / For His name's sake." It is only changed people who can live changed lives. We are ready for the "paths of righteousness" when our souls are restored. What are those paths? For us, they are simply doing the will of God and manifesting God's kingdom through our lives as we submit to Him. As Jesus teaches us to pray, "Your kingdom come. Your will be done on earth" (Matt. 6:10).

Through our transformed lives the name of God is glorified. We are to walk the paths of righteousness "for His name's sake." When we take "His name" we are to do His will. In Ezekiel 34, after judging Israel's corrupt shepherds, God promises that He Himself will become His people's shepherd. "…so will I seek out My sheep and deliver them….I will bring them… to their own land; I will feed them on the mountains of Israel, in the valleys and in all the inhabited places of the country…. They shall lie down in a good fold and feed in rich pasture….I will feed My flock, and I will make them lie down,' says the Lord God" (34:12–15). God will be a good shepherd for God's name sake because God's name requires love, kindness, faithfulness and righteousness.

## II. GOD'S PROTECTION (PSALM 23:4–6)

Now David turns from God's provision to God's protection. David now recounts how God has protected him from the valley of the shadow of death and his enemies. In verse four, the psalmist confronts the reality of hardship and adversity. The valley of the shadow of death symbolizes the darkest and most challenging moments of life. However, the psalmist's unwavering trust in God's presence and protection enables him to face fearlessly in any circumstance. The rod and staff, tools of the shepherd, represent God's guidance, discipline, and protection. In the face of adversity, the psalmist finds comfort and assurance in the Lord's constant presence.

The paths of righteousness are not protection from the valley, but God will protect us as we travel in the valley. God's presences gives comfort and security in evil, the unknown and scary valleys of life. When God sends Israel to the Promised Land as they escaped Egypt, He gives them a guarantee in Exodus 33:14, "My presence will go with you, and I will give you rest." Even more than material possessions God gives us His presence. God's presence is greater than any enemy, trial or fear. The psalmist writes in Psalm 68, "Let God arise, let his enemies be scattered: let them also that hate him flee before him."

Not only does God grant His presence but also His power. The rod was used as a method to beat off external enemies. The shepherd's job is to protect the sheep from predators that might try to attack. God protects us from external enemies even when we are unaware. Look over your life and remember how God has protected you from attacks from the enemy, sickness, attacks, conflicts, from malicious people and circumstances. Not only does the shepherd protect the sheep from external enemies, but he also protects sheep from internal enemies. There are times when the sheep will began to wander from the flock, making itself easy prey or potential to be lost. The staff is used to snatch the sheep back if it wanders. What great comfort it is to know that God has the power to protect His children from enemies and our own wandering foolishness.

In verse 5, the metaphor changes from a shepherd to a host at a lavish banquet. God, the gracious Host, provides sustenance and abundance even in the presence of enemies. The anointing with oil signifies God's favor and blessing. The overflowing cup represents God's abundant provision and joy. This verse highlights God's faithfulness and His ability to bestow blessings and honor upon His people in the midst of opposition and adversity.

The anointing oil is often a metaphor for the Holy Spirit. David remembered when Samuel took oil to anoint him king over Israel (1 Samuel 16:13). A full cup is sign of God's fullness and blessing. This banquet was a great celebration where his enemies would have no choice but to witness him being feted.

In the final verse, the psalmist expresses his unwavering confidence in God's goodness and steadfast love. He declares that God's goodness and mercy will pursue him throughout his life. The psalmist's ultimate hope and aspiration is to dwell in God's presence forever, experiencing eternal communion with Him. This verse encapsulates the psalmist's assurance of God's faithfulness in this life and the life to come.

Through its vivid imagery and profound theological insights, Psalm 23 continues to inspire and comfort believers across generations. By exploring each verse, we have witnessed the intimate relationship between God and His people, the provision and guidance of the Good Shepherd, and the unwavering trust and hope found in the face of adversity.

## The Lesson Applied

Psalm 23 continues to resonate with believers today, offering comfort and hope in challenging times. Its message of trust, provision, and protection serves as a source of encouragement and reassurance. By meditating on the psalm's timeless truths, individuals can find solace amidst the uncertainties of life and draw closer to the Good Shepherd.

For contemporary believers, the "valley of the shadow of death" may be the anticipation of literal death, or it might be the fear of change, loss, or trauma in other areas of life. In congregational life cycles—pastoral transitions, shrinking membership, or death of beloved members—Psalm 23 may have special significance. Trusting in God does not mean believers will not face trials, but rather, that God as the faithful Shepherd goes with them every step of the way. Believers can have confidence that even when the "valley of the shadow of death" is most imposing, God is at his nearest.

## LET'S TALK ABOUT IT

Psalm 23 describes God as our shepherd who lovingly provides for us, guides, and protects us.

1. **Is "shepherd" imagery something that resonates with you naturally, or are there different terms for God that you relate to more easily? What does it mean to you that God is a "shepherd"?**

The shepherd leads his sheep to lush, nourishing pastures. This signifies that God guides us to places of peace, provision, and spiritual nourishment. He leads us toward a life of abundance and purpose. He helps us to overcome anxieties and find rest in His presence. God, as our shepherd, restores our souls, helps us heal from emotional wounds, and empowers us to move forward with renewed strength and hope. As our shepherd, God shields us from spiritual dangers, enemies, and temptations. He provides a safe haven in the midst of life's storms.

2. **Consider a situation when you needed provision, guidance, or protection. How have you experienced God providing for you, guiding you, or protecting you?**

God knows us intimately, understands our individual struggles and desires, and cares for us personally. He walks beside us, not just from afar. His love for us is constant and unwavering, even when we stray or are rebellious. God's love for us is not conditional or based on our performance. It is an enduring love that is always present, even when we falter.

Even when we walk through dark valleys, the Shepherd's rod and staff provide comfort and assurance. We can trust that God's presence is with us in times of difficulty and fear. He is always with us, even in the darkest hours, bringing light and hope.

## GET SOCIAL

Share your views and tag us @rhboydco. Use #rhboydco.

@rhboydco

## HOME DAILY DEVOTIONAL READINGS
### NOVEMBER 4–10, 2024

| MONDAY | TUESDAY | WEDNESDAY | THURSDAY | FRIDAY | SATURDAY | SUNDAY |
| --- | --- | --- | --- | --- | --- | --- |
| The Lord God Almighty Reigns | How Good to Sing God's Praises | Praise God from Heaven and Earth | My Soul Magnifies the Lord | Blessed Be the God of Israel | Praise the Lord, O My Soul! | Let Everything that Breathes Praise God! |
| Revelation 19:1–10 | Psalm 147:1–6, 12–20 | Psalm 148 | Luke 1:46–55 | Luke 1:68–79 | Psalm 146 | Psalms 149–150 |

LESSON XI                                         NOVEMBER 10, 2024

# SONGS OF PRAISE

ADULT TOPIC:  
WHO CAN YOU TRUST?

BACKGROUND SCRIPTURE: PSALMS 146–150  
LESSON PASSAGE: PSALMS 146; 150

## PSALMS 146;150

### KJV

Praise ye the Lord. Praise the Lord, O my soul.
2 While I live will I praise the Lord: I will sing praises unto my God while I have any being.
3 Put not your trust in princes, nor in the son of man, in whom there is no help.
4 His breath goeth forth, he returneth to his earth; in that very day his thoughts perish.
5 Happy is he that hath the God of Jacob for his help, whose hope is in the Lord his God:
6 Which made heaven, and earth, the sea, and all that therein is: which keepeth truth for ever:
7 Which executeth judgment for the oppressed: which giveth food to the hungry. The Lord looseth the prisoners:
8 The Lord openeth the eyes of the blind: the Lord raiseth them that are bowed down: the Lord loveth the righteous:
9 The Lord preserveth the strangers; he relieveth the fatherless and widow: but the way of the wicked he turneth upside down.
10 The Lord shall reign for ever, even thy God, O Zion, unto all generations. Praise ye the Lord.

• • • • • •

1 Praise ye the Lord. Praise God in his sanctuary: praise him in the firmament of his power.

2 Praise him for his mighty acts: praise him according to his excellent greatness.
3 Praise him with the sound of the trumpet: praise him with the psaltery and harp.
4 Praise him with the timbrel and dance: praise him with stringed instruments and organs.

### NRSVue

PRAISE the Lord! Praise the Lord, O my soul!
2 I will praise the Lord as long as I live; I will sing praises to my God all my life long.
3 Do not put your trust in princes, in mortals, in whom there is no help.
4 When their breath departs, they return to the earth; on that very day their plans perish.
5 Happy are those whose help is the God of Jacob, whose hope is in the Lord their God,
6 who made heaven and earth, the sea, and all that is in them; who keeps faith forever;
7 who executes justice for the oppressed; who gives food to the hungry.
The Lord sets the prisoners free;
8 the Lord opens the eyes of the blind.
The Lord lifts up those who are bowed down; the Lord loves the righteous.
9 The Lord watches over the strangers; he upholds the orphan and the widow, but the way of the wicked he brings to ruin.
10 The Lord will reign forever, your God, O Zion, for all generations.
Praise the Lord!

• • • • • •

1 Praise the Lord!
Praise God in his sanctuary; praise him in his mighty firmament![a]
2 Praise him for his mighty deeds; praise him according to his surpassing greatness!
3 Praise him with trumpet sound; praise him with lute and harp!
4 Praise him with tambourine and dance; praise him with strings and pipe!

**MAIN THOUGHT:** I will praise the LORD as long as I live; I will sing praises to my God all my life long. (Psalm 146:2, NRSVue)

## Psalms 146; 150

| KJV | NRSVue |
|---|---|
| 5 Praise him upon the loud cymbals: praise him upon the high sounding cymbals.<br>6 Let every thing that hath breath praise the Lord. Praise ye the Lord. | 5 Praise him with clanging cymbals; praise him with loud clashing cymbals!<br>6 Let everything that breathes praise the Lord! Praise the Lord! |

### LESSON SETTING

**Time: Post–exilic Period**

**Place: Unknown**

### LESSON OUTLINE

I. Praise God for His Intrinsic Qualities and Sovereignty (Psalm 146:1–6; 150:1–2)

II. Praise God for His Acts in Creation and History (Psalm 146:7–9; 150:3–5)

III. Universal Call to Praise (Psalm 146:10; 150:6)

## UNIFYING PRINCIPLE

People extol the virtues of their leaders. What attributes are most worthy of praise? Psalms 146–150 reflect Israel's worship and praise for God as their Creator, Sustainer, and Everlasting Guardian.

## INTRODUCTION

The historical context of Psalm 146 is believed to be the post–exilic period, when the Israelites had returned from Babylonian captivity. This psalm reflects the longing of the people for a just and righteous ruler after experiencing the failures of human kings. The psalmist directs the people's attention to God, who is the ultimate source of hope and salvation

Psalms 146 and 150, known as the "Final Hallelujah" or "Great Hallel," mark the triumphant crescendo of the Psalter. Nestled at the very end, these two short but potent poems burst forth with unbridled praise, urging all creation to join in a cosmic chorus of adoration.

Both psalms exhibit a distinct literary unity, built upon a shared thematic foundation and interconnected by structural similarities. Each opens with a fervent exclamation of "Hallelujah!" – a Hebrew imperative meaning "Praise the Lord!" Immediately setting the tone of exuberant celebration, these pronouncements frame the subsequent verses with a directive purpose.

## EXPOSITION

### I. PRAISE GOD FOR HIS INTRINSIC QUALITIES AND SOVEREIGNTY (PSALM 146:1–6; 150:1–2)

The psalmist extols God's power, righteousness, faithfulness, and eternal dominion. The psalm begins with a call, Praise the Lord which is a summons to praise the Lord (v. 1). The psalm is a hymn of instruction with the purpose of galvanizing the listener to praise the Lord. It has the introduction of an individual hymn of praise. Like Psalm 103 and 104, it begins with a self–invocation addressed to the soul (v. 1) and then vows praise that lasts as long as life (v. 2). But the body of the hymn is composed of instruction. The psalmist then calls on himself ("my soul") to praise the Lord. He resolves to translate the appreciation for the Lord that fills his inner being into verbal, public expression. By his solo hymn he invites others to join him in exalting the Lord because this is what praise naturally seeks to do. With words almost identical to Psalm 104:33, the psalmist determines to praise the Lord all his life. All day, every day, forever he will praise the Lord, for him praise is not an occasional activity, but rather his continual pattern of life. There is no time when he will not be praising; for him to be alive is to praise the Lord. The psalmist's praise, then, is not an isolated event. It is a lifestyle that echoes David's words in Psalm 34:1 "I will bless the LORD at all times: His praise shall continually be in my mouth."

Verses 3 and 4 present an abrupt change of mood as the psalmist gives an unusual word of warning juxtaposed against the praise of the Lord called for in verses 1–2. Employing the tone of a teacher rather than that of a worship leader, the psalmist admonishes against human rulers who are often trusted, even though they do not deserve it. Even powerful monarchs are merely transient humans who are unable to help as the eternal Lord can. To trust in them is to hang one's hopes on a weak and slender thread. By contrast (vv. 5–10), the Lord is worthy of human trust. No human monarchy can provide salvation, but the Lord can deliver His people who trust in Him. It is foolish to trust humans, government leaders, for what only the Lord can do. Yes the sitting President of the United States of America (POTUS) is counted as the most powerful person on earth, but POTUS cannot give salvation. In Psalm 146 rejects all forms of human rule and power over human beings and a deliberate acceptance of divine royal rule.

Echoing Gen 3:19, the psalmist asserts that even the most powerful humans cannot rise above their inherent weakness because every earthling returns to the ground (v.4). Trust in humans is inherently placing confidence in what is transient and fleeting, and this is not a foundation for reliable hope. Humans are mortal, and their commitments will expire with them. Though the source of these great ideas may be an inspiring leader, pastor, or ministry leader they should never become the foundation of one's trust, no matter how brilliant or earnest. Even great ideas come apart at the death of their originator.

This section in Psalm 146 provides the antithesis to vv. 3–4. The term "happy," introduces an exclamation about the happiness that comes from trusting in the Lord rather than in impotent human resources. There is a joy in trusting the Lord. The term "help," is reminiscent of Ps 121:1–2, as it describes the blessing of the Lord, who is the help of his people. As in Psalm 46, the God of Jacob is viewed as the stronghold of His people who provides the help they need. The object of one's hope is all important. The Lord is a secure help and hope. He is the true king (v. 10a) who provides the deliverance that human princes cannot (v. 3).

The phrase "Maker of heaven and earth" depicts God as the Creator of all. The Lord also "remains faithful" forever, as he continually cares for all He has created. Because the Lord is unchanging in His creation and His commitment, He provides reliable help and hope for His people (v. 5)

Psalm 150 begins and ends with a call to praise God similar to Psalm 146. The call is because God will be a faithful God for them in the past, present, and future. The basis for Israel's faith and worship is that the Lord is true to His kept covenant, so He is not arbitrary or fickle or inconsistent in His relationship to His people.

After the introductory exclamation "Hallelujah!", the two main lines of v. 1 call for praise in His sanctuary. The term sanctuary could refer either to the earthly temple or to the heavenly sanctuary. Descriptive praise psalms often include an extended cause for praise, but in Psalm 150 only verse 2 speaks of why the Lord is to be praised. Praise for the Lord is prompted by His "powerful acts." In the Psalms, the divine acts refer at times to the Lord's creative and continuing work in nature and at other times to His work on behalf of Israel in history. The powerful acts of the Lord are evidence that there is no limit to his praiseworthiness. By praising the greatness of the Lord, worshipers implicitly acknowledge their own dependence on him. What the Lord does serves as both the motivation and the content of their praise as they express the greatness of God's amazing acts.

## II. PRAISE GOD FOR HIS ACT IN CREATION AND HISTORY (PSALM 146:7–9; 150:3–5)

God the great Creator is also the good King (vs. 7–10b), the psalmist is ensuring that readers are not fooled by the unreliable human princes of the time. God is greater than any ruler. The psalmist asserts that the Lord's faithfulness extends to all people because he cares for those who are often overlooked—the oppressed (including widows, orphans, the exploited, and foreigners, the hungry, and the prisoners, unlike earthly rulers (v. 9). Unlike many human rulers, the Lord sides with the oppressed and victims against their unjust oppressors rather than being in the pocket of the powerful. As Mary later exclaimed in Luke 1:53, the Lord provides both food and freedom for those in need. Continuing the thought begun in verse 7, the psalmist says that the Lord "opens the eyes of the blind (v.8)." Blindness is used as a metaphor for ignorance or physical helplessness, as in Deut 28:29. The Lord also lifts up those who are crushed by oppression (Psalm 145:14). The righteous are not exempt from trouble, but they are assured of the Lord's care, protection, provision and presence in their affliction because the Lord loves them.

The verb "protects" links this verse with v. 6, for the Lord who "remains" faithful forever protects those who are vulnerable, as great kings in the ancient world were obligated to do. The oppressed, including the foreigners, orphans and widows, find their protection in the Lord. The Lord helps those who cannot help themselves. God is an active moral ruler of the world, not a distant and passive observer, the Lord steps in to ruin the machinations of the wicked (Psalm 150:3–5).

Just as now, music was an integral part of life in the ancient world, but more than leisurely artistic pursuit. These verses call on a variety of instruments to be employed in a symphony of sound and movement in praise to the Lord. The procession bringing the Ark of the Covenant into Jerusalem in 2 Samuel 6, especially v. 5, provides a specific example of the general description here in Psalm 150. Included are wind instruments such as the trumpet and the flute. This trumpet is a ram's horn that makes a loud blast to convene an assembly. The psalmist also lists various other musical instruments and locations as instruments of praise, emphasizing the universality and inclusivity of worship. The use of various musical instruments symbolizes the diversity of ways in which praise can be expressed. Our worships should also reflect the diverse ways in which praise can be expressed.

Along with the various musical instruments, the Lord is also praised with dancing. This liturgical movement as evidenced by David's dancing before the ark of the covenant in 2 Samuel 6:14 must be distinguished from the erotic dancing of Salome before Herod (cf. Matt 14:6). Music and movement are elements of human creativity that have often been misused for purposes that do not honor the Lord, but Psalm 150 indicates that they should be employed properly in worshiping God. These nonverbal expressions are legitimate means for praising the Lord.

### III. Universal Call to Praise (Psalm 146:10; 150:6)

The final verse of Psalm 146 is addressed to Zion, the people of Israel. Because the Lord reigns as He does for as long as He does, there is great hope for the future. There is no end to God's reign. God will reign forever and ever. No one and nothing can modify or destroy the beneficent rule of the Lord, so His great and good rule is the grounds for joy, praise, and hope for the people of Zion. Just as the psalm begins, it ends with hallelujah.

Psalm 146 is a reminder that the Lord is to be praised because God is the eternal, almighty King who takes care of all of His people, including those who traditionally are looked over.

The climax arrives with a resounding call for all creation to join in the cosmic symphony of praise (Psalm 150:6). The praise of the Lord is not limited to or solely dependent on humans; but rather, everything that breathes is called to praise Him. The word "breath," is the same word used in Gen 7:22 to refer to all creatures that have been endowed with life by the Lord. The Lord breathed life into humans, and they should use that breath to magnify and praise the One who gave them life. As Psalm 148 details, humans join the corporate chorus of all creation in praising the Lord, and in that act they fulfill their potential as God's creations.

## The Lesson Applied

The texts for today's lesson retain profound relevance for contemporary readers. In a world grappling with division, despair, and ecological crises, the psalms offer a beacon of hope and a call to action. Their message of unwavering praise amid challenges inspires us to find solace and strength in God's unchanging character. Their universal call to worship urges us to bridge societal divides and build communities where praise transcends differences.

At the same time, though, believers are called to stand with those with whom God stands: the marginalized. God is not afraid to take a side on behalf of the most vulnerable, and the Church's prophetic witness needs to reflect God's commitment to the poor. The Church does not become the Church through neutrality, but rather by demonstrating the love of Christ for the dispossessed. Wherever oppression stands, the Church is called to respond and join in building God's kingdom.

This work of co-creating God's justice should not be regarded as a dreary burden. In fact, our acts of seeking justice are themselves acts of praise and worship of God! Implementing God's justice is a joyful, assignment, surrounded by praises of God's people for the God who gives life.

## LET'S TALK ABOUT IT

Psalms 146 and 150, known as the "Final Hallelujah" or "Great Hallel," mark the triumphant crescendo of the Psalter. Nestled at the very end, these two short but potent poems burst forth with unbridled praise.

1. In verses 1-2, the psalmist calls upon his soul to praise the Lord. What does it mean to you to praise God so deeply that your worship emanates from your soul? Have you ever experienced worship that felt like this?
2. In verses 3-4, the psalmist discusses what it's like to put trust in human rulers with their mortal limitations.
3. Have you ever put your trust in a human leader only to be disappointed? What was that experience like, and what did you learn from the disappointment? How can we respect wise leaders yet recognize that they are only human and have limitations?
4. The psalm describes God as the one who seeks justice for the oppressed, who heals the sick and wounded, and restores proper relations between people. When you read these verses, do you think of any specific situations you know about in your community or world? Where do you see the need for God's justice?
5. In God's kingdom, the psalmist tells us proper social relations will be restored. Wicked people will not be allowed to trample over the vulnerable. As God's Church, we are called to be part of this justice. Can you think of examples of how your church can seek justice in your community?

## GET SOCIAL

Share your views and tag us @rhboydco. Use #rhboydco.

@rhboydco

| MONDAY | TUESDAY | WEDNESDAY | THURSDAY | FRIDAY | SATURDAY | SUNDAY |
| --- | --- | --- | --- | --- | --- | --- |
| Give Thanks through Song | Hymns, and Spiritual Songs | Magnify God with Thanksgiving Psalms | Give Thanks to the Righteous Judge | Thanks for Faithful Brothers and Sisters | Prayer and Supplication with Thanksgiving | Worship the Lord with Gladness |
| Psalm 28 | Ephesians 5:1-2, 15-20 | Psalm 69:1-6, 30-36 | Psalm 7:1-2, 6-17 | 1 Thessalonians 1 | Philippians 4:4-9 | Psalm 100 |

# Lesson XII
## A Song of Thanksgiving

November 17, 2024

**Adult Topic:**
A Gratitude Attitude

**Background Scripture:** Psalm 100
**Lesson Passage:** Psalm 100

## Psalm 100

### KJV

MAKE a joyful noise unto the Lord, all ye lands.
2 Serve the Lord with gladness: come before his presence with singing.
3 Know ye that the Lord he is God: it is he that hath made us, and not we ourselves; we are his people, and the sheep of his pasture.
4 Enter into his gates with thanksgiving, and into his courts with praise: be thankful unto him, and bless his name.
5 For the Lord is good; his mercy is everlasting; and his truth endureth to all generations.

### NRSVue

MAKE a joyful noise to the Lord, all the earth.
2 Serve the Lord with gladness; come into his presence with singing.
3 Know that the Lord is God. It is he who made us, and we are his; we are his people and the sheep of his pasture.
4 Enter his gates with thanksgiving and his courts with praise. Give thanks to him; bless his name.
5 For the Lord is good; his steadfast love endures forever and his faithfulness to all generations.

## LESSON SETTING

**Time:** Possibly 539–570 BCE

**Place:** Unknown

## LESSON OUTLINE

I. A Call to Praise
   (Psalm 100:1–2)

II. A Cause for Praise
   (Psalm 100:3–5)

## UNIFYING PRINCIPLE

When we receive gifts and benefits, we like to show gratitude to our benefactor. To whom should we express our appreciation for life's graces? Psalm 100 is a song of worship and praise directed to the Lord who made us and whose faithfulness was and is for all generations.

## INTRODUCTION

Unlike some psalms that mention specific historical events or figures, Psalm 100 offers no such clues. It lacks references to kings, battles, or specific locations, making precise dating and localization elusive.

### Internal Clues and Possible Contexts

*Second Temple Period (539–70 BCE):* Some scholars suggest a post–exilic context. The mention of a temple in verse 4 ("Enter his gates with thanksgiving,

**MAIN THOUGHT:** Enter his gates with thanksgiving, and his courts with praise. Give thanks to him, bless his name. (Psalm 100:4, NRSVue)

and his courts with praise") aligns with the rebuilding of the Second Temple during this period. The psalm's message of renewed hope and communal worship also resonates with the restoration efforts of this time.

*Cultic Context:* Other scholars propose a broader cultic context, suggesting the psalm was used in various temple rituals or festivals throughout Israel's history. The emphasis on joy, singing, and thanksgiving would fit within the celebratory atmosphere of such occasions.

Ultimately, while the precise circumstances remain unclear, the psalm's timeless message of universal praise and joy transcends a specific date and location. Its focus on God's majesty and goodness, its call to communal worship, and its vision of universal harmony remain relevant and inspiring for people of faith across different times and cultures.

Psalm 100 is a beloved offering that has brought comfort and inspiration to countless individuals throughout history. In this scholarly commentary, we will explore the profound wisdom and enduring relevance of each verse in Psalm 100. By examining the historical context, literary structure, and theological implications of this psalm, we aim to deepen our understanding and appreciation of its timeless message.

Psalm 100 is a hymn of praise and thanksgiving, inviting all people to worship and acknowledge the Lord's goodness. Composed in the poetic tradition of Hebrew literature, this psalm is rich in imagery, metaphors, and theological insights. It consists of five short verses, each containing distinct themes and messages. Psalm 100, a vibrant and concise hymn, stands out within the Psalter as a passionate summons to joyful worship. Its brevity belies its depth, offering rich theological insights and practical directives for engaging with the divine.

## EXPOSITION

### I. A CALL TO PRAISE (PSALM 100:1–2)

The opening verse sets the tone for the entire psalm, emphasizing the universal call to worship. The phrase "make a joyful noise" implies a passionate and exuberant expression of praise. It encourages people from all corners of the earth to unite in worship, regardless of their backgrounds or circumstances. This verse conveys the inclusivity of God's invitation, emphasizing the communal nature of worship. The psalm opens with a resounding exclamation, a universal call to worship directed not only to Israel, but to "all the lands." This inclusivity transcends national and ethnic boundaries, reflecting God's universal claim on all creation. The Hebrew verb "hario" (make a joyful noise) implies exuberant expression, evoking instruments, song, and jubilant shouts of praise. This verse sets the tone for the entire psalm, emphasizing the communal and celebratory nature of worship.

Verse 2 highlights the attitude with which worship should be approached: gladness and joy. It reminds us that worship is not merely a duty but a privilege. The call to serve the Lord with gladness speaks of public worship (Exod. 3:12) that includes joyful singing in praise to him. In contrast to the rebellious kings in Psalm 2:11, who are compelled to serve the Lord with reverential awe and trembling, the whole earth in Psalm 100 is exhorted to proclaim the goodness of the Lord with joy. This is not a dreary duty, but it is their delighted devotion to the Lord as they worship him wholeheartedly. Those who have tasted the grace of the Lord can worship him gladly. The phrase "come into his presence with singing" emphasizes the intimate connection between worship and the divine presence. Singing is a powerful form of expression that transcends language barriers, enabling believers to connect with God on a deeper level. The verse elaborates on the call to praise, urging service to God with "gladness" (*sameach*) and "singing." This joyful service contrasts with the solemn rituals of many ancient Near Eastern religions, emphasizing the unique relationship between Yahweh and his people. Singing, a prominent feature in Israelite worship, signifies joyful surrender and heartfelt communion with the divine.

## II. A Cause to Praise (Psalm 100:3–5)

Verse 3 shifts focus to the basis for such joyous praise: God's lordship and creatorship. The emphatic repetition of "the Lord, he is God" underscores his unique status and sovereignty. The affirmation "It is he who made us" acknowledges God's absolute power and our dependence as his creations. Belonging to God as "his people" and "the sheep of his pasture" evokes images of care and protection, further solidifying the foundation for joyful worship. This verse emphasizes the knowledge of God's sovereignty and creative power. Acknowledging the Lord as the creator affirms our dependence on Him and our identity as His people. The metaphor of "sheep of his pasture" conveys the tender care and guidance that God provides for His people, underscoring the comforting and protective nature of His relationship with us. It is evident that the Lord who created humanity also cares for humanity as his flock and that what the Lord has done in shepherding Israel he also does for all the earth, because he has always had a mission that included the entire earth.

The psalm now describes the act of worship itself. Entering God's "gates" and "courts" signifies entering the sacred space, either the Temple in Jerusalem or a metaphorical representation of God's presence (v.4). "Thanksgiving" and "praise" are the offerings brought, highlighting the reciprocal nature of worship. Gratitude for God's blessings fuels our praise, and praise in turn deepens our gratitude. The concluding command to "give thanks to him and bless his name" encapsulates the essence of joyful worship: a continual outpouring of thanksgiving and adoration. Verse 4 emphasizes the importance of gratitude and thanksgiving in approaching God's presence. The act of entering His gates and courts symbolizes entering into a sacred space, a realm of divine encounter. The psalmist encourages believers to express their gratitude through praise and the blessing of God's name. This verse reminds us that worship should be characterized by a grateful heart and a reverence for God's presence.

The final verse of Psalm 100 encapsulates its central message. It affirms the goodness, love, and faithfulness of the Lord. The phrase "his steadfast love endures forever" emphasizes the enduring nature of God's love, which remains constant throughout all generations. This verse is an encouraging reminder of God's unchanging character and His eternal commitment to His creation. The verse offers a reason for such exuberant praise: God's unchanging goodness, steadfast love, and faithfulness. These attributes are foundational to the covenant relationship between God and his people.

*Hesed* signifies a loyal, covenant love that transcends circumstances. God's faithfulness extends "to all generations," assuring his people of his enduring commitment. The people are prompted to praise the Lord because He is good. God's goodness is not limited to Israel alone, for it is extended to all of humanity. God's love is not limited by time, but it endures forever. God's faithfulness is not for the current time but it will continue for all generations. Because the Lord's character is good, God will always be loving and faithful because the Lord is good and faithful and will always be loving and faithful. God's goodness never ceases, there will always be more than enough reasons to praise God.

The verse begins with the statement, "For the Lord is good." This declaration affirms the inherent goodness of God's character. It establishes a foundational understanding that God's love is rooted in His essential nature, which is unchanging and unwavering. Next the psalmist uses the phrase "his steadfast love endures forever" to describe God's love. The Hebrew word used for "steadfast love" is *hesed*, which encompasses deep affection, loyalty, and unfailing kindness. By emphasizing the enduring nature of God's *hesed*, the psalmist communicates that God's love is not temporary or conditional but steadfast and eternal. The psalmist further underscores the enduring nature of God's love by stating that His faithfulness extends "to all generations." This phrase emphasizes the timeless and universal scope of God's love. It conveys that God's faithfulness is not limited to a specific period or group of people but extends throughout time, embracing every generation that has existed and will exist.

This theme of the universality of God's love is a common one in Hebrew writings of the Second Temple period, to which this psalm is often attributed. In the Second Temple Period, biblical literature often reflects a broadening of perspective to encompass God's love for those previously considered to be outsiders due to culture or religion. For example, consider the book of Jonah. The Lord sends Jonah to the people of Nineveh to call them to repentance. Jonah avoids this mission for as long as possible, but when he arrives in Nineveh, the people unexpectedly repent, avoiding their own certain destruction. Jonah initially sulks under a bush until God intervenes, reminding him of God's mercy for all people. The message of Psalm 100 would be an appropriate one for Jonah, reminding him, like each of us, that God's mercy is for all. Through all time and places, as Romans 8:28 will later remind readers of Scripture, there is nothing that can separate us from the love of God.

By combining these elements, the psalmist paints a picture of God's love as a constant and unchanging force that surpasses the limitations of time and extends to all people. The enduring nature of God's love is portrayed as a foundational truth that provides reassurance, hope, and security to His people throughout the ages. It is a love that remains steadfast and faithful, regardless of changing circumstances or human frailties.

Psalm 100 remains richly relevant for contemporary faith communities. Its call to joyful and inclusive worship resonates with diverse religious traditions. The psalm reminds us that worship is not merely a duty, but a joyous celebration of God's presence and goodness. It encourages us to approach worship with gratitude, enthusiasm, and a sense of community. Psalm 100 is a poetic masterpiece that invites all people to enter into the joyous act of worship. Through its five concise verses, this psalm encapsulates profound theological truths, encouraging believers to express their gratitude, joy, and reverence in the presence of the Lord. The psalmist's words transcend time and continue to resonate with individuals across cultures and generations.

## THE LESSON APPLIED

Christians can apply Psalm 100 to their lives in several meaningful ways: Cultivating a heart of gratitude: Psalm 100 encourages believers to enter into worship with thanksgiving and praise. Christians can apply this by cultivating a daily practice of gratitude, intentionally acknowledging and appreciating the blessings and goodness of God in their lives. By adopting an attitude of gratitude, Christians can experience a deeper sense of joy and contentment, even in the midst of challenges.

Engaging in joyful worship: The psalmist calls for a joyful noise and singing in the presence of the Lord. Christians can apply this by actively participating in worship gatherings, engaging their hearts, minds, and voices in praising God. By approaching worship with gladness and enthusiasm, believers can experience a deeper connection with God and draw closer to His presence.

Recognizing God's sovereignty and care: Psalm 100 reminds Christians that God is their creator and they are His people. By acknowledging God's sovereignty and care, believers can find comfort and security in their relationship with Him. This recognition helps Christians to trust in His guidance and provision, knowing that they are under His watchful care, just as sheep are tended by their shepherd.

Embracing God's enduring love and faithfulness: The psalmist emphasizes the enduring nature of God's love and faithfulness. Christians can apply this truth by anchoring their faith in the unchanging character of God. When faced with uncertainties or challenges, believers can find strength and reassurance in knowing that God's love and faithfulness extend throughout all generations. This encourages Christians to persevere in their faith, trusting that God remains steadfast and true.

Sharing the message of God's goodness: Psalm 100 is a call for all the earth to worship and acknowledge the Lord's goodness. Christians can apply this by sharing the message of God's love, grace, and salvation with others. By living out the principles of Psalm 100 in their daily lives and testifying to the transformative power of God, believers can invite others to join in the worship of the one true God.

In summary, Christians can apply Psalm 100 by cultivating gratitude, engaging in joyful worship, recognizing God's sovereignty and care, embracing His enduring love and faithfulness, and sharing the message of His goodness with others.

## LET'S TALK ABOUT IT

By incorporating the principles of Psalm 100 into our lives daily, we as believers can experience a deeper connection with God and a greater sense of purpose and joy in their journey of faith.

**The Hebrew word *hesed* appears several times in the lesson. What do you understand as the nature of *hesed*? How might it be related to other types of love (*phileo, eros, agape, storge,* etc.) you have experienced? Is *hesed* primarily an attribute of God, or is it something that humans can embody too? How can we reflect God's *hesed*?** In Ephesians 5:1-2, Paul encourages us to imitate Christ, emphasizing His love for us. While we can't perfectly replicate God's *hesed*, nevertheless we are called to reflect it in our lives. This means loving others unconditionally, affirming their inherent worth as human beings made in God's image. Further, we can demonstrate loyalty and faithfulness to our relationships, especially when it's difficult and challenging. Compassion and mercy are vital components of *hesed*, showing kindness and forgiveness, even when people have hurt us. God continuously loves and forgives His repentant children no matter how many times we hurt Him through our disobedience.

*Hesed* underscores the importance of human relationships being built on foundations of love, trust, and mutual care. Embodying *hesed* is a journey, and we grow in our capacity to do so as we grow in Christ. Even the most faithful of believers inevitably falls short, but God's lovingkindness encourages us to continue on the path of love.

2. **Can you share an example of a moment when you felt a deep sense of gratitude and connection to God's enduring love?**
3. **What do you understand as the purpose of worshiping God? What does worship do in the hearts of believers? When we worship, how are we changed?**

## GET SOCIAL

Share your views and tag us @rhboydco. Use #rhboydco.

@rhboydco

LESSON XIII                                          NOVEMBER 24, 2024

# GOD'S PROMISED PRESENCE

**ADULT TOPIC:**　　　　　　　　　　　　　　**BACKGROUND SCRIPTURE: PSALM 139**
**WONDERFUL, MARVELOUS!**　　　　　　　　　**LESSON PASSAGE: PSALM 139:1–12**

## PSALM 139:1–12

### KJV

O LORD, thou hast searched me, and known me.
2 Thou knowest my downsitting and mine uprising, thou understandest my thought afar off.
3 Thou compassest my path and my lying down, and art acquainted with all my ways.
4 For there is not a word in my tongue, but, lo, O Lord, thou knowest it altogether.
5 Thou hast beset me behind and before, and laid thine hand upon me.
6 Such knowledge is too wonderful for me; it is high, I cannot attain unto it.
7 Whither shall I go from thy spirit? or whither shall I flee from thy presence?
8 If I ascend up into heaven, thou art there: if I make my bed in hell, behold, thou art there.
9 If I take the wings of the morning, and dwell in the uttermost parts of the sea;
10 Even there shall thy hand lead me, and thy right hand shall hold me.
11 If I say, Surely the darkness shall cover me; even the night shall be light about me.
12 Yea, the darkness hideth not from thee; but the night shineth as the day: the darkness and the light are both alike to thee.

### NRSVue

O LORD, you have searched me and known me.
2 You know when I sit down and when I rise up; you discern my thoughts from far away.
3 You search out my path and my lying down and are acquainted with all my ways.
4 Even before a word is on my tongue, O Lord, you know it completely.
5 You hem me in, behind and before, and lay your hand upon me.
6 Such knowledge is too wonderful for me; it is so high that I cannot attain it.
7 Where can I go from your spirit? Or where can I flee from your presence?
8 If I ascend to heaven, you are there; if I make my bed in Sheol, you are there.
9 If I take the wings of the morning and settle at the farthest limits of the sea,
10 even there your hand shall lead me, and your right hand shall hold me fast.
11 If I say, "Surely the darkness shall cover me, and night wraps itself around me,"[a]
12 even the darkness is not dark to you; the night is as bright as the day, for darkness is as light to you.

## LESSON SETTING
　Time: Unknown
　Place: Unknown

## LESSON OUTLINE
　I. The Divine Microscope:
　　God's Intimate Scrutiny
　　(Psalm 139:1–4)

　II. Enclosed by Divine Presence:
　　Ubiquitous Embrace
　　(Psalm 139:5–6)

　III. The Unfathomable Mystery:
　　Divine Transcendence
　　(Psalm 139:7–12)

**MAIN THOUGHT:** O LORD, you have searched me and known me.
(Psalm 139:1, NRSVue)

## UNIFYING PRINCIPLE

We all want to feel accepted and valued. Where do we find someone who loves and accepts us just as we are? The psalmist praises God as a Creator who stays intimately involved with our lives and who possesses precise knowledge of each person's spiritual and physical traits and well–being.

## INTRODUCTION

The precise date and location of the writing of Psalm 139 are unknown. The Book of Psalms, including Psalm 139, is a collection of songs and poems attributed to various authors throughout Israel's history. The authors of the Psalms include King David, Asaph, the sons of Korah, and a collection of anonymous writers.

Psalm 139 is traditionally attributed to King David. According to the superscription that appears before the psalm in many versions of the Bible, it is described as a Psalm of David. However, it is important to note that the superscriptions are not part of the original text and were added later. Therefore, the authorship of individual psalms, including Psalm 139, cannot be definitively determined. Nevertheless, the style and language of the psalm are similar to other psalms attributed to David, such as Psalms 23, 34, and 51. The poetic structure, the heartfelt expressions of dependence on God, and the emphasis on God's mercy are all characteristic of David's authorship.

The composition of the Book of Psalms spans a significant period, from the time of David's reign around the 10th century BCE to the post–exilic period after the Babylonian exile, which took place in the 6th century BCE. It is likely that the psalms were compiled and edited over an extended period, reflecting the worship practices and experiences of the Israelite community.

Given the uncertainty surrounding specific details, it is challenging to pinpoint the exact time and place of the writing of Psalm 139. Regardless of what is unknown about its origins, this psalm stands as one of the most beautiful and introspective prayers found in the book of Psalms. In verses 1–12, the psalmist reflects on the profound attributes of God, emphasizing His omniscience and omnipresence. This commentary will explore the textual intricacies of these verses, their historical and cultural background, and their theological implications.

## EXPOSITION

### I. THE DIVINE MICROSCOPE: GOD'S INTIMATE SCRUTINY (PSALM 139:1–4)

The psalm opens with a declaration of transparency: "O Lord, you have searched me and known me" (v. 1). The all–seeing, all–knowing God knows all about the psalmist. The psalmist affirms that the Lord has "searched" him, using the term ḥāqar that indicates a diligent probing or a cross–examination in a legal case. By this investigative activity, the Lord knows him totally and intimately. The psalmist states that the Lord knows what he really is, in contrast to the accusations made by his enemies, so in effect this is his assertion of innocence. By these words divine omniscience is put into an understandable human expression, as the psalmist translates abstract theology into concrete language. The Lord's knowledge of him is the kind of exhaustive knowledge one might expect to have after extensive research and investigation. Of course, with God such effort is not required. The Hebrew verb "*darash*" denotes intense examination, suggesting God has thoroughly inspected the psalmist's inner and outer realms. This intimacy extends to everyday routines ("sit down and rise up"), internal thought patterns ("understand my thoughts afar off"), and the entirety of life's path ("all my ways") (v. 2). The Lord is portrayed as knowing the psalmist's life from A to Z. The Lord knows the psalmist private life as he sits, and also his public life as he rises to go out. Even from far away the omniscient God knows all about the smallest details of the psalmist thoughts. The Lord knew the psalmist desires, likes, dislikes, joys, pains and values. God has complete knowledge and this knowledge brings the psalmist comfort.

Not only does the Lord know thoroughly all the psalmist's thoughts, God is also familiar with the psalmist's ways (v.3). The Lord knows the psalmist even more than the psalmist knows himself. God searches and knows the psalmist in every aspect of his mind, thoughts and deeds. God is an all seeing God who knows every detail whether small or large about each of His children. Here, the psalmist emphasizes that God's knowledge surpasses human comprehension, encompassing both actions and thoughts. The psalmist's recognition of God's perfect knowledge highlights a fundamental aspect of divine omniscience.

The image of God intimately knowing a word before it's uttered (v. 4) escalates this scrutiny to a divine omniscience that transcends human limitations. Not only does the Lord hear the words the psalmist utters, but he also discerns the thoughts that precede and prompt the words. Even before the psalmist forms his words, the Lord knows fully what he intends to say and what he means by what he says. Although humans can often mask from others the full import of what they say and can use words to deceive, the omniscient God knows every word and all words perfectly. The psalmist marvels at God's omniscience, acknowledging that God knows his words even before they are spoken. God's intimate knowledge of the psalmist serves as a source of comfort and assurance, fostering trust and reliance on God's guidance.

## II. Enclosed by Divine Presence: Ubiquitous Embrace (Psalm 139:5–6)

The psalmist applies vv. 1–4 to his own life, as he says that the Lord "encircles," or hems him in. This image can be taken in two contrasting ways. If thought of negatively, it could mean that the Lord is like an enemy who has encircled him; but viewed positively, it speaks of a friend who protects by hedging him in from threats. Similarly, the hand of the Lord laid on him could refer to divine punishment or to divine blessing and care, and perhaps even to the work of a potter in shaping his life. In the context of this song, the psalmist feels nestled in the Lord's protective grip, safe from assault from every direction.

As the psalmist contemplates how omniscience of the Lord applies to his experience, he exclaims that the divine knowledge is too wonderful for him to comprehend. It evokes a response of astonishment and praise from him. If verse six extends a positive tone from the previous verse, then for the psalmist the Lord's perfect knowledge of him is a comfort, not an irritation or threat. It is evident by the end of the psalm that the psalmist welcomes and submits to the Lord's total knowledge of his life; but it is possible that the psalm traces the development of his confidence in the Lord, similar to the progression in the psalmist's thinking in Psalm 73, and that here in verse 6 his response to the Lord's total knowledge of his life is more ambivalent than it is at the conclusion of the Psalm 139. The psalmist marvels at God's omniscience, acknowledging that God knows his words even before they are spoken.

## III. The Unfathomable Mystery: Divine Transcendence (Psalm 139:7–12)

This section explores God's omnipresence, emphasizing that there is nowhere the psalmist can escape from God's presence. The psalmist's contemplation of God's omnipresence affirms the belief that God is not confined to a specific location but is present everywhere. This recognition of God's abiding presence provides solace, reminding believers that God is with them even in the darkest of times. The psalmist considers the effect of the Lord's omnipresence on him. He poses two hypothetical questions, the answer to which is "nowhere." He could never escape the Lord's presence. Throughout the Bible, from Adam and Eve in Gen 3:8–10 to humans seeking to avoid the wrath of the Lord in Rev 6:15–17, those who are sinful seek to hide from the Lord, but they cannot. As Jer 23:24–32 demonstrates, the divine judge sees and knows the truth, and nothing is hidden from his gaze. Though the Lord may be silent, and humans cannot see Him, God is never absent or unaware of where they are and what they need. What a comfort it is to know that we can not go anywhere and escape the presence of the Almighty.

In verses 8–9, the psalmist uses the clause "if" to introduce impossible conditions to emphasize his point. He could not actually do the things he names, that there is no place that the one can go to that God is not present. Even at the most remote locations the Lord will be there. No matter where he is, the psalmist is unable to outrun the Lord's presence. What confidence and peace it is to know that no matter where one goes God is able to locate you and be present. God never gets tired and God is always present; God never loses us.

The psalmist says even if he rhetorically goes to these far off places even there God will guide him (v10). When he does not see the path ahead, the Lord will lead him. When he is weak God will strengthen and support him. The psalmist's struggle resonates with humanity's enduring questions about God's presence, knowledge, and control. The omnipresence of God indicates that wherever the psalmist is so is God, and wherever the Lord is present he protects the psalmist, and that brings the psalmist great comfort. In a world where technology allows ever–increasing surveillance, the psalm offers a poignant reminder of God's all–encompassing gaze. Yet, it also affirms that this gaze is not one of mere judgment but of profound understanding and unconditional love. It beckons us to engage in a continuous dialogue with the divine, embracing both the comfort of divine presence and the mystery of ultimate sovereignty.

Continuing his string of conditions, the psalmist considers how darkness might hide him from the Lord. The Lord is present with him, even in times of utter darkness. Through the psalmist's example, we are encouraged to cultivate our own deep and personal relationship with the Divine. Psalm 139:1–12 offers a remarkable glimpse into the psalmist's deeply personal and profound relationship with God. By exploring the themes of divine omniscience, omnipresence, and the intimate connection between God and humanity, we uncover timeless wisdom and spiritual insights. As we reflect on the psalmist's words, we are reminded of the boundless love and care that God has for His creation. This psalm invites us to embrace a deeper understanding of God's attributes and to cultivate a personal relationship with Him, rooted in trust, vulnerability, and awe. May the words of the psalmist in Psalm 139 continue to inspire and guide us on our own spiritual journey, as we seek to know and experience the profound depths of our Creator.

## THE LESSON APPLIED

The psalm paints a vivid picture of God's encircling presence, offering Himself as a source of profound comfort and reassurance. Embracing this omnipresence can cultivate a deep sense of gratitude for the constant divine companionship that guides and protects us even in our darkest moments. This unwavering trust in God's presence can foster calmness and peace amidst life's uncertainties.

Ultimately, the psalm leaves us suspended in the awe–inspiring mystery of God's sovereignty. Accepting this unknowable aspect of the divine can cultivate a sense of wonder and openness to the transcendent. Engaging with the mystery rather than seeking complete understanding can deepen our faith and enrich our appreciation for the vastness and beauty of the universe. Remember, applying the psalm to your life is a personal journey. Choose the aspects that resonate most deeply with you and allow them to inform your thoughts, actions, and relationship with the divine. By regularly engaging with its profound message, you can find continuous inspiration for self–reflection, gratitude, humility, and a deepening connection with God.

In both your relationships with the Divine and with humans, consider what it means for you to be fully known. Reflect on whether there are aspects of your personhood that you try to withhold from God or from those whom you trust. If you are attempting to do this in your relationships, consider what may be behind this resistance. Since God fully knows us despite whatever we try to hide from him, allow yourself the joy of the knowledge that you are fully known and loved by God. At the same time, you may be able to open yourself to being more fully known and cared for by your community, as well.

## LET'S TALK ABOUT IT

Psalm 139:1–12 invites us to explore the profound attributes of God, particularly His omniscience and omnipresence. Reflecting on these verses, consider the following questions for discussion:

1. **How does the psalmist's acknowledgment of God's perfect knowledge of every aspect of humanity's being**

impact your understanding of God's omniscience? Does this knowledge impact your personal relationship with God?

2. The psalmist marvels at the inescapable nature of God's presence, stating, "Where can I go from your Spirit? Or where can I flee from your presence?" How does the psalmist's recognition of God's omnipresence resonate with you? How does it shape your perception of God's nearness in your own life?

The psalmist emphasizes the intimate relationship between himself and God, using language that indicates a relationship of familiarity and trust. Consider that God knows every aspect of you, even the number of hairs on your head (Luke 12:7). And no matter what He sees in you, God still loves you.

3. How does this portrayal of intimacy with God inspire you to cultivate a deeper relationship with Him? How can you apply the psalmist's example in your own spiritual journey?

The psalmist's reflection on God's omniscience and omnipresence is rooted in a sense of awe and wonder. We truly serve an amazing God! Consider times in your life when your faith has been fortified by your awe and wonder of God. t

4. How can we cultivate a similar sense of awe and reverence for God in our daily lives? What practices or perspectives can help us maintain a deep appreciation for God's attributes?

Consider the imagery used by the psalmist to describe God's presence, such as ascending to the heavens or making his bed in Sheol.

5. In what ways can the profound insights from Psalm 139:1–12 shape our understanding of our own identity and purpose? How does the psalmist's awe–inspiring encounter with God inform our own pursuit of meaning and significance?

Engaging in a thoughtful discussion around these questions can deepen our appreciation for the timeless wisdom and spiritual depth found in Psalm 139:1–12. It allows us to explore and share our own experiences and insights, fostering a collective journey of faith and discovery.

## GET SOCIAL

Share your views and tag us @rhboydco. Use #rhboydco.

@rhboydco

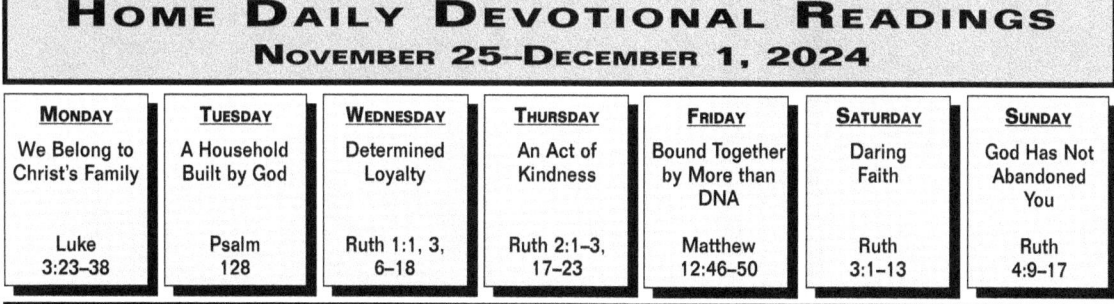

# Second Quarter

*December*

*January*

*February*

LESSON I

DECEMBER 1, 2024

# THE ANCESTRY OF KING DAVID

**ADULT TOPIC:**
A NOBLE FAMILY TREE

**BACKGROUND SCRIPTURE:** RUTH 1–4; LUKE 3:23–38
**LESSON PASSAGE:** RUTH 4:9–17; LUKE 3:23, 31–32

## RUTH 4:9–17; LUKE 3:23, 31–32

### KJV

AND Boaz said unto the elders, and unto all the people, Ye are witnesses this day, that I have bought all that was Elimelech's, and all that was Chilion's and Mahlon's, of the hand of Naomi.

10 Moreover Ruth the Moabitess, the wife of Mahlon, have I purchased to be my wife, to raise up the name of the dead upon his inheritance, that the name of the dead be not cut off from among his brethren, and from the gate of his place: ye are witnesses this day.

11 And all the people that were in the gate, and the elders, said, We are witnesses. The Lord make the woman that is come into thine house like Rachel and like Leah, which two did build the house of Israel: and do thou worthily in Ephratah, and be famous in Bethlehem:

12 And let thy house be like the house of Pharez, whom Tamar bare unto Judah, of the seed which the Lord shall give thee of this young woman.

13 So Boaz took Ruth, and she was his wife: and when he went in unto her, the Lord gave her conception, and she bare a son.

14 And the women said unto Naomi, Blessed be the Lord, which hath not left thee this day without a kinsman, that his name may be famous in Israel.

15 And he shall be unto thee a restorer of thy life, and a nourisher of thine old age: for thy daughter in law, which loveth thee, which is better to thee than seven sons, hath born him.

### NRSVue

THEN Boaz said to the elders and all the people, "You are witnesses today that I have acquired from the hand of Naomi all that belonged to Elimelech and all that belonged to Chilion and Mahlon.

10 I have also acquired Ruth the Moabite, the wife of Mahlon, to be my wife, to maintain the dead man's name on his inheritance, in order that the name of the dead may not be cut off from his kindred and from the gate of his native place; today you are witnesses."

11 Then all the people who were at the gate, along with the elders, said, "We are witnesses. May the Lord make the woman who is coming into your house like Rachel and Leah, who together built up the house of Israel. May you produce children in Ephrathah and bestow a name in Bethlehem;

12 and, through the children that the Lord will give you by this young woman, may your house be like the house of Perez, whom Tamar bore to Judah."

13 So Boaz took Ruth, and she became his wife. When they came together, the Lord made her conceive, and she bore a son.

14 Then the women said to Naomi, "Blessed be the Lord, who has not left you this day without next-of-kin, and may his name be renowned in Israel!

15 He shall be to you a restorer of life and a nourisher of your old age, for your daughter-in-law who loves you, who is more to you than seven sons, has borne him."

**MAIN THOUGHT:** The women . . . gave him a name, saying, "A son has been born to Naomi." They named him Obed; he became the father of Jesse, the father of David. (Ruth 4:17, NRSVue)

# Ruth 4:9–17; Luke 3:23, 31–32

## KJV

16 And Naomi took the child, and laid it in her bosom, and became nurse unto it.
17 And the women her neighbours gave it a name, saying, There is a son born to Naomi; and they called his name Obed: he is the father of Jesse, the father of David.

• • • Luke 3:23 • • •

23 And Jesus himself began to be about thirty years of age, being (as was supposed) the son of Joseph, which was the son of Heli,

• • • Luke 3:31–32 • • •

31 Which was the son of Melea, which was the son of Menan, which was the son of Mattatha, which was the son of Nathan, which was the son of David,
32 Which was the son of Jesse, which was the son of Obed, which was the son of Booz, which was the son of Salmon, which was the son of Naasson,

## NRSVue

16 Then Naomi took the child and laid him in her bosom and became his nurse.
17 The women of the neighborhood gave him a name, saying, "A son has been born to Naomi." They named him Obed; he became the father of Jesse, the father of David.

• • • Luke 3:23 • • •

23 Jesus was about thirty years old when he began his work. He was the son (as was thought) of Joseph son of Heli,

• • • Luke 3:31–32 • • •

31 son of Melea, son of Menna, son of Mattatha, son of Nathan, son of David,

32 son of Jesse, son of Obed, son of Boaz, son of Sala, son of Nahshon,

## LESSON SETTING
   Time: 550–330 BCE
   Place: Israel

## LESSON OUTLINE
   I. Summary of Characters (Ruth 4:9-10)
   II. Boaz, A Kinsman Redeemer (Ruth 4:11–13)
   III. Jesus, the Ultimate Kinsman Redeemer (Luke 3:23, 31–32)

## UNIFYING PRINCIPLE
People belong to families that extend across generations. What can we learn about ourselves by knowing our ancestral families? Jesus' and King David's family tree features an unlikely marriage between Boaz and Ruth, a testimony to the wideness of God's grace to affect divine purposes.

## INTRODUCTION
The book of Ruth offers insights into the tragedy of one family and how God turns their tragedy into triumph. Throughout the book of Ruth, we discover how three people kept their integrity and remained true to God even in the face of a collapsing society. Through the lives of Ruth, Naomi, and Boaz, we see that there are people who will stand for God and not compromise His commands even when all of society normalizes sin. God will use anyone who is willing to go all the way with Him. The book of Ruth reminds us that God is with us during the hard times. Trusting God through times of tragedy and hardship can bring great blessings. Although Ruth and Naomi were unaware of God's greater plan, they trusted in His divine providence. God's grace during tragedy and hardship

preserved the lineage from which Jesus would be born into the world. Through Ruth and Boaz, Jesus became our kinsman redeemer to purchase our freedom from the power of sin.

## EXPOSITION

### I. SUMMARY OF CHARACTERS (RUTH 4:9–10)

The book of Ruth was written after the period of the Judges around 1375–1050 BC. The story takes place during the period of the judges when many of the Israelites wandered away from the Lord. The setting is in Bethlehem of Judah and Moab. Naomi, whose name means "my pleasant one" and her husband Elimelech, whose name means "my God is King" lived in Bethlehem. There was a famine in Bethlehem, so Elimelech sold his land and moved his wife Naomi and their two sons, Mahlon, whose name means "sickly" and Chilion, whose name means "pining" to the land of Moab.

While living in Moab, Elimelech died. Although the Bible does not specifically state the cause of his death, some scholars believe that there was a plague in Moab, and Elimelech died during this plague. Escaping the famine in Judah and relocating to Moab was one thing, but losing her husband was quite another. Naomi was left as a widow with her two sons. Her sons then married Moabite women. One was named Orpah and the other was named Ruth. During the tenth year of their marriages, the two sons died, leaving Naomi not only a widow, but also childless.

During Bible times, widows were among the poorest. They were often taken advantage of or ignored. In Judah, God's law required the next of kin to marry the widow as a means of continuing the family bloodline. This relative would in fact become the kinsman redeemer. Naomi lived in Moab away from her relatives. She would have to move back to Bethlehem to find a kinsman redeemer among her people.

### II. BOAZ, A KINSMAN REDEEMER (RUTH 4:11–13)

Ruth, a Gentile woman, married into an Israeli family. Unlike many Moabites, Ruth forsook the pagan worship of Chemosh, and accepted the faith and customs of her Israelite family. During their journey to Bethlehem when Naomi urged her daughters-in-law to return to their families, Ruth insisted on staying with Naomi. She told her mother-in-law, "Intreat me not to leave thee, or to return from following after thee; for wither thou goest, I will go; and where thou lodgest, I will lodge; thy people shall be my people, and thy God my God; where thou diest, will I die, and there will I be buried. The Lord do so to me, and more also, if aught but death part thee and me." Ruth's steadfast commitment to stay with Naomi reveals her love for her mother-in-law, and faith and trust in the God of her mother-in-law. In Ruth's response to Naomi, she makes an oath to her with the consequences of being severely punished by God if anything but death separates them. Ruth demonstrated to Naomi that she was committed to the continuation of Elimelech's and Mahlon's bloodline even unto death where she vowed to be buried in the family burial plot.

What is distinct about Ruth from other Gentile women is that she was committed to following the God of her Israelite family, especially during a period when God's own people (the Israelites) were disobedient to Him. Her faith in God and her loyalty to her mother-in-law granted her the favor of God and He used her to continue a family bloodline from which Jesus was born. God loves all people; even those who are not part of His covenant group.

It was harvest season when Naomi and Ruth arrived in Bethlehem. Ruth finds a corn field to glean corn. As God's providence would have it, the field belongs to a relative of Naomi. Boaz was not only a wealthy man, but he was also a relative of her husband. Boaz takes note of Ruth and she asks him if she can glean in his field. Ruth found favor with Boaz and he told her to stay and glean in his field. He was impressed by her commitment to her mother-in-law and her courage to leave her native country. Boaz was also impressed by her faith in God.

Boaz told his workers to let Ruth glean with the handmaidens in his field for the entire barley and wheat harvest seasons. Naomi devised a plan for Ruth to invoke the right of the kinsman redeemer. Ruth followed Naomi's plan promptly. She cleaned up herself and went to the threshing floor where she uncovered Boaz's feet and laid down at his feet. By so doing, she was informing him that he could be her kinsman redeemer. Boaz promptly investigated the matter and learned that there was a kinsman redeemer closer than he; however, the closest kin could not redeem or purchase Elimelech's property and neither could he marry Ruth the Moabitess. This meant that the Boaz would be able to redeem the land and marry Ruth. Immediately, he went to the elders and declared that he would take on Ruth as his wife, thus restoring the bloodline and redeeming Naomi's legacy.

The elders witnessed the transaction and gave a beautiful blessing over their relationship. When Ruth put her faith in God ahead of her desires, He rewarded her with a better relationship than she could've imagined! You can imagine that Ruth was devastated to be a young widow without children, and probably worried for her future, especially living in a strange land with people who weren't very welcoming of Moabites. Whatever reservations she may have had, she put all that aside to follow Naomi and Naomi's God. If she hadn't done so, she never would've met Boaz, the bloodline wouldn't have been restored, and she wouldn't have had the privilege of being in the lineage of Jesus Christ! It's truly amazing when you consider all the puzzle pieces that had to fall into place for this story to have a happy ending. But God is the author, and He is able to redeem any situation, no matter how dire it may feel in the moment.

And so, Boaz and Ruth became husband and wife. Ruth bore a son, named Obed, thus providing a son in Elimelech's name, further proof of blessing. But Ruth is not the only one who is restored in this story. Naomi also has a happy ending! She thought her life was over the day her husband died, and then again when her sons died. In the Middle Eastern world, she was not set up for success in that situation. She would likely struggle the rest of her days to get by. Women couldn't own property or have a job. She felt totally hopeless, which is why when she first returned to Israel, she told the other women to call her Mara, which means "bitter." She was completely up front about her disappointment in life and in God; she did not sugar-coat it! Yet, God took her bitterness and turned it into joy! Perhaps as a side note, a takeaway from this story could be Naomi's honesty with the Lord. She was blunt and raw and real, and God didn't express anger towards her for those feelings. Instead, she was given a beautiful grandson to raise through her daughter-in-law whom she truly loved. When Naomi was going through her hardships, she wouldn't have any idea what was coming her way. Ultimately, God brought her complete redemption. Obed would grow up to be the father of Jesse, who would be the father of David, the greatest king Israel ever had and a forerunner for the Christ. How could the blessing get any better than that?

Through this story, we see God's fingerprints everywhere in history. He works through generation after generation, lining up all the dominos just right. It's obvious through stories such as this that nothing is random, and clearly there's a divine hand pulling all the strings to create a glorious tapestry of redemption for His glory. Just look at Naomi returning to Bethlehem to seek a kinsman redeemer. If she hadn't, Ruth wouldn't have met Boaz, and they wouldn't have had a son born in Bethlehem. Then Joseph wouldn't have had a need to return there for the census in Luke 2! Let this story be an encouragement if you're going through a hard time and don't see the reason why. God is always working behind the scenes.

### III. JESUS, THE ULTIMATE KINSMAN REDEEMER (LUKE 3:23, 31–32)

Boaz was a wonderful kinsman redeemer for Naomi and Ruth, and fulfilled every part of the obligation that he was supposed to. Now let's look at how Jesus is the ultimate kinsman redeemer for us.

According to Jewish law, a kinsman redeemer must be a family member. Jesus took on humanity by being born as a baby so that He could relate to us and save us! Jesus *had* to be a man in order to fulfill the requirements; that's why God couldn't send an angel or another being instead. Jesus also had to be fully God in order to save us, which is why a great prophet or wise teacher would've also been insufficient. A kinsman redeemer's job is to buy family members out of slavery; Jesus bought us using His blood on the cross and taking our place. But Boaz did more than what the law required; he loved Ruth! And Jesus loves us with a great love that can't even be comprehended. Boaz took Ruth as his bride, and one day, Jesus will return for His Bride: the Church.

We have the family lineages in the Gospels to trace Jesus' heritage back to Ruth and Boaz. Through the Israelites' careful records from thousands of years ago, we have definite proof that Jesus was born into exactly the right family and has every claim to the throne of David; there can be no dispute.

Luke 3 traces this heritage, and even continues Jesus' genealogy further back than Ruth and Boaz: he goes all the way back to Adam! What a beautiful picture of how God sees every detail, every relationship, every marriage and child. Nothing is beyond His gaze and nothing happens simply by chance! God is behind the scenes, orchestrating everything so that we all get where we're supposed to go every time! It's truly mind-boggling.

## THE LESSON APPLIED

The book of Ruth offers timeless lessons. Elimelech's misguided decision serves as a caution against compromising God's promises in challenging times. Ruth, Naomi, and Boaz exemplify integrity, kindness, and loyalty amid societal challenges. God rewards their faithfulness, restoring joy and blessings even in the face of profound loss. Ultimately, Boaz was the kinsman redeemer that the women desperately needed, and in the same way, Jesus is the kinsman redeemer that the world desperately needs. The narrative encourages trust in divine power during difficulties, emphasizing that today's challenges may pave the way for tomorrow's blessings.

Though you may not understand your hardships in the moment, it's through stories such as this one that you can see the hand of God at work in the circumstances and affairs of those who believe in Him. He will somehow turn it all into good, if we maintain trust in Him. If He told you ahead of time how all the puzzle pieces of your life would fall into place, you probably wouldn't believe Him! It's beyond the comprehension of our little earthly minds, but thankfully we have a benevolent Father who wants to shower us with love and work out everything for our good and His glory!

## LET'S TALK ABOUT IT

In times of tragedy and loss, uncertainty may cloud our understanding of God's plan. Trusting divine power can lead to greater outcomes, and challenges may be preparing us for unforeseen blessings. The book of Ruth inspires us to stay the course, trusting God even when situations appear bleak. And when we put Ruth and Luke next to each other and see how the events of Ruth led to the events in Luke, we can rest assured that God is in control of even the smallest details, and everything will work out in the end. We just have to trust Him along the way. Whatever catches us off-guard is never a surprise to Him. If there's anything that we've learned by living through a pandemic, it's that anything can happen at anytime.

## GET SOCIAL

Share your views and tag us @rhboydco. Use #rhboydco.

**@rhboydco**

## HOME DAILY DEVOTIONAL READINGS
### DECEMBER 2–8, 2024

| MONDAY | TUESDAY | WEDNESDAY | THURSDAY | FRIDAY | SATURDAY | SUNDAY |
| --- | --- | --- | --- | --- | --- | --- |
| The Lord Looks on the Heart | A Shepherd for God's People | Christ's Unending Reign | God Defends God's Anointed | Endless Peace for David's Throne | The Son of David | An Everlasting Kingdom |
| 1 Samuel 16:1–13 | 2 Samuel 5:1–10 | Luke 1:26–38 | Psalm 2 | Isaiah 9:1–7 | Romans 1:1–7 | 2 Samuel 7:4–17 |

LESSON II                                         DECEMBER 8, 2024

# GOD'S PROMISE TO DAVID

ADULT TOPIC:                                     BACKGROUND SCRIPTURE: 2 SAMUEL 7:1–17
A VERY FINE HOUSE                                          LESSON PASSAGE: 2 SAMUEL 7:4–17

## 2 SAMUEL 7:4–17

### KJV

AND it came to pass that night, that the word of the Lord came unto Nathan, saying,

5 Go and tell my servant David, Thus saith the Lord, Shalt thou build me an house for me to dwell in?

6 Whereas I have not dwelt in any house since the time that I brought up the children of Israel out of Egypt, even to this day, but have walked in a tent and in a tabernacle.

7 In all the places wherein I have walked with all the children of Israel spake I a word with any of the tribes of Israel, whom I commanded to feed my people Israel, saying, Why build ye not me an house of cedar?

8 Now therefore so shalt thou say unto my servant David, Thus saith the Lord of hosts, I took thee from the sheepcote, from following the sheep, to be ruler over my people, over Israel:

9 And I was with thee whithersoever thou wentest, and have cut off all thine enemies out of thy sight, and have made thee a great name, like unto the name of the great men that are in the earth.

10 Moreover I will appoint a place for my people Israel, and will plant them, that they may dwell in a place of their own, and move no more; neither shall the children of wickedness afflict them any more, as beforetime,

11 And as since the time that I commanded judges to be over my people Israel, and have caused thee to rest from all thine enemies. Also the Lord telleth thee that he will make thee an house.

12 And when thy days be fulfilled, and thou

### NRSVue

BUT that same night the word of the Lord came to Nathan,

5 "Go and tell my servant David: Thus says the Lord: Are you the one to build me a house to live in?

6 I have not lived in a house since the day I brought up the people of Israel from Egypt to this day, but I have been moving about in a tent and a tabernacle.

7 Wherever I have moved about among all the people of Israel, did I ever speak a word with any of the tribal leaders of Israel, whom I commanded to shepherd my people Israel, saying, 'Why have you not built me a house of cedar?'

8 Now therefore thus you shall say to my servant David: Thus says the Lord of hosts: I took you from the pasture, from following the sheep to be prince over my people Israel,

9 and I have been with you wherever you went and have cut off all your enemies from before you, and I will make for you a great name, like the name of the great ones of the earth.

10 And I will appoint a place for my people Israel and will plant them, so that they may live in their own place and be disturbed no more, and evildoers shall afflict them no more, as formerly,

11 from the time that I appointed judges over my people Israel, and I will give you rest from all your enemies. Moreover, the Lord declares to you that the Lord will make you a house.

12 When your days are fulfilled and you lie

**MAIN THOUGHT:** Your house and your kingdom shall be made sure forever before me; your throne shall be established forever. (2 Samuel 7:16, NRSVue)

## 2 Samuel 7:4-17

### KJV

shalt sleep with thy fathers, I will set up thy seed after thee, which shall proceed out of thy bowels, and I will establish his kingdom.
13 He shall build an house for my name, and I will stablish the throne of his kingdom for ever.
14 I will be his father, and he shall be my son. If he commit iniquity, I will chasten him with the rod of men, and with the stripes of the children of men:
15 But my mercy shall not depart away from him, as I took it from Saul, whom I put away before thee.
16 And thine house and thy kingdom shall be established for ever before thee: thy throne shall be established for ever.
17 According to all these words, and according to all this vision, so did Nathan speak unto David.

### NRSVue

down with your ancestors, I will raise up your offspring after you, who shall come forth from your body, and I will establish his kingdom.
13 He shall build a house for my name, and I will establish the throne of his kingdom forever.
14 I will be a father to him, and he shall be a son to me. When he commits iniquity, I will punish him with a rod such as mortals use, with blows inflicted by human beings.
15 But I will not take my steadfast love from him, as I took it from Saul, whom I put away from before you.
16 Your house and your kingdom shall be made sure forever before me; your throne shall be established forever."
17 In accordance with all these words and with all this vision, Nathan spoke to David.

## LESSON SETTING
**Time:** 975 BC
**Place:** Israel

## LESSON OUTLINE
I. A Royal Bloodline (2 Samuel 7:4-12)
II. God's Covenant is Forever (2 Samuel 7:13-14)
III. God's Unconditional Promises (2 Samuel 7:15-17)

## UNIFYING PRINCIPLE

People value permanence and seek to build structures that will outlast themselves. In what ways can such plans be superseded? When David wanted to build a house for God, God promised to build a "house" for David—a never-ending kingdom!

## INTRODUCTION

In the midst of the tumultuous period when the judges governed Israel, King David emerged as a pivotal figure in the nation's history. Following the shortcomings of King Saul, God chose David, a humble shepherd and courageous warrior, to ascend the throne. As a mighty warrior king, David achieved numerous victories, solidifying his name, and building a palace in Jerusalem. Despite his desire to construct a temple, God revealed a grander plan: an everlasting kingdom through David's lineage. While Solomon eventually erected the temple, it was through David's bloodline that Jesus, the eternal King, entered the world. God's promises endure, leading those who trust and obey Him into the fulfillment of His perfect plan.

## EXPOSITION

### I. A Royal Bloodline (2 Samuel 7:4-12)

David was God's sovereign choice to be the anointed king of Israel. Unbeknown to David for most of his life, God planned to establish a dynasty through which the Messiah was to be born. David was a warrior king. During his reign, he consulted the Lord before going into each battle, and the Lord gave him victory over his enemies. After his victory over the Philistines, the Lord gave David rest from all his enemies.

When David became king of all Israel, the king of Tyre (Hiram) provided the materials to build a palace for David in Jerusalem which became the capital and center of worship. David's palace was made of cedar, which was the highest quality wood for construction. The palace became a symbol of wealth, stability, and power. David felt that it was not right that he was living in a fine palace (made of cedar) while the ark of God was in a tent. He wanted to build a temple for the House of God, so he told Nathan the prophet of his intentions. David often inquired of the Lord through the prophet Nathan before making important decisions. Nathan knew that the Lord was with David and that David had a zeal for God. At first, he encouraged David to do whatever he wanted to do for God; however, Nathan had not yet consulted with the Lord.

The word of the Lord came to Nathan the same night he encouraged David to build a temple for the Lord. The Lord told Nathan that David was not allowed to build the temple for Him. He reminded Nathan that from the time the children of Israel left Egypt and came to The Promised Land, He dwelt in a tent throughout their journey and never demanded a house from the Israelites. Throughout the history of the children of Israel, God has consistently demonstrated that He wanted to be with His people (see Exodus 26, Genesis 3:8). God revealed to Nathan that He would make a covenant with David for his son Solomon to build Him a temple. God also told Nathan that Solomon's throne would be established forever and if Solomon sinned, God would correct him and have mercy on him. After David's death, God would establish his kingdom forever through the birth of Christ, who was born in David's bloodline.

When the prophet Nathan told David what the Lord revealed, David sat before the Lord in awe. He was overwhelmed by the covenant that God made with him. David understood his own unworthiness and responded to the Lord with humility, praise, and prayer. When God blesses us, we should respond like David, with humility, praise, and prayer. Although David really wanted to build a house for the Lord, he was not allowed to. David fought in many wars and his hands shed blood during his battles; therefore, David was not permitted to build a temple for God. God called David to be a warrior, not a builder. Throughout his many battles, David was preparing the way by laying a foundation in his leadership of Israel whereby his son Solomon could build the temple without warring with their enemies. Throughout David's reign, the Philistines were a major threat to Israel. David drove them out. He conquered or established peaceful relationships with the surrounding nations. In support of God's plan, David prepared the materials needed to build the temple for the Lord.

Although he wanted to build a temple for the Lord, God did something far better for David. He established his kingdom forever, which was far greater than building a physical temple. God lavished His grace upon David, the children of Israel, and upon David's future generations. David closed his prayer by asking God to fulfill His promise to bless his house forever. Through David's bloodline, Jesus, the Messiah, was born, and His Kingdom was established forever. God brought salvation to all people through the birth of His Son, Jesus, who was a descendant of David. David's desire to build a house for God was prompted by his gratitude towards God's faithfulness in his life. By acknowledging God as the Source of his success, David demonstrated his humility.

God delivered the children of Israel from Egypt and brought them to the promised land of Canaan. He took a shepherd boy and made him a king. God always has a greater plan. Even when we do not see Him working, He is always working. Instead of David constructing a house for the Lord, the Lord God allowed David to be a part of His plan to save humanity. He built a kingdom dynasty—a lineage through which the descendants of David would rule over Israel and through his lineage, Jesus was born. God promised to David that his son Solomon would build His temple. God also promised David that He would be Solomon's father and Solomon would be His son. Through Solomon, Israel entered its golden age.

David trusted God to fulfill His promises to him. Like David, we too can trust God to fulfill His promises to us. "For no matter how many promises God has made, they are "Yes" in Christ. And so, through him the "Amen" is spoken by us to the glory of God." (1 Corinthians 2:20, NIV).

## II. GOD'S COVENANT IS FOREVER (2 SAMUEL 7:13–14)

God's covenant is a gift that is initiated by God to establish a relationship of trust with Him. All of God's covenants are initiated by Him and are everlasting. They are also memorialized with a sign. The Hebrew word covenant means "betweenness." It is a permanent agreement between two parties in which both make promises on behalf of each to the other. Unlike a contract, which has an end date and is often only specific to a particular performance, a covenant involves the entire being of a person. God's covenants often involve a sign or symbol of the agreement. For example, God promised to bless Abraham's descendants and make them His chosen people. Abraham was to obey God so that He would make his descendants as the sand of the sea, and they would receive the promised land. The covenant was sealed and all of Abraham's male descendants were to be circumcised as a sign of the covenant.

When Jesus died, the old covenant was done away, and a new covenant (New Testament) was established. Through the shedding of His blood, we are redeemed. A covenant is more than a contract, which has an expiration date. A covenant is a permanent arrangement and covers one's total being. God's covenants are not a reward for work, but a firm commitment to establishing a relationship in which God has sought out. Although God keeps His covenant to man, man has not always kept his covenant with God. Marriage is a covenant between a man and a woman who vow to be committed to each other. This commitment allows for true trust and intimacy to grow. God is holy, all-knowing and all-powerful, yet He chooses to enter into a covenant with sinful people.

God's plan to save humanity included establishing a chosen people through whom Jesus would come to the world to save humanity from the power and penalty of sin. When Jesus died, His blood sealed a new covenant with humanity. When we repent of our sins and have faith in God, we receive forgiveness of our sins and are cleansed from all unrighteousness. Through His death and resurrection, Jesus established a covenant of redemption which restores our relationship with God. This is a covenant of grace. We are made right with God through His grace and mercy. No longer are we under the Law, which was based on sacrificial offerings through the shed blood of an innocent lamb. Through Jesus' sacrifice on the cross, we have eternal life and fellowship with God.

### III. GOD'S UNCONDITIONAL PROMISES (2 SAMUEL 7:15–17)

God promised David that when he died, he would set things up for Solomon so that his kingdom would be established. Solomon would build a house for God and his throne would be established forever. God also promised that He would father Solomon. Should Solomon disobey Him, He would "chasten him with the rod of men and with the stripes of the children of men" (vs. 14). A rod is a stick with many uses or a club–like weapon. Stripes refers to lashes or blows dealt as punishment. During Bible times, a rod or a whip was used to inflict stripes. To chasten is to inflict punishment or discipline for the purpose of instruction, training, and corrective guidance. If Solomon disobeyed God, He would discipline him, but He would not stop loving him. Solomon was God's choice to inherit his father's kingdom; however, God would hold him accountable for his actions. God's promise to discipline Solomon demonstrates His grace. He would not reject Solomon as He rejected Saul. God's discipline leads to teaching and maturing His people. The fulfillment of the Davidic covenant did not rely just on David or Solomon. It required Jesus to fulfill it.

Isaiah prophesied that Jesus would come to the world and be rejected. He would bear our griefs and carried our sorrows. He was wounded for our transgressions and the chastisement of our peace was upon Him; and with His stripes we are healed (See Isaiah 53:4–5). God was establishing a kingdom that would, through Jesus, last forever. Although we may fall and be accountable to God for our sins, we have the grace of God and the mercy of God to get back up again through repentance from our sins and God's forgiveness of our sins.

### THE LESSON APPLIED

Often time, unbeknown to us, God is orchestrating the events of our lives to bring us to an expected end. "For I know the thoughts that I think toward you, saith the Lord, thoughts of peace, and not of evil, to give you an expected end" (Jeremiah 29:11 KJV). God knows the future and His plans for us are good. Like David, when we allow God to direct our lives, we will fulfill His plans for us. Regardless of the pain, suffering, or hardship that we may experience, God will see us through to a glorious ending. Our job is to follow Him along the ride.

David was a mere shepherd boy when God hand-selected him to be the future king of Israel. He practiced the presence of God throughout his life. He trusted God's Word and based his life upon it. He regularly inquired of the Lord before going into battle or making important decisions throughout his life. Although he sinned, David was quick to repent. He realized his own unworthiness and humbled himself before God. God has a plan that far exceeds any plans that we may have. We may be spared from many ills in life by inquiring of the Lord first before making important decisions. Because David trusted God, his faith was rewarded. God established a special covenant with David and his dynasty was established forever. Through David's bloodline, Jesus was born.

## LET'S TALK ABOUT IT

David's response to God provides a shining example of how we should respond to God especially during times of success. When David came into success and had rest from his enemies, he considered what could he do for God. David reflected over the years of his life and ascribed God's grace in the good times and in the bad times. He attributed all his success to God. "Every good gift and every perfect gift is from above, and cometh down from the Father of lights, with whom is no variableness, nor shadow of turning" (James 1:17, KJV). By desiring to build a temple for God, David wanted to do something special for God. David had a heart for God and he was fully committed to fulfilling God's plan for his life.

We may pursue many things in life that others define as success; however, like David, let us remember that only what we do for Christ will last. Even though David wanted to do something to honor the Lord, God still said no. Even when we have the best intentions, God still knows better than us. We must simply trust Him and be obedient, even when His will does not align with our plans.

## GET SOCIAL

Share your views and tag us @rhboydco. Use #rhboydco.

@rhboydco

## HOME DAILY DEVOTIONAL READINGS
### DECEMBER 9–15, 2024

| MONDAY | TUESDAY | WEDNESDAY | THURSDAY | FRIDAY | SATURDAY | SUNDAY |
|---|---|---|---|---|---|---|
| God's Covenant of Love | 27–37 God Has Heard Your Prayer | A Message of Promise and Grace | God Is a Sun and Shield | The Herald of God's Coming | A Child of Wonder | Praises to the God Who Saves |
| Psalm 89:1–4, | Luke 1:5–17 | Luke 1:18–23 | Psalm 84 | Malachi 4 | Luke 1:57–66 | Luke 1:67–80 |

LESSON III                                                    DECEMBER 15, 2024

# THE PROPHET WHO PREPARES THE WAY

ADULT TOPIC:                      BACKGROUND SCRIPTURE: LUKE 1:5–23, 57–80
GET READY!                                        LESSON PASSAGE: LUKE 1:67–80

## LUKE 1:67–80

### KJV

AND his father Zacharias was filled with the Holy Ghost, and prophesied, saying,
68 Blessed be the Lord God of Israel; for he hath visited and redeemed his people,

69 And hath raised up an horn of salvation for us in the house of his servant David;
70 As he spake by the mouth of his holy prophets, which have been since the world began:
71 That we should be saved from our enemies, and from the hand of all that hate us;
72 To perform the mercy promised to our fathers, and to remember his holy covenant;

73 The oath which he sware to our father Abraham,

74 That he would grant unto us, that we being delivered out of the hand of our enemies might serve him without fear,
75 In holiness and righteousness before him, all the days of our life.
76 And thou, child, shalt be called the prophet of the Highest: for thou shalt go before the face of the Lord to prepare his ways;
77 To give knowledge of salvation unto his people by the remission of their sins,
78 Through the tender mercy of our God; whereby the dayspring from on high hath visited us,
79 To give light to them that sit in darkness and in the shadow of death, to guide our feet into the way of peace.

### NRSVue

THEN his father Zechariah was filled with the Holy Spirit and prophesied:
68 "Blessed be the Lord God of Israel, for he has looked favorably on his people and redeemed them.
69 He has raised up a mighty savior for us in the house of his child David,
70 as he spoke through the mouth of his holy prophets from of old,
71 that we would be saved from our enemies and from the hand of all who hate us.
72 Thus he has shown the mercy promised to our ancestors and has remembered his holy covenant,
73 the oath that he swore to our ancestor Abraham,
to grant us
74 that we, being rescued from the hands of our enemies,
might serve him without fear,
75 in holiness and righteousness in his presence all our days.
76 And you, child, will be called the prophet of the Most High, for you will go before the Lord to prepare his ways,
77 to give his people knowledge of salvation by the forgiveness of their sins.
78 Because of the tender mercy of our God, the dawn from on high will break upon us,

79 to shine upon those who sit in darkness and in the shadow of death, to guide our feet into the way of peace."

**MAIN THOUGHT:** And you, child, will be called the prophet of the Most High; for you will go before the Lord to prepare his ways, to give knowledge of salvation to his people by the forgiveness of their sins. (Luke 1:76–77, NRSVue)

## LUKE 1:67–80

**KJV**

80 And the child grew, and waxed strong in spirit, and was in the deserts till the day of his shewing unto Israel.

**NRSVue**

80 The child grew and became strong in spirit, and he was in the wilderness until the day he appeared publicly to Israel.

**LESSON SETTING**
   Time: 60 CE
   Place: Asia Minor

**LESSON OUTLINE**
   I. Who is Zechariah?
      (Luke 1:67)
   II. Zechariah's Song
      (Luke 1:68–80)

## UNIFYING PRINCIPLE

In times of trouble, people require rescue. Who can save us in such times? Zechariah prophesied that his son, John, would prepare the way for the coming Savior who would redeem Israel.

## INTRODUCTION

Luke, a physician, historian, and a Gentile, provides the most comprehensive account of Jesus' life than any other Gospel. He was not one of the original disciples, and not an eyewitness of Jesus; however, he was dedicated to record the accounts of those who were first-hand witnesses of Jesus' ministry and their writings about Jesus. After Jesus ascended to heaven, the apostles used their records of His words, sermons, and activities as the subject of their teachings.

Their records of Jesus' life became adopted as the teachings in large and small gatherings and assemblies of the followers of Jesus throughout the region, and also throughout the world. There were many attempts to keep a record of the words and things that Jesus did while He was on earth. The disciples taught the new believers what Jesus taught them. However, as the years passed on, so did they. As the Church continued to grow and the eyewitnesses of Jesus passed on, many of the new converts had only heard of Jesus. A more comprehensive and authoritative account of Jesus was needed to preserve the historical significance and to teach the growing body of followers of Jesus.

In Luke's account of the life of Christ, he brings together the records and accounts of the disciples, but also researches eyewitnesses of Jesus' miracles, sermons, and activities. His work sets in chronological order, as best as we can know, a historical account of the life of Christ. Luke begins with the birth of John the Baptist, the forerunner of Christ and then introduces Mary and the visitation of the angel Gabriel. Throughout the book of Luke, he affirms that Jesus is not only the Son of Man, but also the Son of God. In the book of Luke and in the book of Acts, Luke provides the most reliable account of Jesus' life and the early Church.

## EXPOSITION

### I. WHO IS ZECHARIAH? (LUKE 1:67)

Zechariah was a priest from the Abijah division. His name means "the Lord remembers." Abijah was one of Samuel's sons. Zechariah was married to Elizabeth, who was a descendant of Aaron (the brother of Moses). Elizabeth means "oath of God." While older in years, they were a righteous couple who loved and obeyed God from their hearts.

All priests were descendants of Aaron's bloodline. During this time, there were approximately 20,000 priests. During the reign of David, they were divided into groups of 1,000. Priestly duties included burning incense in the house of the Lord, managing the upkeep of the temple, teaching the Scriptures, and conducting the worship services. Because there were so many priests, each were scheduled to minister in the temple at different times. About once per year, it was Zechariah's turn to minister in the temple, in the most holy place. Lots were cast to see which priest would enter the most holy place in the temple to burn incense. The incense was burned upon the altar of incense twice per day. On this occasion, the lot fell on Zechariah to go into the most holy place. Although this may all seem coincidental to man, God was working to prepare the way for Jesus. When the people saw the smoke ascending from the incense, they would pray to God.

Zechariah and Elizabeth could not bear children because Elizabeth was barren and they were well-advanced in years. Nevertheless, they remained faithful and obedient to the Lord.

Zechariah entered the most holy place inside the temple and prayed as he burned the incense. When the multitudes outside of the temple saw the incense, they all prayed. While he was burning the incense, Zechariah saw the angel Gabriel standing on the right side of the altar of incense. This frightened Zechariah. The angel Gabriel told him that his prayers were heard and that his wife Elizabeth would bear a son and he should call his name John (see Luke 1: 22–14).

Zechariah could not believe what Gabriel told him. Since Zachariah did not believe, Gabriel made Zechariah unable to speak until the day when John was born. This was also done as a sign that God would fulfill the prophecy regarding John's birth.

It was customary for the priest to pronounce a blessing after the incense burned on the altar and after the prayers. The multitudes waited a long time for Zechariah to come out of the most holy place to pronounce the blessing. When Zechariah came out of the most holy place, he could not speak. Sometime after Zechariah returned home, Elizabeth became pregnant. God showed His favor towards her for her years of being unable to have a child.

In the fullness of time, Elizabeth gave birth to her son. Little did anyone know that the account of Zechariah's inability to speak in and of itself would be connected to the birth of his son. The miracle of the birth of their son, coupled with the incident of Zechariah's inability to speak may have now caused others to wonder what manner of child this is. On this occasion of the birth of their son, John, Elizabeth and Zechariah had more to rejoice about than the fact that they had a son. This son was a son of destiny who would one day become the forerunner of Christ.

## II. Zechariah's Song (Luke 1:68–80)

When Zechariah's tongue was loosed, he was full of the Holy Ghost and prophesied. Previous to this, the voice of God had been silent for 400 years. The people hadn't heard a word directly from God in generations, but here He was speaking through Zechariah. This shows that although Zechariah had doubted God at first, God forgave him for that doubt and still chose him to be the vessel of this incredible prophecy about Jesus and John. Keep in mind that Zechariah had been silent for around nine months, the entire duration of Elizabeth's pregnancy, and with his first opportunity to speak, he used it to praise the Lord!

This song is also known as the "Benedictus." The Benedictus was a summary of the life and ministry of Christ. His praise culminated hundreds of years of God's sovereignty throughout the history of humanity. God chose a helpless baby to be born to an old priest and his aged wife to prepare the way of the Savior.

First, he blessed the Lord God of Israel for fulfilling the Old Testament prophecies of a coming Savior. We can be assured that this word from God is prophetic because it's about Jesus, not Zechariah's new son, John. John wouldn't be the "horn of salvation," but Jesus would. Jesus would save the Israelites from their enemies, not John, and so on. Even without knowing Jesus yet, Zechariah was able to praise and glorify Him for all the things He would yet do on earth. It was promised to Abraham that his seed would bless humanity. It was also prophesied in the Old Testament that salvation would come through the line of David. King David is arguably the best king that Israel had ever had, and even he falls short in comparison to Jesus. David honored the Lord, fought for His kingdom, established peace in the nations, and didn't allow idol worship. But he wasn't perfect, and once he left the throne, Israel did go back to their bad habits and fell into trouble again. That's why the Israelites, and all of us, need to put our trust in Jesus and not any earthly leader. God remembered all these promises of the Old Testament and they were about to be fulfilled through Jesus, the son of Mary.

Zechariah then prophesied that his son, John, would be a prophet of the Lord to prepare the way for Him, and to spread the good news of salvation. Before Jesus would come of age and begin His earthly ministry, John would prepare the people's hearts to receive Him. He would devote his life to teaching people about God's plan of salvation; he would point out to the Israelites the depths of their sin. He would call out the darkness and point them toward the light! He would direct them to God's path of peace. Once again, we must remember that the Lord had been silent for 400 years. Prophets had gone by the wayside, but John would revitalize that calling. The Israelites had a very specific idea of what they wanted in a Messiah: they wanted a political leader, a king that would free them from persecution by the Romans. John would counter these ideas and instead tell them about the doctrine of salvation: spiritual rescue over a physical one. One day, when Jesus returns for the second time, there will be a physical restoration, but at this time in Luke 1, the people should've been expecting a different kind of Savior.

When the Lord speaks to us, or gives us a message meant to be shared with someone else, the appropriate response is to first praise Him! Like Zechariah, we can give Him glory for what He's done and what

He's yet to accomplish. It doesn't have to be a song; all that matters is that we speak from the heart and genuinely thank Him for what He's doing in our lives and in the lives of our loved ones. There's nothing that escapes His notice, and He's always working behind the scenes to make things come to pass according to His perfect will and timing.

All of these things came to pass just as God said. Scripture tells us that his spirit was strong, which means he must've spent countless hours in fellowship with the Lord. We also know that he spent many years in the desert, isolated with just the Lord, in order to properly prepare for his duty as forerunner. John didn't spend years with the rabbis in school studying prophecy; he never attended seminary. He simply devoted himself to the Lord and His service. With an example such as that, don't disqualify yourself as useless for the Kingdom of God. If the Lord has called you, He will use you! When the proper time came, John returned from the desert and began teaching the people about Jesus, just as he was born to do.

## THE LESSON APPLIED

One of the key lessons that we learn from the story of Zechariah and Elizabeth is that God chooses the humble to accomplish His purposes. Oftentimes we see others advance based upon their reputation, education, or other privileges in life. However, when God chooses to advance His agenda, He often selects those who are humble.

When we doubt God, we often miss out on the blessings that He has for us or suffer the consequences. Because God is sovereign and all things are possible, we can confidently trust in Him and believe His Word.

God fulfilled His promise to Abraham and to David. He is keenly involved in the affairs of man and has worked throughout the hundreds and hundreds of years of the history of humanity to fulfill His Word. God has a consistent track record of faithfulness to humanity. We can trust that He will do what He says He will do. No matter what is happening in the world around us, we have hundreds of examples to look back on in the Bible of all the times God kept His promises. If a promise hasn't been fulfilled, it's only because it hasn't happened yet; not because it won't. Aren't you thankful that God is faithful?

Although Zechariah and Elizabeth prayed for a child and were barren into their old age, they remained faithful to God. We must remember that God is faithful to His Word. Even when we don't see Him working, He is still working behind the scenes to fulfill His Word. Sometimes it takes longer for certain promises to be kept, or for certain dominoes to fall into place. While this can be frustrating and disappointing at times, we must remember that God's timing is perfect. We know that He is working out all things for our good, so we must simply trust the process and lean on Him when we don't understand the delay.

## LET'S TALK ABOUT IT

We may have many uncertainties in life. We cannot thrive spiritually when we doubt God. He is our Creator and has been working throughout the history of humankind to accomplish His divine will for humanity. God has been faithful in His plan to save humanity; however, for each individual, we are all accountable for where we put our trust. Zechariah put his trust in science. Because he was an old man, he thought it was impossible for him to have a son. What may seem impossible with man, is always possible with God.

God understands our fallen nature and that we needed a Savior. For hundreds of years, He planned for Jesus to come to the world to rescue us from the power and penalty of sin. Sin separates us from God. Through the shed blood of Jesus, we are not only delivered from the power of sin, but also freed from condemnation. Without this two–fold rescue, we would not be able to enjoy freedom in Christ. As long as we are in bondage or slavery to sin, we will disobey Christ.

When we learn to hate sin, we are able to repent and walk in righteousness. Let us die to our sinful nature so that we can live in Jesus. Through Christ, we are fully emancipated and fully forgiven. All our guilt is removed by His redemption at the cross, and we no longer fear being separated from Him. "There is no fear in love, but perfect love casts out fear. For fear has to do with punishment, and whoever fears has not been perfected in love" (1 John 4:18, KJV).

When we surrender to the lordship of Jesus Christ, we live to serve Him at His pleasure and not our own. In Christ, we live to please God just as Christ did, and great will be our reward as we will one day sit with Him in heaven. "To him that overcometh will I grant to sit with me in my throne, even as I also overcame, and am set down with my Father in his throne" (Revelation 3:21, KJV).

This week, spend some quiet time with the Lord and ask Him to reveal some areas where you might have doubt. Ask Him to bolster your faith and give you opportunities to grow in your walk with Him. Or how could you encourage another believer in their walk with Him this week? There could be no sweeter music to His ears! He desires a personal relationship with you.

## Get Social
Share your views and tag us @rhboydco. Use #rhboydco.

**@rhboydco**

## Home Daily Devotional Readings
### December 16–22, 2024

| Monday | Tuesday | Wednesday | Thursday | Friday | Saturday | Sunday |
|---|---|---|---|---|---|---|
| Mercy for Those Who Suffer | Show God's Mercy to All | God Delights in Compassion | Remember Your Mercy, O Lord | God Relieves a Troubled Heart | Mercy for Sinners | Lord, Let Me See Again |
| Luke 4:14–21 | Luke 6:27–36 | Micah 7:14–20 | Psalm 25:1–10 | Psalm 25:11–22 | Luke 18:9–14 | Luke 18:35–43 |

LESSON IV                                                           DECEMBER 22, 2024

# BORN IN THE CITY OF DAVID

ADULT TOPIC:  
BREAKING NEWS!

BACKGROUND SCRIPTURE: LUKE 2:1–20  
LESSON PASSAGE: LUKE 2:1–16

## LUKE 2:1–16

### KJV

AND it came to pass in those days, that there went out a decree from Caesar Augustus that all the world should be taxed.

2 (And this taxing was first made when Cyrenius was governor of Syria.)

3 And all went to be taxed, every one into his own city.

4 And Joseph also went up from Galilee, out of the city of Nazareth, into Judaea, unto the city of David, which is called Bethlehem; (because he was of the house and lineage of David:)

5 To be taxed with Mary his espoused wife, being great with child.

6 And so it was, that, while they were there, the days were accomplished that she should be delivered.

7 And she brought forth her firstborn son, and wrapped him in swaddling clothes, and laid him in a manger; because there was no room for them in the inn.

8 And there were in the same country shepherds abiding in the field, keeping watch over their flock by night.

9 And, lo, the angel of the Lord came upon them, and the glory of the Lord shone round about them: and they were sore afraid.

10 And the angel said unto them, Fear not: for, behold, I bring you good tidings of great joy, which shall be to all people.

11 For unto you is born this day in the city of David a Saviour, which is Christ the Lord.

12 And this shall be a sign unto you; Ye shall find the babe wrapped in swaddling clothes, lying in a manger.

### NRSVue

IN those days a decree went out from Caesar Augustus that all the world should be registered.

2 This was the first registration and was taken while Quirinius was governor of Syria.

3 All went to their own towns to be registered.

4 Joseph also went from the town of Nazareth in Galilee to Judea, to the city of David called Bethlehem, because he was descended from the house and family of David.

5 He went to be registered with Mary, to whom he was engaged and who was expecting a child.

6 While they were there, the time came for her to deliver her child.

7 And she gave birth to her firstborn son and wrapped him in bands of cloth and laid him in a manger, because there was no place in the guest room.

8 Now in that same region there were shepherds living in the fields, keeping watch over their flock by night.

9 Then an angel of the Lord stood before them, and the glory of the Lord shone around them, and they were terrified.

10 But the angel said to them, "Do not be afraid, for see, I am bringing you good news of great joy for all the people:

11 to you is born this day in the city of David a Savior, who is the Messiah, the Lord.

12 This will be a sign for you: you will find a child wrapped in bands of cloth and lying in a manger."

**MAIN THOUGHT:** When the angels had left them and gone into heaven, the shepherds said to one another, "Let us go now to Bethlehem and see this thing that has taken place, which the Lord has made known to us." (Luke 2:15, NRSVue)

## Luke 2:1–16

### KJV

13 And suddenly there was with the angel a multitude of the heavenly host praising God, and saying,
14 Glory to God in the highest, and on earth peace, good will toward men.
15 And it came to pass, as the angels were gone away from them into heaven, the shepherds said one to another, Let us now go even unto Bethlehem, and see this thing which is come to pass, which the Lord hath made known unto us.
16 And they came with haste, and found Mary, and Joseph, and the babe lying in a manger.

### NRSVue

13 And suddenly there was with the angel a multitude of the heavenly host, praising God and saying,
14 "Glory to God in the highest heaven, and on earth peace among those whom he favors!"
15 When the angels had left them and gone into heaven, the shepherds said to one another, "Let us go now to Bethlehem and see this thing that has taken place, which the Lord has made known to us."
16 So they went with haste and found Mary and Joseph and the child lying in the manger.

### LESSON SETTING
Time: 60 CE
Place: Asia Minor

### LESSON OUTLINE
I. A Census is Taken (Luke 2:1–3)
II. Jesus is Born in Bethlehem (Luke 2:4–7)
III. The Angels Announce His Birth (Luke 2:8–14)
IV. Witnessing the Good News (Luke 2:15–16)

## UNIFYING PRINCIPLE

Everyone likes to hear good news. What good news can we expect in our day? God announced the good news of Jesus' birth to shepherds who were amazed at hearing it.

## INTRODUCTION

We live in a digital age marked by rapid advancements in technology that have impacted every aspect of our lives. This age is characterized by the rapid exchange of information on a global scale. Through advancements in media and other technological platforms, the world is now more interconnected than ever before.

But in today's story, amidst the backdrop of the rule of Caesar Augustus, emperor of Rome, the biblical account of Jesus' birth emerges as breaking news in the little town of Bethlehem, also known as the city of David. For centuries, the birth of Jesus was prophesied and many of the prophets awaited His appearance with great expectations that He would elevate the state of the Jews. Luke's account of the birth of Jesus provides the context in detail enabling us to understand that Jesus' birth had more than just political implications. His arrival to the world was not just to improve the state of the Jews, but to save all of humanity.

## EXPOSITION

### I. A CENSUS IS TAKEN (LUKE 2:1–3)

During his reign, Caesar Augustus decreed for a census to be taken and taxes collected for revenue in the treasury and for military purposes. Everyone who lived outside of their hometown traveled to their hometown to be registered. Although the

Jews were not drafted into the Roman army, they were required to be counted in the census and to pay taxes. It is likely that Joseph had property or other business ventures in Bethlehem. Caesar Augustus' timing to conduct the census necessitated that Joseph and Mary make the journey to Bethlehem to comply with the law.

## II. Jesus is Born in Bethlehem (Luke 2:4–7)

Mary was from the line of David and grew up in Nazareth. Joseph, a humble carpenter, was also from the line of David. King David was from Bethlehem of Judea. It was no accident that Jesus, who was to be born in the lineage of David, should also be born in the same city as King David.

Mary was espoused to Joseph and being at the full term of her pregnancy, her delivery was imminent. Given her condition, Joseph was reluctant to make the ninety-mile journey from Nazareth in Galilee to Bethlehem of Judea. Yet Joseph complied with the decree and made the journey. According to John 5:17, God is always working. Often we may not see the hand of God in any given situation. However, God is sovereign, and He works to accomplish His will in His time. This journey to Bethlehem proved to align with God's perfect plan to bring Jesus into the world.

The journey to Bethlehem was long and arduous, and the rocky terrain made it even more difficult of a passage for Mary and Joseph. Joseph was strengthened by God along the way. He understood the possibility of Mary delivering Jesus while they were in Bethlehem, and took great care to ensure their safety.

Because this census was based on ancestry, Joseph and Mary were likely staying with relatives in Bethlehem. During biblical times, a typical home included the living space next to where the animals were housed. This design provided a means for families to keep a close eye on their animals. A manger was a feeding trough for the animals. It was located either indoors where the animals were housed, or outside of the house. Joseph and Mary's relatives' homes were already full to capacity in their guest spaces, which left only the animal holdings as the remaining available space for them to stay.

While in Bethlehem, Mary went into labor. There in the manger, the humblest and yet most unlikely of all abodes, the King of Kings and Lord of Lords, the Savior of the world was born. Though lowly and humble, God's intention would be found in this unlikely setting.

When Mary delivered Baby Jesus, she wrapped Him in swaddling cloths. These cloths were strips of fabric used to secure the Baby and keep Him warm.

## III. The Angels Announce His Birth (Luke 2:8–14)

Today, couples may host a gender reveal party, or a baby shower to welcome their newborn; however, Jesus' birth announcement was beyond spectacular! God chose to announce the birth of the Savior to lowly shepherds who were watching their sheep that historic night. Usually, shepherds stayed out with their sheep during the lambing season, which was around early spring.

God has a long history of using shepherds in significant roles, including Abraham, Jacob, Moses, David, and Amos. Using the shepherds as witnesses to Jesus' arrival to the world underscores the connection to Israel's past history with God. It also shows how God chose to lift up the lowly (Luke 1:52).

The shepherds were entrusted to the care of the lambs that were used in the sacrificial ceremonies in the temple. The lambs offered for sacrifices had to be without spot or blemish. The shepherds were required to ensure the newborn lambs were wrapped in swaddling cloths to avoid blemish or injury. At this moment, the angel announced to them the Lamb of God, who would take away the sins of the world, had been born.

At first the shepherds were afraid, but the angel of the Lord told them not to be afraid. Throughout the Bible when others have encountered angels, fear has been their first response. Perhaps these supernatural beings are intimidating, and their presence reminds us of how finite and sinful we are, and how incompatible we are with these extensions of God's holy presence.

When the angel of the Lord appeared to them, the glory of God *enshrowed* in a white shining cloud that was intolerably bright. This was known as the *Schechinah* (the visible presence of God). The *Schechinah* glory was present with Moses in the burning bush on Mt. Sinai. It was also present with Jesus on the Mount of Transfiguration, and with Saul on the road to Damascus. The shepherds experienced the awe of God as they witnessed the angel of the Lord and the *Schechinah* glory. In the glorious presence of the glory of God, we come to realize our own humanity, and our own inadequacy.

For ages, the Jews had long awaited the Messiah and expected that He would be born in a royal setting; however, God chose His birthplace as a lowly manger and entrusted His birth announcement to humble shepherds instead of the religious and political leaders. He was wrapped in swaddling cloths as the Lamb of God without blemish, who would take away the sins of the entire world. The announcement of Jesus' birth to the shepherds is aligned with Mary's *Magnifcat* found in Luke 1:52 where the lowly are exalted, and the mighty are humbled.

Shepherds were often viewed as social outcasts in ancient near eastern culture. They were elevated as the first recipients of the good news, which signals God's preference for the marginalized. Jesus' mission to save humanity was and continues to be an inclusive mission. He values each of us as His very own. The vehicles by which God accomplishes His plans and purposes through ordinary humble human beings challenges the contemporary notions of status and worthiness. By using humble vessels, God underscores the importance of humility. God does not place value upon us in the same ways in which we place value on ourselves. We are not valued based upon what we achieve in this life. We are valued by God because we belong to Him and He loves us with an everlasting love (see Jeremiah 31:3).

The angel announced the birth of the Savior of the world to the lowly shepherds, and told them where to find Him. A multitude of angels praising God suddenly appeared to the shepherds. They were both surprised and amazed. The multitude of angels surrounded the shepherds on every side. Jesus is known as the Lord of hosts. This number of angelic hosts could have easily numbered in the thousands upon ten thousands, as found in Daniel 7:10.

At the time of Jesus' birth, the Roman empire was at peace. The angelic multitude sang glory to God and resounded peace on earth and good will toward men. This song has been known as "Gloria" throughout history.

With such a great cloud of witnesses, the shepherds were convinced that this visitation of the angel of the Lord and the angelic hosts and what they were told was the fulfillment of the long-awaited prophesies of the Messiah.

## IV. WITNESSING THE GOOD NEWS (LUKE 2:15–16)

The angelic hosts returned to heaven and the shepherds ran immediately to Bethlehem where they found Mary, Joseph, and Baby Jesus in the manger. They wanted to see for themselves what was revealed to them by the angel of God and the multitude of angels.

When they arrived to the manger, Mary realized her song of Magnificat was not only coming true for her, but also for these lowly shepherds. She also realized that God had chosen them to be the first to see the Christ Child. Later, when the travelers from the East arrived, she also realized the fulfillment of the prophesies of Isaiah regarding His birth.

During this period, shepherds were held in such low esteem that they would not be permitted to enter the courts as witnesses. Their daily labor was somewhat of a sacred occupation in that they provided and cared for the very lambs that would be sacrificed in the temple for the sins of the people. Their work brought them into the premises of the temple where they were exposed to the long-awaited appearance of the Messiah. When the shepherds found Jesus lying in a manger, this confirmed what the angel of the Lord told them. Newborns were not typically laid in a manger after they are born; therefore, this provided evidence of the angel's instructions and proof of his word.

In one single night, the shepherds were chosen to be the first preachers heralding to the world the Messiah's arrival! The news of Christ's birth slowly spread widely throughout Bethlehem. Zechariah's encounter with the angel during the sacrificial ceremony, the birth of John the Baptist to he and Elizabeth who were well past their child-bearing years, and now the birth of Jesus to a virgin handmaiden provided evidence of the fulfillment of the prophesies of old.

After they saw the Christ Child, they spread the news of the Messiah to all. They were among the first eyewitnesses of the Savior of the world. The shepherds were never the same after seeing the angels and seeing the Christ Child for themselves.

Just as the angelic host pronounced peace and goodwill to all people, and the shepherds spread the news of the Messiah to everyone, so are we to carry the Gospel to all the world.

## THE LESSON APPLIED

We may have our own expectations of what God can or cannot do. Oftentimes God will use the most unlikely to accomplish the most good. God's eyes are on the righteous and His ears are attentive to our cry (see 1 Peter 3:12). At times we may feel ordinary, as though we have no special value or perhaps do not have anything that qualifies us as great in the eyes of humanity. God used a humble handmaiden and shepherds who were in the field to bring the salvation of humankind into the world. Let us remember that God is sovereign and He does not work according to the whims and expectations of human beings.

By choosing a manger as the location of Jesus' birth, it foregrounded the depraved condition of humanity in which Jesus found us. Yet, although He was King of Kings and Lord of Lords, He took upon Himself our likeness and humbled Himself to our conditions to save us.

We are not promised a luxurious lifestyle in this world; however, God promises that He will be with us and that He will provide for our needs.

God's plan was to bring Jesus to the world to save the world. He is looking for faith in His followers. He is also looking for humility. Joseph trusted God to fulfill His Word. Despite extraordinary and perhaps baffling conditions, he did not give up. He continued to trust what the angel of the Lord told him. He was faithful in supporting Mary as the mother of Christ and protecting the Christ Child. The shepherds were faithful to find Jesus as the angels had told them, and then shared that message with others as soon as possible! As Christians, we carry their legacy with us each day. This isn't a duty that should be taken lightly.

## Let's Talk About It

**How can we know that we are prioritizing the things that are important to God?**

As we survey the methods and means that God uses to fulfill His purposes, we learn what is most important to Him. God's ways are not our ways and His thoughts are not our thoughts. Modern societies may have standards for greatest and success such as wealth, education, fame, or power; however, true greatness is characterized by humility. Regardless of our station in life, our reputation, or what we suffer, humble service to the King of Kings and the Lord of Lords, is fulfilling God's intention for our lives. Let us surrender to the lordship of Jesus Christ each day.

### Get Social
Share your views and tag us @rhboydco. Use #rhboydco.

@rhboydco

## Home Daily Devotional Readings
### December 23–29, 20249

| Monday | Tuesday | Wednesday | Thursday | Friday | Saturday | Sunday |
| --- | --- | --- | --- | --- | --- | --- |
| Mercy for Those Who Suffer | Show God's Mercy to All | God Delights in Compassion | Remember Your Mercy, O Lord | God Relieves a Troubled Heart | Mercy for Sinners | Lord, Let Me See Again |
| Luke 4:14–21 | Luke 6:27–36 | Micah 7:14–20 | Psalm 25:1–10 | Psalm 25:11–22 | Luke 18:9–14 | Luke 18:35–43 |

LESSON V    DECEMBER 29, 2024

# THE MERCIFUL SON OF DAVID

ADULT TOPIC: A MIRACLE IN JERICHO

BACKGROUND SCRIPTURE: LUKE 18:31–43
LESSON PASSAGE: LUKE 18:35–43

## LUKE 18:35–43

### KJV

AND it came to pass, that as he was come nigh unto Jericho, a certain blind man sat by the way side begging:

36 And hearing the multitude pass by, he asked what it meant.

37 And they told him, that Jesus of Nazareth passeth by.

38 And he cried, saying, Jesus, thou son of David, have mercy on me.

39 And they which went before rebuked him, that he should hold his peace: but he cried so much the more, Thou son of David, have mercy on me.

40 And Jesus stood, and commanded him to be brought unto him: and when he was come near, he asked him,

41 Saying, What wilt thou that I shall do unto thee? And he said, Lord, that I may receive my sight.

42 And Jesus said unto him, Receive thy sight: thy faith hath saved thee.

43 And immediately he received his sight, and followed him, glorifying God: and all the people, when they saw it, gave praise unto God.

### NRSVue

AS he approached Jericho, a blind man was sitting by the roadside begging.

36 When he heard a crowd going by, he asked what was happening.

37 They told him, "Jesus of Nazareth is passing by."

38 Then he shouted, "Jesus, Son of David, have mercy on me!"

39 Those who were in front sternly ordered him to be quiet, but he shouted even more loudly, "Son of David, have mercy on me!"

40 Jesus stood still and ordered the man to be brought to him, and when he came near, he asked him,

41 "What do you want me to do for you?" He said, "Lord, let me see again."

42 Jesus said to him, "Receive your sight; your faith has saved you."

43 Immediately he regained his sight and followed him, glorifying God, and all the people, when they saw it, praised God.

## LESSON SETTING
Time: 60 CE
Place: Asia Minor

## LESSON OUTLINE
I. A Blind Man Seeks Jesus
(Luke 18:35–39)
II. Jesus Restores Sight
(Luke 18:40–43)

**MAIN THOUGHT:** Those who were in front sternly ordered him to be quiet; but he shouted even more loudly, "Son of David, have mercy on me!"
(Luke 18:39, NRSVue)

## Unifying Principle
People who ask for help are sometimes silenced. How can we respond to those who call for help? When the crowds tried to silence the cries of a man who called out, "Son of David, have mercy on me!" Jesus stopped to ask the man what he could do for him.

## Introduction
In today's lesson, we learn that the disciples were the closest followers of Jesus, yet there were some things that they failed to see. They couldn't grasp that He was going to be crucified. They were close followers of Jesus, yet they were blind to some importance truths about His mission. In contrast to the disciples who were able to see with their natural eyes, the blind man in Luke 18 could not see with his natural eyes. Despite his blindness, he understood spiritually that Jesus was the Son of God—the Messiah—the One who saves.

The blind man was desperate to be healed. He knew that Jesus was the Messiah, his only hope to transform his life; and therefore, he persisted in his faith to be sure that Jesus heard him. Somehow he knew that if he yelled loud enough, Jesus would hear him and upon hearing him, Jesus would not turn a deaf ear.

Faith opens the eyes of our understanding and unlocks a response from heaven. Whatever we cannot see with our natural eyes does not necessarily mean that we cannot access it with our spiritual eyes of faith. For we know, "what is impossible with man is possible with God" (v. 27). When was the last time you believed in God to do the impossible?

## Exposition
### I. A Blind Man Seeks Jesus (Luke 18:35–39)
Imagine Jesus traveling from town to town teaching, preaching, healing, and delivering many people throughout His ministry. The disciples handled the logistics and served Him in much the same way as bodyguards of today would serve national leaders, iconic figures, and other dignitaries. Although they were a part of Jesus' ministry team, the disciples had much to learn about Jesus and His mission. There were some things about Jesus that they simply couldn't get.

Throughout Jesus' ministry, He encountered all kinds of people. There were several incidences where the disciples rebuked people who were trying to get close to Jesus. Sometimes, Jesus had to deal with their misguided mistakes—especially those that were public.

In today's lesson, Jesus and His disciples are on their way to Jerusalem, where the prophesies of His crucifixion would be fulfilled. Even while on their way to Jerusalem, they were unaware of the crucial events that were soon to be fulfilled.

As they approached Jericho, a blind man was sitting by the roadside begging. The Greek word for begging is *epaiteo*, which means "to ask for, implore, claim, to ask for alms; to desire, demand; to consider oneself entitled to; to require, to inquire for." Begging for his sustenance was his occupation. He did not resign himself to doing nothing to help himself. The Israelites were compassionate towards the blind. It was a curse to cause the blind to wander (see Deuteronomy 27:18). Though blind, he actively relied on the compassion of others to provide for his needs by begging for it. By so doing, he was drawing upon their compassion.

Since the blind man was begging by the roadside, one could infer that his blindness was a chronic condition versus a temporary condition. In the first century, blindness was often considered a punishment for doing evil—as in the case when the men of Sodom demanded Lot to let them sleep with the angels who had visited Lot (Genesis 19:11). Blindness was also considered a judgment from God for sins committed either by the individual or by his parents (for example, John 9:2). Receiving his sight would have been the equivalent to being rescued from God's judgment.

Regardless of the reason for his blindness, the man was persistent in his efforts to be healed and made whole. Included in Jesus' mission to save humanity, He was also to preach the Gospel to the poor, heal the brokenhearted, to preach deliverance to the captives, and to recover the sight of the blind (Luke 4:18).

When the blind man heard a crowd of people passing him, he wanted to know what was going on. They told him that Jesus was passing by. He knew that the Messiah could heal him of his blindness and his life would be changed forever! Immediately, the blind man cried out, "Son of David, have mercy on me!" The Greek word for Son is *uihos* (*hwee–os'*). "Son" refers to descendant of; connected to; immediate, remote, or figurative kinship. In this case, the blind man was referring to Jesus as a descendant of David. Jesus was not only the Son of David, He was also the Son of God. The reference to Son is two–fold, or double entendre (has a double–meaning). The specific Greek reference to "Son" in this passage is also "*huios tou Theou*," which means Son of God. In essence, the blind man was also referring to Jesus as the Messiah. A son is the object of parental love and care. Jesus is the beloved Son of God. Even though he was blind and hadn't met Jesus before, he instinctively understood something that the people closest to Jesus didn't grasp: His godhood; His deity. The almighty power that existed within Him simply by virtue of His identity. Forgive the phrase, but he had "blind faith" in Jesus from their first encounter.

Although the people tried to silence his cry for mercy, the blind man continued to cry out; "Son of David, have mercy on me" even louder than before. As it is today, people during this time period did not highly regard beggars. He was considered "low on the totem pole" and therefore, it was easy to just simply ignore his presence. Some commentators point out the difference in the Greek words used to describe "cried out" and "cried out all the more." In the first use, it's described as "an ordinary shout to attract attention" while the second cry was "an instinctive cry of ungovernable emotion, a scream, an almost animal cry." This man was beyond desperate for Jesus' help and there was nothing he wasn't willing to do. He would not be too embarrassed to cry out for his Savior's help!

His persistence in shouting louder and louder draws Jesus' attention and presence. In James 4:7–8, we are admonished to humble ourselves before God. Come close to God and He will come close to you.

Since our hearts are divided between God and the world, we need to humbly submit to the lordship of Jesus Christ. When we humble ourselves and cry out to the Lord, He does not turn a deaf ear. He responds with loving kindness and compassion.

## II. JESUS RESTORES SIGHT (LUKE 18:40–43)

While others ignored him and even tried to silence him; Jesus did not. Jesus commanded His disciples to bring the man to Him. Jesus does not only pay attention to people who the world considers important, famous, or wealthy. The Gospel is an all-inclusive Gospel. Jesus simply came to save the lost—regardless of their social class, economic status, race, religion, gender, or health condition. Salvation is a free gift for everyone!

The blind man asked Jesus to have mercy on him. His request for mercy was a request to restore his sight. This effectively reveals his awareness of his physical impairment as requiring a miracle to be healed, his humility, his need to be rescued from his sin condition, and his faith in the Son of God. Although he could not see with his natural eyes, the blind man understood who Jesus was more so than His own disciples who were very close to Him, and had the ability to see. Luke's placement of this story is intentional and strategic. In verses 31–34, he tells a story about how the disciples knew Jesus best yet were blind to his real purpose on earth.

Also, the man fully recognized the fact that if Jesus healed him, it was out of His mercy–not because God owed him something. This shows the blind man's humility in his petition before the Lord. Think about how you pray for needs in your life. Do you demand them as a petulant child or do you humbly ask for God's mercy on your situation, recognizing that without Him, you would be nowhere? It changes your prayer life when you pray from this perspective of humility.

Luke 18:35–43 isn't just a story about healing a blind beggar. It is also about truly seeing Jesus for who He is, and how we are saved (18:26). The blind man was healed because he had faith in Jesus as the Son of David—the Son of God.

By naming Jesus "Son of David," the blind man places himself under Jesus' authority as the Davidic heir. The Lord had promised David that his kingdom would last forever. Jesus was the fulfillment of this Davidic covenant. The blind man's insistence echoed on Jesus' ears as He heard him say, "have mercy on me."

Jesus asked the blind man, "What do you want me to do for you"? (18:41). It was obvious that the man was blind and needed his sight restored; however, Jesus wanted him to make his request known so that everyone could hear it. The man who was blind could have treated Jesus' question as a superficial query into his position as a beggar (see Acts 3:4–6), but instead he let the question sink deeply in to expose his true need, his helplessness, and his vulnerability. Jesus answered him and healed him, at the level he internalized Jesus' words. Instead of asking Jesus for money, he asked Jesus for what he really needed. He drew on his core belief in who Jesus was—the Son of David, the Son of God, and the Messiah.

Jesus responded to the blind man by telling him to "recover your sight, your faith has made you well" (v. 42). Jesus demonstrated that our belief in His ability to rescue us is what releases the blessing. Instead of hoping that Jesus will do what we ask of Him, we know by faith that He will fulfill His Word. Our faith is in God's strength and goodness to rescue/save, while accepting God's sovereignty and what might seem the strangeness of God's plan. We know God can do it; we ask that God's will be done. What do you want Jesus to do for you today? What is your core need? Part of having faith is believing that God is big enough and powerful to answer our requests, but also wise enough to know when to say no. Sometimes the timing isn't right, or something better is coming in the future. We don't know all the information that He does, but our faith teaches us to trust in His goodness and sovereignty.

Jesus saw the blind man's faith and heard his desperate cry for mercy. Moved by his faith in Jesus' ability to heal him, Jesus immediately healed him. After the blind man was healed, he followed Jesus while glorifying God, and everyone who saw his praise also praised God!

When God heals us or intervenes in our lives, our response to God should be to give Him glory. If He redeems an impossible situation or provides miraculous healing that no one else could do, then we're obligated to recognize His miracles and to praise Him for such. It's never out of our own doing or our own goodness that He rescues us. When we give God the glory in our various situations, others are impacted by our praise as it influences them to also praise God as well. Jesus wanted the children of Israel to know that if they respond to Him, by acknowledging their need for a Savior and receiving Him as their personal Savior, they would be granted eternal life. Despite all the work that Jesus did to teach, heal, and do all kinds of miracles, many did not respond to Him. Today, Jesus has extended His invitation to all. If you haven't yet already, will you receive Him as your personal Savior?

## THE LESSON APPLIED

We learn some key lessons from today's story. The disciples were close followers of Jesus, yet they did not know Him as well as they should have. Although they had eyes to see, they were not able to understand many of the things He talked about—particularly His crucifixion. They thought that Jesus came to set up an earthly kingdom in Jerusalem; therefore, they could not imagine that He would be crucified there. The blind man was able to recognize Jesus as the Messiah, and had faith in Him enough to transform his life. When you look at your own life, do you resonate more with the disciples or with the blind man? Why?

Jesus used a blind man (one who could not see) to magnify what faith in Him looks like. When the blind man learned that Jesus was passing by, he cried out for help despite others who tried to silence him. Instead of walking by the blind man, Jesus stopped to help him because He noticed his faith and his persistence. We too must be desperate for God and cry out to Him for help. When others tried to silence the blind man, he cried louder. When others try to silence us, we should not stop crying out for help when we need; and we should not stop being desperate for God.

The blind man's cry for help did not fall on deaf ears. Amidst the sounds of the crowd, Jesus heard him say "Son of David, have mercy on me!" Jesus healed the man immediately. Before he was healed, he didn't see Jesus with his eyes; he believed in Jesus by faith. If you are believing for a miracle today, your brothers and sisters in Christ stand with you in faith. If your miracle doesn't come how you want, expect, or in the time frame you'd like, trust that God is still good.

## Let's Talk About It

**How desperate are you for Jesus to transform your life?**

Sometimes we can get in a rut going to church and perhaps serving in Christian ministry. We end up going through the motions of worship, prayer and service, but it doesn't penetrate into our hearts like it should. The blind man could have sat by the side of the road and spent his entire life begging for his sustenance. Although he could not see, he was curious enough and motivated enough to inquire what was going on as he listened to the crowd of people walking by him. Instead of sitting in silence, he opened his mouth and said something. Sometimes, we too must open our mouths and say something. Other times, we may speak up, but others may try to drown out our voices or shut us down all together. We must push past the pain and inertia to do nothing, and raise our voices to God and others for help.

The blind man wasn't healed because he was the loudest in the room, but because his faith was the biggest. He understood more about Jesus' power and deity than the disciples did, even though they were with Him 24/7.

We should have such faith now! We've never met Jesus physically, but we've heard stories. We know what He can do because we believe the Bible to be true. We know He's the Son of God. We have every reason to trust in Him no matter our circumstances. Are you willing to trust Him this week? If you don't currently have that trust in Him, would you have the courage to ask Him why not?

## Get Social

Share your views and tag us @rhboydco. Use #rhboydco.

@rhboydco

## Home Daily Devotional Readings
### December 30, 2024– January 5, 2025

| Monday | Tuesday | Wednesday | Thursday | Friday | Saturday | Sunday |
|---|---|---|---|---|---|---|
| The Kingdom Belongs to the Messiah | A Heart Full of Thanks | A Plea to God for Grace | Immortal, Invisible | The Life of Faith | God's Judgments Are True | God Will Arise and Hear Us |
| Revelation 11:14–19 | Psalm 9:1–9 | Psalm 9:10–20 | 1 Timothy 1:12–17 | 1 Timothy 6:11–16 | Psalm 10:1–11 | Psalm 10:12–18 |

LESSON VI                                                JANUARY 5, 2025

# THE LORD IS KING

**ADULT TOPIC:**
IN TIMES OF TROUBLE

**BACKGROUND SCRIPTURE:** PSALMS 9; 10
**LESSON PASSAGE:** PSALM 10:12–18

## PSALM 10:12–18

| KJV | NRSVue |
|---|---|
| ARISE, O Lord; O God, lift up thine hand: forget not the humble.<br>13 Wherefore doth the wicked contemn God? he hath said in his heart, Thou wilt not require it.<br>14 Thou hast seen it; for thou beholdest mischief and spite, to requite it with thy hand: the poor committeth himself unto thee; thou art the helper of the fatherless.<br>15 Break thou the arm of the wicked and the evil man: seek out his wickedness till thou find none.<br>16 The Lord is King for ever and ever: the heathen are perished out of his land.<br>17 Lord, thou hast heard the desire of the humble: thou wilt prepare their heart, thou wilt cause thine ear to hear:<br>18 To judge the fatherless and the oppressed, that the man of the earth may no more oppress. | RISE up, O Lord; O God, lift up your hand; do not forget the oppressed.<br>13 Why do the wicked renounce God and say in their hearts, "You will not call us to account"?<br>14 But you do see! Indeed, you note trouble and grief, that you may take it into your hands; the helpless commit themselves to you; you have been the helper of the orphan.<br>15 Break the arm of the wicked and evildoers; seek out their wickedness until you find none.<br>16 The Lord is king forever and ever; the nations shall perish from his land.<br>17 O Lord, you will hear the desire of the meek; you will strengthen their heart; you will incline your ear<br>18 to do justice for the orphan and the oppressed, so that those from earth may strike terror no more. |

**LESSON SETTING**
   Time: 1010–930 BCE
   Place: Israel

**LESSON OUTLINE**
   I. God, Our Present Help in Trouble (Psalm 10:12–15)
   II. Confidence in God's Judgments (Psalm 10:16–18)

## UNIFYING PRINCIPLE

People are greatly troubled by overwhelming violence, injustice, and oppression. How can we survive and overcome such abusive conditions? The psalmist appeals to God to rise up as king and ruler and restore justice to the defenseless who suffer under the attack of the wicked.

**MAIN THOUGHT:** O LORD, you will hear the desire of the meek; you will strengthen their heart, you will incline your ear. (Psalm 10:17, NRSVue)

## INTRODUCTION

The book of Psalms was written by several authors, David, Asaph, Solomon, Heman Ethan, and Moses between 1440 BC and 586 BC (Moses to the Babylonian captivity). David is the key person for the Psalms as he is believed to have written 73 of them. The setting was Jerusalem where God's holy temple resided. The Psalms are a collection of songs and prayers that express the heart of humanity's lived experiences.

David and the other writers of the Psalms give license to freedom of expression with God and bears the soul to one in whom they have found friendship. The book of Psalms is like a diary in which sins are confessed, doubts and fears are expressed, and the cry to God for help in trouble are central themes. It also expresses praise, worship, and adoration to the living God. The authentic expression of the feelings of the writers connects us with them, and with God. The words of Psalms give comfort to those who are weary, and relief for those who are suffering.

A deep abiding faith and confidence in God is the foundation upon which the authors discover the power of God's love and forgiveness. The ability to trust God with their innermost anguish and pain helps readers of today to know that we too can have an authentic relationship with God—one in which we can call upon Him when we are in trouble and we can trust Him even when He is silent.

## EXPOSITION

### I. GOD, OUR PRESENT HELP IN TROUBLE (PSALM 10:12–15)

Our world is troubled by injustice, war, poverty, disease, and a myriad of ways in which inequality and aggressions are perpetuated. The rich appear to get richer and the poor stay poor, or get poorer. The innocent are killed; accidents happen; and the toll of mental illness threatens the well-being of millions of people around the world. On a personal level, we may ask God, why did my loved one die? Why have such calamites come upon me?

Where is God and why is He silent on these and other related issues? Why does He stand by and watch the innocent suffer and why do good people die far too soon? These are questions that have been asked throughout the history of mankind.

The wicked seem to prosper while the godly suffer. The psalmist notes in today's text that the wicked persecute the poor and kill the innocent. They are full of cursing, deceit, and fraud, yet they still seem to prosper. This does not seem fair and oftentimes, the righteous get upset at the prosperity of the wicked. They get away with cursing God and it seems that they are not held accountable for their actions. The psalmist seemingly calls out the Lord for His lack of action. It's clear the psalmist is frustrated that the evil ones are prospering and the Israelites are suffering. He knows it's unfair, so why isn't God intervening? Many of us can relate to this sentiment.

We become impatient with God when His timing doesn't match ours. It's hard to remember that He sees all the things that we can't and knows all the information that we don't know. There's a reason why He's God and we're not: our brains aren't big enough for the scope and magnitude that it takes to be God! Over and over throughout the Psalms, writers will sing to God: "there's no one like You" or "no one is greater than You." These verses aren't hyperbole; they're absolutely correct! Not one single human comes close.

The writer is crying out for God to take action, but even in this request, the writer recognizes God's sovereignty. The psalmist isn't taking matters into his own hands, he's not relying on himself to defeat all the wicked in the world or evil-doers. He knows deep down that justice belongs to the Lord. While it's okay and healthy to express our frustrations with God, we must ultimately remember that He's in control and nothing escapes His view.

One may ask, why do the wicked disregard God? The wicked disregard God because they fundamentally believe that there will be no consequences for their actions. They also believe that there will be no divine judgment against them. The wicked believe that they are secure in their ways and can do whatever they want to do. They believe that it is okay to harm or oppress the innocent because there will be no real or lasting consequence of their actions. The wicked may not even believe that there is a God. If he does believe that there is a God, he does not believe that God will judge his actions. God may allow the wicked to amass wealth and the righteous to be poor. In order to understand this, we must first examine the construct of wealth and poverty. Wealth is not an indicator of God's pleasure or displeasure, and poverty is not an indicator of God's displeasure. God will hold everyone accountable for his actions regardless of their station in this life. The wicked will surely come into God's divine judgment.

Psalm 10 begins with this inquiry "Why hidest thou thyself in times of trouble?" (10:1). The Philistines had a long history of 40 years of cruelly oppressing Israel. Because Israel did evil in the sight of the Lord, He handed them over to the Philistines who oppressed them (see Judges 13:1). In this case, Israel's suffering was caused by their own disobedience to God.

The psalmist felt that God was far away in times of trouble. Sometimes the weight of our circumstances and the depth of our pain and sorrow may cause us to feel as though God is far away. In Psalm 10, David insists that God act against the wicked. When we are in trouble, oppressed, or when our life is in jeopardy, we can cry out to God for help and He hears our prayers. When we feel the pressure of the situation, it is important to tell God about it, and keep telling God about it. We must remember that God is our refuge, according to Psalm 46:1, "God is our refuge and strength, an ever-present help in trouble." David is crying out to God to take action because of the suffering of the poor and innocent by the hands of the wicked. We are also to seek God's justice for the good of the poor and the oppressed. We are reminded in Psalm 34:15 that God watches over the righteous: "The eyes of the LORD are on the righteous, and His ears are open to their cry for help."

Before David became king, he suffered for years under Saul's volatile temper (see 1 Samuel 18–19; 24; 26) and later, his persecution. Both David and those he loved bore the brunt of Saul's jealousy and fear (see 1 Samuel 18:8–9, 12, 15: 29–30). David's family was also vulnerable because of Saul's persecution. Ultimately, David saw God bring justice to his situation and he learned to trust God's justice and God's timing.

Why does suffering exist? Throughout the history of humanity, there have been an incalculable amount of suffering across the world. From the beginning, our first parents encountered suffering as an outcome of disobeying God in the Garden of Eden. This original sin set in motion a complex domino effect of sin in epic proportions. Suffering is defined as "agony, affliction, or distress; intense pain or sorrow." Suffering has been a part of the human dilemma from the day of the original sin of Adam and Eve.

There are many reasons for suffering and many types of suffering. For example, suffering as a result of sin. After the fall of Adam and Eve in the Garden of Eden, we see that one type of suffering comes from disobedience to God. We live in a sinful world that is at amenity with God, or against God. When we sin, we effectively open ourselves to God's judgment and we also provide the enemy with open access to us. We may experience loss in key areas of our lives because of our sin. Since the penalty for sin is death, no amount of good can come out of sinning.

A critical response to willful sinning is confession and repentance. In I John 1:9–10, it states: "If we confess our sins, he is faithful and just and will forgive us our sins and purify us from all unrighteousness" (NIV). To confess our sins is to admit that we have sinned. Confession is taking responsibility for our own actions, especially our disobedience, failures, and mistakes. If we are unwilling to confess our sins, we will not want to repent of our sins. We're no different from the wicked ones who believe judgment is never coming.

Repentance is "a turning away from sin, disobedience or rebellion and turning back to God." It means a change of mind or a feeling of remorse or regret for past conduct. When we are truly repentant, we will have godly sorrow for our sins, and turn around and in the opposite direction of sinning. Repentance with godly sorrow changes our relationship with God by bringing us into a restored relationship and fellowship with Him.

Some people suffer for the sake of righteousness, as in the case of Jesus when he died on the cross. Although He was perfect, He suffered unto death to save humanity from the penalty and the power of sin. Therefore, those who follow God often suffer at the hands of those who do not follow God. As believers we share in the suffering of Christ by identifying with Him. As His disciples suffered, so do we. This suffering for righteousness bonds us with the heart of our Lord and Savior.

Another type of suffering involves suffering for the sake of other people. Jesus' suffering was a part of His mission. He endured the suffering so that we could be saved from sin so that we could be reunited with God. In Isaiah 48:10, we read, "Behold, I have refined thee, but not with silver; I have chosen thee in the furnace of affliction." This means that God chose us to endure the affliction. He knew that we would not give up on Him because of our suffering.

Suffering can also help to shape and refine our characters. During times of adversity, we may feel as though God is very far away, or even silent, just as the psalmist today felt. As we endure hardships, losses, pain, and sorrow, we may also wonder if God still cares. In Psalm 10, David resisted the urge to believe that God no longer cared for him. Despite his emotions, he continues to pray to God with a sense of urgency for help.

He reminds himself in verse 14 that God has seen him and his suffering, and He's never left his side. He remembers that God cares about the poor, the helpless, and those that suffer. They aren't being ignored by the Lord. The psalmist writes that God is able to help those who need it, and He won't stop until there's no more wickedness. Ultimately, we know that this will be answered in the millennial reign of Christ: He will come back in all His glory and set the world to righteousness, the way it was always intended, and there will be a new heaven and a new earth. But until that day comes, we are to be the hands and feet of Jesus to those in this world who are suffering and need assistance. We must first pray for them and their salvation, which is of the most importance, but there are always practical ways in which we can help as well.

## II. CONFIDENCE IN GOD'S JUDGMENTS (PSALM 10:16–18)

While the psalmist started these verses with despair and desperation, here he ends with a calm confidence in the Lord. He believes that God will provide justice in the end and everything will be made right according to God's perfect timing. He recognizes that God is the King forever and ever, even when hope seems lost. This is a great reminder for us today as well! When everything seems hopeless, we can remind ourselves that God is still sitting on the throne and there's no one that can overthrow Him!

When David writes that God hears the desires of our hearts, that means that He knows our deepest wishes. Sometimes these are things that we think are too big or too out of reach for us, or things that we don't dare hope for because the disappointment would be crushing. These things that we hide deep down the Lord knows intimately! And He prepares our hearts to pray for these things (v. 17). What a good God we serve that He would desire to hear these secret wishes and give them to us as they align with His will. When our hearts want what God wants, how can the prayer go unanswered?

Finally, David ends with assurance that God's justice will be applied to all evildoers. They may think they're winning the day, but God has the final say. They can run around the world with their egos and power, thinking that rules don't apply to them and there are no consequences for whatever evil deeds they commit or lives they destroy. God knows how to bide His time; He's very patient. And when the time is right, the wicked will get what judgment is due them.

## THE LESSON APPLIED

Throughout the history of humanity, there has always been a war between good and evil. As wickedness prevails, suffering increases. We suffer for many reasons—oftentimes because of the cruelty and injustice of others. When bad things happen, we often feel as though God is far away, or that He is silent. The Bible reminds us that God's eyes are on the righteous and His ears are attentive to our cry (see 1 Peter 3:12).

You may find yourself in a bad situation today. Perhaps you have lost a loved one, or lost your job. Perhaps you were passed over for a promotion or denied a position, or lost your health. Whatever calamity, big or small, know that God is always near. Even when we do not see Him working, He is still working.

Like David, it can be helpful to reflect on past instances of God's faithfulness or examples of Him caring for the downcast and hurting. It's so easy to forget, or to wallow in our own self-pity. But when we look back on these past examples, our hearts and faith can be encouraged that the story isn't over yet. God is a God of justice and when the timing is right, He will restore all things. Don't lose hope.

## LET'S TALK ABOUT IT

Sometimes people are abused and taken advantage of. The streets of America are full of poor homeless people who have no haven and no food. If you simply turn on the news, you are bombarded with stories of suffering, injustice and despair. It can feel completely overwhelming, and it does make you wonder, where is God when these bad things are happening? As Christians, we can trust that God knows, God sees, and God has a plan to restore order. In the meantime, we are to act on His behalf by representing His love to everyone we come into contact with.

**What can we do to help others who are mistreated, overlooked, and denied opportunities?**

God is a God of justice. He has established laws that govern humanity. We can be advocates for those who are less fortunate, abused, or oppressed. Ask God to help you to show up and do the right thing whenever the situation demands it. Pray that you would see people around you the way He sees them, and see how that changes your perspective.

**Will you be a voice of social justice today to help elevate the dignity and humanity of others?**

## GET SOCIAL

Share your views and tag us @rhboydco. Use #rhboydco.

@rhboydco

## HOME DAILY DEVOTIONAL READINGS
### JANUARY 6–12, 2025

| MONDAY | TUESDAY | WEDNESDAY | THURSDAY | FRIDAY | SATURDAY | SUNDAY |
|---|---|---|---|---|---|---|
| Faithful and True | God Makes Great and Gives Strength | Our God Reigns | Shout Joyfully to God | Exalted through Obedience | The Wind and Sea Obey Jesus | Robed in Majesty |
| Revelation 19:11–21 | 1 Chronicles 29:10–20 | Isaiah 52:1–12 | Psalm 47 | Philippians 2:1–13 | Mark 4:35–41 | Psalm 93 |

LESSON VII

JANUARY 12, 2025

# THE LORD IS ROBED IN MAJESTY

ADULT TOPIC:
THE MAJESTY OF A KING'S REIGN

BACKGROUND SCRIPTURE: PSALMS 47; 93
LESSON PASSAGE: PSALM 93

## PSALM 93

### KJV

THE Lord reigneth, he is clothed with majesty; the Lord is clothed with strength, wherewith he hath girded himself: the world also is stablished, that it cannot be moved.
2 Thy throne is established of old: thou art from everlasting.
3 The floods have lifted up, O Lord, the floods have lifted up their voice; the floods lift up their waves.
4 The Lord on high is mightier than the noise of many waters, yea, than the mighty waves of the sea.
5 Thy testimonies are very sure: holiness becometh thine house, O Lord, for ever.

### NRSVue

THE Lord is king; he is robed in majesty; the Lord is robed; he is girded with strength. He has established the world; it shall never be moved;
2 your throne is established from of old; you are from everlasting.
3 The floods have lifted up, O Lord, the floods have lifted up their voice; the floods lift up their roaring.
4 More majestic than the thunders of mighty waters, more majestic than the waves of the sea, majestic on high is the Lord!
5 Your decrees are very sure; holiness befits your house, O Lord, forevermore.

## LESSON SETTING
Time: 1010–930 BCE
Place: Israel

## LESSON OUTLINE
I. He Reigns! (Psalm 93:1-2)
II. God is Sovereign! (Psalm 93:3-5)

## UNIFYING PRINCIPLE

Throughout the world, we find chaos and disorder. Who can restore order and peace? Psalm 93 proclaims God as the almighty and creative power whose reign stands firm amidst crisis and unrest.

## INTRODUCTION

Psalm 93, a brief yet profound hymn within the book of Psalms, offers deep theological insights and practical lessons for contemporary believers. By examining its themes, we unearth the enduring relevance of Psalm 93 as it affirms God's sovereignty and His creation of a stable world.

The book of Psalms, an integral component of the Hebrew Bible and Christian Old Testament, serves as a rich source of spiritual guidance, theological reflection, and liturgical practice. Psalm 93, classified

**MAIN THOUGHT:** The LORD is king; he is robed in majesty; the LORD is robed; he is girded with strength. (Psalm 93:1, NRSVue)

as a royal psalm, is particularly notable for its celebration of God's kingship over the world. In today's lesson, we will explore the message of Psalm 93, and the lessons it imparts for contemporary life.

From a literary lens, Psalm 93 is structured as a hymn of praise, consisting of five verses that can be divided into two sections: the proclamation of God's reign (vv. 1–2) and the affirmation of God's eternal strength against chaotic forces (vv. 3–5).

At its core, Psalm 93 celebrates God's unassailable kingship and authority over the universe. This theme of divine sovereignty, juxtaposed against the transient rule of earthly kings, offered hope and assurance to the ancient Israelites, and continues to resonate with believers today.

## EXPOSITION

### I. HE REIGNS! (PSALM 93:1–2)

We live in a world characterized by increasing advancements in technology that has penetrated almost every area of our existence. Information is available to us at the tip of our fingers. News spreads around the world while the dramatic events are still unfolding. Artificial Intelligence (AI) appears to be rapidly outpacing human intelligence. We are now able to get more things done in less time and with less people, and all the while we are increasingly disconnected from one another. As humans interact with technology, this raises more concerns about the impact on our health and well-being.

War strikes suddenly with catastrophic results, taking its toll on humanity, and victims of war are separated from their families forever. We are bombarded with news and programming filled with turmoil, sorrow, greed, and all manner of human vices. During the COVID-19 pandemic, we were isolated from one another. The eerie silence of the airways and city streets and the mandates for social distancing created its own social pandemic of panic and fear.

We face a host of natural disasters, and pressures and injustices in the workplace. Natural disasters such as tornados and tsunamis have devastated communities in a matter of minutes and precious lives are suddenly taken with the disaster. There's a storm of politics, scientific experiments with drugs, foods filled with growth chemicals and pesticides creating sickness and diseases that have no cure. The myriad of things that plague our world today reminds us of the devastating flood of calamities that the children of Israel faced during ancient times.

Psalm 93, whose author is unknown, describes overwhelming forces in life as a "flood lifting." The Hebrew word for lift is *"nasa,"* which means to lift up; to carry or take away. While the exact historical context of Psalm 93 remains debated, it is widely regarded as a post-exilic composition, reflecting a period when the Israelite community sought to reaffirm God's sovereignty amidst political instability and national reconstruction. The psalm echoes ancient near eastern motifs of cosmic battle, portraying God as a divine king who establishes order over chaos.

The political instability of the Israelites was largely due to the rise of the Neo-Assyria empire and the rise of the Neo-Babylonian Empire, which resulted in the subsequent destruction of Jerusalem and captivity or "taking away" of its people. The

Babylonians overthrew the Neo-Assyrian empire in 626 BCE, inheriting the regions controlled by Assyria, which included the Kingdom of Judah. Nebuchadnezzar became king of Babylon in 604 BCE, and captured Jerusalem in 597 BCE, taking the articles from the temple and the royal palace in Jerusalem. He also captured King Jehoiachin of Judah and thousands of people, including many of the officials, because Judah was aligned with Egypt and sought their help during the Assyrian and Babylonian wars. Later in 586 BCE, King Zedekiah of Judah rebelled against Babylon, and Nebuchadnezzar destroyed Jerusalem and took the remaining articles from the temple and more captives to Babylon. The state of Israel, which was utterly destroyed, was now under Babylonian control.

Despite the political climate of the time of this psalm's writing, the writer maintains that God still reigns! Whatever may be happening on the earth below, God is sitting on His throne, completely secure. Nothing shakes Him and nothing causes Him to worry. The writer reminds us all that God's throne was established long ago and there's nothing that will dethrone Him; God will reign for all eternity. What comfort we can take in that thought!

Psalm 93 specifically reminds us that even though disaster may strike, God still reigns. The Hebrew word for "reigns" is *malak*, which means "to ascend the throne; to induct into royalty; to become king; to rule; to have power and dominion over people and nations." As King of Kings and Lord of Lords, the Lord reigns over everything and everyone. He reigns over all the kings and rulers of the entire world and throughout all of humanity. He establishes the system and process of rulership; therefore, we can put our full confidence in Him.

In Psalm 93, the metaphor of floods represent chaotic forces and challenges in life while affirming God's sovereignty and steadfastness amidst such turmoil. God is in control, even when life feels chaotic. We can look beyond the immediate turmoil and trust in God's sovereignty. God's throne was established from long ago, and it has been unmovable since the beginning of creation. God's faithfulness and stability are everlasting. Unlike the shifting sands of human circumstances, God's presence and His throne are unshakable.

## II. God is Sovereign! (Psalm 93:3–5)

As Psalm 93 highlights floods that are overwhelming, the Bible often portrays God's power and sovereignty over the natural world, including the waters, which were seen by ancient peoples as mysterious and often chaotic forces. Each situation highlights God's creation of and dominion over the waters.

"In the beginning, God created the heavens and the earth. The earth was formless and empty, darkness was over the surface of the deep, and the Spirit of God moved upon the face of the waters. God then spoke; "Let there be light," and He separated the water under the sky from the water above it" (Genesis 1:1–4).

During Noah's time in Genesis 6–9, God judged the world's wickedness by sending a great flood; however, He saved Noah, his family, and the animals on the ark. The waters prevailed upon the earth for 150 days before God receded the waters. This demonstrated His control over the floodwaters and His covenant with creation.

The children of Israel walked across the Red Sea on dry ground in Exodus 14. God delivered the Israelites from Egyptian slavery by miraculously parting the Red Sea so that they could cross over. This event showed the world that God was in charge. He has the power to control the waters and provide salvation for His people.

Once again. God parted the Jordan River in Joshua 3–4 so that His people could cross over on dry ground to enter the Promised Land. As the Israelites entered the Promised Land, God stopped the flow of the Jordan River, allowing them to cross on dry ground. This miracle serves as a reminder of God's ongoing provision and leadership.

In Mark 4:35–41, Jesus speaks to the storm to calm it down. The winds and the waves obeyed Him. On another occasion, Jesus walked on the Sea of Galilee (on the water) to meet His disciples who were caught up in a storm at sea (Matthew 14:22–33). These stories collectively portray a God who is not bound by the forces of nature, but commands them with authority, offering both judgment and salvation, demonstrating power, and providing care and sustenance to His creation.

The psalm speaks of floods lifting up their voice and pounding waves, symbolizing overwhelming challenges. At times such as the loss of a loved one, or the loss of one's health, we may feel as though our troubles are unbearable. Psalm 93 reminds us that even the mightiest waters are subject to God's dominion. Just as God holds authority over the natural world, He is more than capable of sustaining us through our most challenging and difficult times.

Let us remember to view our situation through the lens of God's ultimate victory. We can overcome our difficulties with God's help. Our problems may feel too big for us, but they are never too big for God. "God is our refuge and strength, a very present help in the time of need" (Psalm 46:1). God's principles and presence are timeless. They are a constant source of security and protection. "Those who hope in the Lord shall renew their strength" (Isaiah 40:31). We are not the keeper of ourselves. We are all under God's care. He is our protector and source of enduring peace.

How do we know? Because His Word says so and His Word is sure (v. 5). As believers, we believe that the Bible is completely true and the living Word of God, so if He said it, then we can stand on it! We are given every confidence that we can trust in the Lord because He is faithful and true, even when we are not. Praise the Lord!

## THE LESSON APPLIED

Psalm 93 covers three important lessons that can be applied to our daily lives: trust in divine governance; stewardship of creation; and community and ethical living. In an era marked by political uncertainty and social upheaval, Psalm 93 offers a profound reminder of God's ultimate authority and the temporality of human power structures. This perspective encourages us to place our trust in divine governance rather than in fallible human institutions.

The psalm's portrayal of God as the Creator and Sustainer of the world serves as a call to environmental stewardship. We are reminded of our responsibility to humbly respect and care for the earth, not as dominators, but as caretakers of God's creation. The themes of order and faithfulness in Psalm 93 have implications for community life and ethics. By recognizing the stability and order God imparts to the world, we are called to reflect these qualities in our relationships, promoting justice, peace, and mutual respect. Psalm 93 offers guidance and inspiration to contemporary believers. By affirming God's sovereignty, the stability of creation, and the call to ethical living, this psalm provides a timeless framework for our faith practice, ecological responsibility, and community engagement. As such, Psalm 93 remains a vital resource for reflection and spiritual growth.

## LET'S TALK ABOUT IT

**During times when chaos and conflict flood our lives, how can I keep my faith in God when all around me is crumbling?**

We can feel overwhelmed when crisis happens or when things go terribly wrong. During such times, we must recall to mind that God is sovereign. This means that He is greater than any problems that we face. Sometimes we may have to wait until things get sorted out. In such times, remember the Word of God: "They that wait on the Lord shall renew their strength" (see Isaiah 40:31). He promises that He will be with us in the floods of life circumstances: "I will strengthen you and help you; I will uphold you with my righteous right hand" (Isaiah 41:10).

While the reality of the situation may be devastating, actively trusting God will help to strengthen us as we go through it. At times, we may need to take practical steps in faith: reading the Bible and praying; seeking support from our community; seeking resources such as professional help or guidance from a trusted pastor or Christian counselor. Regardless of our situations, let us never lose hope in God.

## GET SOCIAL

Share your views and tag us @rhboydco. Use #rhboydco.

@rhboydco

| MONDAY | TUESDAY | WEDNESDAY | THURSDAY | FRIDAY | SATURDAY | SUNDAY |
|---|---|---|---|---|---|---|
| God's Heavenly Throne | Life Springs from God's Throne | My Eyes Have Seen the King | Draw Near to God in Humility | Boldly Approach the Throne of Grace | Heaven Is God's Throne | Bless God's Holy Name |
| Revelation 4 | Revelation 22:1–14 | Isaiah 6:1–8 | James 4:1–10 | Hebrews 4:11–16 | Isaiah 66:1–14 | Psalm 103:1–11, 19–22 |

Home Daily Devotional Readings — January 13–19, 2025

LESSON VIII

JANUARY 19, 2025

# The Lord's Throne Is Established

**Adult Topic:**
Don't Forget!

**Background Scripture:** Psalm 103
**Lesson Passage:** Psalm 103:1–14

## Psalm 103:1–14

### KJV

BLESS the Lord, O my soul: and all that is within me, bless his holy name.
2 Bless the Lord, O my soul, and forget not all his benefits:
3 Who forgiveth all thine iniquities; who healeth all thy diseases;
4 Who redeemeth thy life from destruction; who crowneth thee with lovingkindness and tender mercies;
5 Who satisfieth thy mouth with good things; so that thy youth is renewed like the eagle's.
6 The Lord executeth righteousness and judgment for all that are oppressed.
7 He made known his ways unto Moses, his acts unto the children of Israel.
8 The Lord is merciful and gracious, slow to anger, and plenteous in mercy.
9 He will not always chide: neither will he keep his anger for ever.
10 He hath not dealt with us after our sins; nor rewarded us according to our iniquities.
11 For as the heaven is high above the earth, so great is his mercy toward them that fear him.
12 As far as the east is from the west, so far hath he removed our transgressions from us.
13 Like as a father pitieth his children, so the Lord pitieth them that fear him.
14 For he knoweth our frame; he remembereth that we are dust.

### NRSVue

BLESS the Lord, O my soul, and all that is within me, bless his holy name.
2 Bless the Lord, O my soul, and do not forget all his benefits—
3 who forgives all your iniquity, who heals all your diseases,
4 who redeems your life from the Pit, who crowns you with steadfast love and mercy,
5 who satisfies you with good as long as you live so that your youth is renewed like the eagle's.
6 The Lord works vindication and justice for all who are oppressed.
7 He made known his ways to Moses, his acts to the people of Israel.
8 The Lord is merciful and gracious, slow to anger and abounding in steadfast love.
9 He will not always accuse, nor will he keep his anger forever.
10 He does not deal with us according to our sins nor repay us according to our iniquities.
11 For as the heavens are high above the earth, so great is his steadfast love toward those who fear him;
12 as far as the east is from the west, so far he removes our transgressions from us.
13 As a father has compassion for his children, so the Lord has compassion for those who fear him.
14 For he knows how we were made; he remembers that we are dust.

**MAIN THOUGHT:** The LORD works vindication and justice for all who are oppressed. (Psalm 103:6, NRSVue)

**LESSON SETTING**
   Time: 1010–930 BCE
   Place: Israel

**LESSON OUTLINE**
  I. Song of Praise (Psalm 103:1–5)
  II. Benefits of Trusting God (Psalm 103:6–14)

## Unifying Principle

Good and fair leadership engenders confidence and peace. How do we express our gratitude to leaders who embody these qualities? Psalm 103 offers praise and thanksgiving to the Lord Almighty who rules with steadfast love, justice, and compassion.

## Introduction

David was a shepherd boy in Bethlehem when Samuel anointed him king of Israel. David was a skilled musician, warrior, poet, and author of 73 Psalms (songs). He ruled Israel for 40 years from 1010 and 970 BCE, and led them to victory in battle. He established Jerusalem as the capitol, which became a thriving metropolis and center of worship. Israel became a strong kingdom during David's rule, and there was a return to godliness among the people of God.

In this lesson, we will explore Psalm 103, in which David introduces his major theme at the beginning. Such themes include the compassion and mercy of God toward man, God's faithfulness, His forgiveness of our sins, His redemption, His righteousness, and His divine judgment. God is unfailingly faithful in expressing His love for His people. He answers our deepest fears and meets our deepest needs (Psalm 103:1–6). We learn from this psalm of God's healing, the challenges of life, our significance in God, our happiness and endurance for living, and God's justice towards humanity.

Psalm 103 also highlights the level of intimacy that David had with God. He draws proofs for his praise and arguments for God's greatness from timeless truths about God (Psalm 103:3–6). He also draws proofs from the experience of generations past (Psalm 103:7–9), and from his own personal history with God (Psalm 103:10–18). After all that David went through in his life, he found God to be faithful and full of compassion.

The key to David's praises is that his confidence in God's complete goodness leads to his joy in God's complete sovereignty (Psalm 103:17–19). The message of Psalm 103 reminds us that we can trust God implicitly.

## Exposition

### I. Song of Praise (Psalm 103:1-5)

The word "psalm" comes from the Greek word *psalmos*, which was a song that was sung with musical instruments. The psalms are songs of praise. The psalms are also poems that express the spontaneous authentic outpouring of the feelings expressed. The psalms were sung during processionals to the temple mount. They were written by authors who were passionate in their faith. Such is the case with King David, who wrote 73 of the psalms.

David begins Psalm 103 with blessing the Lord with all that is within him. The word "bless" means an act of adoration, or to congratulate. To adore someone is to have deep love and respect for them. David commands his soul and all that is within him to bless the Lord. By blessing the Lord, King David expresses his deep love and respect for Him. The word "within" (*qereb*) refers to the innermost self; the heart; the inner organs of the body. The soul (*nephesh*) is the breath, thoughts, and emotions. Our love for God should saturate our very beings, our souls, our thoughts, and our emotions.

Jesus' ultimate agenda is that we become one with Him and God "that they all may be one; as thou, Father, art in me, and I in thee, that they also may be one in us: that the world may believe that thou hast sent me" (John 17:21–23, KJV).

In this psalm, David shows a deep understanding for true worship. It is supposed to take over every fiber of our beings. It's not about superficially following along with the lyrics on the screen or raising your hands when you're really wondering how much longer the service will be. Our minds have a million distractions ready to go any second, but David commanded every part of him to bless the Lord: to be wholly in the moment with God and not letting his mind wander to other things.

David then moves on to why he should bless the Lord. First of all, He forgives us of our sins! There can be no greater reason to praise Him! Without that basic foundation, we are dead men walking. If you are truly about to sit down and comprehend how sinful you are, and how impossible it would be to save yourself on your own merit, there could be no other response than to wholly praise the Lord for His free grace.

David came to know the power of God's forgiveness as he cried out in deep sorrow for the sins that he committed against God. Psalm 103:2 reminds us to bless the Lord and not to forget His benefits. We have the assurance that when we confess our sins, God is faithful to forgive us and to cleanse us from all unrighteousness. "If we confess our sins, he is faithful and just to forgive us our sins, and to cleanse us from all unrighteousness. If we say that we have not sinned, we make him a liar, and his word is not in us" (1 John 1:9–10, KJV).

Next, David asserts that God is the ultimate Healer. Any illness, physical or spiritual, is able to be healed with a touch from the Lord; nothing is beyond His reach. (Just look at the multiple people He raised from the dead; even death can't stop Him!) God is also our Redeemer. Not only has He redeemed us from spiritual death and destruction, but He is all the time working to redeem our lives in the present too. Can you think of a relationship you lost but God restored, or replaced with a better one? Can you remember a time when you thought all hope was lost but God brought an answer in the eleventh hour? We are all full of testimonies like this that demonstrate the love of God and His redemptive grace.

We can also praise God for crowning us with mercy and lovingkindness. Even in this world that's full of sickness, suffering, and hardship, we still receive God's blessings. He satisfies us with good things. Because God gives us blessings that are greater than what the world could offer us. Worldly pleasures are always nice for a moment, but even the richest of kings is miserable without God residing in his heart. Each one of us was born with a God-sized hole in our hearts, and when we don't have Him, we try to fill that hole with other things, but they will always fall short. They might feel nice for a minute, but that feeling will fade and we'll yearn again for something deeper. That something is God, and He's readily available to all of us, anytime of the day or night. That satisfaction is what gives us strength and renews our spirits like the eagle (v. 5).

There is so much that is wrong with the world today. There are wars between Ukraine and Russia, and Israel and Hamas in Gaza. We can complain about many things that are not right with the world, or perhaps not right with us. In Psalm 103, David reminds us of all of the benefits of God that we should never forget no matter what is going on in our lives, or how difficult life's journey becomes. He forgives us of our iniquities. He heals us from our sickness and diseases. God redeems our life from destruction. He crowns our heads with loving kindness and tender mercies. God is good to us because He loves us and because He knows what we need even if we don't know. We receive from the hand of God whether or not we deserve it because He has promised "that ye may be the children of your father that is in heaven: for he maketh his sun to arise on the evil and the good, and sendeth rain on the just and unjust" (Matthew 5:45, KJV).

## II. BENEFITS OF TRUSTING GOD (PSALM 103:6–14)

God first gave His laws to Moses and the children of Israel because He wanted them to be clear of His character and His will. As they emerged from 430 years of Egyptian slavery, they needed to be re-trained on the ways of God. He gave Moses the Ten Commandments which were guidelines for living.

David reminds us of the kind of God we serve. He asserts that God wanted to be known of His people. He did not try to keep them in the dark about Who He is. Today, God wants us to know Him personally. He invites us to enter into His secret place: "He that dwelleth in the secret place of the most High shall abide under the shadow of the Almighty" (Psalm 91:1).

David also reminds us that God is merciful, and slow to anger. As much as we'd like God to dole out punishments on the wicked, we quickly forget that we could just as easily be recipients of those punishments apart from the precious blood of Jesus. That's the only thing that separates us, so we should be grateful that the Lord is slow to anger and offers plentiful chances for repentance.

As a father has mercy on his children, so does the Lord have mercy on us. If an earthly father, who is also a sinner and prone to mistakes, can show mercy to his children, how much more is the Lord able to do so when He is perfect, righteous and just? If you are a parent, then you understand when your child grows up, they are going to make mistakes. This is how they learn. As much as you want to shield them from pain and heartbreak, you know that it's part of life and they're going to get knocked down every once in a while. You don't like it, but you accept that it's part of growing pains of life. In a similar manner, God sees us making mistakes every day and pities us for those, yet understands that it's how we learn and grow. It's how He wired our brains to expand and evolve. If everything was perfect and came naturally and you never endured any hardship, there wouldn't be any opportunity for character building. There also wouldn't be any opportunity for you to lean on the Lord and His understanding if everything came easily to you.

Psalm 103 also shows us the spiritual maturity of David. After all that he experienced throughout his life, he gained wisdom and came to understand God's process for raising leaders. God wants us to know that He pardons us from our sins; therefore, we can put the past behind us and move forward in faith. God wants to heal us from all things that are unhealthy or that may be holding us back, whether they are old emotional wounds, or physical wounds.

Verse 14 tells us that He knows our frame. God is our Creator, who formed Adam from dust. There is not a single molecule of your being that God doesn't know, or didn't put in that place. He knows you so much more deeply than any person ever could, and wants to fix all your wounds and restore you to the image-bearer of Christ you were made to be. The depth of His love knows no bounds! Therefore, we can go to Him with literally anything and share it with Him! Whatever feeling or emotion you're experiencing, tell Him! There's no need to put on a brave face or a false front because He already knows your thoughts anyway. Be honest with Him as David was and allow your relationship with Him to grow and deepen. You couldn't tell Him anything that would surprise Him, upset Him, or anger Him.

David remembered where he came from and he also remembered how God brought him through. Because he was fully surrendered to the Lord, he inquired of the Lord before making important decisions. He had a firm commitment in the depths of his soul to love God with all of his being.

## THE LESSON APPLIED

Psalm 103 is a psalm of epic proportions! God knew that we would encounter injustice in this world, so He touched the heart of a king to pen these precious words to us. David poured out his heart to God, holding nothing back, but fully and authentically, opened himself up to the Father. Although the psalms are songs, reading them today is like reading someone's diary.

We can see how David feels about God, and how much he trusts Him. Through this psalm, we gain wisdom that we can apply to our daily lives. In our various communities, there are inequalities and injustices in just about every system. Crimes, wars, pandemics, technological advances, humanitarian crises, global warming, etc. all challenge our day-to-day existence.

Dr. Martin Luther King, Jr., feted leader of the Civil Rights Movement to end racial segregation, dreamed of day when all people would be free. He used his voice for the greater good of humanity. Through the work of Dr. King and all those who gave their lives for this cause, we owe a debt of gratitude. Likewise, as followers of Jesus, we seek to influence every realm of modern life. We are called to take the Gospel to the world. We seek to influence with the Gospel the seven mountains of modern life: family, religion, education, media, entertainment, business, and government. Although there are many injustices in society, we should never forget the words of King David: "For the Lord executes righteousness and judgment for all that are oppressed" (Psalm 103:6, KJV).

When you're having a tough time, it can be helpful to return to these psalms and look at how David spoke to God. He was honest about his feelings and held nothing back. He didn't sugarcoat his frustrations or hide his depression. He unloaded it all on the Lord and walked away feeling lighter and more confident in the goodness of God! Who couldn't use some of that? Today, it's too easy to self-medicate in a variety of forms, when what we should really be doing is crying out to God. This week, before you reach for a bottle, a quick fix, or some other method of coping, try having a heart-to-heart with your loving Heavenly Father. Let that become your first response instead of last resort.

## LET'S TALK ABOUT IT

- Do you feel as though you have nothing to thank God for? Do you feel as though everything has gone wrong and do you find yourself complaining all the time and being dissatisfied with life?
- At times, life can be very difficult, *but God*! People who experience trauma in their lives feel broken. Some turn to drugs, alcohol, or sexual pursuits in an attempt to ease the pain that they may be experiencing. While these substances may offer momentary pleasure, they do not heal one from their trauma. David provides a remedy for the brokenhearted and those who feel as though life has dealt them a bad hand. He reminds us to recall the benefits of God throughout our lives. As we recall how good God has been to us, we should take a moment to thank God. Because praise is a weapon of spiritual warfare, we can pour out our praise on the Lord and invite the Holy Spirit to come into our lives. Scripture tells us that when we praise the Lord, our enemies flee! It's a powerful weapon to worship the Lord, and too often this weapon is under-utilized.

Evaluate your ability and willingness to accept God's forgiveness. Call on your whole being to never forget that God's love and grace doesn't depend on your actions. Rejoice in God's steadfast love!

## GET SOCIAL

Share your views and tag us @rhboydco. Use #rhboydco.

@rhboydco

## HOME DAILY DEVOTIONAL READINGS
### JANUARY 20–26, 2025

| MONDAY | TUESDAY | WEDNESDAY | THURSDAY | FRIDAY | SATURDAY | SUNDAY |
| --- | --- | --- | --- | --- | --- | --- |
| The Kingdoms of This World | The Kingdom of God's Son | Christ, the Hope of Glory | The Lord Reigns over the Earth | An Unshakable Kingdom | Seek First God's Kingdom | Bless God's Name Forever |
| Daniel 2:31–45 | Colossians 1:11–20 | Colossians 1:21–29 | Zechariah 14:8–11, 16–21 | Hebrews 12:18–29 | Matthew 6:25–34 | Psalm 145:1–10, 17–21 |

LESSON IX                                                                                                    JANUARY 26, 2025

# MY GOD, THE KING

**ADULT TOPIC:**
DOESN'T ANYTHING LAST ANYMORE?

**BACKGROUND SCRIPTURE:** PSALM 145
**LESSON PASSAGE:** PSALM 145:1, 10–21

## PSALM 145:1, 10—21

### KJV

I WILL extol thee, my God, O king; and I will bless thy name for ever and ever.

• • • • • •

10 All thy works shall praise thee, O Lord; and thy saints shall bless thee.
11 They shall speak of the glory of thy kingdom, and talk of thy power;
12 To make known to the sons of men his mighty acts, and the glorious majesty of his kingdom.
13 Thy kingdom is an everlasting kingdom, and thy dominion endureth throughout all generations.

14 The Lord upholdeth all that fall, and raiseth up all those that be bowed down.
15 The eyes of all wait upon thee; and thou givest them their meat in due season.
16 Thou openest thine hand, and satisfiest the desire of every living thing.
17 The Lord is righteous in all his ways, and holy in all his works.
18 The Lord is nigh unto all them that call upon him, to all that call upon him in truth.
19 He will fulfil the desire of them that fear him: he also will hear their cry, and will save them.
20 The Lord preserveth all them that love him: but all the wicked will he destroy.
21 My mouth shall speak the praise of the Lord: and let all flesh bless his holy name for ever and ever.

### NRSVue

I WILL extol you, my God and King, and bless your name forever and ever.

• • • • • •

10 All your works shall give thanks to you, O Lord, and all your faithful shall bless you.
11 They shall speak of the glory of your kingdom and tell of your power,
12 to make known to all people your mighty deeds and the glorious splendor of your kingdom.
13 Your kingdom is an everlasting kingdom, and your dominion endures throughout all generations. The Lord is faithful in all his words and gracious in all his deeds.[c]
14 The Lord upholds all who are falling and raises up all who are bowed down.
15 The eyes of all look to you, and you give them their food in due season.
16 You open your hand, satisfying the desire of every living thing.
17 The Lord is just in all his ways and kind in all his doings.
18 The Lord is near to all who call on him, to all who call on him in truth.
19 He fulfills the desire of all who fear him; he also hears their cry and saves them.

20 The Lord watches over all who love him, but all the wicked he will destroy.
21 My mouth will speak the praise of the Lord, and all flesh will bless his holy name forever and ever.

**MAIN THOUGHT:** Your kingdom is an everlasting kingdom, and your dominion endures throughout all generations. (Psalm 145:13, NRSVue)

## LESSON SETTING
   Time: 1010–930 BCE
   Place: Israel

## LESSON OUTLINE
   I. God is Exalted (Psalm 145:1)
   II. The Lord is Good! (Psalm 145:10–21)

## UNIFYING PRINCIPLE
We live in an ever–changing world of turmoil and uncertainty. Where can we find a reason for relief and joy? Psalm 145 invites us to find constancy in God's everlasting kingdom of steadfast mercy, power, goodness, and compassion.

## INTRODUCTION
Psalms 145, written by King David, is a call to praise God. Unlike many other psalms, Psalm 145 does not focus on specific historical actions by God, but rather on general actions that consistently flow out of who God is: actions that God will always do, because they are a natural outworking of who He is (145:8–9, 14–20).

Several themes such as God's greatness and mercy, God's goodness, God's sovereignty, and eternal kingdom are extolled as reasons why we should praise God. David's critical foundation is his acknowledgment of God as sovereign (145:1) and because of His sovereignty, he is submitted to God's plans and direction (Psalm 145:21). The rest of Psalm 145 is David's explanation of why he rejoices in God's sovereignty. God's goodness and faithfulness are constant, making trusting God the only option that makes sense in this world (145:3–7). We can learn from this psalm to follow David's example of praise!

## EXPOSITION

### I. GOD IS EXALTED (PSALM 145:1)

David begins Psalm 145 with extolling God as God, the King of Kings and Lord of Lords. In a world of so many false gods, David acknowledges God as the supreme God—God Almighty who transcends time! The Hebrew word for "God" is *Elohim*, which means God is the one true God, Creator of all; Lord; Savior. He is compassionate, gracious, and faithful to His covenant.

David also acknowledges God as his King. The Hebrew word for "king" is *melek*, which means an individual with power and authority. *Melek* is similar to Lord, captain, prince, chief, or ruler. David is basically identifying God as the Supreme God having all power over all living beings; but he also identifies God as his King. Although David was a king, he humbled himself to God, submitting to His lordship. Therefore, David was a king under God's authority.

In this opening verse, David also committed to blessing God's name forever and ever. To bless is *barka*, or "to kneel as an act of adoration." In essence, David committed to adore God forever. The Hebrew word for "forever" is *owlam*, which means to the vanishing point; eternity, perpetual. It may refer to a person's lifetime; for many generations, or beyond the earthly time constructs. The Hebrew word for "ever" is the word *ad*, which means continual, perpetual. David is expressing his adoration for God by stating that he would bless God; not just for now when things are going well, but for all times (whether good or bad) into eternity and beyond earthly constructs. David points us to the infinite greatness of God. Because of His greatness, He is to be praised every day, continually, and perpetually for all generations. This is a song that David admonishes to be sung all the time. Our praise to God should never cease.

David insists on praising God continually and perpetually because God deserves our unconditional commitment and praise. As His followers, we must surrender to His lordship, recklessly abandoning ourselves to Him. God provides everything we need to fulfill His will. Our role is to simply surrender to Him. God's role is one of a Provider. He is King of Kings and Lord of Lords. His greatness is so vast that we cannot fathom it. He is majestic and His Kingdom lasts forever. He is mighty, and merciful. He is righteous, and He satisfies us. What does He want in return for all these gifts? We are to love God with all our hearts, minds, and souls, and strength (see Mark 12:30–31).

## II. THE LORD IS GOOD! (PSALM 145:10–21)

When we speak honorably about God, we are in essence praising God. In today's culture, many people use God's name in vain. David not only demonstrated his devotion to God during times of worship, but also by his words and in common conversations. As followers of Jesus, we should be careful what we say and how we say it. Many people complain when things do not go the way that they planned or when others do not do what they want them to do. Instead of complaining, we should take our concerns to the Lord in prayer, and by faith, thank Him for working things together for our good and His glory. We often hear others berate people such as politicians, people at work, family members, and people in the church. It is best to keep silent on matters where we feel as though we do not have anything good to say and pray for those who are berating others as well as those whom they are criticizing.

In Luke 6:45 (KJV), Jesus says, "A good man out of the good treasure of his heart bringeth forth that which is good; and an evil man out of the evil treasure of his heart bringeth forth that which is evil; for out of the abundance of the heart his mouth speaketh." Others can tell what we believe, our attitude and our motivations by our actions and by our words. When we are deeply committed to God, it will manifest in what we say and how we say it, also in what we do. When we cherish God in our hearts, we will speak well of Him. We should not only praise God during the times when we are receiving answers to our prayers, but also during the times when we are waiting for the answers to our prayers.

One may ask how often should I praise God? We are receiving blessings from God every day; therefore, we are to praise Him every day. David made a commitment to God to praise Him forever and ever. This forever refers not only throughout David's life, but it also points to praise God into eternity. David looked forward to praising God into everlasting life.

In verse 4 (not in today's text), David states that each generation should pass down the mighty acts of God to the next generation. This means that we should teach our children and others about the great and wonderful things that God has done. We are to instill in the next generation a holy awe and respect for God, and teach them to praise Him. As we proclaim the mighty acts of God from one generation to the next, His kingdom will expand.

This idea is reiterated in verse 12, when David talks about how people will tell one another about the works of God. As believers, this should be one of the easiest parts of the job. Simply telling others about the goodness of God should be as simple as breathing. There's no need to think about it; it's baked into His nature and the proof is in our free salvation! He sent His only Son to die a horrendous death so that we might be saved. What other world religion has such a devoted, loving, and selfless God? The answer is none! Christianity is so unique in many areas, but especially for the fact that it's the only religion where the deity came to man's level instead of man striving to get to the gods.

As we read Psalm 145, David reminds us of the Lord's goodness. He lists all the ways in which the Lord expresses His love for humanity. The Lord is gracious and merciful. The Hebrew word for "gracious" is *channuwn*, which means compassionate. The Lord is abounding in compassion (Psalm 86:15, Psalm 103:8). When the oppressed cry out to the Lord, He responds with compassion (see Exodus 22:26–27). The Lord is compassionate to those who reverence Him: "He hath made His wonderful works to be remembered; the Lord is gracious and full of compassion" (Psalm 11:4, KJV). The Lord is gracious and merciful to those who turn to Him: "And rend your heart, and not your garments, and turn unto the Lord your God; for He is gracious and merciful, slow to anger, and of great kindness and repenteth him of the evil" (Joel 2:13, KJV).

David also states that "The Lord is slow to anger and abounding in steadfast love" (Psalm 145:8, KJV). The Hebrew word for "steadfast love" is *chesed*, which means lovingkindness, mercy, goodness. God is true, faithful, merciful, just, righteous, and good. David acknowledges God's character as merciful, kind, and loving. His character endures forever. God meets the needs of all His creation. God is good to all and His Kingdom is an everlasting Kingdom. God has dominion over all and He provides meat for them in due season (see verse 15). In Matthew 6, Jesus teaches us to pray for our "daily bread" and in that way, God provides for us and answers that prayer.

God also satisfies the desire of every living thing. David goes so far to say that all of creation is provided for! Humans are selfish by nature, and we tend to forget that God didn't just create man, but He created an entire universe for His glory! The animals, the land and water, the celestial bodies in space all speak to the glory of God. They were made to worship Him and so were we. In the context of David writing this, these acts were in direct opposition to the popular gods in the pagan religions. They were angry and petulant, and didn't care about humanity or creation. God was demonstrating through David's words how He was different and more worthy of being followed and praised.

God is righteous and holy. He is near to all who call upon Him in truth. He fulfills the desire of those who fear him. He will hear their cry and save them. Can we stop and think about this for a moment? In the

Old Testament, when a person wanted to repent of their sins and be forgiven, they had to wait for a specific day, offer a specific sacrifice with a priest, and then the priest would go before God on their behalf and plead their case for forgiveness. There was separation between God and His people because He was too holy to dwell with the sinners. But thanks to Jesus' death and resurrection, that barrier has been broken! Now we are free to go to Him anytime, pray anywhere, and He hears us! The God of the universe, Creator of the galaxies, hears you when you talk to Him. We are so unworthy, but He made a way anyway out of His great love for us. Aren't you thankful?

The Lord preserves those who fear Him. Because He is just, He will destroy the wicked. David reminds us that because of who God is, we should praise Him for the rest of our lives. While we may seek help from others, it is often temporary, incomplete, and unstable; however, when we seek help from God, it is lasting and complete because God is everlasting. Regardless of our circumstances, we can trust that God will aid us through all of our trials and tribulations.

Having listed all these reasons for why God was worthy of praise and deserving for all of creation to glorify Him, David ends this psalm with a final declaration that he will bless the Lord forever and ever. In fact, this is the last word that David ever writes; his final will and testament, as it were. The sum of his life is to praise God and invite others to do so as well. If you died tomorrow, would that be your legacy? There's no condemnation if the answer is no; it's merely an opportunity for self-reflection and to consider what kind of example you're leaving behind for your future generations.

## THE LESSON APPLIED

David reminds us of all the many reasons why we should demonstrate our commitment to God by praising Him and by sharing His mighty acts with the next generation. As we meditate on each verse of Psalm 145, we come to know the character of God as loving, compassionate, merciful, patient, and kind.

Regardless of the circumstances that we face in this life, God is faithful and He is committed to our well–being and the well-being of others. We can demonstrate our commitment to God by praising Him daily and by sharing His love with humanity. Consider the words that you speak. What will others know about God as they listen to you? Do you complain about the things that you are going through or do you thank God for all the ways in which He keeps you?

When we do not praise God, this is a red flag. It can be an indication that our hearts have become hardened to Him. This often happens when we don't believe God, or have experienced a kind of hurt that we attribute to God even though He wasn't the cause. Regardless of whether or not we struggle with unbelief or a hardened heart, we can bring it to the Lord in prayer and surrender it. As John writes, "If we confess our sins, he is faithful and just to forgive us our sins and to cleanse us from all unrighteousness" (1 John 1:8–9). Psalm 145 is a song, but can also be prayed daily. Let us practice praising God in all circumstances of life.

## LET'S TALK ABOUT IT

How can we share the Gospel with the next generation?

First of all, for those who have children or grandchildren, we can make church attendance a priority. Attending weekly service shouldn't be something we *have* to do; it's something we *get* to do. Consider how many Christians are underground around the world, and could be killed for having a scrap of paper with one Bible verse on it, yet we're too lazy or busy or bothered to attend Sunday services. There's really no excuse when we live in such a privileged country.

We can also share our testimony of our own personal encounters with God. The next time you encounter the Lord through a song on the radio, a verse during devotional time, or hear a word during prayer, share it with someone! Encourage them in their faith by talking about it together. We can talk about Jesus in our common day-to-day communication. Through our experiences, we can share our faith day by day and demonstrate to others how trusting in God makes all of the difference in life. You never know how your story will impact someone else or bolster their faith when they might be struggling with something similar. The enemy would love for us to be separated and silent, so we must combat this by seeking community and camaraderie with our fellow believers. Not only will it help us, but it will bring glory to God as well.

Sometimes we may go through situations that seem unbearable. During these times, it is critical that we remember who God is and that we turn to the Lord and lean onto His promises to care for us. Everyone's circumstances are different, and there is no one-size-fits-all solution; however, there is a one-size-fits-all God who is willing to walk with you through it.

## GET SOCIAL

Share your views and tag us @rhboydco. Use #rhboydco.

@rhboydco

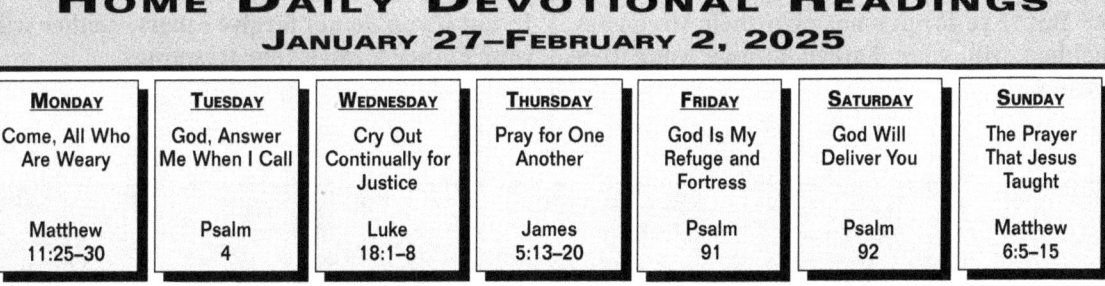

## HOME DAILY DEVOTIONAL READINGS
### JANUARY 27–FEBRUARY 2, 2025

| MONDAY | TUESDAY | WEDNESDAY | THURSDAY | FRIDAY | SATURDAY | SUNDAY |
|---|---|---|---|---|---|---|
| Come, All Who Are Weary | God, Answer Me When I Call | Cry Out Continually for Justice | Pray for One Another | God Is My Refuge and Fortress | God Will Deliver You | The Prayer That Jesus Taught |
| Matthew 11:25–30 | Psalm 4 | Luke 18:1–8 | James 5:13–20 | Psalm 91 | Psalm 92 | Matthew 6:5–15 |

LESSON X                                              FEBRUARY 2, 2025

# PRAYING FOR RELIEF

ADULT TOPIC:                         BACKGROUND SCRIPTURE: MATTHEW 6:5–15
TOO MUCH DEBT                           LESSON PASSAGE: MATTHEW 6:5–15

## MATTHEW 6:5–15

### KJV

AND when thou prayest, thou shalt not be as the hypocrites are: for they love to pray standing in the synagogues and in the corners of the streets, that they may be seen of men. Verily I say unto you, They have their reward.
6 But thou, when thou prayest, enter into thy closet, and when thou hast shut thy door, pray to thy Father which is in secret; and thy Father which seeth in secret shall reward thee openly.
7 But when ye pray, use not vain repetitions, as the heathen do: for they think that they shall be heard for their much speaking.

8 Be not ye therefore like unto them: for your Father knoweth what things ye have need of, before ye ask him.
9 After this manner therefore pray ye: Our Father which art in heaven, Hallowed be thy name.
10 Thy kingdom come, Thy will be done in earth, as it is in heaven.
11 Give us this day our daily bread.
12 And forgive us our debts, as we forgive our debtors.
13 And lead us not into temptation, but deliver us from evil: For thine is the kingdom, and the power, and the glory, for ever. Amen.
14 For if ye forgive men their trespasses, your heavenly Father will also forgive you:
15 But if ye forgive not men their trespasses, neither will your Father forgive your trespasses.

### NRSVue

"AND whenever you pray, do not be like the hypocrites, for they love to stand and pray in the synagogues and at the street corners, so that they may be seen by others. Truly I tell you, they have received their reward.
6 But whenever you pray, go into your room and shut the door and pray to your Father who is in secret, and your Father who sees in secret will reward you.
7 "When you are praying, do not heap up empty phrases as the gentiles do, for they think that they will be heard because of their many words.
8 Do not be like them, for your Father knows what you need before you ask him.

9 "Pray, then, in this way: Our Father in heaven, may your name be revered as holy.
10 May your kingdom come. May your will be done on earth as it is in heaven.
11 Give us today our daily bread.
12 And forgive us our debts, as we also have forgiven our debtors.
13 And do not bring us to the time of trial, but rescue us from the evil one.

14 "For if you forgive others their trespasses, your heavenly Father will also forgive you,
15 but if you do not forgive others, neither will your Father forgive your trespasses.

**MAIN THOUGHT:** May your kingdom come. May your will be done on earth as it is in heaven. (Matthew 6:10, NRSVue)

**LESSON SETTING**
   Time: 85 CE
   Place: Antioch

**LESSON OUTLINE**
   I. Don't Be a Hypocrite
      (Matthew 6:5–8)
   II. Pray the Way Jesus Prayed
      (Matthew 6:9–15)

## Unifying Principle

Many people struggle to achieve sustainable lives in a world of debt and obligation. How can we be released from the obligation to make ends meet? Jesus teaches us to pray for the forgiveness of debts that is a hallmark of God's reign.

## Introduction

The Gospel of Matthew was written by Matthew, who was a Jewish tax collector. He became one of Jesus' disciples. Matthew connects the old and the New Testament by emphasizing Jesus as the Messiah, fulfilling the prophecies of old. During His time on earth, Jesus began to set up His Kingdom whereby all those who confess their sins and repent can be saved. As the Son of God, Jesus was sent to the world by our Heavenly Father so that through Christ, the world may be saved.

While we live on earth, we are to take great care in not allowing anything to take the priority in our lives over the lordship of Jesus Christ. We are to seek to make Him first in all that we do. In a culture where people try to make themselves the center of attention, or project their image as one who is larger than life, we must be careful and discerning to avoid the pitfalls of self–aggrandizement and worshiping of ourselves or others outside of Jesus. Jesus is the King of Kings and Lord of Lords.

Throughout His ministry, Jesus taught many lessons about living in His Kingdom. He often used parables, sermons, and instruction to teach key principles such as forgiveness, peace, putting others first, and what it means to be a citizen of the Kingdom of God. By implementing godly principles in our daily lives, we are preparing to live forever with the Lord.

## Exposition

### I. Don't Be a Hypocrite (Matthew 6:5–8)

Jesus gave solid counsel and guidance on how to live a godly life. One key area that He provided guidance on is prayer. Jesus taught His disciples and the crowds against being a hypocrite. The word "hypocrite" comes from the Greek word, *hupokrites*, which means "an actor under an assumed character, a stage player." In Bible times, Hypocrite was a character used in Greek theatre. Essentially, Jesus was stating that we should never use prayer to get attention.

We should also not pray as though we are in a theatrical performance, and we should not use pretense in prayer. During Bible times, people prayed in public and in the synagogues just to be seen as righteous. This practice continues in our modern times. People intentionally pray in public, online, in religious gatherings so that they can be seen by others as having a special connection with God.

We can also apply this principle to people who have wrong motives for doing good deeds, or people who seek to build their reputation by doing good deeds. While it is good to do good for others, it is not good to have insincere reasons for doing good. Hypocrites do not genuinely care for others or sincerely believe in the cause that they are giving to. They merely care about themselves and simply want to look good. Praying with such intentions are self-righteous. While there are times that one should pray in public, it is the motive behind it that Jesus was addressing in Matthew 6:5. When we pray, we should pray to God as He should be the only audience of our prayer. When we pray to get attention or to be noticed, we are not praying to God. We are essentially praying to others.

Being a hypocrite can be compared to being a narcissist today. Narcissism is being selfish; lacking empathy; and having a need to be admired. Narcissists have an unreasonably high sense of importance and seek attention. Narcissists are not able to care about others. The narcissist is preoccupied with the focus on self; therefore, their actions are based on being seen as better than others.

If one's motive is to impress others during times of prayer, or while doing a good deed, it is the wrong motive. Our motive should be fixed on pleasing God and not man. Jesus states that the only reward that one will get by praying to get attention or to gain prominence is the reward of their intention. He sees our hearts and knows our true motives; therefore, we should never pretend or put on a pretense when we are praying–or at any other time. We should always pray with sincerity and do good deeds out of a genuine sense of compassion and empathy. Jesus was not against public praying; however, He will not reward the prayer that is echoed just to get attention or to appear righteous. Jesus Himself often prayed in private.

Jesus further explains that when we pray, we should pray in our closet (privately) and meet God in secret. When God sees us praying to Him privately, He will reward us openly. David wrote in Psalms 91:1, "He that dwelleth in the secret place of the Most-High shall abide under the shadow of the Almighty" (KJV). Jesus was not against public prayer. The point that He was driving home centered our motives for praying in public. Jesus prayed privately and publicly. When we pray in private and in public, we should not focus on what others think about our prayer. We should focus on addressing God.

In verse 6, the focus is also not on keeping our faith a secret, but rather that our faith is focused, without distraction, only on God. The purpose of praying in "secret" is to avoid the temptation to put on a show for others' benefit of your devotion.

Jesus also cautions against praying repetitively in vain. Here, He is saying we shouldn't treat our prayers as if we have to reach a certain word count in order for them to be effective or for others to be impressed by the length of our prayers. Just because someone prays for a long time, it doesn't mean that their hearts are sincere. Maybe they are sincere and they're just long-winded; we don't know, but God does, and that's Jesus' point. He will always look at our hearts and motives first before the substance of the prayer.

Jesus encourages us to go to God with literally any thought or request, because God already knows what we're going to say before we say it. Your prayers aren't informing God of new information; He already knows. But what it does is allows you to have communication with Him. We aren't required to pray or talk to Him, but when we do, it bonds us. It strengthens our relationship with Him. He is our Heavenly Father who longs to commune with us! When we do, He listens.

## II. PRAY THE WAY JESUS PRAYED (MATTHEW 6:9–15)

In verse 9–13, Jesus teaches us how to pray. Within Hellenistic religions, prayers were characterized by begging and attempts to bargain with the gods as in the case when Elijah mocked the prophets of Baal (see 1 Kings 18:27–28); many priests also specialized in voluble magical incantations that, if done properly, were believed to essentially coerce the power into performing the desired action. Jesus' prayer is simple and nearly casual compared to pagan Hellenistic prayers, but it is centered on one thing: submitting oneself to God's kingship (sovereignty; Matthew 6:10) and trusting that God knows what we truly need and is able and willing to meet it. There is no bargaining or coercion; no idea that "doing it right" will guarantee that God does what we desire. Let us keep in mind that God is sovereign; He is not a magical genie waiting to do all that we command. We should never model our prayer life after those who do not know God and do not serve Him.

Jesus provided a simple prayer that is timeless. He begins the prayer by acknowledging God as our Father. This indicates God's personal and loving regard for us. Jesus called God, "Father". By so doing, He establishes the people of God as the family of God. He is our Father and we are His children. He could've started the prayer with "My Father," but instead He uses "our" because collectively, God belongs to all of us. What a privilege! It adds a social layer to the prayer and invites all of us to participate in it, not just Jesus.

Jesus also establishes that God is sovereign and He is holy. When we pray to Him, we must acknowledge Him as sovereign and as holy. In today's culture, some often refer to God in ways that do not necessarily honor Him. For example, they refer to God as "the man upstairs." Although they may be well–meaning in the use of this phrase; it is actually an exploitative and flippant reference to a holy God. First, God is not a "man upstairs." He is the King of Kings and Lord of Lords. We should never attempt to bring God down to our level. Instead, we should elevate our references to God by acknowledging Him for who He is. He is holy, the Lord God Almighty.

When we pray for the Lord's will to be done on earth as it is in heaven, we are praying in alignment with God's desires. In heaven, there is no disobedience or suffering or any sort of obstacles to accomplishing God's will. As Christians, we should desire that on earth as well. What greater goal could we have than spreading His Gospel and achieving His perfect will in our lives?

As we pray for God's will to be done, we must check our attitudes as well. On the one hand, we could look at it as "well, your will wins even when I don't like, so there's nothing I can do about it," and that isn't honoring to God. But if we look at it as "God, do your will because I know it's best, even when I don't understand it. Help to change my perspective when I don't understand or accept your will," this is much more pleasing to the Lord. He knows your true feelings behind the prayer.

Everything about the Lord's Prayer announces that we are not in ultimate control of meeting our most basic needs—food (6:11), forgiveness (6:12), protection (6:13)—but that God is, and we admit and accept our limitations and God's sovereignty when we acknowledge that trusting like a child (6:8–9) in God's unfailing goodness and rightness is exactly where He wants us to be.

Forgiveness is at the heart of our relationship with God, our piety, and our life in the Christian community. The Bible commands God's people to forgive all economic debts every seventh and 50th year so that no one would be permanently impoverished. This system does not exist in the United States. Wouldn't it be great if it did? Instead, we owe debt until it is paid off or discharged. While those in overwhelming debt are able to file bankruptcy, there is no economic relief every seventh or every 50th year. Credit card debt is one of the leading reasons for being in debt. Approximately 28 percent of the debt Americans hold is credit card debt. Our consumerism and collective spending is beyond out of control.

We are living in a culture of debt that has been a part of the history of the United States since its inception. Today's national debt is roughly $34.55 trillion. This is the amount of outstanding borrowing by the U.S. Federal Government. The average debt of individual Americans is an estimated $21,800. The Bible provides guidance on debt. In Deuteronomy 15:1, debts are to be released after a period of time. In 1 Kings 4:7, we are to instructed to pay our debts. In Nehemiah 10:31, we are to forgo the exaction of every debt. Proverbs 22:26 says that we are to not become guarantors of debts.

Matthew 6:12 says that we ask God to forgive us of our debts as we forgive our debtors. In Matthew 18, we are admonished to forgive others of debts because we have been forgiven of our debts. Luke 7:42–43 reminds us that those who are forgiven of much, love much, but those who are forgiven of little, love little. Colossians 2:14 further reminds us of the ultimate forgiveness of our debts when Jesus died to pay our debt of sins. Matthew 18:21–35 illustrates the significance of debt forgiveness in God's kingdom. Since God forgives us of our personal and moral debts, we should also forgive others.

Jesus also taught us to pray that we are not led into temptation, but to be delivered from evil. We all face temptation and struggle with temptation. Remember, even Jesus was tempted while He was on earth, but He resisted the temptations. At times, the enemy is so subtle, we hardly realized that we are being tempted. In 1 Corinthians 10:13, God has promised that we would not be tempted above what we can bear, and He would always provide a way out of the temptation. God promises to give us the strength to overcome temptation. We won't always succeed simply because we're imperfect humans; we're bound to make mistakes. However, when we slip up, we are to go to the Lord with repentance, and He will forgive us.

Jesus included in the final passages of the Lord's prayer that we are to forgive others. When we forgive others, we ourselves will also be forgiven; however, when we refuse to forgive others, we forfeit the forgiveness of God that is available to us. Additionally, when we refuse to forgive others, and hold on to grudges, it becomes more difficult to forgive others. This is not to say that we shouldn't have boundaries with difficult people or complicated family members; He isn't giving us license for people to walk all over us and we just have to take it. Rather, we know that we've been forgiven by the grace of God, so we must pass on that grace to others. If they deserved it, it wouldn't be called grace. Forgiveness also frees the forgiver from harboring anger and resentment, which can cause negative effects on our health—spiritual, physical, emotional, and mental health.

## THE LESSON APPLIED

Jesus provided guidelines for godly living. All of His guidelines are to prepare us for living in His heavenly Kingdom. Jesus taught us how to pray. Instead of praying with the intention to impress others, we should pray in private with a central focus on God. He also taught us to not be long–winded and repetitive in praying to God because He already knows what we need, and vain repetitions is mimicking those who do not serve God.

Finally, Jesus told us how to pray and provided the model prayer. He acknowledges God as our Father and establishes the family of God of which those who follow Him are included. He admonishes us to forgive others and to remember that Jesus paid the debt for all of our sins. He taught us to prioritize the will of God here on earth, and for us to recognize the sovereignty of God in our lives.

## LET'S TALK ABOUT IT

We witness injustices on a global, national, and community scale. People are marginalized in a host of different ways. Understanding the Lord's prayer provides a strategy by which we can navigate the injustices of our society. We can cry out to God and ask for His wisdom to do our part to rectify whatever situations we can until He returns to bring true justice.

There's always a way to help practically, and we know that when we help others in need, Jesus recognizes those acts of kindness as if He received them Himself.

### GET SOCIAL
Share your views and tag us @rhboydco. Use #rhboydco.

@rhboydco

## HOME DAILY DEVOTIONAL READINGS
### FEBRUARY 3–10, 2025

| MONDAY | TUESDAY | WEDNESDAY | THURSDAY | FRIDAY | SATURDAY | SUNDAY |
| --- | --- | --- | --- | --- | --- | --- |
| Be Strong and Courageous | As Sheep among Wolves | Resistance and Reward | God Is Our Salvation | Rescue Me from My Enemies | Don't Rejoice When Enemies Fall | The Kingdom Presses On |
| Joshua 1:1–9 | Matthew 10:16–30 | Matthew 10:31–42 | Psalm 35:1–14 | Psalm 35:15–28 | Proverbs 24:8–22 | Matthew 11:7–15, 20–24 |

LESSON XI  
FEBRUARY 9, 2025

# RESISTANCE TO THE KINGDOM

ADULT TOPIC:  
STAND UP

BACKGROUND SCRIPTURE: MATTHEW 11  
LESSON PASSAGE: MATTHEW 11:7–15, 20–24

## MATTHEW 11:7–15, 20–24

### KJV

AND as they departed, Jesus began to say unto the multitudes concerning John, What went ye out into the wilderness to see? A reed shaken with the wind?
8 But what went ye out for to see? A man clothed in soft raiment? behold, they that wear soft clothing are in kings' houses.
9 But what went ye out for to see? A prophet? yea, I say unto you, and more than a prophet.
10 For this is he, of whom it is written, Behold, I send my messenger before thy face, which shall prepare thy way before thee.
11 Verily I say unto you, Among them that are born of women there hath not risen a greater than John the Baptist: notwithstanding he that is least in the kingdom of heaven is greater than he.
12 And from the days of John the Baptist until now the kingdom of heaven suffereth violence, and the violent take it by force.
13 For all the prophets and the law prophesied until John.
14 And if ye will receive it, this is Elias, which was for to come.
15 He that hath ears to hear, let him hear.

• • • • • •

20 Then began he to upbraid the cities wherein most of his mighty works were done, because they repented not:
21 Woe unto thee, Chorazin! woe unto thee, Bethsaida! for if the mighty works, which were done in you, had been done in Tyre and Sidon, they would have repented long ago in sackcloth and ashes.

### NRSVue

AS they went away, Jesus began to speak to the crowds about John: "What did you go out into the wilderness to look at? A reed shaken by the wind?
8 What, then, did you go out to see? Someone dressed in soft robes? Look, those who wear soft robes are in royal palaces.
9 What, then, did you go out to see? A prophet? Yes, I tell you, and more than a prophet.
10 This is the one about whom it is written, 'See, I am sending my messenger ahead of you, who will prepare your way before you.'
11 "Truly I tell you, among those born of women no one has arisen greater than John the Baptist, yet the least in the kingdom of heaven is greater than he.
12 From the days of John the Baptist until now, the kingdom of heaven has suffered violence, and violent people take it by force.
13 For all the Prophets and the Law prophesied until John came,
14 and if you are willing to accept it, he is Elijah who is to come.
15 Let anyone with ears listen!

• • • • • •

20 Then he began to reproach the cities in which most of his deeds of power had been done because they did not repent.
21 "Woe to you, Chorazin! Woe to you, Bethsaida! For if the deeds of power done in you had been done in Tyre and Sidon, they would have repented long ago in sackcloth and ashes.

**MAIN THOUGHT:** Then he began to reproach the cities in which most of his deeds of power had been done, because they did not repent.
(Matthew 11:20, NRSVue)

## MATTHEW 11:7–15, 20–24

| KJV | NRSVue |
|---|---|
| 22 But I say unto you, It shall be more tolerable for Tyre and Sidon at the day of judgment, than for you. | 22 But I tell you, on the day of judgment it will be more tolerable for Tyre and Sidon than for you. |
| 23 And thou, Capernaum, which art exalted unto heaven, shalt be brought down to hell: for if the mighty works, which have been done in thee, had been done in Sodom, it would have remained until this day. | 23 And you, Capernaum, will you be exalted to heaven? No, you will be brought down to Hades. "For if the deeds of power done in you had been done in Sodom, it would have remained until this day. |
| 24 But I say unto you, That it shall be more tolerable for the land of Sodom in the day of judgment, than for thee. | 24 But I tell you that on the day of judgment it will be more tolerable for the land of Sodom than for you." |

## LESSON SETTING
**Time:** 85 CE
**Place:** Antioch

## LESSON OUTLINE
I. Opposition and Rejection (Matthew 11:7–15)
II. The Silencing of a Prophetic Voice (Matthew 11:20–24)

## UNIFYING PRINCIPLE

People resist changes that affect them. What resistance might we expect when we stand up for changes that are good and right? Matthew records Jesus' pronouncement that there is violence against the Kingdom of heaven, which is under constant attack.

## INTRODUCTION

The Gospel of Matthew establishes the connection between the Old and the New Testament by making references to the Old Testament to establish that Jesus was a fulfilment of the prophesies of old which told of a coming Messiah; that Jesus was a type of Moses; Jesus was from the line of David; and that Jesus was Immanuel, God with us. The Gospel of Matthew was written by the Apostle Matthew (who was a tax collector before he was called by Jesus). He was one of the twelve disciples and was chosen to record the ministry of Jesus. Although the Gospel of Matthew does not claim to be a complete narrative of the life of Christ, it contains important themes that help us to understand key events in Jesus' ministry as He began to set up the Kingdom of God. Matthew wrote to a Christian audience who were Jews who converted to Christianity. It was originally written in the Aramaic dialect used by the Hebrews to appeal to a Christian–Jewish audience. It was later written in Greek for a wider audience. Matthew preached in Israel for about fifteen years before traveling to other parts of the world. As a tax collector, he was a public servant and understood Aramaic and Greek. The Jews were under Roman rulership and the Romans spoke Greek. The early chapters of the Gospel of Matthew cover the genealogy of Christ's birth, His early years, the inauguration of His ministry, the constitution of the kingdom, the miracles of Jesus, the selection of the apostles, and opposition to Jesus.

## EXPOSITION

### I. OPPOSITION AND REJECTION (MATTHEW 11:7–15)

As Jesus continued His ministry, He sent the twelve disciples out from Galilee to other cities ahead of Him. While Jesus was in Galilee, John the Baptist was imprisoned because he rebuked King Herod for marrying his sister–in–law. While in prison, John the Baptist was discouraged and began to wonder if Jesus was truly the Messiah. He sent two of his disciples to find out if Jesus was truly the Messiah. Jesus sent messages back to John the Baptist, letting him know that He was performing miracles that were prophesied of the Messiah. Jesus restored sight to the blind; healed the lame to be able to walk again; cleansed people of leprosy; healed those who were deaf; and preached the Gospel to the poor. He also told John the Baptist that anyone who was not offended by Him was blessed. Upon receiving word from Jesus, John the Baptist recognized that He was truly the Messiah because the things that He was doing were things that were prophesied of Him.

We may often face severe trials and persecutions that try our very souls. During these times, we, like John the Baptist, may need encouragement. We may wonder why did God allow such things to come upon us? We may even be tempted to turn away from Christ. Instead of looking away from Christ when we feel discouraged, we should lean into Him more. Jesus reminds us of one simple truth that we can keep in mind: "These things I have spoken unto you, that in me ye might have peace. In the world ye shall have tribulation: but be of good cheer; I have overcome the world" (John 16:33, KJV). Jesus knew that we would have troubles and that we would suffer for our faith in Him. It was never promised to be an easy path, but it was promised to be rewarded in the end through eternity in heaven with our loving Savior.

Many who looked for the fulfillment of the prophesies of the Messiah expected that He would come as a king to overthrow the Romans and restore rulership to the Jews. Jesus did not come to the world as someone who was full of pride; but as a humble servant. His mission was not to save the Jews from Roman rulership; His mission was to save humanity from the power and penalty of sin. Although Jesus was and is the King of Kings and Lord of Lords, He did not present Himself as a mighty ruler to save the Jews from the Romans. Instead, He humbled Himself and became like a servant to save us and to begin implementing the kingdom of God. Only those who were humble and had spiritual insight recognized Jesus as the Messiah. Today, we must still humbly accept Jesus as the Lord of our lives in order to be saved.

After sending His message to John, Jesus turned to the crowd and praised John the Baptist for he was sent into the world as a messenger to prepare the way for the Messiah. John the Baptist did an excellent job at preparing the way for the Messiah. Many of those who followed John the Baptist became followers of Jesus and were present on this occasion when He spoke to them.

In verse 12, Jesus stated; "And from the days of John the Baptist until now the kingdom of heaven suffereth violence, and the violent take it by force." Jesus knew that John the Baptist would be beheaded. Just as in the days of Jesus, Christ-followers must be courageous, unwavering in their faith, and endure growing opposition against Christians. Today, Christians are still being persecuted for their faith. Over 360 million Christians in 76 countries suffer high levels of persecution and discrimination for their faith. Approximately 1 in 7 Christians experience high levels of persecution and discrimination. This happens mostly on a global scale, and therefore, we can be grateful that our persecution in America is on a smaller scale. That might not always be the case.

Jesus asked the crowd (referring to John the Baptist), "what did they go into the wilderness to see?" (v. 7). Jesus' question foreshadows the point of this passage: the people didn't go out to see something common and unremarkable (a common reed), nor did they go to see a spectacle of human power or status, but instead went out to witness God intervening in history through John, the eschatological prophet (meaning someone who heralds the end times or the coming of a significant event in religious history).

Reeds were used figuratively for what was weak and undependable in times of trouble such as 1 Kings 14:15 and 2 Kings 18:21. In this context, the statement suggests that what the people sought in John the Baptist was not weakness or frailty, but rather a divine intervention that transcends human power and status, as indicated in Isaiah 40:3–5, which speaks of a voice crying out in the wilderness, preparing the way for the Lord. John the Baptist (the Baptizer) fulfilled his mission to prepare the way of the Lord.

"Let anyone with ears listen!" The children of Israel were not always ready to hear (Isaiah 6:10; Jeremiah 6:10; Ezekiel 12:2). Those who listen will realize that the one who comes after Elijah, after the voice in the wilderness, is the Messiah, God's Anointed Servant (Isaiah 53). John the Baptist was not Elijah resurrected; he was chosen by God to represent Elijah's role by confronting sin at its highest level and pointing people to God.

## II. THE SILENCING OF A PROPHETIC VOICE (MATTHEW 11:20–24)

John the Baptist was a significant figure in the New Testament, known for his role in baptizing Jesus and preparing the way for His ministry. Jesus commended John the Baptist by telling the crowd that he was more than a prophet. John was a messenger sent by God to prepare the way of the Lord. Although John the Baptist was great, Jesus also said that even the least significant person in the kingdom of heaven is greater than John the Baptist. This means that the privileges and blessings of being part of the Kingdom of heaven are far greater than any earthly status, including that of John the Baptist. Being a part of the Kingdom of God is far more important than any worldly accomplishment.

The killing of John the Baptist by Herod represented an attack against the kingdom of God. Since John the Baptist was a significant figure, His message of preparing a way for the Lord was silenced when Herod killed him. This hindered the proclamation of God's message to the world. It was against Jewish law to marry one's brother's wife. When John the Baptist publicly denounced Herod's unlawful marriage to Herodias, Herod attempted to suppress the truth and maintain his power without being held accountable for his actions. John the Baptist preached a message of righteousness and moral uprightness. His call for repentance challenged the corrupt practices of the ruling authorities. By killing John, Herod tried to eliminate a voice that challenged his immoral behavior and threatened his authority.

By killing John, Herod rejected God's authority and His Kingdom values because John was chosen by God to prepare the way of the Lord. Instead of aligning himself with the principles of justice and righteousness, Herod prioritized his own desires and political ambitions. This rejection of God's authority was effectively an attack against the Kingdom of God.

Jesus acknowledged the significance of John's ministry and his role in preparing the way for the Messiah and proclaiming the Kingdom of heaven. He also stated that from the day of John the Baptist, the kingdom of God suffers violence. There are several perspectives on this passage.

First, proclaiming the message of God's Kingdom challenges the established order, including religious traditions, societal norms, and personal beliefs. This opposition can manifest as persecution, ridicule, or rejection. Millions of Christians are persecuted, killed, or discriminated against severely as a result of standing up for or expressing their identity as a follower of Jesus. Another interpretation of verse 12 suggests that "the violent take it by force" refers to the enthusiastic and persistent pursuit of the Kingdom of heaven by individuals who are eager to enter a relationship with God. It implies that those who earnestly seek after God's Kingdom do so with fervor and determination, not passively waiting but actively engaging as citizens of the Kingdom of God. The Kingdom of God is a divine initiative to save humanity. Despite historic and modern-day forceful opposition, it continues to advance, breaking through barriers and transforming lives.

In these last verses, Jesus rebukes the great cities where the Gospel had been preached but rejected. Because they were the eyewitnesses of Jesus' miracles, they had a greater responsibility to share the light with others. Because they hadn't, they would be held accountable appropriately. Even those the cities Jesus named weren't the ones where He was persecuted and died, they were cities that disregarded Him as the Messiah. Where are those cities now? Lost to history. That's why Jesus says, "Woe to you," because He knew judgment would come unto them. If you've been given the privilege of knowing the Gospel, then you must share it with others! It's part of your duty as a Christian; it's too good to keep to yourself! If you do...woe to you!

## THE LESSON APPLIED

Today's lesson focused on challenges involved in proclaiming the message of God's Kingdom while also affirming the ultimate triumph and victory of God's purposes. John faced severe consequences for being the forerunner for Christ and for standing for repentance and righteousness. Throughout His ministry, Jesus also faced opposition and rejection. Some of His fiercest opposition came from religious and political leaders who saw Him as a threat to their authority. There are times when being a follower of Christ will cause others to reject us or to violently or aggressive oppose us. During such times, we are to stand firm in our faith for God. Following Christ requires complete surrender. We cannot be fully committed to Christ until we are fully surrendered to Him. Being a follower of Christ is more significant and important than any worldly attainment or recognition. As John the Baptist prepared the way for Jesus, so Jesus prepared the way for each of us to be saved.

## LET'S TALK ABOUT IT

**In what ways have you experienced persecution or discrimination because of your faith?**

There are many who do not follow Christ. In almost every aspect of daily life, we may encounter those who hate Christians. Revealing your identity as a Christ follower may result in unwanted attention or injustices. Leaning into the Lord, being confident in Who God is, and trusting Him to see us through will help as we navigate the circumstances. As Christ followers, we may experience some of the same things that Jesus experienced. When we consider the things that Christ suffered for our salvation, let us remember that opposition to our faith is often a sign that we are doing the right thing.

We should never allow anyone to force us to surrender our faith in God. Our relationship with Christ leads to eternal life. Jesus has promised: "But he that shall endure unto the end, the same shall be saved" (Matthew 24:13, KJV). In taking our stand for Christ, let us do so with passion for Christ. Let us not be apathetic in our relationship with Christ. There is no room for middle ground. We are to stand fervently and faithfully for the Lord. Remember that only what we do for Christ will last. We live in a relationship with God, not a formula. When we recognize His voice and actions and respond appropriately to God at work, we are being citizens of the Kingdom of God.

## GET SOCIAL

Share your views and tag us @rhboydco. Use #rhboydco.

@rhboydco

LESSON XII     FEBRUARY 16, 2025

# THE FIRST WILL BE LAST

**ADULT TOPIC:**     **BACKGROUND SCRIPTURE:** MATTHEW 19:16–30
**WHAT MORE DO I HAVE TO DO?**     **LESSON PASSAGE:** MATTHEW 19:16–30

## MATTHEW 19:16–30

### KJV

AND, behold, one came and said unto him, Good Master, what good thing shall I do, that I may have eternal life?

17 And he said unto him, Why callest thou me good? there is none good but one, that is, God: but if thou wilt enter into life, keep the commandments.

18 He saith unto him, Which? Jesus said, Thou shalt do no murder, Thou shalt not commit adultery, Thou shalt not steal, Thou shalt not bear false witness,

19 Honour thy father and thy mother: and, Thou shalt love thy neighbour as thyself.

20 The young man saith unto him, All these things have I kept from my youth up: what lack I yet?

21 Jesus said unto him, If thou wilt be perfect, go and sell that thou hast, and give to the poor, and thou shalt have treasure in heaven: and come and follow me.

22 But when the young man heard that saying, he went away sorrowful: for he had great possessions.

23 Then said Jesus unto his disciples, Verily I say unto you, That a rich man shall hardly enter into the kingdom of heaven.

24 And again I say unto you, It is easier for a camel to go through the eye of a needle, than for a rich man to enter into the kingdom of God.

25 When his disciples heard it, they were exceedingly amazed, saying, Who then can be saved?

26 But Jesus beheld them, and said unto them,

### NRSVue

THEN someone came to him and said, "Teacher, what good deed must I do to have eternal life?"

17 And he said to him, "Why do you ask me about what is good? There is one who is good. If you wish to enter into life, keep the commandments."

18 He said to him, "Which ones?" And Jesus said, "You shall not murder. You shall not commit adultery. You shall not steal. You shall not bear false witness.

19 Honor your father and mother. Also, you shall love your neighbor as yourself."

20 The young man said to him, "I have kept all these; what do I still lack?"

21 Jesus said to him, "If you wish to be perfect, go, sell your possessions, and give the money to the poor, and you will have treasure in heaven; then come, follow me."

22 When the young man heard this word, he went away grieving, for he had many possessions.

23 Then Jesus said to his disciples, "Truly I tell you, it will be hard for a rich person to enter the kingdom of heaven.

24 Again I tell you, it is easier for a camel to go through the eye of a needle than for someone who is rich to enter the kingdom of God."

25 When the disciples heard this, they were greatly astounded and said, "Then who can be saved?"

26 But Jesus looked at them and said, "For

**MAIN THOUGHT:** "It is easier for a camel to go through the eye of a needle than for someone who is rich to enter the kingdom of God." (Matthew 19:24, NRSVue)

## Matthew 19:16–30

### KJV

With men this is impossible; but with God all things are possible.

27 Then answered Peter and said unto him, Behold, we have forsaken all, and followed thee; what shall we have therefore?

28 And Jesus said unto them, Verily I say unto you, That ye which have followed me, in the regeneration when the Son of man shall sit in the throne of his glory, ye also shall sit upon twelve thrones, judging the twelve tribes of Israel.

29 And every one that hath forsaken houses, or brethren, or sisters, or father, or mother, or wife, or children, or lands, for my name's sake, shall receive an hundredfold, and shall inherit everlasting life.

30 But many that are first shall be last; and the last shall be first.

### NRSVue

mortals it is impossible, but for God all things are possible."

27 Then Peter said in reply, "Look, we have left everything and followed you. What then will we have?"

28 Jesus said to them, "Truly I tell you, at the renewal of all things, when the Son of Man is seated on the throne of his glory, you who have followed me will also sit on twelve thrones, judging the twelve tribes of Israel.

29 And everyone who has left houses or brothers or sisters or father or mother or wife or children or fields for my name's sake will receive a hundredfold and will inherit eternal life.

30 But many who are first will be last, and the last will be first.

---

**LESSON SETTING**
   **Time:** 85 CE
   **Place:** Antioch

**LESSON OUTLINE**
   I. Treasure in Heaven
      (Matthew 19:16–22)
   II. The Cost of Discipleship
      (Matthew 19:23–30)

## UNIFYING PRINCIPLE

People seek to acquire wealth and possessions. How might the pursuit of wealth stand in the way of a purposeful life? Jesus says it is practically impossible for the rich or poor to enter God's Kingdom if they attempt to do so through their own effort, because it is only possible for those who put their trust in God.

## INTRODUCTION

As Jesus' ministry grew, He attracted large crowds of people; among them were the Pharisees, who often questioned Him in hopes to catch Him in an error or breaking the Law. There were many complex laws that governed man's relationship with God and man's relationship with others. Some laws provided guidance on specific situations. In today's lesson, the rich young ruler asked Jesus what he had to do to have eternal life. Jesus told him to keep the commandments. We will examine what point Jesus was trying to bring home to the young man's heart. It is perhaps the most challenging aspect of adult life—coming to terms with the condition of our hearts.

It is important to note that keeping the commandments does not guarantee eternal life. Jesus wanted the rich young ruler to know that salvation is about loving God with all our hearts, minds, and souls, and loving our neighbors as ourselves (see Matthew 22:37–40). In essence, Jesus looked beyond his works and went straight to the heart of the matter. If we are to live with God forever, we must first learn to love Him with our whole heart and then to love others the way we love ourselves.

## EXPOSITION

### I. TREASURE IN HEAVEN (MATTHEW 19:16–22)

On one occasion, Jesus was met by a rich young ruler who had a sincere question. The rich young ruler was quite proud of his accomplishments in this life. He was a ruler, and he was rich. He asked the Lord as "Good Master." By greeting the Lord in this manner, the young man did not recognize Jesus for who He is. He saw Jesus as a teacher, referring to Him as just another great man. He was not truly aware of Jesus' identity as the Messiah. He also did not understand how to gain eternal life. His perspective on eternal life was interpreted through works, rather than as a gift. Salvation is a gift from God: "For by grace are ye saved through faith; and that not of yourselves: it is the gift of God" (Ephesians 2:8).

Jesus addressed the first point with the young man—that of calling Him "good." By telling him that only God is good, He was trying to get the young man to see that He was not just a mere man. The young man did not get it.

Jesus then moved on to answer the second part of his question—how to gain eternal life. At face value, Jesus told him to keep the commandments. The young man wanted to know which commandments he should keep. Jesus answered by listing the second five of the Ten Commandments, which have to do with our relationship with others. This does not mean that we can be saved by keeping the commandments. Jesus wanted him to see that the commandments convict us of sin. This then gives us the opportunity to repent and surrender to God. Jesus was testing the young man to see how completely devoted his heart was to God (and not to appearances and his reputation).

The rich young ruler responded by telling Jesus that he had kept all the five commandments that Jesus mentioned from the time he was a youth. The word "kept" is the Greek word *phulasso*, which means to "be on guard, to observe, preserver, take care, and watch over." The young man had carefully ensured that he obeyed the commandments; however, he lacked one thing. He had a blind spot that prevented him from seeing the condition of his own heart. The young man thought that by obeying the Law, he could gain eternal life; however, we cannot gain eternal life by "doing" such and such. Eternal life is a gift from God.

In response, Jesus told the young man to sell what he had and give the money to the poor and follow Him. By so doing, he would have treasure in heaven. This was a call from the Lord that really tested the young man to his core because it revealed how attached he was to his possessions. The Lord was showing the young man that he really didn't love his neighbor.

He was also showing him that he really didn't have faith in God. The young man could not be saved by keeping the commandments, or by selling all that he had and giving it to the poor. The only way to eternal life is to have faith in God. The young man was very conflicted by the decision to sell his riches and follow Christ. "…the young man went away sorrowful because he had great possessions" (Matt. 19:22). This is one of the saddest responses to the call of Christ to follow Him.

The young man's sorrow (Matthew 19:22) demonstrates that he clearly understood Jesus's point. Sorrow also means the conflict and the pain of letting go of oneself; as such, it's a legitimate response in the process of repentance. The young man sorrowfully rejected Jesus' invitation to sell everything he had, give it to the poor, and follow Him.

The young man failed in keeping the Law by having other gods before God as found in Exodus 20:3, which states: "Thou shalt have no other gods before me" (KJV). This was evident by the fact that he walked away sorrowful, unable to let go of his treasures and follow Christ. Jesus wanted him to let go of his need for personal control over his life and hold on to a deep dependance on God.

Jesus did not require everyone He met to sell everything and follow Him. We are to be sure that nothing gets in the way of using our God-given wealth or talents in a selfish way. We should all be willing to give up anything that God asks us to in order to follow Him. Loving God with all our hearts means using our wealth and resources in ways that honor Him.

The young man should have immediately acknowledged that he had sinned by not loving his neighbor and by not having faith in God. If he had done so, he would have been saved. The young man effectively traded his soul's salvation for his temporal riches. There are many people today that sell their souls for temporal gains. They live for the pleasures and comforts of life instead of living for God. Everyone will have to answer for themselves the call of Christ to follow Him. When we repent and surrender to Christ, and follow Him, we gain eternal life. The treasures of heaven are of eternal value, for there we will forever be with the Lord. No earthly possession or riches can compare to eternity with God.

## II. THE COST OF DISCIPLESHIP (MATTHEW 19:23–30)

Jesus took the occasion with the rich young ruler to make an important point—"that a rich man shall hardly enter into the kingdom of heaven" (Matthew 19:26 KJV). He further expounded that "It is, easier for a camel to go through the eye of a needle, than for a rich man to enter into the Kingdom of God" (Matthew 19:24, KJV).

It is easy for the things of this world to become idols, especially riches. He is simply stating that it is easy for wealth to become idols or little 'gods' in our lives, which makes it impossible to serve God. God will not share the throne of our hearts with any other idols. Jesus was using a hyperbole to make an impression. Without Christ, it is impossible to be saved. It is more difficult for a wealthy person to give up their wealth or surrender their will to Christ because of their attachment to their wealth. When we store up our wealth and don't help each other, we are hoarding wealth and not loving our neighbors as ourselves.

It is easier for a poor person to surrender their will to God than for a rich person. The wealthy person finds it impossible to surrender their trust in their riches, which they can see, to trust in God whom they cannot see.

In light of Jesus' guidance on wealth, the disciples wondered who can be saved. In first-century Israel, wealth was viewed as a blessing/reward from God and a sign of God's favor. Jesus' response (19:23) turns this cultural view upside down by pointing out that wealth can instead be an obstacle to one's obedience to and reliance on God. We are such a wealthy nation; we should take this to heart.

Peter asked Jesus, "Behold, we have forsaken all, and followed thee; what shall we have therefore?" (Matthew 19:27). This demonstrates that he missed the point that Jesus was making: Peter was still concerned about the stuff they've left behind in order to follow Christ, not about his heart's devotion to God. At this point, the disciples were still expecting a revolutionary Messiah who would set up a political kingdom and free them from Roman rulership.

Jesus' response (Matthew 19:28–30) is compassionate. He offers hope for so many in the Church who have sacrificed everything for Him. Yet it is still a reminder that we cannot expect our justice or our reward in this fallen world, but that our hope is in the eternal God and the life God gives us through His Son—and the rewards God promises for our eternity with him.

Jesus wanted the disciples to know that the reward for those who follow Him may not be earthly riches, but they will inherit eternal life and shall receive one hundred-fold of the sacrifices that they made to follow Christ. We cannot bargain or buy our way to eternal life. Heaven is not for sale. There is no good deed that will purchase heaven for us. The way to eternal life is to be fully surrendered to Christ and have faith in Him.

## The Lesson Applied

What is standing in the way of fully surrendering your life to Christ? We are often attached to things or ideologies that keep us separated from God. In today's lesson, Jesus was referring to riches owned by the young ruler; however, we can broaden this context to anything that we love more than we love God. This can be a person, wealth, or things in the material world. Jesus' discussion with the rich young ruler revealed something that was hidden from his view. The Holy Spirit is the Spirit of Truth and will guide us in all areas of life and godly living. The rich young ruler was so attached to his wealth that he could not see that hoarding wealth, withholding funds that could have benefited the poor, would demonstrate that he loved his neighbor as he loved himself. Sometimes we miss the foundational truths of the Ten Commandments. While we are to honor them, it is more important to love God with all our hearts, minds, and souls, and to love our neighbors as we love ourselves. These two commandments sum up the entire Ten Commandments. When we have the opportunity to do good and do not do it, we are forfeiting the blessing that God has for us by giving.

## Let's Talk About It

**Are you more invested in fame and fortune in this life than in the life hereafter?** Jesus provides clear guidance on how to handle treasures in this life. "Lay not up for yourselves treasures upon earth, where moth and rust doth corrupt, and where thieves break through and steal, but lay up for yourselves treasures in heaven, where neither moth nor rust doth corrupt, and where thieves do not break through nor steal; for where your treasure is there will your heart be also" (Matthew 6:19, KJV). Jesus warns us against placing excessive emphasis on material possessions and wealth, which can be stolen, lost or destroyed. Material possessions decay and corrode over time. Worldly treasures are temporary and vulnerable to loss. Instead of investing solely in earthly treasures, we should focus on accumulating spiritual wealth, such as acts of kindness, love, charity, and righteousness, which have eternal significance. Unlike earthly treasures, spiritual treasures are not subject to decay or loss. They endure beyond the physical realm and are secure in heaven. There is a connection between one's priorities and their heart's desires. If one's focus is on accumulating earthly wealth, their heart will be attached to worldly pursuits. Conversely, if they prioritize spiritual treasures, their heart will be oriented towards heavenly matters.

**In light of the situation of the rich young ruler, is there anything that you are holding onto that stands between you and God?**

The young man's wealth had become the source of his personal identity, power, purpose, and meaning in life. Jesus called him to sacrifice his "idols" and follow Jesus. It requires trust in God to surrender anything that has become an idol. When we are more invested in this life than we are in eternity, God will require that we change course, give up something, and fully commit to Him. Today, ask God to show you if there are any idols in your life and if so, ask Him to help you to surrender to His lordship and follow Him all the way. Anything that we give up in order to follow Christ cannot be compared to the eternal value of living with Him forever.

## GET SOCIAL

Share your views and tag us @rhboydco. Use #rhboydco.

**@rhboydco**

## HOME DAILY DEVOTIONAL READINGS
### FEBRUARY 17–23, 2025

| MONDAY | TUESDAY | WEDNESDAY | THURSDAY | FRIDAY | SATURDAY | SUNDAY |
|---|---|---|---|---|---|---|
| Equipped for Every Good Work | Delight in God's Ways | Keep Awake; The Bridegroom Is Coming | Praise for a Faithful Servant | Choose the Way of Faithfulness | The Fast That God Chooses | Compassion for the Least |
| 2 Timothy 3:10–17 | Psalm 119:17–24 | Matthew 25:1–13 | Matthew 25:14–15, 19–30 | Psalm 119:41–48 | Isaiah 58 | Matthew 25:31–46 |

LESSON XIII

FEBRUARY 23, 2025

# KINGDOM LIFE

ADULT TOPIC:
DON'T BE A GOAT

BACKGROUND SCRIPTURE: MATTHEW 25
LESSON PASSAGE: MATTHEW 25:31–46

## MATTHEW 25:31—46

### KJV

WHEN the Son of man shall come in his glory, and all the holy angels with him, then shall he sit upon the throne of his glory:
32 And before him shall be gathered all nations: and he shall separate them one from another, as a shepherd divideth his sheep from the goats:

33 And he shall set the sheep on his right hand, but the goats on the left.
34 Then shall the King say unto them on his right hand, Come, ye blessed of my Father, inherit the kingdom prepared for you from the foundation of the world:
35 For I was an hungred, and ye gave me meat: I was thirsty, and ye gave me drink: I was a stranger, and ye took me in:
36 Naked, and ye clothed me: I was sick, and ye visited me: I was in prison, and ye came unto me.
37 Then shall the righteous answer him, saying, Lord, when saw we thee an hungred, and fed thee? or thirsty, and gave thee drink?

38 When saw we thee a stranger, and took thee in? or naked, and clothed thee?

39 Or when saw we thee sick, or in prison, and came unto thee?
40 And the King shall answer and say unto them, Verily I say unto you, Inasmuch as ye have done it unto one of the least of these my brethren, ye have done it unto me.

### NRSVue

"WHEN the Son of Man comes in his glory and all the angels with him, then he will sit on the throne of his glory.
32 All the nations will be gathered before him, and he will separate people one from another as a shepherd separates the sheep from the goats,
33 and he will put the sheep at his right hand and the goats at the left.
34 Then the king will say to those at his right hand, 'Come, you who are blessed by my Father, inherit the kingdom prepared for you from the foundation of the world,
35 for I was hungry and you gave me food, I was thirsty and you gave me something to drink, I was a stranger and you welcomed me,
36 I was naked and you gave me clothing, I was sick and you took care of me, I was in prison and you visited me.'
37 Then the righteous will answer him, 'Lord, when was it that we saw you hungry and gave you food or thirsty and gave you something to drink?
38 And when was it that we saw you a stranger and welcomed you or naked and gave you clothing?
39 And when was it that we saw you sick or in prison and visited you?'
40 And the king will answer them, 'Truly I tell you, just as you did it to one of the least of these brothers and sisters of mine, you did it to me.'

**MAIN THOUGHT:** "The king will say to those at his right hand, 'Come, you that are blessed by my Father, inherit the kingdom prepared for you from the foundation of the world; for I was hungry and you gave me food..."
(Matthew 25:34–35, NRSVue)

## MATTHEW 25:31–46

### KJV

41 Then shall he say also unto them on the left hand, Depart from me, ye cursed, into everlasting fire, prepared for the devil and his angels:

42 For I was an hungred, and ye gave me no meat: I was thirsty, and ye gave me no drink:
43 I was a stranger, and ye took me not in: naked, and ye clothed me not: sick, and in prison, and ye visited me not.
44 Then shall they also answer him, saying, Lord, when saw we thee an hungred, or athirst, or a stranger, or naked, or sick, or in prison, and did not minister unto thee?
45 Then shall he answer them, saying, Verily I say unto you, Inasmuch as ye did it not to one of the least of these, ye did it not to me.
46 And these shall go away into everlasting punishment: but the righteous into life eternal.

### NRSVue

41 Then he will say to those at his left hand, 'You who are accursed, depart from me into the eternal fire prepared for the devil and his angels,
42 for I was hungry and you gave me no food, I was thirsty and you gave me nothing to drink,
43 I was a stranger and you did not welcome me, naked and you did not give me clothing, sick and in prison and you did not visit me.'
44 Then they also will answer, 'Lord, when was it that we saw you hungry or thirsty or a stranger or naked or sick or in prison and did not take care of you?'
45 Then he will answer them, 'Truly I tell you, just as you did not do it to one of the least of these, you did not do it to me.'
46 And these will go away into eternal punishment but the righteous into eternal life."

## LESSON SETTING
**Time:** 85 CE
**Place:** Antioch

## LESSON OUTLINE
I. The Great Separation
   (Matthew 25:31–33)
II. The Reward of the Sheep
   (Matthew 25:34–40)
III. The Reward of the Goat
   (Matthew 25:41–46)

## UNIFYING PRINCIPLE

We are often judged based on known and unknown criteria. Whose (or what) standards should matter to us the most? Matthew 25 tells us that the criterion for the Son of Man's final judgment of responsible Kingdom living will be based on service to the "least of these."

## INTRODUCTION

In Matthew 25:31–40 Jesus discusses the final judgment. He tells of a time when He will come to the earth in glory, accompanied by angels and He will sit on His glorious throne. All the nations will be gathered before Him, and He will separate people from one another as a shepherd separates the sheep from the goats, placing the sheep on his right and the goats on his left.

The sheep represent the righteous and the goats represent the unrighteous. Jesus explains that the righteous, those on His right, will inherit the Kingdom prepared for them from the foundation of the world. This is because they provided food to the hungry, drink to the thirsty, welcomed the stranger, clothed the naked, cared for the sick, and visited the prisoners. They did these things not knowing they were serving Jesus himself. The righteous are surprised and ask when they did these things for him. Jesus responds, "Truly I tell you, whatever you did for one of the least of these brothers and sisters of mine, you did for me." By saying this, Jesus emphasized the importance of compassion and service to others, illustrating that acts of kindness to those in need are seen as direct services to Jesus.

## EXPOSITION

### I. THE GREAT SEPARATION (MATTHEW 25:31–33)

Sheep and goats often graze together in open fields. They are separated them during times when the sheep need to be sheared and during times when the goats need to be milked. They are also separated to keep the goats together at night to stay warm. In those days, sheep and goats looked similar from a distance and often grazed together. But they were separated at night because the goats required a warmer place to rest. The sheep have wool to keep them warm and are therefore, able to bear the cooler temperatures.

During biblical times, sheep were used in the sacrificial ceremonial services. Goats were sacrificed during Yom Kippur, which is the Day of Atonement. Sheep were sacrificed during Passover. When Jesus died on the cross, He became the perfect sacrifice, or sacrificial lamb, to atone for our sins.

In Matthew 25: 31–46, Jesus described a time of judgment when He will come to the earth, which will be His second coming, with all the holy angels with Him. All the nations of the world will be gathered before Him, and He shall separate them one from another. He will place the sheep on His right hand and the goats on His left hand. Jesus uses the symbolism of sheep and goat to describe the nations. In essence, He will separate the nations. While we all share this planet as our home, there are countries that follow the Lord and there are countries that do not follow the Lord. The same is true for individuals. Some follow the Lord, and some do not.

Use of the term "sheep" is a metaphor to describe people who have shown kindness, compassion, and aid to those in need. Jesus identifies such acts of mercy as being done unto Him directly, saying, "Truly I tell you, whatever you did for one of the least of these brothers and sisters of mine, you did for me" (v. 42). It also represents those who live by God's commands, particularly in terms of showing love and compassion to others and are thus welcomed into eternal life.

Use of the term "goat" represent those who are unrighteous; those who failed to show compassion and aid to those in need. They are depicted as being unaware or indifferent to the suffering of others, and Jesus says to them; "Truly I tell you, whatever you did not do for one of the least of these, you did not do for me" (v. 45). These are to be cast away into eternal punishment (see v. 46).

### II. THE REWARD OF THE SHEEP (MATTHEW 25:34–40)

Jesus emphasizes the importance of helping the least of these by linking such acts of compassion with salvation. Individually and collectively, we are to love the Lord with all our hearts, minds, and souls, and to love our neighbors as we love ourselves. Jesus highlighted the importance that our actions reflect faith in Him and fulfill our call to love our neighbors as we love ourselves. By so doing, we are serving the Lord. In the service of humanity, we should not do good for others with any intention to be seen and heard. We should do good to others out of a pure motive—because we love the Lord and we love others.

Sacrificial generosity (see Matthew 25:35–45) is the heartbeat of a life that loves and follows God, since we follow the infinitely generous and self–sacrificing God: "But who so keepeth his word, in him verily is the love of God perfected: hereby know we that we are in Him. He that saith he abideth in Him ought himself also so to walk, even as He walked" (1 John 2:5–6, KJV).

Jesus' ministry was underscored by His compassion for humanity. He healed the sick, restored sight to the blind, taught the Gospel, and fed the hungry. These acts of compassion are to characterize Christ followers in the modern world. If you aren't known for these acts, what are you known for? How are you showing Jesus' love?

After Jesus separates the sheep from the goats, He invites the sheep who were separated from the goats and placed at His right hand to inherit the Kingdom prepared for them from the foundation of the world. He identifies them as blessed. The Greek word for "blessed" is *eulogeo*. In this context, the blessing is from God towards humanity. *Eulogeo* means "to distinguish with favor; to prosper; to make happy." God will show His favor to those who demonstrate lovingkindness and compassion to others. This was God's plan from the time that He created the world. While doing good deeds does not automatically get us into eternal life, it is our sincere motivation that comes from a desire to show God's love to others that truly matters. We cannot earn our way to eternity. Salvation is a gift from God, who judges the motives and intentions of the heart.

We are co–laborers with Christ. No man is an island; we are all interdependent on one another on a global scale and on an individual level. We cannot do life without others. Throughout the pandemic, we experienced isolation on a global scale. Many churches opened food drives and gave food to the hungry. This is an example of what it means to be the hands and feet of Jesus. People don't care how much we know until they know how much we care. One never has to look very far to find others who are in need. There is always someone who needs help in some way. We are the hands and feet of Jesus. He calls each one to be the one that He can use to bless someone else.

### III. THE REWARD OF THE GOAT (MATTHEW 25:41–46)

The disciples did not fully understand Jesus when He said that those who fed the hungry, gave water to the thirsty, took the stranger in, clothed the naked, visited the sick and those in prison, were essentially doing it unto the Lord. Although they were considered righteous, they did not see the connection between their love for God and their service to humanity. This is an important point that the disciples missed. Those who do not love the Lord don't do kind deeds out of pure motives of love. They may not be compassionate or merciful to others. God sees the true motives and intentions of the heart. Good deeds done for the wrong motives will not be rewarded by God. Those who do not love the Lord cannot fully be committed to living life according to His principles. Ultimately, they will be lost if they do not repent. The unrighteous (those who refuse to repent) will not inherit eternal life. Heaven is for those who trust and love God and sincerely want to serve Him with sincere motives to please Him.

## THE LESSON APPLIED

What can we do to demonstrate lovingkindness and compassion to those in need? Jesus modeled the behaviors that we should embody as His followers. We are to visit those in prison, feed the hungry, clothe the naked, care for the sick, and be hospitable to strangers. Whatever we do to show compassion to others is showing compassion to Jesus. There are many people who need help in our world today, among them are refugees. Oftentimes refugees flee their countries with very little, if anything. The political situation in their countries threaten their lives. In times of war, and political instability, their countries may be so damaged, it is not possible for them to return to their homes. At other times, they face economic and political instability that results in loss of food supplies, and safe housing. The infrastructure of their country make it inhabitable. Some refugees are targeted by their government for their faith in Jesus, or for supporting ideologies that are viewed as a threat to their government.

There are many opportunities to apply Jesus' model to our daily lives. Many people in the United States face food insecurity, lack healthcare, and assistance. The 2024 poverty level in the United States is $15,060 for an individual, and $31,200 for a family of four. The consumer price inflation rate has increased 19.6 percent between January 2020 and January 2024 with the highest increase in housing costs. The rising costs of living in today's economy has left many homeless, and experiencing food insecurity. We can see in Acts 2:42–47, that the Early Church ministered to those in need. Today, the Church is still called to minister to the needs of others, whether they are physical, spiritual, or emotional needs.

It is striking that the "sheep" did not see their actions as relating to Jesus personally (Matthew 25:37–39); it seems that their generosity was simply part of how they lived life–a structure or an attitude of the heart that they cultivated that overflowed into charity.

In collectivist cultures, people prioritize the needs of the group or society over their individual needs. Individualistic cultures prioritize the needs of the individual over the needs of the group. They feel responsible for themselves and their individual family, but not the larger society. Jesus' mandate to love our neighbor as we love ourselves embraces a collectivist perspective. Jesus modeled how to care for others throughout His life on earth. Among many things that He did were such things as healing the sick and feeding the hungry. Most importantly, He died for all humankind. He paid the penalty for the sins of all so that we may have eternal life.

We are called to be kind and generous to others. Generosity is merely sacrificing part of yourself—your time, resources, energy, even emotion—on behalf of someone else's need. In 1 John 3:16–18, we learn that real generosity flows out of gratitude for what we have been given and out of following

God's generous example. Generosity is also an act of trusting in God for our resources. When we truly believe that God will supply what we need generously; we can give freely to others (Proverbs 11:24–25; Luke 6:37–38; 2 Corinthians 8:12–15). When we are generous to others, the Lord is generous to us as well!

## Let's Talk About It
**Am I a sheep or am I a goat?**

One way to tell whether we are truly loving the Lord is to look at how we spend our time and our money and how we treat others. Do we spend more time pleasing ourselves, pleasing others, or pleasing God? While salvation is a gift and cannot be earned through works, when we truly love the Lord, our actions will align with His perfect will and we will model His example of what it means to love others.

How we treat others reflects what we think about Jesus and His mandate to demonstrate compassion and mercy to others regardless of a person's socio– economic status; educational attainment or not attained; physical abilities or lack thereof; race; gender identification; political affiliation; marital status; mental health status; etc. We are to love everyone and serve anyone that we can serve. We are to freely give to others without expecting anything in return. When we love others, we are reflecting our love for Jesus and glorifying Him.

There is an eternal reward (eternal life) for loving the Lord and demonstrating our love for others. This week, ask God to give you opportunities to demonstrate His love to others. Even in the most unexpected of places, there can be a chance to plant a seed for Christ. Our job is to plant these seeds and allow the Holy Spirit to water them after we've left. You never know the impact you might have on someone else's life, and you wouldn't want to miss the opportunity to share the Gospel with someone who might otherwise not hear it! Seize every chance God gives you.

## Get Social
Share your views and tag us @rhboydco. Use #rhboydco.

@rhboydco

## Home Daily Devotional Readings
### February 24–March 2, 2025

| Monday | Tuesday | Wednesday | Thursday | Friday | Saturday | Sunday |
|---|---|---|---|---|---|---|
| We Are Priests | Give Thanks to God's Holy Name | Be Holy | Love Your Neighbor as Yourself | Priests of God and Christ | Do Justice, Love Kindness, Walk Humbly | Treasured Possession |
| Revelation 1:3–8 | Psalm 106:36–48 | Leviticus 19:1–10 | Leviticus 19:11–18 | Revelation 20:1–6 | Micah 6:1–8 | Exodus 19:1–14 |

# Third Quarter

*March*

*April*

*May*

LESSON I — MARCH 2, 2025

# A Kingdom of Priests, A Holy Nation

**Adult Topic:**
Bound by Love

**Background Scripture:** Exodus 19
**Lesson Passage:** Exodus 19:1–14

## Exodus 19:1–14

### KJV

IN the third month, when the children of Israel were gone forth out of the land of Egypt, the same day came they into the wilderness of Sinai.
2 For they were departed from Rephidim, and were come to the desert of Sinai, and had pitched in the wilderness; and there Israel camped before the mount.
3 And Moses went up unto God, and the Lord called unto him out of the mountain, saying, Thus shalt thou say to the house of Jacob, and tell the children of Israel;
4 Ye have seen what I did unto the Egyptians, and how I bare you on eagles' wings, and brought you unto myself.
5 Now therefore, if ye will obey my voice indeed, and keep my covenant, then ye shall be a peculiar treasure unto me above all people: for all the earth is mine:
6 And ye shall be unto me a kingdom of priests, and an holy nation. These are the words which thou shalt speak unto the children of Israel.
7 And Moses came and called for the elders of the people, and laid before their faces all these words which the Lord commanded him.
8 And all the people answered together, and said, All that the Lord hath spoken we will do. And Moses returned the words of the people unto the Lord.
9 And the Lord said unto Moses, Lo, I come unto thee in a thick cloud, that the people may hear when I speak with thee, and believe thee for ever. And Moses told the words of the people unto the Lord.

### NRSVueue

ON the third new moon after the Israelites had gone out of the land of Egypt, on that very day, they came into the wilderness of Sinai.
2 They journeyed from Rephidim, entered the wilderness of Sinai, and camped in the wilderness; Israel camped there in front of the mountain.
3 Then Moses went up to God; the Lord called to him from the mountain, "Thus you shall say to the house of Jacob and tell the Israelites:
4 'You have seen what I did to the Egyptians and how I bore you on eagles' wings and brought you to myself.
5 Now, therefore, if you obey my voice and keep my covenant, you shall be my treasured possession out of all the peoples. Indeed, the whole earth is mine,
6 but you shall be for me a priestly kingdom and a holy nation.' These are the words that you shall speak to the Israelites."
7 So Moses went, summoned the elders of the people, and set before them all these words that the Lord had commanded him.
8 The people all answered as one, "Everything that the Lord has spoken we will do." Moses reported the words of the people to the Lord.

9 Then the Lord said to Moses, "I am going to come to you in a dense cloud, in order that the people may hear when I speak with you and so trust you ever after." When Moses had told the words of the people to the Lord,

**MAIN THOUGHT:** "Indeed, the whole earth is mine, but you shall be for me a priestly kingdom and a holy nation." (Exodus 19:5-6, NRSVue)

## Exodus 19:1–14

### KJV

10 And the Lord said unto Moses, Go unto the people, and sanctify them to day and to morrow, and let them wash their clothes,

11 And be ready against the third day: for the third day the Lord will come down in the sight of all the people upon mount Sinai.

12 And thou shalt set bounds unto the people round about, saying, Take heed to yourselves, that ye go not up into the mount, or touch the border of it: whosoever toucheth the mount shall be surely put to death:

13 There shall not an hand touch it, but he shall surely be stoned, or shot through; whether it be beast or man, it shall not live: when the trumpet soundeth long, they shall come up to the mount.

14 And Moses went down from the mount unto the people, and sanctified the people; and they washed their clothes.

### NRSVueue

10 the Lord said to Moses, "Go to the people and consecrate them today and tomorrow. Have them wash their clothes

11 and prepare for the third day, because on the third day the Lord will come down upon Mount Sinai in the sight of all the people.

12 You shall set limits for the people all around, saying, 'Be careful not to go up the mountain or to touch the edge of it. Any who touch the mountain shall be put to death.

13 No hand shall touch them, but they shall be stoned or shot with arrows; whether animal or human being, they shall not live.' When the trumpet sounds a long blast, they may go up on the mountain."

14 So Moses went down from the mountain to the people. He consecrated the people, and they washed their clothes.

## LESSON SETTING
**Time:** Circa 1462 BCE
**Place:** Mount Sinai or Horeb

## LESSON OUTLINE
I. **Moses Receives God's Message on Sinai** (Exodus 19:1–6)
II. **Ratification of the Covenant** (Exodus 19:7–11)
III. **The Importance of Consecration** (Exodus 19:12–14)

## UNIFYING PRINCIPLE

People know that relationships come with responsibilities. How can we best honor our relationships? Yahweh calls the people a "treasured possession," a kingdom of priests, and a holy nation.

## INTRODUCTION

While attending his father–in–law's flock, the glow of the mountain attracted Moses, who ascended the mountain called Sinai or Horeb (the mountain of God). It was on this peak that Moses encountered the theophany of Yahweh in the form of a burning bush. It is during this encounter that Moses was given his orders to return to Egypt on the mission of liberating Israel from Egyptian captivity. Ironically, instead of escaping into the land of Canaan proper, Moses would lead Israel to the base of this Holy Mountain to receive God's commandments and laws. Moses was familiar with this territory and believed that Israel would be safe in the land. Now that Israel had arrived, they must be placed in a spiritual position to receive Yahweh and His new set of instructions, which are to guide Israel as a nation.

# EXPOSITION

## I. MOSES RECEIVES GOD'S MESSAGE ON SINAI (EXODUS 19:1–6)

In the third month after the sons of Israel had gone out of the land of Egypt, on that very day, they came into the wilderness of Sinai and Israel camped in front of the mountain. There is a valid reason why Moses recorded the site of the encampment in the beginning of this chapter and in this missive. In the three months since leaving Egypt, Moses and Israel faced several challenges. First, there existed a need for food and water. Second, as they approached Rephidim, there was an ambush by the Amalekites, who attacked the rear of an Israelite column. Yet, Yahweh rescued Israel from that dilemma. Third, the overriding fear that the Egyptians would return to attack Israel in their quest to return these once-oppressed people back into slavery.

After Israel reached the base of the mountain, where God would mold the families of Jacob into the Nation of Israel, Moses went up to be with God. At this point, God gave Moses a message for the "House of Jacob" and the "Sons of Israel." This address to the "House of Jacob" is not confusing. Recall, the House of Jacob consisted of the "Sons of Jacob," (Israel's sons) who would settle in Canaan as the "Twelve Tribes," according to the land granted geographically by the Lord. Joseph, Jacob's penultimate son, was sold into Egyptian slavery and yet, Yahweh converted this heinous act into the saving of both Egypt and Israel, as the latter came to settle in Egypt, primarily around the region of Goshen. Joseph had insisted that the entire family, including his elderly father, relocate to Egypt where, as one of the governors, Joseph could ensure their care. God made the same promises concerning the land and the nation to Abraham, Isaac, and Jacob, but it is by Jacob's God–given name, Israel, that the nation is known. Therefore, the message to the "Sons of Israel" and the "Sons of Jacob" are one and the same.

Verse 5 describes the components of the covenant, which are constructed as a series of "if–then" agreements. If the people would do this (i.e., follow the commandments of Yahweh), then Yahweh will bless and protect the people (Israel). The nation would be exalted to a position of being God's chosen people. However, this position was not to be seen as one of arrogance or superiority, but to be God's chosen is to be in a position of service. Moreover, it is through the attributes and examples of God's chosen that the world might be led to Yahweh and thus, be saved. In the Jewish Bible,

Yahweh declares that Israel shall be His treasured possession among all the peoples. Therefore, if Israel accepts His covenant, Yahweh will cherish Israel because of His personal relationship with them. Many Bible scholars are familiar with David's declaration of "the earth is the Lord's and the fullness thereof…," which is found in Psalm 24:1. Here, David acknowledges that the entire world belongs to God and everything in it. However, when the Egyptian Pharaoh realized he was powerless against the plagues sent by God, he begged Moses to intervene and ask Yahweh to call off the afflictions, whereas Moses declared that "the earth is the Lord's" (Exodus 9:29). Therefore,

Yahweh's declaration in verse 5 solidifies and reinforces His position in the mindset and understanding of the people.

Continuing, the Lord promises that Israel will be to Him a kingdom of priests and a holy nation that will be a showcase for the world. This designation must not be thought of as only for the Levites, who were given duties to serve as priests to all of the tribes; it would apply to all of the people who were to live holy lives and raise their families in the same manner of life before God. The covenant was an agreement or contract between the Hebrews and Yahweh. Covenants serve a specific purpose for the time that they are issued. Notice the terms set forth in the covenants between Abraham and God, and Noah and God, as well as the current bond linking Moses and God. Moses, like John the Baptist, serves as leader of the movement but also, as God's messenger and spokesman. Ultimately, this is an agreement between the people and God, as the people must not only accept the covenant but the union (i.e., the people and not its leaders) must ratify the contract.

## II. Ratification of the Covenant (Exodus 19:7–11)

Now, it is time to actually ratify the covenant, which is where the people agreed to honor its guidelines, procedures, and directions. Moreover, aside from the laws of the covenant, the people must commit their allegiance to Yahweh by moving beyond the "Letter of the Law" to the "Spirit of the Law." In a nod to His later declarations, Jesus will exclaim that "true worshipers will worship the Father in spirit and truth; for such people the Father seeks to be His worshipers" (John 4:23). As Moses presented the contents of the covenant to the people, it seems that there was a general consensus, and the people agreed to accept (ratify) the covenant with Yahweh. By agreeing to the covenant, Israel was now connected to the true and authentic worship of the Lord. Verse 8 records that "all the people answered together and said, 'All that the Lord has spoken we will do!'" Here, we witness the promise that was made to Yahweh, which also echoes the later declarations of Joshua when he clearly states his commitment, saying, "As for me and my house, we will serve the Lord" (Joshua 24:15). Moreover, the people would declare their allegiance to Yahweh by proclaiming, "Far be it from us that we should forsake the Lord to serve other gods" (Joshua 24:16). Upon hearing their acceptance of the covenant, Moses brought back the words of the people to the Lord. Ratification of the covenant was important because history has shown that unfortunately, throughout Israelite history, the people had failed to keep the contents of the covenant after ratification. The initial spirit of the people may be willing; however, their flesh will consistently remain weak.

The Lord then said to Moses, "I will appear in a thick cloud so that the people will hear Me when I speak to You." This must not be confused with a concept of limiting God, as if He could not speak to Moses and the people from heaven or another place. Being all–powerful, God could have chosen another method to be heard; however, the key here is that Yahweh chooses not to reveal Himself in the same manner of theophany (e.g., a burning bush) that He appeared to Moses. Recall that in their escape from the Egyptians, Israel was guided by a pillar of cloud in the daytime, which became a pillar of fire at night, as the Israelites apparently traveled some distance every day. Besides guiding them, the cloud, symbolizing God's presence, assured them of His goodness and faithfulness. Therefore, the thick cloud that He had chosen to appear in was an extension of the method that Yahweh had utilized to lead the Exodus. God's voice should not be considered the only voice that the people would automatically recognize if they heard it again because He speaks in different types of sounds and structures. One example is the boom of thunder in His voice, (Job 37:2) as compared to the quiet of a still small voice (1 Kings 19:12). In that Yahweh spoke to Moses, it was to be that the people would believe in the authority and position of Moses as God's servant and messenger forever, or as long as God retained Moses in his position. Moreover, from another perspective, this confidence–giving comment cements Moses' position in Israelite history as her greatest prophet.

Moses was then commanded to consecrate the people in preparation for God's appearance. The Hebrew term *quadash* is used here, translated as to sanctify, hallow, and dedicate themselves in a manner of being set apart for the service of God, or in this case, for being in the presence of God. What is noticeable here is that the command is for Moses to consecrate the people. The ritual would usually begin with a series of prayers and the washing of the people's garments (clothes) that would be dirty from their journey; nonetheless, they were to appear before the Lord with clean garments. To wash their garments was to clean their appearance; however, spiritual consecration had to occur inwardly in order to fully appreciate the seriousness of God's appearance, in a thick cloud, which was to occur on the "third day" following Moses' instructions to the people.

## III. THE IMPORTANCE OF CONSECRATION (EXODUS 19:12–14)

Continuing, Yahweh has Moses set boundaries and parameters for the people in gathering at the base of the mountain. Remember, this is the holy mountain of God, and Moses had been instructed to "remove [his] sandals," because it was holy ground. That holiness was not included the entire expanse of Mount Sinai. The warning was given not to go up into the mountain, nor to touch the base of its borders. Any person or their animals who disregarded this warning would be "put to death."

This command may seem harsh; however, it is grounded in the obedience and respect that either the people would have for Yahweh, or would decide that they could ignore and go their own way. Additionally, the people would wait until they heard the blast of the ram's horn (shofar), which would signal the clearance for them to come up to the mountain. Notice that the people were not to ascend the mountain, but they could approach the slope as long as they honored the restrictions and boundaries set by the Lord. However, the signal of the ram's horn could also mean that God was leaving Sinai, and it was safe for the people to approach.

Chapter 19 of Exodus serves as preparation for Yahweh's coming to the mountain where Moses will receive the Ten

Commandments and eventually, the Law. Israel had been in Egyptian slavery for approximately 450 years. As a nation, Israel had absorbed and aligned with many of the laws and practices of Egypt, and therefore, needed a "restart" before becoming the holy nation of the Lord. In order to receive the commandments and the law, Israel had to be prepared for the expectations of the Lord. Although many readers may focus on the washing of their garments, it is the importance of the cleansing of their minds, hearts, and spirit that are in desperate need of cleansing. Moreover, the acceptance of the covenant is based on Israel's dedication to holiness.

## THE LESSON APPLIED

Committed believers proudly express their identities as members of a "kingdom of priests" and a "holy nation." Although contemporary Christians are not individually labeled as priests, we must also embrace the provisions of this concept. We are to dedicate our families and raise our children in the admonition of the Lord.

Although we may attend worship services at our local churches on a regular basis, as a "kingdom of priests," we must be intentional in that worship, in practice as well as in theory, also must occur in the home. If Christian families would return to this concept, where the head of the house serves as priest of the house, our Christian community would better resemble God's holy nation.

## LET'S TALK ABOUT IT

**What is the most important aspect of worship?**

In some church circles, there remains a debate about wearing casual attire to worship services. Some perceive the practice as disrespectful. This deliberation is sometimes generationally based—the elders who attend church are dressed in suits while the younger generation is comfortable in polo shirts and slacks. Despite the debate, the most important aspect of worship will not be found in clothing or dress, but rather, in whether there is a casual approach to worshiping Jesus. Do we give Him our best, or do we simply go through the motions because we have shown up physically but not spiritually?

### GET SOCIAL
Share your views and tag us @rhboydco and use #rhboydco.

@rhboydco

## HOME DAILY DEVOTIONAL READINGS
### APRIL 28–MARCH 9, 2025

| MONDAY | TUESDAY | WEDNESDAY | THURSDAY | FRIDAY | SATURDAY | SUNDAY |
|---|---|---|---|---|---|---|
| God Is Our Sanctuary | Desire for God's Presence | God's Glory Fills the Temple | Who May Draw Near? | The Temple of Christ's Body | Worship God in Spirit and Truth | Prepare a Sacred Space |
| Ezekiel 14:25 | Psalm 26 | Ezekiel 43:1–12 | Ezekiel 44:15–27 | John 2:12–22 | John 4:13–26 | Exodus 25:1-9; 26:1, 31–37 |

LESSON II												MARCH 9, 2025

# PITCHING A TENT

**ADULT TOPIC:** A SPACE FOR GOD

**BACKGROUND SCRIPTURE:** EXODUS 25–27
**LESSON PASSAGE:** EXODUS 25:1–9; 26:1, 31–37

## EXODUS 25:1–9; 26:1, 31–37

### KJV

AND the Lord spake unto Moses, saying,
2 Speak unto the children of Israel, that they bring me an offering: of every man that giveth it willingly with his heart ye shall take my offering.
3 And this is the offering which ye shall take of them; gold, and silver, and brass,
4 And blue, and purple, and scarlet, and fine linen, and goats' hair,
5 And rams' skins dyed red, and badgers' skins, and shittim wood,
6 Oil for the light, spices for anointing oil, and for sweet incense,
7 Onyx stones, and stones to be set in the ephod, and in the breastplate.
8 And let them make me a sanctuary; that I may dwell among them.
9 According to all that I shew thee, after the pattern of the tabernacle, and the pattern of all the instruments thereof, even so shall ye make it.

• • • 26:1 • • •

1 Moreover thou shalt make the tabernacle with ten curtains of fine twined linen, and blue, and purple, and scarlet: with cherubims of cunning work shalt thou make them.

• • • 26:31-37 • • •

31 And thou shalt make a vail of blue, and purple, and scarlet, and fine twined linen of cunning work: with cherubims shall it be made:

32 And thou shalt hang it upon four pillars of shittim wood overlaid with gold: their hooks shall be of gold, upon the four sockets of silver.

### NRSVue

THE Lord said to Moses,
2 "Tell the Israelites to take for me an offering; from all whose hearts prompt them to give you shall receive the offering for me.
3 This is the offering that you shall receive from them: gold, silver, and bronze,
4 blue, purple, and crimson yarns and fine linen, goats' hair,
5 tanned rams' skins, fine leather, acacia wood,
6 oil for the lamps, spices for the anointing oil and for the fragrant incense,
7 onyx stones and gems to be set in the ephod and for the breastpiece.
8 And they shall make me a sanctuary so that I may dwell among them.
9 In accordance with all that I show you concerning the pattern of the tabernacle and of all its furniture, so you shall make it.

• • • 26:1 • • •

1 "The tabernacle itself you shall make with ten curtains of fine twisted linen and blue, purple, and crimson yarns; you shall make them with cherubim skillfully worked into them.

• • • 26:31-37 • • •

31 "You shall make a curtain of blue, purple, and crimson yarns and of fine twisted linen; it shall be made with cherubim skillfully worked into it.

32 You shall hang it on four pillars of acacia overlaid with gold, which have hooks of gold and rest on four bases of silver.

**MAIN THOUGHT:** And they shall make me a sanctuary, so that I may dwell among them. (Exodus 25:8, NRSVue)

## Exodus 25:1–9; 26:1, 31–37

### KJV

33 And thou shalt hang up the vail under the taches, that thou mayest bring in thither within the vail the ark of the testimony: and the vail shall divide unto you between the holy place and the most holy.
34 And thou shalt put the mercy seat upon the ark of the testimony in the most holy place.
35 And thou shalt set the table without the vail, and the candlestick over against the table on the side of the tabernacle toward the south: and thou shalt put the table on the north side.
36 And thou shalt make an hanging for the door of the tent, of blue, and purple, and scarlet, and fine twined linen, wrought with needlework.
37 And thou shalt make for the hanging five pillars of shittim wood, and overlay them with gold, and their hooks shall be of gold: and thou shalt cast five sockets of brass for them.

### NRSVueue

33 You shall hang the curtain under the clasps and bring the ark of the covenant in there, within the curtain, and the curtain shall separate for you the holy place from the most holy place.
34 You shall put the cover on the ark of the covenant in the most holy place.
35 You shall set the table outside the curtain and the lampstand on the south side of the tabernacle opposite the table, and you shall put the table on the north side.
36 "You shall make a screen for the entrance of the tent, of blue, purple, and crimson yarns and of fine twisted linen, embroidered with needlework.
37 You shall make for the screen five pillars of acacia and overlay them with gold; their hooks shall be of gold, and you shall cast five bases of bronze for them.

## LESSON SETTING
**Time:** Circa 1462 BCE
**Place:** Mount Sinai or Horeb

## LESSON OUTLINE
I. Offerings for the Tabernacle (Exodus 25:1–8)
II. The Design of the Tabernacle (Exodus 25:9; 26:1, 31–37)

## UNIFYING PRINCIPLE

People treasure mountaintop experiences. How can we keep the power of such experiences fresh? Yahweh gives instructions for building a holy tent, a mobile Mount Sinai, that conveys Yahweh's intention to dwell with the covenant people.

## INTRODUCTION

The lesson is primarily about some of the instructions Moses was given in the construction of the Tabernacle. This should have been a joyous occasion, but there exists a specter of treachery, disappointment, rebellion, and unfaithfulness looming in the background. Initially, there was excitement and enthusiasm before Moses returned to the heights of the mountain. Remember, Moses had come down from the mountain to the people, where they were consecrated as they washed their garments (Exodus 19:14). Then, the Lord came down to Mount Sinai, to the top of the mountain; and the Lord called Moses to the top of the mountain, and Moses went [back] up (Exodus 19:20) to receive further instructions from Yahweh.

## EXPOSITION

### I. OFFERINGS FOR THE TABERNACLE (EXODUS 25:1–8)

The Lord spoke to Moses and issued a series of commands that the people were to follow in the construction of the Tabernacle. First, they were to lift a contribution for the supplies that would be used in the work. The gifts were to come from the hearts of men who wished to be a part of this monumental task. The Hebrew term used here is *nadab*, which means to give freely from the heart, as these men will willingly offer their goods to Moses for the project. Moses begins his litany by encouraging Israel to give or to provide for the project; he does not want anyone who is unwilling to be a part of this effort. From those who are willing, Moses requests precious metals, such as gold, silver, and bronze, and fine linens, oils, incense, precious stones, and other materials that will be needed to construct the Tabernacle.

Yahweh is specific about the materials that are requested. Verses three through seven provide such a list. That Yahweh requested these items should not be a surprise because Israelite craftsmen were developed during their Egyptian sojourn, and the idea that they were in bondage does not reduce the entire nation to a group of unskilled laborers who were relegated to working in the fields and the tar pits. Moreover, these craftsmen were quite skilled and creative; however, unfortunately, as we will see later, their work will be misused and misplaced. Notice that besides the linens that were used, additional materials included animal skins or hides, which were dyed red after the tanning process. An interesting animal listed in the inventory of verse five is the porpoise, as the use of the porpoise seems overly exotic or remote. The Hebrew term used is tachash, which indicates the skin of a porpoise or dugong (sea cow) found in the Red Sea. These animals were available to Moses and his workmen and are found all around the coast. These animal skins were used because only the best of materials were rendered unto God in the construction of the Tabernacle. The skins were an important aspect in the construction. The wooden framework of the Tabernacle to be afterward described had three coverings – one, the immediate covering of the Tabernacle or "dwelling;" a second, the "tent" covering of goats' hair; and a third, a protective covering of rams' and porpoise skins, cast over the whole.

Everything that was used in the construction of the Tabernacle was special yet practical, as well as a sign that the people were giving God their best. The Israelites chose to use acacia wood (often used in Egyptian construction) because it was the only kind of wood available in the Sinai desert. It also had a high tolerance for heat. This type of wood was heavier and harder than woods such as oak; it is durable and not easily damaged by insects. Acacia is an excellent material that could also be used in other types of woodworking, such as cabinets and storage bins. Other items to be brought included olive oil, spices, and precious stones.

God commanded that Israel build a "sanctuary for Me" (Him) in that He would live among the people. The portable sanctuary was said to have been built at Mt. Sinai in the time of Moses and used until Solomon built the First Temple. However, verse 8 is clear that this area would be constructed for Him alone. Yahweh is specific in that the construction of the sanctuary, which should be distinguished from the Tabernacle proper. The Tabernacle was a gathering place for all of the people to worship God. It had specific places inside and outside of the tent that allowed the people to gather for sacrifice, for hearing the covenant word, for worship and prayer, and for the celebration of the major feasts. The Hebrew term for Tabernacle is *mishkan*, which is translated as "dwelling" [place] and is also known by other names, such as "tent of meeting" and sanctuary, which is the translation of two Hebrew words, *kodesh* and *mikdosh*, both of which are derived from the verb "to be clean" and/or "to be holy." Sanctuary refers to the place where God appeared and/or dwelt as indicated by the presence of the ark. God's Word was kept there and issued forth from it.

It must be emphatically stressed that God's people were to have one central sanctuary (Deuteronomy 12:4–7; 16:5–8). More than one sanctuary was permitted so they could, without long–distance traveling, gather for eating and worship (12:15–25); however, the one and the same God was to be worshiped at these various places. But the Israelites also made use of pagan sanctuaries, which was considered an abomination. In this case, the sanctuary is the inner sanctum of the Tabernacle, and it is constructed and consecrated for Yahweh. However, the wording of this command gave rise that God actually lived in what would be known as the "Holy of Holies." The inner part of the area was separated by a veil that housed the Ark of the Covenant and the Mercy Seat, which covered the Ark. Although God's presence is ubiquitously all–over and everywhere, the mistake the people made was boxing in Yahweh and limiting God to the Holy of Holies.

## II. THE DESIGN OF THE TABERNACLE (EXODUS 25:9; 26:1, 31–37)

The architecture, floor plan, and plan for its furnishings must be followed according to the design of Yahweh, the Master Builder. Nothing is to be left to chance, and each of the accouterments has a specific purpose in the form articles of worship. As an example, there were to be ten linen curtains that would follow a specific weaving design, along with the colors of blue, purple, and scarlet. The curtains were to be embroidered by cherubim, mythological winged creatures that also adorned the Mercy Seat. Moreover, Yahweh provides instructions for the veil and screen, following the same specific weaving design, along with the colors of blue and purple. As with the curtains, the veil is to be adorned by cherubim. The screen is to be of blue, purple, and scarlet (but possibly excluded the cherubim), and the outer curtain is supported by five posts and not four, as with the inner curtain. The veil will be hung on four pillars of acacia wood, overlaid with gold, with golden hooks on four sockets or bases of silver. The curtain divided the Tabernacle into two sections, which partitioned off the holy place and the Holy of Holies.

Verse 34 places God's emphasis on the Mercy Seat and the Ark of the Covenant (or testimony) in its reserved section of the Tabernacle. Recall the aforementioned description and purpose of the Mercy Seat and the Ark. Yahweh directs the position of the table and the lampstand. The table was a piece of furniture in the Tabernacle, and later, the Temple, upon which was the Bread of the Presence (Ex 25:23–30), which means bread that has been set before the Lord's face. The term "showbread" (KJV, shewbread) refers to the arrangement of the bread in rows on the table. The Bread of the Presence consisted of 12 very large loaves, each made of 1/5 ephah of fine flour, and (although outside the Holy of Holies) they were considered to be in the presence of God. As an offering placed before the presence of God, the loaves were considered holy and could be eaten only by priests. The bread was arranged in two rows, the one leaning against the other, and placed on the table. Arranged in that way, the bread became an "offering of food" to the Lord, and the loaves were changed weekly on the sabbath day.

The Tabernacle housed an ornate golden lampstand, or menorah, which was a seven–branched golden lampstand, which (like the cherubim and the Mercy Seat) was made of pure gold. Six golden branches, three on either side, extended from a central shaft, and the whole lampstand was ornamented with almond flowers. From the biblical evidence, it is not clear whether the lampstand gave continuous illumination or night light only. However, Leviticus 24:4 strongly supports the former. In Scripture, the golden lampstand symbolizes the continuing witness of the covenant community.

As a concluding piece, the priests were to be identified by their official garments. Verse 7 notes that the rulers who brought the onyx and stones for setting the ephod and breastplate are best identified as leaders, probably of their respective tribes. The Hebrew term *nasiy'* can also mean captain or chief. In this case, these men, i.e., tribal chiefs, are in a position to collect these precious stones either from their collection or from those of their tribes. The ephod was a beautiful, two–piece, sleeveless garment, held to the body by a skillfully woven band (Exodus 28:8) and joined at the shoulders by straps. On the straps were placed two onyx stones (possibly emeralds), with the names of six tribes on each stone. The breastplate of judgment was a square piece of beautiful material, folded in half, that opens at the top like a pouch and is placed over the front of the ephod. It was adorned with 12 precious stones (in four rows), on which were engraved the names of the 12 tribes.

Included but not forgotten in the inventory were the precious oils, scents, and incenses. Obviously, oil was needed for fuel to burn in the lamps, but also needed was holy oil for anointing. Exodus 25:6 instructs that these oils remain separate and distinct: "oil for lightening, spices for the anointing oil and for the fragrant incense." The oil for the light, literally "oil for the luminary," was olive oil, to be used in the lamps for the lampstand (25:37). Olive oil was also used in the recipe of sweet–smelling spices to be mixed with incense for the anointing oil for ordaining the priests (30:24). Incense was also needed to keep the aroma of the Tabernacle from becoming offensive; remember, the smell of the animals, used for both work and sacrifice, was overpowering! The people wanted to present a sweet smell to the nostrils of the Lord.

Yahweh has provided the people with His plan for the construction of the Tabernacle, and the record indicates that the people freely gave of their materials and skills to complete the project. By all accounts, it seems that there existed a joyful atmosphere; however, the elation quickly diminished as this segment of Moses' meeting God and being a messenger to the people does not end well. During the time Moses was on the mountain, the people rebelled, somehow believing that Moses had perished; and they resorted to idol worship by constructing a golden calf or bull. Aaron is usually depicted as the culprit in its construction; however, he would have had the assistance of the same skilled workers who were constructing the Tabernacle.

## The Lesson Applied

It is a sad and troublesome state of affairs into which Israel has fallen. Remember, it was in not too long passing that the people complained about the lack of food and water during their escape from Egypt; yet, how could they forget that it was Yahweh, their God, that had supplied their needs? Unfortunately, even in church circles, great projects and ideas can suffer from the infusion of evil minds and desires, quickly deteriorating, becoming acidic, and preventing their implementation. The lesson here is that believers must continually place our faith and trust in the Lord, not leaning unto our own understanding while trying to "read" His mind and thoughts.

## Let's Talk About It

Christian adults must appreciate how the holiness of God is honored through the design of worship spaces. Churches buildings are constructed differently, and their unique designs are usually based on the particular needs of each congregation and their approach to worship. In many cases, church buildings may have been purchased by new or developing congregations, and the existing design might hinder their needs. A congregation needing a large choir platform may have purchased a church that was constructed with a different type of choir loft. Nonetheless, what must not be lost is that while appreciating and respecting the edifice, the building is not the church. We, the people, are the church of Jesus Christ.

## Get Social

Share your views and tag us @rhboydco and use #rhboydco.

@rhboydco

## Home Daily Devotional Readings
### March 9–16, 2025

| Monday | Tuesday | Wednesday | Thursday | Friday | Saturday | Sunday |
|---|---|---|---|---|---|---|
| A Compassionate High Priest | A Chosen High Priest | A Cleansed High Priest | A Chaste Priest | A Commendable High Priest | A Continuous High Priest | A Consecrated High Priest |
| Hebrews 5 | Leviticus 8:1–13 | Leviticus 8:14–23 | Psalm 133 | Hebrews 7:1–14 | Hebrews 7:15–30 | Exodus 29:1–9, 35–37 |

LESSON III                                                           MARCH 16, 2025

# THE ORDINATION OF PRIESTS

**ADULT TOPIC:**
PREPARATION FOR SERVICE

**BACKGROUND SCRIPTURE:** EXODUS 29:1–37; LEVITICUS 8:1–36
**LESSON PASSAGE:** EXODUS 29:1–9, 35–37

## EXODUS 29:1–9, 35–37

### KJV

AND this is the thing that thou shalt do unto them to hallow them, to minister unto me in the priest's office: Take one young bullock, and two rams without blemish,

2 And unleavened bread, and cakes unleavened tempered with oil, and wafers unleavened anointed with oil: of wheaten flour shalt thou make them.

3 And thou shalt put them into one basket, and bring them in the basket, with the bullock and the two rams.

4 And Aaron and his sons thou shalt bring unto the door of the tabernacle of the congregation, and shalt wash them with water.

5 And thou shalt take the garments, and put upon Aaron the coat, and the robe of the ephod, and the ephod, and the breastplate, and gird him with the curious girdle of the ephod:

6 And thou shalt put the mitre upon his head, and put the holy crown upon the mitre.

7 Then shalt thou take the anointing oil, and pour it upon his head, and anoint him.

8 And thou shalt bring his sons, and put coats upon them.

9 And thou shalt gird them with girdles, Aaron and his sons, and put the bonnets on them: and the priest's office shall be theirs for a perpetual statute: and thou shalt consecrate Aaron and his sons.

• • • • • •

35 And thus shalt thou do unto Aaron, and to his sons, according to all things which I have commanded thee: seven days shalt thou consecrate them.

### NRSVueue

"NOW this is what you shall do to them to consecrate them to serve me as priests. Take one young bull and two rams without blemish,

2 and unleavened bread, unleavened cakes mixed with oil, and unleavened wafers spread with oil. You shall make them of choice wheat flour.

3 You shall put them in one basket and bring them in the basket and bring the bull and the two rams.

4 You shall bring Aaron and his sons to the entrance of the tent of meeting and wash them with water.

5 Then you shall take the vestments and put on Aaron the tunic and the robe of the ephod and the ephod and the breastpiece and gird him with the decorated band of the ephod,

6 and you shall set the turban on his head and put the holy diadem on the turban.

7 You shall take the anointing oil and pour it on his head and anoint him.

8 Then you shall bring his sons and put tunics on them,

9 and you shall gird them, Aaron and his sons, with sashes and tie headdresses on them, and the priesthood shall be theirs by a perpetual ordinance. You shall then ordain Aaron and his sons.

• • • • • •

35 "Thus you shall do to Aaron and to his sons, just as I have commanded you; through seven days you shall ordain them.

**MAIN THOUGHT:** The priesthood shall be theirs by a perpetual ordinance. You shall then ordain Aaron and his sons. (Exodus 29:9, NRSVue)

## Exodus 29:1-9, 35-37

### KJV

36 And thou shalt offer every day a bullock for a sin offering for atonement: and thou shalt cleanse the altar, when thou hast made an atonement for it, and thou shalt anoint it, to sanctify it.

37 Seven days thou shalt make an atonement for the altar, and sanctify it; and it shall be an altar most holy: whatsoever toucheth the altar shall be holy.

### NRSVueue

36 Also every day you shall offer a bull as a purification offering for atonement. Also you shall offer a sin offering for the altar, when you make atonement for it, and shall anoint it, to consecrate it.

37 Seven days you shall make atonement for the altar and consecrate it, and the altar shall be most holy; whatever touches the altar shall become holy.

## LESSON SETTING
**Time:** 1462 BCE
**Place:** Region of Mount Sinai or Horeb

## LESSON OUTLINE
I. The Elements of Consecration (Exodus 29:1–3)
II. The Consecration of the Priests (Exodus 29:4–9)
III. The Holiness of the Altar (Exodus 29:35–37)

## UNIFYING PRINCIPLE

Communities set apart certain persons to carry out special duties on behalf of the group. What are some ways of marking this special status? Exodus 29 describes Yahweh's instructions to Moses for the preparation of Aaron and his sons to the holy priesthood.

## INTRODUCTION

Today's lesson describes the ordination and consecration of Aaron and his sons (and possibly, other Levites), as priests. The importance of this account is to establish the order of the ministers of the nation and designate the line of Aaron as future priests. Moreover, Yahweh cements the sacrifice system as foundational to Israelite worship. Although the Scriptures do not indicate the time of year that the events chronicled in this section of Exodus detail, they probably happened during the season when the wheat harvest occurred and the grain was readily available. Additionally, these events seem to have occurred during or near the celebration of Passover, which would have taken place on the 14th day of the first month of Abib (later called Nisan). The weather seems to be mild and favorable, as the events are to take place in an outdoor setting. It is amazing that God has set this period of ordination during Passover, just as He selected a later Passover to send His Son to the cross.

## EXPOSITION

### I. THE ELEMENTS OF CONSECRATION (EXODUS 29:1–3)

As part of the consecration of the priests—to dedicate them and make them holy, setting them apart to serve as priests, as their office dictates—Yahweh provides instructions as to what elements will be used in the sacrifice. The description for unleavened bread (Hebrew *matstsah*, from where we get our term "matzoh") refers to flat, round cakes made without any yeast-like substance to make them rise. The composition of the bread makes it soft and easy to chew. During the first Passover (see Exodus 12–13), instructions were given to prepare bread without any type of leavening agent. The use for unleavened bread was couched in the need for Israel to be ready to leave Egypt at a moment's notice. However, at this juncture, there does not seem to be a necessity, yet the unleavened bread remains part of the instructions. The use of unleavened bread became part of Jewish tradition, where the ritual remains to this day.

After the period of consecration and ordination of the priests, the bull was brought to the doorway of the Tabernacle, where Aaron and his sons blessed it and (after laying hands on it) offered it up to the Lord. The offerer's laying or pressing his hand on the head of the sacrifice symbolized his complete identification with the animal as a substitute. Here, the bull served as a sin offering for Aaron and his sons. They were to place some of the blood on the horns of the altar and the remainder at its base (v. 12). Additionally, Aaron and his sons were to repeat the process with the first ram and sprinkle the blood on the altar. The second ram, which is the ram of ordination, would be slaughtered in the same fashion; however, some of the blood was to be put on Aaron's right ear and the lobes of his sons' right ears, and on the thumbs of their right hands, and on the big toes of their right feet, with the rest to be sprinkled on the altar. Moreover, the pieces of the second ram were to be mixed with one cake of bread, one cake of bread mixed with oil, and one wafer from the basket to serve as a wave offering. In a wave offering, the breast of the animal was waved or moved back and forth, toward and away from the altar, as a symbol of presenting the offering to God and of His returning it to the priest. However, the flesh and remains of the bull were to be taken outside of the camp and burned as a sin offering (v. 14).

## II. THE CONSECRATION OF THE PRIESTS (EXODUS 29:4–9)

Continuing, Aaron and his sons were to be brought to the doorway of the Tabernacle and washed. Remember that these men were bloodied from the sacrificing of the animals. Also, the blood placed on their earlobes symbolized obedience to God, while the blood on their thumbs and toes symbolized working for God. Due to the condition of these men, they had to undergo a ritual bath that symbolized purity but was physically essential to wash the blood from their bodies. Although water was at a premium in the Middle East, the element is essential for life and survival. Recall that during the Exodus, Israel found herself in the desert, lacking for water. Yahweh provided water (and food) for the people's continued survival; yet here, there is a need for water to be used prior to the consecration and worship observances. Aaron and his sons needed water for practical purposes, to wash their bodies, and second, for ritual bathing.

Regulations for holiness and purity can be found in Leviticus 11–15, which provides instructions for clean and unclean animals (chapter 11), purification from blood flow after childbirth (chapter 12), diagnosing and cleansing from defiling skin diseases and molds (chapters 13–14), and cleansing from bodily discharges causing impurity (chapter 15). If not handled properly, such impurities could contaminate and offend the Tabernacle presence of God, causing infection to break out amongst the community of Israel (15:31). Once a year, on the Day of Atonement (chapter 16), the high priest performs ritual procedures for completely cleansing the tabernacle and community from all their impurities and sins of the past year. Cleanness before Yahweh was important because being "unclean" is equal to being defiled, and the unclean person would be observed by the entire nation, not just the priests.

Recall that the priests were to be identified by their official garments which included the onyx and stones that were set in the ephod and breastplate. Aaron was to be girded by the ephod, which was a beautiful two–piece sleeveless garment, held to the body by a skillfully woven band (Exodus 28:8) and joined at the shoulders by straps on which were placed two onyx stones with the names of six tribes on each stone. Additionally, Aaron was to wear the breastplate or breastpiece of judgment, a square piece of beautiful material, folded in half, that opens at the top like a pouch and is placed over the front of the ephod. Likewise, the breastplate was adorned with 12 precious stones (in four rows), on which were engraved the names of the 12 tribes. It is possible that Aaron's priestly garments were woven by the same workers who were responsible for the crafting of the curtains of the Tabernacle.

Continuing, Aaron was to wear a turban and the holy crown that would be affixed to what would be referred to as a cap (v. 9). Verses 6 and 7 may possibly seem to be out of sequence, as the anointing oil would have probably been poured on Aaron's head before the turban and holy crown were set on his head, unless he removed the turban to be anointed. For anointing the tabernacle and its priests, a special oil was compounded and used only for that sacred purpose. Skilled perfume makers blended the choicest spices (myrrh, cinnamon, sweet cane, and cassia) in olive oil (Exodus 30:22–25). Obviously, if the oil was poured after Aaron donned the cap, the oil would have soaked into the turban and not onto the head of Aaron. Following this command, Aaron's sons, who are also priests following in the Levitical line, were brought to the doorway following their ritual baths. Aaron's sons would be dressed in tunics, girded with brilliant sashes and also adorned with turbans. However, Aaron's sons would not have the holy crown or the ephod, which signaled and recognized Aaron as the High or Chief Priest of Israel. Aaron's sons were to be granted their status as priests in a continuous state, as they would serve Israel for the remainder of their lives. Remember, the vestments of the priest symbolized the perpetual or unending stature and length of the office. Within this context, specific priestly activities belonged to three orders—high priest, priest, and Levite. Priests were male descendants of Aaron (Numbers 3:10), and Levites were male members of the tribe of Levi. The chief functions of the priesthood were in the temple. Priests looked after the ceremonial vessels and performed the sacrifices. In doing their duties, they dressed in special symbolic vestments. They were also teachers, passing on the sacred traditions of the nation, which included such matters as medical information (Leviticus 13–15). The High Priest was the spiritual head of

Israel, and he had special functions, for example, entering the Holy of Holies on the Day of Atonement (Leviticus 16). The Levites assisted the priests and served the congregation in the temple. They sang the psalms, kept the temple courts clean, helped to prepare certain sacrifices and offerings, and also had a teaching function.

## III. THE HOLINESS OF THE ALTAR (EXODUS 29:35–37)

The consecration service for the priests was seven days, and each day, a young bull was to be offered as a sin offering. Additionally, during the process, the altar was to be cleaned and purified for the acceptance of new sacrifices. Cleaning the altar was important because the constant sacrifices would deposit greasy oil from the fat of the animals and possible dirt and grime from the elements. Therefore, the altar had to also be cleansed in the spirit of purification. Today's English version adds that the altar was to be anointed with olive oil (v. 36). Nevertheless, for seven days, the altar was to be atoned and consecrated for holy service by means of sacrifices. The cleansing of the altar was to be an ongoing obligation, as these commands will be recounted at a later date when Moses will state that "you shall take the anointing oil, and anoint the tabernacle and all that is in it; and you shall hallow it and all its utensils, and it shall be holy. You shall anoint the altar of the burnt offering and all its utensils and consecrate the altar, and the altar shall be most holy" (Exodus 40:9–10). Although Scripture supplies few details of the ceremonial anointing of official things and persons, the Lord specified that everything set apart for God—the tabernacle, the ark, the table and its instruments, the lampstand and utensils, the incense altar and main altar, the washbasin – was to be anointed. The result was a holy place with holy furnishings, holy implements of worship, and holy ministers. The offices of prophet, priest, and king were those associated with anointing in the nation of Israel.

However, the focus that must not be missed here is the holiness of the altar. Recall that there are two altars in the Tabernacle. One is the Altar of Incense or the Golden Altar which is located in the Inner Court near the Golden Lampstand and the Table of the Bread of the Presence. The second altar, the Altar of Burnt Offering, is where the sacrifices occur and is located in the Outer Court. It is the second altar that requires the needed cleaning and re–preparation for additional sacrifices that is central to the aforementioned commands. Although burnt offerings are exacted here, the altar is found to have traits of holiness. The outside altar is not to be confused with the Ark, especially when realizing that "whoever" touches the altar will become holy. God has allowed instances when people could touch the Ark; however, the proscriptions for the ark and the altar in this missive should not be mistaken. It is Yahweh that allows the altar to become a source of holiness, which is due to the holiness and attitude of the person. Therefore, in this situation, whoever will touch the altar during this period will also become holy.

The lesson presented in these verses details the seriousness of the sacrificial system and the practice of these procedures ordained by Yahweh. Moreover, here, we are introduced to the seriousness of anointing Aaron and his sons as priests. Obviously, Yahweh must have forgiven Aaron for the crafting of the golden calf (bull) for idol worship while Moses was on the mountain. As for modern sensibilities, this style of worship and the sacrifice system of ancient Israel is abhorrent and repulsive; however, this approach will not last forever. The sacrifice system will endure for centuries until the crucifixion of Jesus who eradicates the ancient system and becomes the ultimate sacrifice. As the sacrificial lamb, Jesus removes all vestiges of sacrificial repulsion, as believers only have to have faith, which becomes the foundation of Christian worship.

## THE LESSON APPLIED

Our lesson does not exhibit the traits and novel storyline of "living happily ever after;" however, the paradigm of the account is to understand ancient practices for identifying and setting apart people for ministry. The nation existed during a period when the Lord instituted a sacrificial system that was pleasing to Him and His purposes. Notice that everything that was touched concerning the Tabernacle and the priests were holy. God's command for Israel went far beyond the system of sacrifices. Yahweh needed to develop Israel as a holy nation that would follow Him and worship Him in spirit and truth.

## LET'S TALK ABOUT IT

The contemporary church is filled with many rituals that we refer to as traditions. There exists a myriad of opinions as to whether these traditions are relevant in contemporary society. As an example of traditions of the past, in many church circles, services such as BTU (Baptist Training Union) or evening communion may be viewed as outdated. Many seasoned members of the church worry that the loss or downgrading of the traditions or rituals have worked to degrade society. However, two of the ordinances of the church, baptism and communion, should never be left to falter. Remember, these two ordinances have been ordained by God and are dedicated to our worship to Him.

## GET SOCIAL

Share your views and tag us @rhboydco and use #rhboydco.

@rhboydco

## HOME DAILY DEVOTIONAL READINGS
## MARCH 17–23, 2025

| MONDAY | TUESDAY | WEDNESDAY | THURSDAY | FRIDAY | SATURDAY | SUNDAY |
|---|---|---|---|---|---|---|
| Building a Spiritual House | Prayer like Incense | The Fragrance of Knowing Christ | God's Delight | A Holy and Acceptable Sacrifice | Worship through Loving Genuinely | An Acceptable Offering |
| 2 Peter 2:1–5 | Psalm 141 | 2 Corinthians 2:12–17 | Zephaniah 3:14–20 | Romans 12:1–8 | Romans 12:9–21 | Leviticus 1:3–17 |

LESSON IV  
MARCH 23, 2025

# OFFERING A SWEET AROMA TO GOD

**ADULT TOPIC:**  
UP IN SMOKE

**BACKGROUND SCRIPTURE:** LEVITICUS 1:1–17; 6:8–13  
**LESSON PASSAGE:** LEVITICUS 1:3–17

## LEVITICUS 1:3–17

### KJV

IF his offering be a burnt sacrifice of the herd, let him offer a male without blemish: he shall offer it of his own voluntary will at the door of the tabernacle of the congregation before the Lord.
4 And he shall put his hand upon the head of the burnt offering; and it shall be accepted for him to make atonement for him.
5 And he shall kill the bullock before the Lord: and the priests, Aaron's sons, shall bring the blood, and sprinkle the blood round about upon the altar that is by the door of the tabernacle of the congregation.
6 And he shall flay the burnt offering, and cut it into his pieces.
7 And the sons of Aaron the priest shall put fire upon the altar, and lay the wood in order upon the fire:
8 And the priests, Aaron's sons, shall lay the parts, the head, and the fat, in order upon the wood that is on the fire which is upon the altar:
9 But his inwards and his legs shall he wash in water: and the priest shall burn all on the altar, to be a burnt sacrifice, an offering made by fire, of a sweet savour unto the Lord.
10 And if his offering be of the flocks, namely, of the sheep, or of the goats, for a burnt sacrifice; he shall bring it a male without blemish.
11 And he shall kill it on the side of the altar northward before the Lord: and the priests, Aaron's sons, shall sprinkle his blood round about upon the altar.
12 And he shall cut it into his pieces, with his

### NRSVueue

"IF the offering is a burnt offering from the herd, you shall offer a male without blemish; you shall bring it to the entrance of the tent of meeting, for acceptance on your behalf before the Lord.
4 You shall lay your hand on the head of the burnt offering, and it shall be acceptable on your behalf as atonement for you.
5 The bull shall be slaughtered before the Lord, and Aaron's sons the priests shall offer the blood, dashing the blood against all sides of the altar that is at the entrance of the tent of meeting.
6 The burnt offering shall be flayed and cut up into its parts.
7 The sons of the priest Aaron shall put fire on the altar and arrange wood on the fire.
8 Aaron's sons the priests shall arrange the parts, with the head and the suet, on the wood that is on the fire on the altar,
9 but its entrails and its legs shall be washed with water. Then the priest shall turn the rest into smoke on the altar as a burnt offering, an offering by fire of pleasing odor to the Lord.
10 "If your gift for a burnt offering is from the flock, from the sheep or goats, your offering shall be a male without blemish.
11 It shall be slaughtered on the north side of the altar before the Lord, and Aaron's sons the priests shall dash its blood against all sides of the altar.
12 It shall be cut up into its parts, with its head

**MAIN THOUGHT:** The priest shall turn the whole into smoke on the altar as a burnt offering, an offering by fire of pleasing odor to the LORD. (Leviticus 1:9, NRSVue)

## Leviticus 1:3-17

### KJV

head and his fat: and the priest shall lay them in order on the wood that is on the fire which is upon the altar:

13 But he shall wash the inwards and the legs with water: and the priest shall bring it all, and burn it upon the altar: it is a burnt sacrifice, an offering made by fire, of a sweet savour unto the Lord.

14 And if the burnt sacrifice for his offering to the Lord be of fowls, then he shall bring his offering of turtledoves, or of young pigeons.

15 And the priest shall bring it unto the altar, and wring off his head, and burn it on the altar; and the blood thereof shall be wrung out at the side of the altar:

16 And he shall pluck away his crop with his feathers, and cast it beside the altar on the east part, by the place of the ashes:

17 And he shall cleave it with the wings thereof, but shall not divide it asunder: and the priest shall burn it upon the altar, upon the wood that is upon the fire: it is a burnt sacrifice, an offering made by fire, of a sweet savour unto the Lord.

### NRSVueue

and its suet, and the priest shall arrange them on the wood that is on the fire on the altar,

13 but the entrails and the legs shall be washed with water. Then the priest shall offer the rest and turn it into smoke on the altar; it is a burnt offering, an offering by fire of pleasing odor to the Lord.

14 "If your offering to the Lord is a burnt offering of birds, you shall choose your offering from turtledoves or pigeons.

15 The priest shall bring it to the altar and wring off its head and turn it into smoke on the altar, and its blood shall be drained out against the side of the altar.

16 He shall remove its entrails close to its tail feathers and throw it at the east side of the altar, in the place for ashes.

17 He shall tear it open by its wings without severing it. Then the priest shall turn it into smoke on the altar, on the wood that is on the fire; it is a burnt offering, an offering by fire of pleasing odor to the Lord.

## LESSON SETTING
**Time:** Circa 1462
**Place:** Region of Mount Sinai or Horeb

## LESSON OUTLINE
I. Offerings of Bulls
   (Leviticus 1:3-9)
II. Offerings from the Flock
   (Leviticus 1:10-13)
III. Offerings of Birds
   (Leviticus 1:14-17)

## UNIFYING PRINCIPLE

People know that their relationships with others require effort. How can we maintain our relationships? In Leviticus, God's people are instructed to offer burnt sacrifices to maintain and restore their relationship with the Lord.

## INTRODUCTION

The introduction to Leviticus as found in chapter one is the way to sacrifice to God (1:1–10:20) and especially through (burnt) offerings (1:1–7:38). The title Leviticus is derived from the Greek translation of the Septuagint meaning "pertaining to the Levites." Though the book is a manual for the priests (who were from the tribe of Levi), many of its laws concern all Israelites. Although the book of Exodus concludes with the erection of the Tabernacle, which was constructed to the pattern that God gave to Moses, the instructions in Leviticus describe how Israel was to use the Tabernacle. The instructions in Leviticus were given to

Moses during the 50 days between the setting up of the Tabernacle (Exodus 40:17) and the departure of the people from Sinai (Numbers 10:11). Moreover, Leviticus is a book about the holiness of God and His requirements for fellowship with Himself.

## EXPOSITION

### I. OFFERINGS OF BULLS (LEVITICUS 1:3–9)

The person who has come to the entrance of the "Tent of the Meeting," which is the Tabernacle, would present the animal of his choice. In this case, if the animal has been taken from the herd, it would be acceptable for the burnt offering. The animal had to be a male without defect or blemish, a choice of the choicest of his herd, which would show his attitude of giving back to God. The worshiper was then to have the offered animal at the doorway of the Tabernacle; however, the actual presentation of the sacrifice probably took place at the actual entrance or gateway to the outer court, before the priest, worshiper, and animal moved to the area north of the altar to enact the sacrificial procedure. The priest would accept the animal only after it had been thoroughly examined for any imperfections. Though a sacrificial animal might vary in age from one week (22:26–27) to probably three years, many of the sacrificial rituals specify a yearling.

Following the presentation of the animal, the offerer was to lay his hand (probably his right hand) on the head of the animal to be sacrificed, to symbolize that the gift would be accepted on behalf of the worshiper, making atonement for him. The word *camak* is translated "to lay his hand on," meaning "resting or supporting oneself" on the animal. Through this act, the worshiper identified himself with the animal as his substitute. Here, the worshiper seeks atonement in the eyes of the Lord. To appreciate the concept of sacrifice, it must be understood that God provided for the sacrifice, while man performed the rite.

Verse 6 of the Jewish Bible records that the burnt offering shall be flayed (by the offerer) and cut into sections. The act of flaying means to peel or strip the skin from the animal (which in this case is the young bull) and then, cut the meat into pieces or sections. Here, the division of labor is clear. The offerer is responsible for the mundane task of transferring ownership of the animal and transforming it from a living animal into food fit for consumption. The priests, however, are responsible for the sacred tasks of dashing the blood and offering the flesh as a gift to the Lord.

Continuing, the sons of Aaron were to place fire on the altar and arrange the wood on the fire. The instruction for the priests to put fire on the altar (1:7) is difficult to understand since at the ordination of the priests (chapters. 8–9), the national festivals (Numbers 28–29), and numerous individual occasions, sin offerings were offered before burnt offerings, so the fire would already be burning. In fact, the fire was not to be allowed to go out between the daily morning and evening sacrifices (Leviticus. 6:12–13). Perhaps the expression is a general one to indicate priestly responsibility to care for the fire. The fire here, as in many passages, probably means burning coals; again, the priests were required to maintain a constant fire on the altar. The altar fire, once ignited, must never be allowed to die out, which serves as a perpetual sign that the enshrined deity is being worshiped constantly. The instructions about the fire and the arrangement of wood are specific and are not to be thought of as some random barbecue.

Following the directives of the placement of the fire and wood, Aaron's sons were to arrange the head and the suet on the altar. The Hebrew term for suet, *peder*, can be described as the grease or fat of the animal. The uniqueness of the burnt offering is made evident in that the priest was to burn the animal in its entirety on the altar. However, the priests were to wash the entrails and the animal's legs (thoroughly) with water. The inner parts and the (rear) legs would be the dirtiest part of the animal and would definitely need to be clean to be suitable for a sacrifice to the Lord. If the instructions were followed, the result offered up would be a soothing aroma to the Lord (as in, the sacrifice would smell good to God), thus, pleasing Him.

## II. Offerings from the Flock (Leviticus 1:10–13)

Verse 10 and following provides instructions for those whose offerings are different from that of a bull. This category allows the worshiper to select an animal from his flock. Also, notice that the animal was to be a male, which aligns with the perspective of the role of the male in Israelite society as a leader and the head of his household, region, and devotion to the Lord. Additionally, the lamb or goat was a much smaller animal than a bull, which could have led to a sense of inferiority or even been devalued by hypocritical or wealthy people, to degrade the less fortunate person's gift to the Lord. Nonetheless, within these rules, Yahweh is promoting equal sacrifice and not equal giving. Verses 11–13 generally follow the instructions of verses 5–9, which describe the area where the animal is to be killed and the sprinkling of its blood on and around the altar. Additionally, instructions for the washing of the lamb or goat, especially the entrails and legs, is the same as was given for the washing of the bull.

## III. Offerings of Birds (Leviticus 1:14–17)

As with Verse 10 and following, instructions are provided for those whose offerings are different from that of a bull, or in this case, a lamb or a goat. In this collection, instructions are provided for birds, as this category allows the worshiper to select an animal from the nest. It is thought that many of these animals were not necessarily captured in the wild but were initially kept as domestic pets. Verses 14–17 allow the offering of turtledoves or young pigeons, which are considered edible and acceptable for human consumption. Again, these fowl are much smaller than the bull, ram, or goat; therefore, the normal execution of the birds is completed by the wringing of their necks, thereby removing their heads. Offerings of birds do not leave a large physical carcass; however, it is God's wish that even the seemingly smallest gift when offered to the Lord is accepted. This was the offering that Joseph and Mary presented to God, a pair of turtledoves; yet, this small gift was wholeheartedly accepted by the Father.

Instead of having a hide or a coat of wool to dispense with, the priest had to discard the unused feathers of a fowl in order to expose the meat or flesh. The small size of the bird required a simplification of the sacrificial ritual so that all was done necessarily by the priest. The crop, which is defined as a pouch in a bird's gullet where food is stored or prepared for digestion, with its contents, was cast aside on the ashpit or the refuse pit; then, the bird which had been partially torn open was burned on the altar as an aroma pleasing to the LORD (cf. Leviticus 1:9).

## THE LESSON APPLIED

The lesson here describes the instructions of how the sacrificial offerings were to be presented and lifted up to the Lord. Although the account may seem to be instructions for Aaron, his sons, and the Levite priests, the men of Israel were also to follow these instructions in the worship of the Lord. In the sacrifice, the gift is wholly to the Lord and represents a total surrender to the Lord, while asking for His forgiveness of their sin. Their dedication to not withholding the best of their pastures, flocks, or nests signaled the trust of the worshiper, in that there would be no other gods before Him. Moreover, the instructions were not only to be a one-time offering but were to be executed at each designated time of the sacrifice. Animal sacrifices will eventually be replaced by the supreme and ultimate sacrifice of Jesus.

## LET'S TALK ABOUT IT

Christian believers must be dedicated to commit an offering to God that is the best of who we are. For example, many members of the church do not display the best of who we are because we are deceptive in our tithes and offerings. While withholding our gifts, there may be a thought that we are "cheating" God, but we are actually deceiving ourselves because the gift offerings are based on faith, not purely on money, which is simply the tool that we use. The genuine offerings of ancient Israel in the form of bulls, rams, and birds revealed the best of the people. In our contemporary church, we must show the Lord the best of our offering, but also the best of who we are.

## GET SOCIAL
Share your views and tag us @rhboydco and use #rhboydco.

@rhboydco

## HOME DAILY DEVOTIONAL READINGS
### MARCH 24–30, 2025

| MONDAY | TUESDAY | WEDNESDAY | THURSDAY | FRIDAY | SATURDAY | SUNDAY |
| --- | --- | --- | --- | --- | --- | --- |
| Delighting to Do God's Will | Safe in God's Love and Faithfulness | A Preferred Sanctuary | Christ's Perfect Sacrifice | Vertical and Horizontal Reconciliation | Approach God in Awe | Cleanse the Sanctuary |
| Psalm 40:1–8 | Psalm 40:9–17 | Hebrews 9:1–14 | Hebrews 9:15–22 | 2 Corinthians 5:12–21 | Leviticus 16:1–10 | Leviticus 16:11–19 |

LESSON V　　　　　　　　　　　　　　　　　　　　　　　MARCH 30, 2025

# THE DAY OF ATONEMENT

ADULT TOPIC:　　　　　　　　　　BACKGROUND SCRIPTURE: LEVITICUS 16
WHAT A DAY!　　　　　　　　　　　　LESSON PASSAGE: LEVITICUS 16:11–19

## LEVITICUS 16:11–19

### KJV

AND Aaron shall bring the bullock of the sin offering, which is for himself, and shall make an atonement for himself, and for his house, and shall kill the bullock of the sin offering which is for himself:

12 And he shall take a censer full of burning coals of fire from off the altar before the Lord, and his hands full of sweet incense beaten small, and bring it within the vail:

13 And he shall put the incense upon the fire before the Lord, that the cloud of the incense may cover the mercy seat that is upon the testimony, that he die not:

14 And he shall take of the blood of the bullock, and sprinkle it with his finger upon the mercy seat eastward; and before the mercy seat shall he sprinkle of the blood with his finger seven times.

15 Then shall he kill the goat of the sin offering, that is for the people, and bring his blood within the vail, and do with that blood as he did with the blood of the bullock, and sprinkle it upon the mercy seat, and before the mercy seat:

16 And he shall make an atonement for the holy place, because of the uncleanness of the children of Israel, and because of their transgressions in all their sins: and so shall he do for the tabernacle of the congregation, that remaineth among them in the midst of their uncleanness.

17 And there shall be no man in the tabernacle of the congregation when he goeth in to make

### NRSVueue

"AARON shall present the bull as a purification offering for himself and shall make atonement for himself and for his house; he shall slaughter the bull as a purification offering for himself.

12 He shall take a censer full of coals of fire from the altar before the Lord and two handfuls of crushed sweet incense, and he shall bring it inside the curtain

13 and put the incense on the fire before the Lord, that the cloud of the incense may shroud the cover that is upon the covenant, or he will die.

14 He shall take some of the blood of the bull and sprinkle it with his finger on the front of the cover, and before the cover he shall sprinkle the blood with his finger seven times.

15 "He shall slaughter the goat of the purification offering that is for the people and bring its blood inside the curtain and do with its blood as he did with the blood of the bull, sprinkling it upon the cover and before the cover.

16 Thus he shall make atonement for the sanctuary, because of the uncleannesses of the Israelites and because of their transgressions, all their sins, and so he shall do for the tent of meeting, which remains with them in the midst of their uncleanness.

17 No one shall be in the tent of meeting from the time he enters to make atonement in the

**MAIN THOUGHT:** He shall make atonement for the sanctuary, because of the uncleannesses of the people of Israel, and because of their transgressions, all their sins; and so he shall do for the tent of meeting, which remains with them in the midst of their uncleannesses. (Leviticus 16:16, NRSVue)

## LEVITICUS 16:11–19

### KJV

an atonement in the holy place, until he come out, and have made an atonement for himself, and for his household, and for all the congregation of Israel.
18 And he shall go out unto the altar that is before the Lord, and make an atonement for it; and shall take of the blood of the bullock, and of the blood of the goat, and put it upon the horns of the altar round about.
19 And he shall sprinkle of the blood upon it with his finger seven times, and cleanse it, and hallow it from the uncleanness of the children of Israel.

### NRSVueue

sanctuary until he comes out and has made atonement for himself and for his house and for all the assembly of Israel.
18 Then he shall go out to the altar that is before the Lord and make atonement on its behalf and shall take some of the blood of the bull and of the blood of the goat and put it on each of the horns of the altar.
19 He shall sprinkle some of the blood on it with his finger seven times and cleanse it and sanctify it from the uncleannesses of the Israelites.

### LESSON SETTING
**Time:** 1461 BCE
**Place:** Region of Mount Sinai or Horeb

### LESSON OUTLINE
I. The Sin Offering of the High Priest (Leviticus 16:11–14)
II. The Sin Offering for the People (Leviticus 16:15–17)
III. Cleansing of the Altar (Leviticus 16:18–19)

## UNIFYING PRINCIPLE

People seek reconciliation when relationships have soured. What can we do to heal broken trust? Yahweh establishes an annual Day of Atonement that symbolizes for Israel the substitutionary atonement God provided for their sins and the total removal of their guilt.

## INTRODUCTION

This section of Leviticus provides a detailed set of instructions and descriptions of the ceremonies and rituals of the sin offering of the high priest and the sin offering of the people. These rituals may seem foreign and somewhat revolting to our sensitivities; however, in the dispensation of sacrifices, these rituals were commanded by the Lord. Much of the instructions supported the purposes of re–uniting the nation under the banner of God's chosen people. Much of the acts were symbolic; however, these enactments were necessary at this juncture in the life and the context of Israel. Moreover, the role of the High Priest and his care of the Tabernacle is shown here, and it expands throughout the succeeding Levitical generations, long after Aaron sleeps with his fathers. When the New Testament High Priest (such as Annas and Caiaphas) is examined, we will find that the rituals and care of the Temple will mirror the traditions of the Tabernacle.

## EXPOSITION

### I. THE SIN OFFERING OF THE HIGH PRIEST (LEVITICUS 16:11–14)

The biblical language may often seem to be doublespeak; however, one must closely examine it to understand its meaning. For example, when the Scripture reveals that Aaron shall offer a bull for this sin offering, the idea is that Aaron is making this offering for himself and his household. The second part of the sentence is a repetition of the first act, that Aaron is to make the sin offering for himself. Verse 11 allows us to realize that the Lord places the high priest in a position to receive sin offerings for the masses; however, the high priest (just as anyone else) is also not above sin, so, the high priest must offer personal sin offerings for himself and his family. In this sense, the sin offering of the high priest is necessary because atonement is needed to cover himself and his family. Moreover, the high priest had to be cleansed from the pollution of sin before he could function as a mediator to offer the "sin offering for the people" (v. 15). After offering the bull for his personal sin offering, Aaron makes the kill. If we closely examine the specifics of the act, during the time that Aaron makes the kill, he is a bloody mess. He cannot immediately offer the blood to gain God's favor because in the killing of the bull, the blood has made Aaron unclean. Also, remember that the high priest and his assistants would become bloody and soiled from offering the sacrifices of others, and since their clothing would be caked with layers of sediment, the need to be physically clean would be very important. During this interval, occupied by his entrance into the Holies of Holies with the incense, the blood was held by an attendant, probably one of his sons, and prevented from coagulating or clotting by being kept in motion.

Continuing, Aaron was to take a firepan full of coals from the fire of the altar; however, one must be careful with the translations, as the Hebrew term *machtah* may mean firepan or censer. The censer or firepan is a vessel used to burn incense, which is a type of perfume that sends up to God a fragrant smoke in order to please Him. Notice that Aaron was instructed to bring two handfuls of finely ground sweet incense to burn inside the veil. Incense offerings seem to have served a multitude of purposes. They may have been used to drive away evil spirits and thereby sanctify all the utensils of the place of worship (Exodus 30:26–29). Undoubtedly, the sweet smell of incense provided an antidote to the putrid odor of the animal sacrifices. Therefore, if God was to receive a sweet savor and thereby be pleased with an offering, incense was necessary to compensate for the smell of the sacrifices. However, spices were never added to the flesh of the animals or birds.

There existed a sense of danger in the Holy of Holies because death could occur to the priest if the exact instructions were not followed. The high priest, who was the only one who was allowed in this sanctum, was to put the incense on the fire before the Lord, that the cloud of incense, which also is to be understood as the paucity and thickness of the cloud of smoke, needed to cover the mercy seat, which is on the ark of the covenant; otherwise, he will die (v. 13). Additionally, this incense was specially prepared to be burned in this segment of the ceremony, and the effect of the thick smoke created a screen between Aaron and the Shekinah (meaning that which dwells, i.e., the glory of God's presence) over the atonement cover; again, keeping himself safe from what was a certain death.

Additionally, operating in the Holy of Holies, the high priest was to take some of the blood of the sacrificed bull and sprinkle it with his finger on the mercy seat, on the east side and in front of the mercy seat; and as part of the ritual, the priest was to sprinkle blood with his fingers, seven times. This ritual differs from the sprinkling of blood on the north side of the altar where the blood was splashed on all four sides of the altar of sacrifice. Instructions for sprinkling the blood seven times may be symbolic; remember, in Scripture, the number seven symbolizes completeness or perfection.

## II. THE SIN OFFERING FOR THE PEOPLE (LEVITICUS 16:15–17)

Continuing the ritual, Aaron moves to slaughter the goat of the sin offering for the people. This is the third entry of Aaron into the Holy of Holies and represents the sin offering. This aspect actually consisted of two male goats (v. 5), one serving as the Lord's goat and the other representing the scapegoat (aza'zel) (v. 8). The slaughter of the first goat, which was the Lord's goat, is explained in verses 7–8, where Aaron selected the goat for the Lord and the scapegoat, by casting lots. The sprinkling of the blood and the procedures that have been previously mentioned are followed. Verses 20–21, however, provide the procedure that Aaron was to follow for the offering of the scapegoat. When he finished the atoning for the holy place, the tent of the meeting, and the altar, Aaron was to offer the scapegoat alive. Aaron places his hands on the live goat and confesses the sins of Israel, as if he is placing these acts on the head of the live goat. Following the ritual, the live goat is then released into the wilderness and serves as a symbol of the iniquities of the nation.

Continuing, verse 16 records that Aaron is to make atonement for the holy place because of the impurities of the sons of Israel and because of their transgressions in regard to all of their sins. From a contemporary perspective, the sin offering of the people may seem redundant and extraneous. Recall that the sin offerings are closely associated with guilt offerings and occasionally, it is difficult to discern one from the other. Remember that the nation has recently been rescued from Egyptian captivity, and much of the Israelite populace had been reduced to living close to Egyptian customs and in other instances, had lifestyles that were closer to animals than what we would accept as civilized beings. One only has to refer to the food laws that were given to return some sense of civility to the populace. However, one of the more serious issues that had to be covered was their guilt of transgressions against Yahweh. The Hebrew term used in verse 16 is *pesha*, the most grievous accusation in the Old Testament, which is better translated as rebellion against God. This initial use of the word in Leviticus indicates that on the Day of Atonement, not only were intentional sins atoned for but the tabernacle was purified to allow God's presence to reside. Cleanliness and restoration to the Lord is needed because now the nation had another opportunity to be the chosen ones of the Lord.

When Aaron goes into the Holy of Holies to make atonement, he is to be alone, and no one is to be in the Tabernacle proper. The idea here is that Yahweh will only recognize the High Priest who is granted this once–a–year privilege to communicate with the Lord on this level. As it was with the individual Moses who singularly witnessed the "burning bush," there were to be no witnesses to the opening of the holy veil, so that the rite of purification might not be interfered with by an impure presence. Even on the Day of Atonement, the dwelling–place of God (typical of heaven) was closed to the eye and foot of man, "the way into the holiest of all being not yet made manifest" (Hebrew 9:8) until the Divine High Priest opened the way for his people by his own entrance. These requirements do not limit or obstruct Israel from worshiping or communicating with God through prayers and supplication; this ritual happens to be a matter of respect for the holiness of God and honoring the sanctum of the holy place.

## III. Cleansing of the Altar (Leviticus 16:18–19)

Upon the completion of the ritual, there is another act of atonement that must occur. When Aaron was finished with his duties in the Holy of Holies, he is to make atonement for the altar. The Holy of Holies and the outer chamber of the Tabernacle having been reconciled, the high priest shall go out unto the altar that is before the Lord – that is, the altar of burnt sacrifice in the court, standing in front of the tabernacle, not the altar of incense, as has been supposed by some – and shall take of the blood of the bullock, and of the blood of the goat, and put it upon the horns of the altar round about. Unlike the previous sprinklings, notice that the blood of the different animals, with the exception of the turtledoves or pigeons, are mixed. This may symbolize the unity of all of Israel that Yahweh has created and wishes to save. And he shall sprinkle of the blood upon it with his finger seven times. This completes the ceremony of "making an atonement for the holy sanctuary and making an atonement for the tabernacle of the congregation, and for the altar" (v. 33.)

Finally, Aaron is to again sprinkle the blood seven times in its cleansing. Recall that blood, even when it is used in these sacrificial enactments, remains impure, and when the priests touch it or sprinkle it upon the designated areas, an aspect of impurity remains. Notice that in cleansing the altar and the outer chamber, Aaron continues to sprinkle the blood of a bull and a goat. This original handling of the blood of these animals was a major contributor to the uncleanliness of the area and the priests who touched the blood. Initially, this ritual does not seem to clean the altar or the priests; however, the cleansing of the altar is not to be considered by our standards of cleaning or wiping away a spill but is to be seen symbolically as a cleansing of the pollution of Israel's sins. As Aaron sprinkles the blood on the altar of sacrifice (not the altar of incense), seven times, here is correctly noted the progression in the purification process. First, the most holy object (the mercy seat) was purified, then, the Tent of Meeting (including the incense altar), and finally, the altar of burnt offering, the most holy object in the court.

Although the lesson focuses on the rituals of the sacrificial system and the manner in which the priests dedicated themselves to the Tabernacle, it is noteworthy to understand the role of the scapegoat. The contemporary definition of the scapegoat is one who is made to take the blame for a situation or an issue. In this Old Testament setting, however, the scapegoat serves as an honorable symbol that reflects God's grace on and for the people. In the New Testament, the scapegoat will be Jesus who will take on the sins of the world. There is nothing negative about the love of Jesus, and His serving as both the sacrificial lamb and scapegoat are nothing but honorable.

## The Lesson Applied

In our contemporary society, if the topic of incense enters into a conversation, it is usually associated with the use of drugs and how the sweet fragrances are used to mask the pungent smell, usually, of marijuana. There are an array of commercial air fresheners that are used; however (culturally), stick– or bowl–incense is favored in modern times. What is noteworthy in the example of the priests using incense in the worship service is that its aroma was also pleasing to Yahweh. Moreover, in Catholicism, the priests use incense in the censers to proclaim and acknowledge the presence of God. If incense would be used in the Protestant Churches, would it be offensive, or could it be an acknowledgment of the presence of God?

## Let's Talk About It

Christian adults are to appreciate God's work to repair the relationship with His covenant people. Although the majority of church members believe that they are saved, in many circles, the truth is that there exists some uncertainty. Although the Old Testament worship rituals may seem barbaric and crude, these mechanisms were designed by the Lord to bring the people together under one banner. Regardless of the manner in which God chooses, God constantly works to repair relationships with His people. For God so loved us that He sent into the world a Son that, through Him, the world might be saved. Christian adults must treasure the love of the Lord and the grace that is offered to those who believe.

### Get Social
Share your views and tag us @rhboydco and use #rhboydco.

@rhboydco

## Home Daily Devotional Readings
### March 31– April 6, 2025, 2024

| Monday | Tuesday | Wednesday | Thursday | Friday | Saturday | Sunday |
|---|---|---|---|---|---|---|
| Enter God's Courts with an Offering | Christ's Suffering and Exaltation | Suffering Servant | Light out of Anguish | A Ransom for Many | Christ in Heaven on Our Behalf | Confidence in God's Presence |
| Psalm 96 | 1 Peter 3:18–22 | Isaiah 52:13–53:3 | Isaiah 53:4–12 | Mark 10:41–45 | Hebrews 9:23–10:4 | Hebrews 10:11–14, 19–25 |

LESSON VI
APRIL 6, 2025

# CHRIST'S ONCE-FOR-ALL SACRIFICE

ADULT TOPIC:
IT ONLY TAKES ONE

BACKGROUND SCRIPTURE: HEBREWS 9:23–10:25
LESSON PASSAGE: HEBREWS 9:23–10:4, 11–14, 19–25

## HEBREWS 9:23–10:4, 11–14, 19–25

### KJV

IT was therefore necessary that the patterns of things in the heavens should be purified with these; but the heavenly things themselves with better sacrifices than these.
24 For Christ is not entered into the holy places made with hands, which are the figures of the true; but into heaven itself, now to appear in the presence of God for us:
25 Nor yet that he should offer himself often, as the high priest entereth into the holy place every year with blood of others;
26 For then must he often have suffered since the foundation of the world: but now once in the end of the world hath he appeared to put away sin by the sacrifice of himself.

27 And as it is appointed unto men once to die, but after this the judgment:
28 So Christ was once offered to bear the sins of many; and unto them that look for him shall he appear the second time without sin unto salvation.

• • • 10:1-4 • • •

1 For the law having a shadow of good things to come, and not the very image of the things, can never with those sacrifices which they offered year by year continually make the comers thereunto perfect.
2 For then would they not have ceased to be offered? because that the worshippers once purged should have had no more conscience of sins.
3 But in those sacrifices there is a remembrance again made of sins every year.

### NRSVueue

THUS it was necessary for the sketches of the heavenly things to be purified with these rites, but the heavenly things themselves need better sacrifices than these.
24 For Christ did not enter a sanctuary made by human hands, a mere copy of the true one, but he entered into heaven itself, now to appear in the presence of God on our behalf.
25 Nor was it to offer himself again and again, as the high priest enters the holy place year after year with blood that is not his own,
26 for then he would have had to suffer again and again since the foundation of the world. But as it is, he has appeared once for all at the end of the ages to remove sin by the sacrifice of himself.

27 And just as it is appointed for mortals to die once and after that the judgment,
28 so Christ, having been offered once to bear the sins of many, will appear a second time, not to deal with sin but to save those who are eagerly waiting for him.

• • • 10:1-4 • • •

1 Since the law has only a shadow of the good things to come and not the true form of these realities, it can never, by the same sacrifices that are continually offered year after year, make perfect those who approach.
2 Otherwise, would they not have ceased being offered, since the worshipers, cleansed once for all, would no longer have any consciousness of sin?
3 But in these sacrifices there is a reminder of sin year after year.

**MAIN THOUGHT:** Christ did not enter a sanctuary made by human hands, a mere copy of the true one, but he entered into heaven itself, now to appear in the presence of God on our behalf. (Hebrews 9:24, NRSVue)

# Hebrews 9:23–10:4, 11–14, 19–25

## KJV

4 For it is not possible that the blood of bulls and of goats should take away sins.

• • • • • •

11 And every priest standeth daily ministering and offering oftentimes the same sacrifices, which can never take away sins:
12 But this man, after he had offered one sacrifice for sins for ever, sat down on the right hand of God;
13 From henceforth expecting till his enemies be made his footstool.
14 For by one offering he hath perfected for ever them that are sanctified.

• • • • • •

19 Having therefore, brethren, boldness to enter into the holiest by the blood of Jesus,
20 By a new and living way, which he hath consecrated for us, through the veil, that is to say, his flesh;
21 And having an high priest over the house of God;
22 Let us draw near with a true heart in full assurance of faith, having our hearts sprinkled from an evil conscience, and our bodies washed with pure water.
23 Let us hold fast the profession of our faith without wavering; (for he is faithful that promised;)
24 And let us consider one another to provoke unto love and to good works:
25 Not forsaking the assembling of ourselves together, as the manner of some is; but exhorting one another: and so much the more, as ye see the day approaching.

## NRSVueue

4 For it is impossible for the blood of bulls and goats to take away sins.

• • • • • •

11 And every priest stands day after day at his service, offering again and again the same sacrifices that can never take away sins.
12 But when Christ had offered for all time a single sacrifice for sins, "he sat down at the right hand of God,"
13 and since then has been waiting "until his enemies would be made a footstool for his feet."
14 For by a single offering he has perfected for all time those who are sanctified.

• • • • • •

19 Therefore, my brothers and sisters, since we have confidence to enter the sanctuary by the blood of Jesus,
20 by the new and living way that he opened for us through the curtain (that is, through his flesh),
21 and since we have a great priest over the house of God,
22 let us approach with a true heart in full assurance of faith, with our hearts sprinkled clean from an evil conscience and our bodies washed with pure water.
23 Let us hold fast to the confession of our hope without wavering, for he who has promised is faithful.
24 And let us consider how to provoke one another to love and good deeds,
25 not neglecting to meet together, as is the habit of some, but encouraging one another, and all the more as you see the Day approaching.

## LESSON SETTING
Time: Unknown
Place: Unknown

## LESSON OUTLINE

I. The Singular Death of Christ
(Hebrews 9:23–28)

II. One Sacrifice of Christ is Sufficient (Hebrews 10:1–4)

III. Perfection Sits at the Right Hand of God
(Hebrews 10:11–14)

IV. A New and Living Way
(Hebrews 10:19–25)

## UNIFYING PRINCIPLE

People base their day-to-day lives on what has worked in the past. What if they were to learn that what worked in the past really didn't work? Compared to the effect of Christ's single sacrifice for sin, the repeated rituals of the Torah are found wanting. Christ's life and death seal God's covenant with us, put God's law into our hearts and minds, and guide us to live faithfully.

## INTRODUCTION

Previous lessons detailed the Aaronic priesthood and the instructions for sacrifice. The writings in Hebrews explain that these past rituals have become obsolete. Hebrews has been thought to be a book of Old Testament themes written in the New Testament era. Although the author is unknown, he connects these themes to Jesus as the New Covenant, who (metaphorically) has replaced the duties of the priests and (literally) became the sacrifice for all of humanity. Moreover, Hebrews discloses that Yahweh adapts to the plight of humans and that those things that worked previously may become archaic. Additionally, Hebrews reveals that Jesus is the answer to the ills of the world and the conclusion to all of the Old Testament prophecies, especially, Jesus as High Priest. The book may have been written to Jewish Christians that had spread into different parts of the world.

## EXPOSITION

### I. THE SINGULAR DEATH OF CHRIST (HEBREWS 9:23–28)

In this section, the author of Hebrews rebuffs the connection of heaven and animal sacrifices of the past. Although animal sacrifices were mandated in the Old Testament, with the advent of Jesus, these rituals no longer served their purpose or function. When the writer speaks of "copies" of the things in the heavens, he uses the Greek term *hupódeigma*, which can be translated as "to show or forewarn." However, here, the term is used to highlight an example or pattern that is imitated in the action of the continuation of the rituals of Temple sacrifice. In this case, if the rituals must change, the priestly functions change along with the definition, interpretation, and understanding of the New Testament sacrifice, along with its purpose. Therefore, a more useful or more profitable sacrifice had to be instituted that aligned with the New Covenant.

Christ's death and sacrifice is now seen as more important than ever or in a more intense, yet portent light. Here, the author notes that Christ did not enter a holy place made with hands. In this statement, he is speaking of the Temple constructed under the guidance of Herod the Great, as the work began in 20 BCE, and while the main sanctuary was quickly erected (it was in full operation within 10 years), the total project was not completed until 64 CE, only six years before it was destroyed by the Romans. Remember, Israel believed that Yahweh actually lived in the Temple and therefore, if Jesus was the Messiah, it is possible that they thought the Christ lived there as well.

Therefore, for the believer, instead of living in the Temple, Jesus is in the presence of God. Here, Christ was appointed as High Priest of the New Covenant to represent sinful people in heaven itself, that is, in the presence of God. Additionally, Christ changes the role of the High Priest in that He does not offer ritual sacrifices as did the Levitical priests because, as the ultimate sacrifice, He would have to offer Himself or die many times over to fulfill the demands of the ritual. For the believer, Jesus is not limited to the holy place, such as the Holy of Holies, once a year but is within Himself at all times. This is why it is extremely important to understand the definition of the one–time sacrifice. Moreover, the essence of Jesus is higher than any bull or ram that He initially created! Jesus was foreordained before the foundation of the world but was manifest in these last times for you (believers) who through Him believe in God, who raised Him from the dead and gave Him glory, so that your faith and hope are in God (1 Peter 1:20–21).

## II. ONE SACRIFICE OF CHRIST IS SUFFICIENT (HEBREWS 10:1–4)

The Law was only a shadow of good things to come. Recall, the Law was given because the people had been in Egyptian bondage, and much of the nation had conformed to the Egyptian customs, which included idolatry. Moreover, as a newly emancipated people, there needed to be laws to govern the lives of the people; however, because Israel was God's chosen, these laws included worship and dedication to God. These laws had been a foretaste of the good things that Yahweh had for His people, but yet, they were not the completion of the grace God had for His people. In this case, the author notes that the Law could never make perfect those who draw or remain near to Yahweh in the worship styles of the Law. What must be understood is that here, when the Hebrew writer speaks of "make perfect," he does not mean sinless perfection, as he is concerned with the definitive removal of guilt, which makes free access to God possible for worshipers who will later trust in the sufficiency of the cross.

Examples of the yearly sacrifices that are offered are Expiation, which is the act of making amends or reparation for guilt, wrongdoing, or atonement. This was the sin offering in which animals were sacrificed according to the Law. The second was the guilt offering, which was a trespass offering that was required whenever someone had been denied his rightful due. In this early form of reparations, the valued amount that had been defrauded had to be made, plus, a fine of one–fifth. Again, there was an animal involved which was usually a ram. However, the author notes in a question that these repeated rituals are not working and serve as a testament to the Law's incapacity to "perfect" its worshippers. Far from enabling them to achieve a standing before God by which they would no longer have felt guilty for their sins, the yearly rituals (of the Day of Atonement) served as a kind of annual reminder of sins, since animal blood has no power to take away sins. In verse 10:1, the Hebrew term that denotes perfection is *teleioō*, which is used in a moral sense, meaning to make perfect, to fully cleanse from sin, in contrast to ceremonial cleansing. This term is also used to describe Jesus, as the author notes that "and being made perfect, he became the author of eternal salvation unto all them that obey Him" (Hebrews 5:9). The thought here is not that Jesus suffered from a deficiency of character or nature or that through suffering, He underwent any type of moral improvement. Rather, the perfection of Christ covers His qualifications as Savior.

## III. Perfection Sits at the Right Hand of God
## (Hebrews 10:11–14)

The Aaronic priests under the Law stand daily in their services, ministering and performing the ritual sacrifices; however, these rituals do not have the power to take away sins. Again, the purpose was to place Israel in a position to serve as a role model to the world, as Children of God. Jesus is a one–time sacrifice that is universally effective for those of the faith who chose to follow Him and become His disciples. Here, we have a reference to Jesus sitting at the right hand of God, which represents the strong hand of a man. Notice that the author says that when He finished as a sacrifice, Jesus sat down at the right hand of God. That He sat down at the right hand of God indicates the completion of any sacrificial work, such as any unneeded repetition of His death. Seated at the right hand of God serves as a bastion of grace and mercy that is provided to all believers who live within His realm. In the completion of His sacrifice, Jesus Christ is exalted.

While at the right hand, Jesus is waiting for His enemies. The Hebrew writer includes this as a warning about the infusion of Satanic interference; however, Jesus will make His enemies into His footstool. An example of this is found where David writes, "The LORD said to my Lord, sit at My right hand, 'till I make Your enemies Your footstool" (Psalm 110:1). Jesus would later quote this Psalm in Matthew 22:44 as a question posed to some Pharisees. In this case, this claim could extend from Jesus to His believers in that He will make our enemies into our footstools. Moreover, by His one–time offering, Jesus has perfected for all–time those who are sanctified.

## IV. A New and Living Way
## (Hebrews 10:19–25)

The Hebrew writer sums up this section by declaring that there is a new and better method of being saved and sanctified. Again, the old ways of Temple worship and sacrifices have been rendered obsolete, especially the thoughts of Yahweh living in the Holy of Holies which was accessible only to the High Priest. With the Advent of Jesus, the mystery behind the forbidden veil has been made available to the believers of Christ. Recall that at the crucifixion of our Lord, the veil of the Temple was torn in two from top to bottom (Mark 15:38). Now that Christ is the Way, the ripping of the veil symbolically acknowledges that believers will be accessible to Jesus. The torn veil opening the way to the Holy of Holies symbolizes Christ's flesh (body) on the cross, which opens access to God for us (Matthew 27:51).

Therefore, believers must hold on to the faith through Jesus Christ. We profess our faith by daily living and not simply uttering some mere words. Believers are connected to a faithful God who never reneges on His promises or dedication to His believers. The excitement of the believer is infectious and regenerative, such as is found when new skin is created to heal old wounds.

In the methodology of the church, believers must not fail to assemble ourselves together because togetherness is the basis for corporate worship. Recall that

Jesus built His house, the Church, on a solid rock, not on sinking sand. In verse 10:25, the writer reveals that infidelity in the faith is not an abstraction but a confrontation with real danger. There was an urgent need for mutual concern and exhortation (toward love and good deeds) within the church to whom he wrote. His readers were not to abandon their meeting together, as some were doing.

## THE LESSON APPLIED

The lesson provokes an interesting paradigm as it confirms the singular sacrifice of our Savior and that the faithful are blessed because of the New Covenant. It seems as if this missive should conclude these declarations with celebrations and thanksgiving; however, the supposition points toward the warning to the believers who fall away from the church and the Lord. With this sense of caution, the faithful in the church are admonished not to overlook the day which is approaching. Sadly, for the contemporary Christian and churchgoer, that day has already arrived. Yet, we as believers and the cadre of the faithful, must continue to encourage as well as maintain our discipleship in the furtherance of the kingdom, knowing that the gift of eternal life awaits us.

## LET'S TALK ABOUT IT

Christian adults must persevere in the confidence of our public witness to the transforming power of the gospel. In our contemporary society, it seems that the enemies of the church are so pervasive that the faithful is overwhelmed. Many congregations are not reaching the masses, and what is offered back is a series of lethargic excuses seeking to blame the church for their absences, such as (in their words) services that do not reach, preaching that does not preach, and music that does not resonate, because all of these entities are outdated. The reality is that Satanic influences have poisoned the world and turned people away from the message of Jesus. Even so, our public witness must never waver because true believers know the truth that Jesus is Lord.

## GET SOCIAL

Share your views and tag us
@rhboydco and use #rhboydco.

@rhboydco

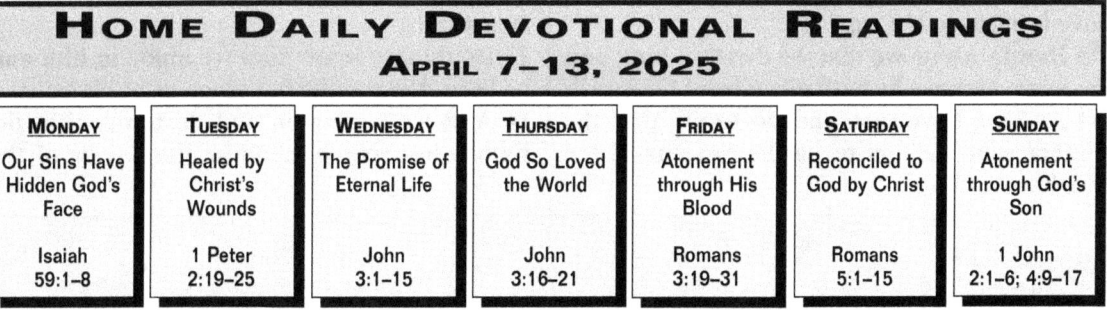

| | MONDAY | TUESDAY | WEDNESDAY | THURSDAY | FRIDAY | SATURDAY | SUNDAY |
|---|---|---|---|---|---|---|---|
| | Our Sins Have Hidden God's Face | Healed by Christ's Wounds | The Promise of Eternal Life | God So Loved the World | Atonement through His Blood | Reconciled to God by Christ | Atonement through God's Son |
| | Isaiah 59:1–8 | 1 Peter 2:19–25 | John 3:1–15 | John 3:16–21 | Romans 3:19–31 | Romans 5:1–15 | 1 John 2:1–6; 4:9–17 |

HOME DAILY DEVOTIONAL READINGS
APRIL 7–13, 2025

LESSON VII                                            APRIL 13, 2025

# CHRIST THE ATONING SACRIFICE

ADULT TOPIC:                                BACKGROUND SCRIPTURE: 1 JOHN 2:1–6; 4:7–21
ALL YOU NEED IS LOVE                               LESSON PASSAGE: 1 JOHN 2:1–6; 4:9–17

## 1 JOHN 2:1–6; 4:9–17

| KJV | NRSVueue |
|---|---|
| MY little children, these things write I unto you, that ye sin not. And if any man sin, we have an advocate with the Father, Jesus Christ the righteous: | MY little children, I am writing these things to you so that you may not sin. But if anyone does sin, we have an advocate with the Father, Jesus Christ the righteous, |
| 2 And he is the propitiation for our sins: and not for ours only, but also for the sins of the whole world. | 2 and he is the atoning sacrifice for our sins, and not for ours only but also for the sins of the whole world. |
| 3 And hereby we do know that we know him, if we keep his commandments. | 3 Now by this we know that we have come to know him, if we obey his commandments. |
| 4 He that saith, I know him, and keepeth not his commandments, is a liar, and the truth is not in him. | 4 Whoever says, "I have come to know him," but does not obey his commandments is a liar, and in such a person the truth does not exist; |
| 5 But whoso keepeth his word, in him verily is the love of God perfected: hereby know we that we are in him. | 5 but whoever obeys his word, truly in this person the love of God has reached perfection. By this we know that we are in him: |
| 6 He that saith he abideth in him ought himself also so to walk, even as he walked. | 6 whoever says, "I abide in him," ought to walk in the same way as he walked. |
| • • • • • • | • • • • • • |
| 9 In this was manifested the love of God toward us, because that God sent his only begotten Son into the world, that we might live through him. | 9 God's love was revealed among us in this way: God sent his only Son into the world so that we might live through him. |
| 10 Herein is love, not that we loved God, but that he loved us, and sent his Son to be the propitiation for our sins. | 10 In this is love, not that we loved God but that he loved us and sent his Son to be the atoning sacrifice for our sins. |
| 11 Beloved, if God so loved us, we ought also to love one another. | 11 Beloved, since God loved us so much, we also ought to love one another. |
| 12 No man hath seen God at any time. If we love one another, God dwelleth in us, and his love is perfected in us. | 12 No one has ever seen God; if we love one another, God abides in us, and his love is perfected in us. |
| 13 Hereby know we that we dwell in him, and he in us, because he hath given us of his Spirit. | 13 By this we know that we abide in him and he in us, because he has given us of his Spirit. |
| 14 And we have seen and do testify that the Father sent the Son to be the Saviour of the world. | 14 And we have seen and do testify that the Father has sent his Son as the Savior of the world. |

**MAIN THOUGHT:** This is love, not that we loved God but that he loved us and sent his Son to be the atoning sacrifice for our sins. (1 John 4:10, NRSVue)

## 1 John 2:1–6; 4:9–17

### KJV

15 Whosoever shall confess that Jesus is the Son of God, God dwelleth in him, and he in God.
16 And we have known and believed the love that God hath to us. God is love; and he that dwelleth in love dwelleth in God, and God in him.
17 Herein is our love made perfect, that we may have boldness in the day of judgment: because as he is, so are we in this world.

### NRSVueue

15 God abides in those who confess that Jesus is the Son of God, and they abide in God.
16 So we have known and believe the love that God has for us. God is love, and those who abide in love abide in God, and God abides in them.
17 Love has been perfected among us in this: that we may have boldness on the day of judgment, because as he is, so are we in this world.

## LESSON SETTING
Time: Circa CE 90
Place: Ephesus

## LESSON OUTLINE
I. Christ as Advocate
   (1 John 2:1–6)
II. God is Love
   (1 John 4:9–17)

## UNIFYING PRINCIPLE

Fake news breeds hostility and leads people to believe in lies. How can we know the truth? The truth of Christ's atoning sacrifice, as an expression of God's love, demonstrates itself in love among believers and for the world.

## INTRODUCTION

John starts by writing, "My little children," the sentiment of which is that of endearment and affection from an apostle who has the concern of a father. John does not treat his readers as if they are totally immature; however, he is appealing to and encouraging his audience in the fact that they have the ability to reject sin because of their walk with the Lord. Moreover, in his encouragement, John continues to promote the power of God's love as an antidote to all of the ills of the world.

John emphasizes God's love through the gift of Jesus into the world because the world needed saving grace. The similarity in literary style and theology that sets the Gospel and Letters of John apart from all other New Testament writings is a strong argument that they were written by the same person, and this is especially true of 1 John and the Gospel of John. Yet, there are differences between these two as well, in small details of linguistic habit.

## EXPOSITION

### I. CHRIST AS ADVOCATE
   (1 JOHN 2:1–6)

John begins this missive by providing reasons that they may not sin. This phrase may seem impossible to understand because humans have a problem refraining from their vices, their greed, and other weaknesses that invite the opportunity to sin. Additionally, since individual and corporate sinning is enjoyable for humans, how could John offer any advice that would support his theories when it seems impossible not to sin? However, there exists a wrong–headed manner for interpreting John's belief. That humans may not sin is found in Jesus' creating situations in which believers never find themselves out of the arc of God's safety or out of touch with God. Since sin is defined by being separated from God, it is not simply the act of excessive drinking or being high on drugs. Sin is not defined as gambling or any other type of action that society and the church has labeled as some sort of moral turpitude. However, it is in these acts that humans find themselves being separated from their walk with the Lord, and it is impossible for humans to be involved with God while being held captive by devices that cause this separation or sin. Nonetheless, for John, when we sin, we have an advocate with the Father. It is possible to misunderstand this need for an advocate. It could be taken that God the Father is an unbending, uncaring, unloving God who is ready to hand down the harshest sentence for anyone who has fallen short of His requirements and commandments. This is far from the truth, as God loves humanity and has gone to extraordinary measures to prove His love and to continue displaying His love, especially by keeping us near Him throughout the gift of eternal life. Nothing would please God more than to have His people, His creation, to return their love back to Him so that all of humanity could share in eternity with Him, meaning that all would be saved.

If one argues for the advocacy of Jesus in a courtroom context, the term "propitiation" would fit, in that Jesus' argument for the salvation of believers is satisfactory to God. However, in the context of "helper," Jesus' blessings and guidance are necessary, as believers move through the maze of life that brings satisfaction to both humans and God. Of course, Jesus is the only offering that satisfied God concerning sin, whom God set forth as a propitiation by His blood, through faith, to demonstrate His righteousness, because in His forbearance God had passed over the sins that were previously committed (Romans 3:25). Jesus Christ, Yahweh's only begotten Son and the second part of the Trinity, is necessary as an advocate, as He is mediating with the Father for our shortcomings. Many believe that the focus on sin dilutes the motivation to seek holiness; however, this is a misunderstanding that possibly provokes the thought that while Jesus is pleading with God to forgive us and sort–of overlook our misdeeds, the Father wants to actually invoke severe punishment, as if Jesus is begging God not to punish us while giving God a reason why we should be saved. Since the Father and the Son are One, this concept is impossible. Although theologians define "advocate" as literally, one summoned alongside (a helper or a patron in a lawsuit), in actuality, Jesus is better defined as a helper to the Father in the heavenly act of securing the salvation of His faithful. Additionally, Christ died for the sins of the whole world, the entire human race. He is the only one who could satisfactorily die for the believers of the past, present, and future.

"By this, we have come to know Him," simply means that belief in His sacrifice and advocacy is the foundation for those of the faith. However, having a basic belief in the system of holiness does not satisfy our place in being part of His union and realizing our relationship with Him. It is in our lifestyles and commitment to the faith that Christians actually come to develop a greater knowledge of Jesus and a clearer understanding of our walk with Him. For readers who wish to decide whether their experience of fellowship with God has led them really to know Him in a personal way, John gave a simple test: We know that we have come to know Him if we obey His commands. Moreover, the one who says, "I have come to know Him," and does not keep His commandments, is a liar, and the truth is not in him (1 John 2:4). In this case, truth is not merely correct knowledge but the demonstration of the reality of God's love. God's love is so incredible that it is impossible to correctly and adequately define its essence. Since Jesus is the given Son, it is in this capacity that He serves as the heart and core of truth. Truth (*alḗtheia*) or verity is the property of being in accord with fact or reality. In everyday language, truth is typically ascribed to things that aim to represent reality or otherwise correspond to it, such as beliefs, propositions, and declarative sentences. Therefore, the Christian who comes to know Jesus understands that those who worship Him must worship in spirit and truth (John 4:24). By worshiping the Lord in spirit and truth, the believer is one who not only knows the commandments but keeps his word by the practice of constant repetition. In this believer, the love of God has been perfected, i.e., realized in practice and love, from which it becomes pleasing to the Christian, who is comforted by his knowledge that we are in Him (v. 5).

## II. GOD IS LOVE (1 JOHN 4:9–17)

John defines the love of God as the giving of His Son as the ultimate sacrifice for the redemption of the human race that Yahweh unconditionally loves. In this manner of agape or sacrificial love, God reveals His intentional plan toward humans. What the plan involves is God doing what He knows is best for man and not necessarily what man desires. For example, John 3:16 states, "For God so loved the world, that He gave …" However, what did He give? It was not what man wanted but what God knew man needed, i.e., His Son to bring forgiveness to man. Remember, God provided Jesus as a gift to the world to accomplish what man could not do. John reminds us that God did not send His Son into the world to condemn the world, but that the world through Him might be saved (John 3:17). Therefore, if we embrace the gift of Jesus in the world, we will be able to live through and with Him.

Of the many attributes of God, several are considered as incommunicable, such as eternity and immensity (His size), which is impossible to be analyzed by others. Through his revelation, God is truly known by faith, yet, no creature will ever comprehend God the Creator. Likewise, no one will ever fully understand any one of God's attributes. However, one of His greatest attributes is love, which is the centerpiece of the Gospel. This attribute is considered as communicable, in that it may not be subject to analysis but is constantly communicated to the body of believers. John is convinced that God is love and therefore, if Yahweh loved believers according to His paradigm, Christians (or humans, for that matter) have the capacity to (and should) love one another. However, the human desire for brotherly love is lacking. When Jesus was asked, "What is the greatest commandment?" He declared, "You shall love your neighbor as yourself as there is no other commandment greater than these" (Mark 12:31). Since no one has seen Yahweh at any time, it is imperative that believers realize we have the capacity to love because God (and His attribute of love) abides in us and therefore, is perfected.

Moreover, by His love for us, we should be convinced and persuaded as to the depth of where we abide in God's love. It is also in this paradigm that we have been gifted with His love within another incommunicable attribute of spirit. Since this attribute is inexpressible, it is to the benefit of the Christian, in that God's spiritual love for us is "locked–in" and is not subject to change. Because He has given us of His Spirit, the mutual abiding of a believer in God – and God in that believer – is indicated by that Christian's experience of the Spirit, which suggests participation in the Spirit of God. Therefore, when a believer loves, he is drawing that love from God's Spirit, who is also the Source of his confession of Christ. A believer's Spirit–led obedience becomes the evidence that he is enjoying the mutual, abiding relationship with God.

Moreover, we have seen and testified that Yahweh sent His Son Jesus, the Messiah, to be the Savior of the world. When John declared that God gave His begotten Son, it was because the Son was sent on the mission to save the world and not condemn it. Although there are resurrection deniers, whoever confesses or acknowledges that Jesus is the Son of God is following in the example of Peter who when asked, "Who do men say that I am?" declared, "You are the Christ, the Son of the living God."

Jesus answered saying, "Blessed are you, for flesh and blood had not revealed this to you, but my Father who is in heaven" (Matthew 16:15–17). Whoever accepts Jesus as Savior is able to do so because we abide in God and He lives in us.

Therefore, Christian believers are convinced beyond a doubt that God loves us. Life has issued too many challenges in the personal lives of believers to doubt His existence and direction in the lifespan of Christians. Although Scriptures present a myriad of examples of God's love, His dedication to His people must not be overlooked. Several examples are found in His promise to never leave us or forsake us (Hebrews 13:5), and where Jesus promises that "if I go and prepare a place for you, I will come again and receive you to Myself; that where I am, there you may be also" (John 14:3). For Jesus to prepare a heavenly place indicates that the Christian will permanently abide in and with God.

Now that Yahweh has proved His love for the believer, Christians may now have confidence in the Day of Judgment because the believer who has practiced love during his earthly life will be able to approach the judgment seat of Christ without any shame. In this situation, such assurance is not presumption or a supposition. In this case, a believer may have confidence that God will approve the quality of his life if, through love, that believer (while in this world) becomes like Him. Additionally, a loving believer is one in whom the work of God's love has been made complete, and the fruit of that is boldness before the One who will judge him. In this way, he achieves the goal of confidence and no shame before Him.

"For God so loved the world that He gave His only begotten Son." John is writing to convince his readers and audience that the love of God is incomparable and that believers have access to Yahweh through Jesus and His love for the entire world. His love for us is very important in the lives of Christians because it is His love that assures the correct trajectory of our existence. As love, Jesus serves as a helper that assists in the movement in the lives of the believer, ensuring a sense of comfort, fluidity, and consistency. Regardless of the pitfalls that confront the believer, God's love serves as the foundation and platform that promises a fruitful walk with Him.

## THE LESSON APPLIED

Unfortunately, the masses of this world do not believe in God, Jesus, or the Holy Spirit. All of humanity has heard of the Trinity, but having a familiarity of the Lord as part of the world's information base does not equate to knowledge in the conversation about love or eternal life. Christians must realize the situation of the non–believing world where believers are in the minority and yet, we must not become faint of heart and dissuaded into falling away from the love of the Lord. Christians must exercise the love that Jesus has instilled in us, which creates a love for our fellow man, regardless of the nature of the world.

## LET'S TALK ABOUT IT

Christian adults must be assured in the realization and knowledge of God's love. Believers do not have to simply rely on readings of the Gospel or other writings by Christian apologists. Christians should be able to see God's love in the eyes of our children and families. Christians should realize that it is because of the love of God that we are able to exist with our coworkers in our vocations. Christians must embrace the power of God's love that allows the Church to survive through the clashes with the powers of darkness that continually seek to destroy her continuation. Christian adults must be able to see, know, and feel the love of God.

### GET SOCIAL
Share your views and tag us @rhboydco. Use #rhboydco.

@rhboydco

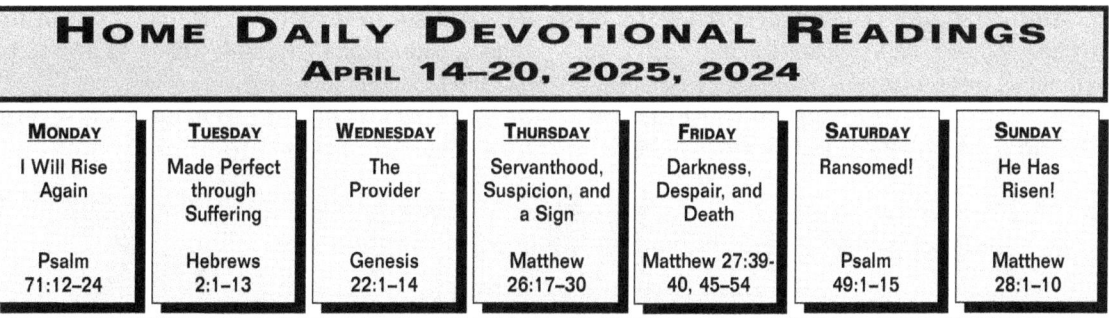

# LESSON VIII
**APRIL 20, 2025**

# CHRIST DIES AND RISES TO NEW LIFE

**ADULT TOPIC:**
THEY COULDN'T KEEP HIM DOWN

**BACKGROUND SCRIPTURE:** MATTHEW 27:24–28:10
**LESSON PASSAGE:** MATT. 27:39–40, 45–54; 28:1–10

## MATTHEW 27:39–40, 45–54; 28:1–10

| KJV | NRSVueue |
|---|---|
| AND they that passed by reviled him, wagging their heads, <br> 40 And saying, Thou that destroyest the temple, and buildest it in three days, save thyself. If thou be the Son of God, come down from the cross. <br> • • • • • • <br> 45 Now from the sixth hour there was darkness over all the land unto the ninth hour. <br> 46 And about the ninth hour Jesus cried with a loud voice, saying, Eli, Eli, lama sabachthani? that is to say, My God, my God, why hast thou forsaken me? <br> 47 Some of them that stood there, when they heard that, said, This man calleth for Elias. <br> 48 And straightway one of them ran, and took a spunge, and filled it with vinegar, and put it on a reed, and gave him to drink. <br> 49 The rest said, Let be, let us see whether Elias will come to save him. <br> 50 Jesus, when he had cried again with a loud voice, yielded up the ghost. <br> 51 And, behold, the veil of the temple was rent in twain from the top to the bottom; and the earth did quake, and the rocks rent; <br> 52 And the graves were opened; and many bodies of the saints which slept arose, <br> 53 And came out of the graves after his resurrection, and went into the holy city, and appeared unto many. <br> 54 Now when the centurion, and they that were with him, watching Jesus, saw the earthquake, | THOSE who passed by derided him, shaking their heads <br> 40 and saying, "You who would destroy the temple and build it in three days, save yourself! If you are the Son of God, come down from the cross." <br> • • • • • • <br> 45 From noon on, darkness came over the whole land until three in the afternoon. <br> 46 And about three o'clock Jesus cried with a loud voice, "Eli, Eli, lema sabachthani?" that is, "My God, my God, why have you forsaken me?" <br> 47 When some of the bystanders heard it, they said, "This man is calling for Elijah." <br> 48 At once one of them ran and got a sponge, filled it with sour wine, put it on a stick, and gave it to him to drink. <br> 49 But the others said, "Wait, let us see whether Elijah will come to save him." <br> 50 Then Jesus cried again with a loud voice and breathed his last.[ <br> 51 At that moment the curtain of the temple was torn in two, from top to bottom. The earth shook, and the rocks were split. <br> 52 The tombs also were opened, and many bodies of the saints who had fallen asleep were raised. <br> 53 After his resurrection they came out of the tombs and entered the holy city and appeared to many. <br> 54 Now when the centurion and those with him, who were keeping watch over Jesus, saw |

**MAIN THOUGHT:** Suddenly, Jesus met them and said, "Greetings!" And they came to him, took hold of his feet, and worshiped him. (Matthew 28:9, NRSVue)

## Matthew 27:39–40, 45–54; 28:1–10

### KJV

and those things that were done, they feared greatly, saying, Truly this was the Son of God.

••• 28:1-10 •••

1 In the end of the sabbath, as it began to dawn toward the first day of the week, came Mary Magdalene and the other Mary to see the sepulchre.
2 And, behold, there was a great earthquake: for the angel of the Lord descended from heaven, and came and rolled back the stone from the door, and sat upon it.
3 His countenance was like lightning, and his raiment white as snow:
4 And for fear of him the keepers did shake, and became as dead men.
5 And the angel answered and said unto the women, Fear not ye: for I know that ye seek Jesus, which was crucified.
6 He is not here: for he is risen, as he said. Come, see the place where the Lord lay.
7 And go quickly, and tell his disciples that he is risen from the dead; and, behold, he goeth before you into Galilee; there shall ye see him: lo, I have told you.
8 And they departed quickly from the sepulchre with fear and great joy; and did run to bring his disciples word.
9 And as they went to tell his disciples, behold, Jesus met them, saying, All hail. And they came and held him by the feet, and worshipped him.
10 Then said Jesus unto them, Be not afraid: go tell my brethren that they go into Galilee, and there shall they see me.

### NRSVueue

the earthquake and what took place, they were terrified and said, "Truly this man was God's Son!"

••• 28:1-10 •••

1 After the Sabbath, as the first day of the week was dawning, Mary Magdalene and the other Mary went to see the tomb.
2 And suddenly there was a great earthquake, for an angel of the Lord, descending from heaven, came and rolled back the stone and sat on it.
3 His appearance was like lightning and his clothing white as snow.
4 For fear of him the guards shook and became like dead men.
5 But the angel said to the women, "Do not be afraid, for I know that you are looking for Jesus who was crucified.
6 He is not here, for he has been raised, as he said. Come, see the place where he lay.
7 Then go quickly and tell his disciples, 'He has been raised from the dead, and indeed he is going ahead of you to Galilee; there you will see him.' This is my message for you."
8 So they left the tomb quickly with fear and great joy and ran to tell his disciples.
9 Suddenly Jesus met them and said, "Greetings!" And they came to him, took hold of his feet, and worshiped him.
10 Then Jesus said to them, "Do not be afraid; go and tell my brothers and sisters to go to Galilee; there they will see me."

## LESSON SETTING
Time: Circa CE 27 or 30
Place: Jerusalem

## LESSON OUTLINE
I. The Crucifixion
   (Matthew 27:39–40, 45–54)
II. Jesus Has Risen
   (Matthew 28:1–7)
III. A Blessed Reunion
   (Matthew 28:7–10)

## UNIFYING PRINCIPLE

People want their lives to have meaning. What meaning can we find? Matthew tells us that Jesus's death and resurrection find meaning in the Temple and the Old Testament sacrificial teachings, leading to worship of the Risen One.

## INTRODUCTION

Although Jesus had been arrested by the Sanhedrin inclusion with the Romans, He was initially charged with blasphemy, declaring Himself to be the Messiah and Son of God. However, it was the charge of sedition against the Roman Empire that sealed His crucifixion. Although the Romans were guilty of crucifying many, and it is possible that the crosses were filled on this particular day, the Gospels only mention two other men who were crucified with Jesus, and the details of their trials remain obscure. These men have been labeled as thieves, robbers (lēstés), or criminals.

Nonetheless, there existed scoffers who were hurling insults at Jesus, mocking Him by saying, "If you are the Son of God, come down from the cross and save Yourself" (Matthew 27:40). Ironically, one of the condemned men joined in the chorus of abuse, yet, the other refused to get caught up in the animosity directed at Jesus, instead, rebuking his compatriot and asking Jesus to "remember me when You come into Your Kingdom" (Luke 23:42–43). The account here in Matthew documents details of the crucifixion, the empty tomb, His resurrection, and His promise to return to His disciples.

## EXPOSITION

### I. THE CRUCIFIXION (MATTHEW 27:39–40, 45–54)

In Christian circles, the crucifixion of Jesus is a monumental occurrence; however, in the reality of the day, the actual event was probably insignificant. Pontius Pilate, the fifth Roman prefect, was a ruthless man who did not care about the sensibilities of Jewish culture or religion. Moreover, Jesus was on the cross by the third hour (9:00 am). The shopkeepers and many of the people who were in the city had barely come to life, therefore, missing the procession from the city to Calvary. However, heaven's reaction to Jesus' execution was being displayed, and by the sixth hour (noon), darkness fell upon the land until the ninth hour (3:00 pm).

It was during this latter hour that Jesus cried out in a loud voice saying, "Eli, Eli, Lama Sabachthani." "Eli, Eli" represents the Hebrew version of Psalm 22:1 ("My God, My God, why have You forsaken Me?"), and "Eloi, Eloi" (Mark 15:34) comes from the Aramaic. Jesus' cry of "Eli, Eli, Lama Sabachthani" is translated by Matthew, yet, the words are profound, as it is taken by some to mean that Jesus actually believed God had abandoned Him at this moment. Others take into consideration the entire Psalm, especially verses 24 and 26, and see here the prayer of One who still trusts in God to vindicate Him. Today's English Version has rendered "forsaken" with the more contemporary "abandoned."

Some of the crowd that had gathered at the crucifixion site heard Jesus cry and thought that He was calling on Elijah instead of Yahweh. Their misunderstanding is actually appreciated because Elijah was one of Israel's champions of faith. Remember, John the Baptist was identified with Elijah in his dress and diet, and when Herod Antipas first heard of John, many around him believed John the Baptist was Elijah (Mark 6:14–15). Additionally, the disciples were so enamored with Elijah that they wanted to build three tabernacles, one for Jesus, one for Moses, and one for Elijah (Luke 9:33). Matthew has Jesus drinking some sour wine that was put on a sponge and lifted up to Him (v. 48). However, Mark records that they gave Him wine mingled with myrrh to drink, but He did not take it (Mark 15:23). If the latter is accurate, Jesus would have refused the drink because myrrh was an analgesic drug that would have numbed Him and reduced the pain of the execution. Since "by His stripes we are healed," Jesus did not want to be under the influence of any drugs when He gave up His life for humanity.

Nonetheless, while the soldiers were attempting to give Jesus the sour wine, the mockers and scoffers continued their tirade. Again, the thought was that Jesus was calling on Elijah. In this case, they decided to taunt Jesus by saying, "Let us see if Elijah will save Him" (v. 49). In reality, their taunts were almost just as painful as the beating, as they were saying that Jesus' cries for Elijah's rescue were in vain. More than likely, the crowd of deriders had mistaken what Jesus was saying when He cried out, "Eli, Eli," and thought it was a cry for Elijah. Nevertheless, Jesus cried out again – although Matthew does not record these exact words, whereas Luke does – "Father, into Your hands I commit My spirit" (Luke 23:46).

Recall that from the sixth hour, darkness fell upon all the land until the ninth hour (v. 45); however, God was not yet finished with His signs. What could be thought of as God being angry for the collusion between the High Priests, the Sanhedrin, and the Romans in the execution of His Son is rather misunderstood. Jesus was the ultimate sacrifice for the world and since He gave His life, it was part of God's overall plan. Consequently, if God were angry, He would have been angry with Himself because Jesus was offered by God. The unnatural darkness that came over the land was simply a reaction from heaven through the displaying of God's power over nature, declaring that the executioners were not in control of the situation.

Additionally, Matthew records that there was a seismic shift causing an earthquake, splitting many of the giant rocks that encompassed the area and opening the tombs to reveal the bodies of various saints who later appeared to many in Jerusalem. However, the primary results of the earthquake affected the temple, where the great veil was torn from top to bottom. The significance of this was that the message of God was not to be hidden behind the curtain to be visited by only the High Priest once–a–year but that, with the gift of Jesus, God would be accessible to all who seek Him at all times. If anything, God was displeased with the High Priest and the Sanhedrin because they should have been closer to God and, therefore, should have known better.

## II. JESUS HAS RISEN (MATTHEW 28:1–7)

Now, after the Sabbath came the dawning of the first day of the week. Matthew identifies Mary Magdalene and "the other Mary" as the two women who came to the tomb to properly anoint the body of Jesus. Besides Mary Magdalene, Luke includes Joanna (a wealthy disciple), Mary, the mother of James, and other unnamed women (Luke 24:9–10), while (besides Mary Magdalene), Mark lists Mary, the mother of James, and Salome, who came to anoint Jesus. During this period, Mary was a common name; however, none of the Marys gathered at the tomb seem to be Mary or Miriam, the mother of Jesus. Continuing, Matthew briefly describes the angel as one whose appearance (*idéa*) was like lightning, while arrayed in garments as "white as snow." The word for appearance, which appears only here in the New Testament, may also mean "face" or countenance. Nonetheless, the appearance of the angel was so frightening to the guards that they were rendered into a comatose stage. Matthew recounts that the women were afraid, and the angel sought to alleviate their fears, saying, "Do not be afraid" (v. 5). Notice that the angel knew the purpose of the women's visit and also told them that Jesus had risen, with an invitation to see where He had been laid. Moreover, the angel reminds them to tell the disciples to go ahead to Galilee where He will meet them.

## III. A Blessed Reunion (Matthew 28:7–10)

After the women discovered the empty tomb, they left quickly. In their excitement and awe, they could not bring themselves to linger and investigate the empty place where they knew that Christ had been laid. This scene was not lifted from some modern–day horror classic where bodies disappear, and the actors in the plot need to have their curiosity satisfied. These women did not feel comfortable in this mysterious place. Gripped with fear and trembling, they gathered enough resolve to leave the tomb. The women's fear was probably not as much about the situation that they had just discovered as it was from the aspect of the "unknown." What had happened to Jesus' body? Had someone slipped in and stolen His corpse in the middle of the night? It was tragic enough that the events of the previous days had served to upset and traumatize His followers. Now, the thought that His body was missing was almost unbearable! Their fear was real and ever–present because initially, they were totally perplexed and could not conceive of what had occurred in this place (Jerusalem).

However, in the midst of their horror and panic, one of the women remembered that there was hope in the message of the angel. Recall, Jesus had told His disciples several times He would rise on the third day (see 16:21; 17:23; 20:19). Now, their despair turned suddenly into a tremendous sense of great (*mégas*) joy that changed their fear into an excitement of the awe and wonder of their Lord. It was not simply because the women were infused with a newfound breath of courage. Their fear had been turned into joy by the rise of their faith. The words of the angel now made sense. Buoyed with an excess of energy, the women knew that Jesus had risen, and they ran to report their experience to the disciples. According to Matthew's account, before they could get to the place where the men were in hiding, Jesus suddenly appeared to them. However, John reports that Mary did not initially recognize Jesus and mistook Him for the gardener (John 20:14–15).

Then, Jesus said to them, "Do not be afraid, but go and tell My brethren [the disciples] to immediately leave for Galilee and there they will meet [see] Me" (v. 10). The Galilean ministry of Jesus was prominent in Matthew's account, so, it was natural for Jesus to meet His disciples there. They were all from Galilee and would be returning to Galilee after the Feast, and there, Jesus would meet them. Moreover, in Galilee they would be safe from the Sanhedrin and the Romans who may have also been seeking their lives. Recall that when Jesus predicted His capture and the disciples' falling away, He disclosed that "after I have been raised [resurrected], I will go ahead of you to Galilee" (Matthew 26:32). Therefore, the reunion with His disciples was not accidental but was part of God's overall plan.

For Christians, Jesus' trials, flogging, and execution are a painful reminder of the lack of awareness of who Jesus was and the extent of His mission.

## The Lesson Applied

Christian believers are convinced that Jesus' crucifixion was necessary for humanity to be saved. However, the characters that surround His crucifixion are both kind and loving and (on the other hand) brutal and unconcerned. The term theodicy is defined as asking, "Why do bad things happen to good people?" Jesus' crucifixion asks that question, but as exclaimed in the Church, "on the third day, He got up with all power in His hands." This is an example of what believers face in our daily lives, the enigmas of this world. However, we are comforted with the fact that there is "joy in the morning" because His resurrection is a sign of great exultation in the lives of the believer.

## Let's Talk About It

Christians must be able to rejoice in Jesus' resurrection. On far too many occasions, Christians focus on the cross and allow their worship to remain with this visible sign of Jesus' sacrifice. The Church is not founded on the cross but is grounded in the resurrection. As with the week when Jesus was executed, many men lost their lives on a cross. Christians should not place too much emphasis on the tool that killed Jesus, but rather, should rejoice in the power that saved Jesus. Remember, one day, we will be saved by this same power.

## Get Social

Share your views and tag us @rhboydco. Use #rhboydco.

@rhboydco

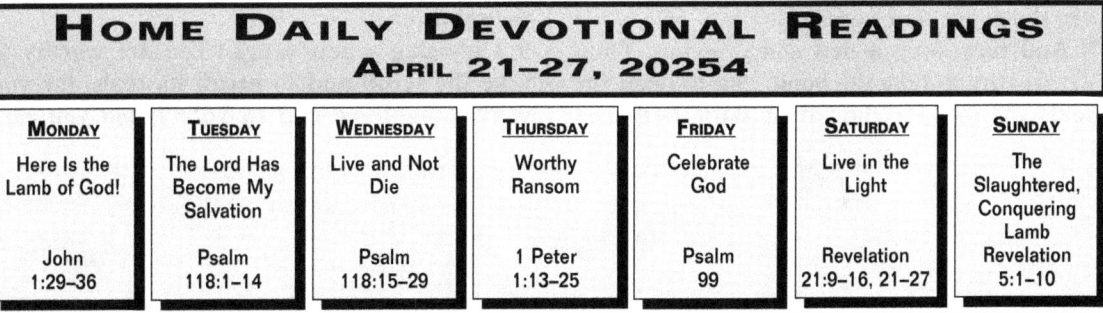

## Home Daily Devotional Readings
### April 21–27, 20254

| Monday | Tuesday | Wednesday | Thursday | Friday | Saturday | Sunday |
|---|---|---|---|---|---|---|
| Here Is the Lamb of God! | The Lord Has Become My Salvation | Live and Not Die | Worthy Ransom | Celebrate God | Live in the Light | The Slaughtered, Conquering Lamb |
| John 1:29–36 | Psalm 118:1–14 | Psalm 118:15–29 | 1 Peter 1:13–25 | Psalm 99 | Revelation 21:9–16, 21–27 | Revelation 5:1–10 |

LESSON IX                                                 APRIL 27, 2025

# THE LAMB IS WORTHY

ADULT TOPIC:                                  BACKGROUND SCRIPTURE: REVELATION 5
SING A NEW SONG                               LESSON PASSAGE: REVELATION 5:1–10

## REVELATION 5:1–10

### KJV

AND I saw in the right hand of him that sat on the throne a book written within and on the backside, sealed with seven seals.
2 And I saw a strong angel proclaiming with a loud voice, Who is worthy to open the book, and to loose the seals thereof?
3 And no man in heaven, nor in earth, neither under the earth, was able to open the book, neither to look thereon.
4 And I wept much, because no man was found worthy to open and to read the book, neither to look thereon.
5 And one of the elders saith unto me, Weep not: behold, the Lion of the tribe of Judah, the Root of David, hath prevailed to open the book, and to loose the seven seals thereof.
6 And I beheld, and, lo, in the midst of the throne and of the four beasts, and in the midst of the elders, stood a Lamb as it had been slain, having seven horns and seven eyes, which are the seven Spirits of God sent forth into all the earth.
7 And he came and took the book out of the right hand of him that sat upon the throne.
8 And when he had taken the book, the four beasts and four and twenty elders fell down before the Lamb, having every one of them harps, and golden vials full of odours, which are the prayers of saints.
9 And they sung a new song, saying, Thou art worthy to take the book, and to open the seals thereof: for thou wast slain, and hast

### NRSVueue

THEN I saw in the right hand of the one seated on the throne a scroll written on the inside and on the back, sealed with seven seals,
2 and I saw a mighty angel proclaiming with a loud voice, "Who is worthy to open the scroll and break its seals?"
3 And no one in heaven or on earth or under the earth was able to open the scroll or to look into it.
4 And I began to weep bitterly because no one was found worthy to open the scroll or to look into it.
5 Then one of the elders said to me, "Do not weep. See, the Lion of the tribe of Judah, the Root of David, has conquered, so that he can open the scroll and its seven seals."
6 Then I saw between the throne and the four living creatures and among the elders a Lamb standing as if it had been slaughtered, with seven horns and seven eyes, which are the seven spirits of God sent out into all the earth.
7 He went and took the scroll from the right hand of the one who was seated on the throne.
8 When he had taken the scroll, the four living creatures and the twenty-four elders fell before the Lamb, each holding a harp and golden bowls full of incense, which are the prayers of the saints.
9 They sing a new song: "You are worthy to take the scroll and to break its seals, for you were slaughtered and by your blood you ran-

**MAIN THOUGHT:** They sing a new song: "You are worthy to take the scroll and to open its seals, for you were slaughtered and by your blood you ransomed for God saints from every tribe and language and people and nation." (Revelation 5:9, NRSVue)

## Revelation 5:1–10

### KJV
redeemed us to God by thy blood out of every kindred, and tongue, and people, and nation;
10 And hast made us unto our God kings and priests: and we shall reign on the earth.

### NRSVueue
somed for God saints from every tribe and language and people and nation;
10 you have made them a kingdom and priests serving our God, and they will reign on earth."

## LESSON SETTING
**Time:** Circa CE 95
**Place:** Patmos

## LESSON OUTLINE
I. The Scroll (Book) with the Seven Seals
   (Revelation 5:1–5)
II. He Alone is Worthy
   (Revelation 5:6–10)

## UNIFYING PRINCIPLE
People make sacrifices for those they love. What sacrifices are to be lifted up for their lasting value? In Revelation, Christ, the "slaughtered lamb" sacrificed for the sin of the world, is lifted to the throne of God and is worthy of praise and honor forever.

## INTRODUCTION
John's Book of Revelation is the final book in the Christian Bible. The term apocalypse (*Apokálupsis*) means to reveal: an uncovering, unveiling, or disclosure, and is one of the words that refer to the Second Coming of Christ (1 Corinthians 1:7; 2 Thessalonians 1:7; 1 Peter 1:7, 13). The book also serves as predictions into what will occur in the final days of the earth and the results of Jesus' sacrifice for the redemption of the believers who will obtain eternal life. Chapter five is an extension of the previous chapter where John witnessed Yahweh sitting on a high and prominent throne, being worshiped by four living creatures and twenty-four elders. Of the themes presented here are the identity of the Lamb, His worthiness to open sealed scrolls, and the results that accompany the unveiling. The Books of Daniel and Revelation (and possibly Ezekiel) reveal the apocalypse in the Bible.

## EXPOSITION

### I. THE SCROLL (BOOK) WITH THE SEVEN SEALS (REVELATION 5:1–5)

In John's vision, he has been allowed to observe some of the events that are occurring in the throne room. Writing for an audience of his generation, there would be an appreciation for the metaphor of the trappings of a royal court, which would signify a king, vassals, and a kingdom. John's vision may serve as a continuation of thematic images presented in the birth account of Matthew's Gospel, which were dominated by the interaction between kings (Herod and the Magi) and the lineage of Jesus as Messiah. Matthew included his story as a reminder to Israel that Jesus is King of the Jews. As John revealed, the action in the throne room of heaven is only natural as God sits on the eternal throne. The God of Israel is described metaphorically as sitting upon a throne (Isaiah 66:1), and the vision of God seated on a throne as seen in prophetic visions is described by Micaiah (1 Kings 22:19), Isaiah (6:1-3),

Ezekiel (1:4-28; 10:1), and Daniel (7:9-10). Later, Ezekiel's vision of the throne of God was of major significance in Jewish "throne mysticism."

John saw in the right (strong) hand of Yahweh, a book written inside and on the back, sealed with seven seals. A scroll was a document made of sheets of parchment or papyrus that were pasted together in one long strip and then rolled up like a tube, usually tied, or else sealed, as this scroll was. Ordinarily, there was writing on only one side of the sheets, but this scroll had writing on both sides. Ancient official documents were sealed with wax and ribbons and usually, a royal stamp from a signet ring or imprint served to identify the sender, as confirmation of their authority. Continuing, John witnessed what he described as a "strong angel." Although the angel is not identified, this term also described the angel as "able." In this case, the might of the angel may have come from the power of his voice, as he served as a herald to ask who was worthy to open the scroll and break its seals.

However, John found that no one was able to open the book and look into it. John is intentional in his statement of worthiness as he mentions that no one on and under the earth was able or had the authority to open the scroll and view its contents and message. When John declares the phrase, "no one in heaven or on earth or under the earth," this is a way of talking about the universe as it was conceived of at that time. The universe was thought to have three parts: the world of heavenly beings, the world of earthly beings, and the world of the dead, each of which is found in Philippians 2:10, respectively: "of those in heaven, and of those on earth, and under the earth." The world of the dead (under the earth) was called Sheol (in Hebrew) or Hades (in Greek). This was John's method of including the entire universe, heaven and hell, and any other environs that may be included in God's celestial realm. When John declares that no one was able to open the scroll, he does not mean that no one could physically open the document; he is indicating that no one was worthy of examining the contents of the manuscript.

John then becomes distraught because no one is available or worthy to open the scroll. It is possible to infer that someone else was sought after to open the scroll, yet, there are no references to a formal search for anyone other than the One who will be authorized to unlock the scroll. John begins to weep in his state of sadness and frustration because he desperately wanted to know the contents of the scroll. At this point in the narrative, John does not reveal why he wants to know the contents of the document; nevertheless, in this revelation, John must sense that the document contains some of the mysteries of heaven: the path Christians are to follow to further obtain eternal life and the promises of Jesus, such as "I go to prepare a place for you…" (John 14:2).

However, one of the elders spoke up and asked John to stop weeping because he had the answer to John's question as to who could open the book, declaring that there is One who has overcome any barriers and obstacles to be able to open the book. John remembers the trials of the earthly Jesus and recalls that he had received an earlier message that stated, "To him who overcomes I will grant to sit with Me on My throne, as I also overcame and sat down with My Father on His throne" (Revelation 3:12). Jesus overcame the cross, and the grave, for such a time as this! Moreover, He is described as the Lion from the tribe of Judah, which is thought of as the most noticeable tribe (Genesis 49:9). Recall, the lion is considered the "king of beasts," as the animal is representative of strength and power. Lions played an important part in the political and religious symbolism of the Near East. In Assyria and Babylonia, the lion was regarded as a royal beast (Daniel 7:4). To the Jews, the lion was the mightiest of beasts, having a king's regal bearing (Proverbs 30:29-31). The lion symbolized leadership and hence, eventually became a title for Christ. The lion was also the ensign of Judah's tribe and was used by King Solomon in the decoration of his house and the temple. Moreover, as the root of David, which is also referred to as a rod from the stem of Jesse, the Messiah has the Spirit of the Lord and is the New Covenant between Yahweh and His people (see Isaiah 11:1). Therefore, the Lion (the Messiah) will have the power to open the scroll. The Messiah (John is assured) is competent and worthy to break the seven seals and open the scroll to release the plagues.

## II. HE ALONE IS WORTHY (REVELATION 5:6–10)

John was granted the ability to further look into the throne room, and he witnessed the four living creatures, the elders, and a Lamb, standing as if it was slain. Arranged around the center throne were twenty-four elders seated on lesser thrones. Gathered around the throne were the four living creatures. The first living creature was like a lion; the second living creature, like a calf; the third living creature had a face like a man; and the fourth living creature was like a flying eagle (Revelation 4:3-6). These creatures had seven horns and seven eyes, which are the seven Spirits of God that were sent out to cover the earth. Additionally, these seven eyes represent the power of God's ability to see everywhere. The standing Lamb is symbolically posed as a reminder of the sacrifice of the Messiah, bearing the marks of the cross, who also symbolically represented the slain lamb at Passover. However, one of the most beautiful mixed metaphors of the Bible is that of the lion (5:5), which is transformed into the lamb! It is the Lion of Judah that has conquered the deception and trickery of Satan whose desires are to lead humanity astray through the sin of separation from God. Although the lion represents power, especially military supremacy, it is the Lamb who has the ultimate control of power and authority. It is the Lamb and not the lion that rode on a donkey instead of a warhorse into the Holy City on what is celebrated as Palm Sunday. While the denizens and pilgrims of Jerusalem wanted a lion, the Lamb declared that His kingdom was not of this world (John 18:36). Moreover, it was the Lamb and not the lion who was crucified but rose on the third day. The transformation of the lion into the Lamb is a continuation of the Messiah as One of peace.

The book (scroll) was taken from the right hand of the One who sat on the center (main) throne by the Lamb who is worthy. When the Lamb received the book, the elders fell down prostrate and began to worship the Lamb. Each elder had a harp and golden bowls full of incense, which is interpreted as the prayers of the saints, as was earlier prophesied, "Let my prayer be set before You as incense, the lifting up of my hands as the evening sacrifice" (Psalm 141:2). While the angels presented the prayers, they were not priests or mediators. Note: Only the harp (lyre) and the trumpet are mentioned as musical instruments in heavenly worship in the Book of Revelation. The harp (kithara), also occasionally identified as a lyre, is the most frequently mentioned instrument in the Bible. The most beloved instrument of the Jewish people, it is often called David's Harp, which could have been a lyre. Recall that whenever the spirit of God was upon Saul, David would play his harp; then, Saul would become refreshed and well, and the distressing spirit would depart from him (1 Samuel 16:22-23). The music flowing from the harp or lyre would be audibly refreshing to Yahweh, contrary to what was declared by Amos when God rejected the noise of their songs and the melody of their stringed instruments (Amos 5:23). The instrument remained silent during times of mourning; however, the scene in the throne room was a celebration. In this case, God accepts the worship of the elders and (possible) angels. Additionally, the incense (although not identified, it could have ranged from cinnamon to nard) served as a sweet-smelling fragrance to Yahweh and represented the prayers for the people of God.

In their worship, the twenty-four elders sang a new (kainós) song. The song they sang was one of acclamation in the recognition of the power of the Lamb who was slain from the foundations of the world. The song is composed of three parts: the acclamation of the worthiness of the Lamb (5:9b), the salvific work of the Lamb (5:9c), and the effects for the followers of the Lamb (5:10). Additionally, the Lamb is worthy to open the book and break its seals, inaugurating the plagues. The opened seals are the conquering Rider on a White Horse, War, Famine, Death, Martyrs (those who had been slain), Terror, and an interlude before the Seven Trumpets. However, before the opening of the final seal, the kings of the earth and the great men and the commanders and the rich and the strong and every slave and free man will hide themselves in the caves and among the rocks of the mountains, while begging the mountains and rocks to "fall on us and hide us from the presence of Him who sits on the throne, and from the wrath of the Lamb, for the great day of their wrath has come, and who is able to stand?" (Revelation 6:15-17). The reason why the Lamb is worthy is because of His role as a sacrifice but also, the Lamb has the power. It is by the blood of the Lamb that was slain that believers are saved. The purchase, using the Old Testament precedent of a ransom, was requested by God but was also for all men of every tribe, tongue, people, and nation.

The Lamb is worthy because He died (in the past) to pay the ransom price for the sins of the world, which positioned us (in the present) as a kingdom and priests before God and gave us a promise of reigning on the earth in the future. In an attempt to identify the worshipers, there are a few manuscripts that read "us" and "we" in verse 10, instead of "them" and "they." In either instance, the elders could be singing of their own redemption in either the first or third person. The Greek text used by the KJV indicates that the new song is sung by those who themselves have been redeemed: "Thou … has redeemed us to God … and hast made us unto our God kings and priests, and we shall reign on the earth." The New International Version, however, reads, "You purchased men for God.… You have made them to be a kingdom and priests to serve our God, and they will reign on the earth."

## THE LESSON APPLIED

Due to its many metaphorical and seemingly impossible images, John's apocalypse remains a frightening read to many Christians. When read literally, images of beasts with many eyes and horns are frightening; however, the book is understood only when read through the interpretation of the pictures that John was provided. As he wrote from a small island off of the city of Ephesus, probably from a cave on Patmos, the text is written in code because of the need to hide it from both the authorities and those opposed to the Christian movement. Christians should not be afraid of the contents of the book but instead, should beware of the manner in which we live, in hopes that our walk with Jesus will be sealed by the revelations found in this text.

## LET'S TALK ABOUT IT

Christian adults must understand what makes Jesus the only One worthy to open the scroll. Christians must not be dissuaded or "turned off" by the overt and explicit symbolism that John presents in his writings. John offers many explanations of "how" things will happen and "why" the occurrences in the end times arrive. Yet, for the believer, the knowledge of Jesus' worth will encourage us in our walk with the Lord. While we believe that Jesus opens doors and protects us in this life, His worthiness to open the scrolls serves as a final testament to His provision of eternal life for the believer. Christian believers must realize that the power of Jesus is unlimited, past, present, and future.

### GET SOCIAL
Share your views and tag us @rhboydco. Use #rhboydco.

@rhboydco

# HOME DAILY DEVOTIONAL READINGS
## APRIL 28–MAY 4, 2025

| MONDAY | TUESDAY | WEDNESDAY | THURSDAY | FRIDAY | SATURDAY | SUNDAY |
| --- | --- | --- | --- | --- | --- | --- |
| Answer Me, O Lord | Be Alert | The Lord Will Not Reject Forever | God Patiently Waits for Repentance | Live the Godly Life | A Presumptive King | A Costly Sacrifice |
| Psalm 86:1–7, 10–17 | 1 Peter 5 | Lamentations 3:21–36 | 2 Peter 3:1–10 | 2 Peter 3:11–18 | 1 Chronicles 21:1–13 | 1 Chronicles 21:14–30 |

LESSON X                                          MAY 4, 2025

# DAVID'S SACRIFICE

ADULT TOPIC:                    BACKGROUND SCRIPTURE: 1 CHRONICLES 21:1–22:1
IT'LL COST YOU EVERYTHING            LESSON PASSAGE: 1 CHRONICLES 21:14–30

## 1 CHRONICLES 21:14–30

### KJV

SO the Lord sent pestilence upon Israel: and there fell of Israel seventy thousand men.
15 And God sent an angel unto Jerusalem to destroy it: and as he was destroying, the Lord beheld, and he repented him of the evil, and said to the angel that destroyed, It is enough, stay now thine hand. And the angel of the Lord stood by the threshingfloor of Ornan the Jebusite.
16 And David lifted up his eyes, and saw the angel of the Lord stand between the earth and the heaven, having a drawn sword in his hand stretched out over Jerusalem. Then David and the elders of Israel, who were clothed in sackcloth, fell upon their faces.
17 And David said unto God, Is it not I that commanded the people to be numbered? even I it is that have sinned and done evil indeed; but as for these sheep, what have they done? let thine hand, I pray thee, O Lord my God, be on me, and on my father's house; but not on thy people, that they should be plagued.
18 Then the angel of the Lord commanded Gad to say to David, that David should go up, and set up an altar unto the Lord in the threshingfloor of Ornan the Jebusite.
19 And David went up at the saying of Gad, which he spake in the name of the Lord.

20 And Ornan turned back, and saw the angel; and his four sons with him hid themselves. Now Ornan was threshing wheat.
21 And as David came to Ornan, Ornan looked and saw David, and went out of the threshing-

### NRSVueue

SO the Lord sent a pestilence on Israel, and seventy thousand persons fell in Israel.
15 And God sent an angel to Jerusalem to destroy it, but when he was about to destroy it, the Lord took note and relented concerning the calamity; he said to the destroying angel, "Enough! Stay your hand." The angel of the Lord was standing by the threshing floor of Ornan the Jebusite.
16 David looked up and saw the angel of the Lord standing between earth and heaven and in his hand a drawn sword stretched out over Jerusalem. Then David and the elders, clothed in sackcloth, fell on their faces.
17 And David said to God, "Was it not I who gave the command to count the people? It is I who have sinned and done very wickedly. But these sheep, what have they done? Let your hand, I pray, O Lord my God, be against me and against my father's house, but do not let your people be plagued!"
18 Then the angel of the Lord commanded Gad to tell David that he should go up and erect an altar to the Lord on the threshing floor of Ornan the Jebusite.
19 So David went up following Gad's instructions, which he had spoken in the name of the Lord.
20 Ornan turned and saw the king, and while his four sons who were with him hid themselves, Ornan continued to thresh wheat.
21 As David came to Ornan, Ornan looked and saw David; he went out from the threshing

**MAIN THOUGHT:** King David said to Ornan, "No; I will buy them for the full price. I will not take for the LORD what is yours, nor offer burnt offerings that cost me nothing." (1 Chronicles 21:24, NRSVue)

## 1 Chronicles 21:14–30

### KJV

floor, and bowed himself to David with his face to the ground.
22 Then David said to Ornan, Grant me the place of this threshingfloor, that I may build an altar therein unto the Lord: thou shalt grant it me for the full price: that the plague may be stayed from the people.
23 And Ornan said unto David, Take it to thee, and let my lord the king do that which is good in his eyes: lo, I give thee the oxen also for burnt offerings, and the threshing instruments for wood, and the wheat for the meat offering; I give it all.
24 And king David said to Ornan, Nay; but I will verily buy it for the full price: for I will not take that which is thine for the Lord, nor offer burnt offerings without cost.
25 So David gave to Ornan for the place six hundred shekels of gold by weight.
26 And David built there an altar unto the Lord, and offered burnt offerings and peace offerings, and called upon the Lord; and he answered him from heaven by fire upon the altar of burnt offering.
27 And the Lord commanded the angel; and he put up his sword again into the sheath thereof.
28 At that time when David saw that the Lord had answered him in the threshingfloor of Ornan the Jebusite, then he sacrificed there.

29 For the tabernacle of the Lord, which Moses made in the wilderness, and the altar of the burnt offering, were at that season in the high place at Gibeon.
30 But David could not go before it to enquire of God: for he was afraid because of the sword of the angel of the Lord.

### NRSVueue

floor and prostrated himself before David with his face to the ground.
22 David said to Ornan, "Give me the site of the threshing floor that I may build on it an altar to the Lord—give it to me at its full price—so that the plague may be averted from the people."
23 Then Ornan said to David, "Take it, and let my lord the king do what seems good to him; see, I present the oxen for burnt offerings and the threshing sledges for the wood and the wheat for a grain offering. I give it all."
24 But King David said to Ornan, "No, but I will buy them for the full price. I will not take for the Lord what is yours nor offer burnt offerings that cost me nothing."
25 So David paid Ornan six hundred shekels of gold by weight for the site.
26 David built there an altar to the Lord and presented burnt offerings and offerings of well-being. He called upon the Lord, and he answered him with fire from heaven on the altar of burnt offering.
27 Then the Lord commanded the angel, and he put his sword back into its sheath.
28 At that time, when David saw that the Lord had answered him at the threshing floor of Ornan the Jebusite, he made his sacrifices there.

29 For the tabernacle of the Lord that Moses had made in the wilderness and the altar of burnt offering were at that time in the high place at Gibeon,
30 but David could not go before it to inquire of God, for he was afraid of the sword of the angel of the Lord.

## LESSON SETTING
Time: Circa 988 BCE
Place: Jerusalem

## LESSON OUTLINE
I. David's Sin Affects Jerusalem
(1 Chronicles 21:14-17)
II. David Seeks Ornan's Threshing Floor
(1 Chronicles 21:18-25)
III. David Builds an Altar
(1 Chronicles 21:26-30)

## Unifying Principle

People find it difficult to accept the generosity of others when it comes to paying a debt. Is it right to accept a gift from one person in order to pay what is owed to another? David refuses Ornan's gift because his conscience would not permit him to offer to the Lord a sacrifice for which he did not pay.

## Introduction

David takes a census of the people, against the will of God, who is displeased with David's actions. Kings often would order that a census be taken during warlike situations when the numbers available to serve in the military would be affected or, as in the case of the Romans of the New Testament, the census would be conducted for taxation purposes. It seems that God was already angry with Israel. In order to punish Israel, He incites David to number the people, which raises for the reader the theological conundrum of God's inciting to sin. The author of 1 Chronicles 21:1 resolves the issue by replacing God with Satan (a late biblical concept).

Though not inherently wrong, the action demonstrated David's reliance on the number of warriors rather than on God. The census took ten months to complete (2 Samuel 24:5-8). David acknowledges that he has sinned and pleads with God to punish him and his family instead of the people. To put an end to the plague, David erects an altar on the site where later the Temple will be built (2 Chronicles 3:1). Though the plague, as well as its cessation, result from actions by David, they are independently decided upon by God, hinting at both human responsibility and divine sovereignty.

## Exposition

### I. David's Sin Affects Jerusalem (1 Chronicles 21:14-17)

This missive opens to Yahweh sending pestilence on Israel. There is a plague sent to affect the people and the land, but the epidemic is not identified; yet, the lives of 70,000 men were taken because of it. More than likely, the numbers of those stricken were much higher, as the number of those in this report are only identified as the males (who are usually identified in biblical accounts). Through the prophet Gad, Yahweh had given David a choice of punishment for his mistake. He was to select from one of these judgments that would be placed on the people: There could be three years of famine, or three months of pursuit by the enemy, or three days of direct divine retribution by a plague (vv. 11–12). Rather than choosing one of the three options, David placed himself in God's hands, who then destroyed 70,000 men by a plague. So, the Lord sent a plague upon Israel from the morning till the appointed time.

Following the pestilence and death, Yahweh sent an angel to destroy Jerusalem; however, in the midst of preparing for the destruction, Yahweh felt compassion and stayed the hand of the destroying angel, sparing the city and its inhabitants. Feeling that the punishment had already been meted, the Chronicler records that Yahweh was sorry for the calamity that had been pressed upon the people. As this scene unfolds, we find the angel standing by the threshing floor of Ornan the Jebusite, which will feature prominently in the further events of David. Here, the Chronicler identifies the owner of this threshing floor as Ornan; however, in a parallel account of this story, Samuel identifies Ornan as Araunah the Jebusite (2 Samuel 24:1). Ornan was an inhabitant of the city formerly known as Jebus that had been conquered by David and became known as Jerusalem.

David is now drawn into the scene, as he looks on, to see the angel of the Lord standing between what the Chronicler identifies as earth and heaven. That the angel is positioned between the earth and the sky is symbolic of heaven and earth being united and in agreement of the wrath that Yahweh has prepared. In this case, the angel has his sword drawn and ready, as if prepared for battle. The Chronicler notes that the hand of the angel is stretched out (*natah*) or stretched forth in what could be construed as the angel's assuming a menacing position toward Jerusalem, as if he is to destroy the city and its inhabitants. Upon the realization of what was to happen to the city and the people, David and the elders covered themselves in sackcloth in a sign of mourning and lamentation. Notice that the elders of David are included in this passage. These men could have been advisors of the king, but notice that neither Gad, the prophet, or Joab, the commander of David's forces, were included. Moreover, since the angel that is standing between the earth and heaven could reflect the celestial connection, it is conceivable that the elders are of heaven. Nonetheless, in a sign of mourning and sorrow, they immediately fall on their faces in worship and supplication to Yahweh.

Begging God, David assumes the blame for this breach of protocol and enormous error. David admits that he is the one who ordered the census and therefore, the people are innocent because they would be powerless to disobey the king's edict. David literally begs God that the distemper might now cease, and that he would be satisfied with those that had already perished, signifying that there had been destruction and death in the city. Recall, the Chronicler has recorded that 70,000 men (not including women and children) have already fallen (v. 14). Remorseful, David said to God that he might justly be punished, who was their shepherd, but that the sheep ought to be preserved, as not having sinned at all; and he implored God that he would send his wrath upon him, and upon all his family, but spare the people. At this juncture, David's plea does not affect the situation, as Yahweh will not stop the carnage until verse 27.

## II. DAVID SEEKS ORNAN'S THRESHING FLOOR (1 CHRONICLES 21:18-25)

Following David's plea to Yahweh, an angel of the Lord commanded Gad to say to David that David should go up and build an altar to the Lord on the threshing floor of Ornan the Jebusite. The "Gad" of this period was a prophet and seer for David and had previously counseled David in military and personal matters, such as convincing David to leave the stronghold and sanctuary of Mizpah of Moab while he was being pursued by Saul. Gad is named after the first of two sons born to Jacob by Zilpah, Leah's maid. Leah named the boy "Gad," meaning "good fortune," but yet, it was Gad's possible misfortune to have to convey the message of the Lord that David had to follow. David is to build an altar on Ornan's property. Here, the Chronicler rewords his forward position in order to make clear that Gad is speaking on divine authority and not just on his own initiative. Therefore, at the advice of Gad, David readied himself to obey Yahweh's command.

When David approached, Aranauh (Ornan) said, "Why has my lord the king come to his servant?" (2 Samuel 24:21). David informed Ornan that the king wanted Ornan's threshing floor (and the property associated with it). Although verse 22 has David asking Ornan to give the king the property, the term used here is *nathan*, which means to grant or transfer the property. David is not annexing or seizing the estate, as he offers Ornan the full price of the transaction. Here, David's honesty is contrasted with the greed of a later king, Ahab (874-953 BCE), who would illegally seize the vineyard of Naboth by having him murdered (1 Kings 21:13). David informed Ornan that he needed the property to build an altar to the Lord to satisfy Mosaic Law that "when you take the census of the children of Israel for their number, then every man shall give a ransom for himself to the LORD, when you number them, that there may be no plague among them when you number them" (Exodus 30:12).

Ornan's trust or confidence in David is displayed in the fact that he wants to be part of the solution and assist his king. Ornan offers the king to "do what is good in your sight," meaning that Ornan would accept whatever David wished. Moreover, Ornan offers his property, oxen, and threshing floor sledges for wood and wheat for the grain offering. In his dedication to the law and knowledge of sacrifice, Ornan is willing to offer his goods for the ritual, saying, "I will give it all" (v 23). David says, "I will not take what is yours for the Lord," meaning that the king will honor the value of the property and the willingness of Ornan's spirit. David insists that he will not offer to Yahweh burnt offerings that "cost me nothing," i.e., that he did not pay for. To offer a sacrifice from someone else's possession or purse would not be accepted by the Lord because the offering would be counterfeit. Sacrificial offerings must be a personal sacrifice from the person giving to God because the gift is both spiritual and personal. David purchased Ornan's property for 600 shekels of gold, which was about 240 ounces (15 lb., or 6.8 kg.), and paid for the whole property, on which the temple will later be built.

## III. DAVID BUILDS AN ALTAR (1 CHRONICLES 21:26-30)

David builds the altar on the site of Ornan's threshing floor. He has fairly completed the transaction and now, the king is following the command of the Lord through Gad. David could have traveled to the Tabernacle to make his sacrifice; however, the Tabernacle and its accompanying altar were farther away on a hill in Gibeon. The site of David's altar, on Mount Moriah, is where his son Solomon will later build the magnificent temple (2 Chronicles 3:1). David offers burnt offerings and peace offerings. Among the holdings that David acquired from Ornan were grain (wheat), which was an acceptable component of the sacrifice. In David's call for forgiveness, Yahweh consumes the elements that are placed on the altar. Satisfied with David's supplication, the

Lord ordered the angel to sheath his sword. More than likely, this is the angel that was responsible for dispensing the plagues upon the land. The act of putting his sword back into its sheath serves as a signal that the land and the people will be spared. The angel of the Lord in this case is a powerful being that serves as the hand of the Lord, especially in the protection of His people.

## The Lesson Applied

In this lesson, David's predicament is due to his lack of faith in the Lord and his conveniently ignoring the mandates of the Law for selfish purposes. Jerusalem and its inhabitants are punished for the sin of David. A lesson herein is that Christians must be careful ignoring the edicts of heaven because we can afflict innocent brothers and sisters. Our sin has a bearing on others. Therefore, we must authentically follow the Lord in all of our ways and thoughts. David knew better and yet, followed his own will. Christians know better in our determination if we sincerely wish to please God. The idea of disobedience should provide a sense of horror for the believer because of the fear of affecting our loved ones. Sadly, the reality of the effects of disobeying God are real; ask the gambler who lost the house payment and is now in a severe crisis.

## Let's Talk About It

Although the lesson may seem to focus on the missteps of David, Christian believers must reflect on the judgment that was transformed by God's grace. Yahweh was pleased with David's contrition and repentance and commanded the avenging angel to call off the plagues. Christians must eternally be grateful for the grace of God in His forgiveness of the misdeeds that occur even in our walk with the Lord.

We must remember that God loves us to such an extent that He sends the same avenging angel to clear away many of the hurdles and obstacles that act to keep us away from God. Christians are blessed because God wants His believers to succeed, in spite of our many lapses of judgment. Therefore, we must be cognizant and circumspect in our walk with God, knowing that we walk in the grace of God

### Get Social
Share your views and tag us @rhboydco. Use #rhboydco.

@rhboydco

LESSON XI                                        MAY 11, 2025

# SOLOMON DEDICATES THE TEMPLE

ADULT TOPIC:                    BACKGROUND SCRIPTURE: 2 CHRONICLES 7:1–20
A GRAND OPENING                          LESSON PASSAGE: 2 CHRONICLES 7:1–7, 11

## 2 CHRONICLES 7:1–7, 11

### KJV

NOW when Solomon had made an end of praying, the fire came down from heaven, and consumed the burnt offering and the sacrifices; and the glory of the Lord filled the house.
2 And the priests could not enter into the house of the Lord, because the glory of the Lord had filled the Lord's house.
3 And when all the children of Israel saw how the fire came down, and the glory of the Lord upon the house, they bowed themselves with their faces to the ground upon the pavement, and worshipped, and praised the Lord, saying, For he is good; for his mercy endureth for ever.
4 Then the king and all the people offered sacrifices before the Lord.
5 And king Solomon offered a sacrifice of twenty and two thousand oxen, and an hundred and twenty thousand sheep: so the king and all the people dedicated the house of God.
6 And the priests waited on their offices: the Levites also with instruments of musick of the Lord, which David the king had made to praise the Lord, because his mercy endureth for ever, when David praised by their ministry; and the priests sounded trumpets before them, and all Israel stood.
7 Moreover Solomon hallowed the middle of the court that was before the house of the Lord: for there he offered burnt offerings, and the fat of the peace offerings, because the brasen altar which Solomon had made was not able to receive the burnt offerings, and the meat offerings, and the fat.

### NRSVueue

WHEN Solomon had ended his prayer, fire came down from heaven and consumed the burnt offering and the sacrifices, and the glory of the Lord filled the temple.
2 The priests could not enter the house of the Lord because the glory of the Lord filled the Lord's house.
3 When all the people of Israel saw the fire come down and the glory of the Lord on the temple, they bowed down on the pavement with their faces to the ground and worshiped and gave thanks to the Lord, saying, "For he is good, for his steadfast love endures forever."
4 Then the king and all the people offered sacrifice before the Lord.
5 King Solomon offered as a sacrifice twenty-two thousand oxen and one hundred twenty thousand sheep. So the king and all the people dedicated the house of God.
6 The priests stood at their posts, the Levites also, with the instruments for music to the Lord that King David had made for giving thanks to the Lord—for his steadfast love endures forever—whenever David offered praises through their playing. Opposite them the priests sounded trumpets, and all Israel stood.
7 Solomon consecrated the middle of the court that was in front of the house of the Lord, for there he offered the burnt offerings and the fat of the offerings of well-being because the bronze altar Solomon had made could not hold the burnt offering and the grain offering and the fat parts.

**MAIN THOUGHT:** When all the people of Israel saw the fire come down and the glory of the LORD on the temple, they bowed down on the pavement with their faces to the ground, and worshiped and gave thanks to the Lord, saying, "For he is good, for his steadfast love endures forever."
(2 Chronicles 7:3 , NRSVue)

## 2 Chronicles 7:1–7, 11

### KJV

••••••

11 Thus Solomon finished the house of the Lord, and the king's house: and all that came into Solomon's heart to make in the house of the Lord, and in his own house, he prosperously effected.

### NRSVueue

••••••

11 Thus Solomon finished the house of the Lord and the king's house; all that Solomon had planned to do in the house of the Lord and in his own house he successfully accomplished.

### LESSON SETTING
**Time: Circa 962 BCE**
**Place: Jerusalem**

### LESSON OUTLINE
I. The Shekinah Glory
(2 Chronicles 7:1-3)
II. Sacrifices and Feast
(2 Chronicles 7:4-7, 11)

## UNIFYING PRINCIPLE

People honor special places with celebrations and gifts. What are appropriate ways to mark such spaces? Solomon dedicates the temple and the altar for the worship of Yahweh.

## INTRODUCTION

The events depicted in these passages of 2 Chronicles 7:1-9 are a re-telling account found in 2 Chronicles 5:2, 5-13. Recall that many of these events are also recounted in 1 Kings. This repetition is inserted for emphasis and as an expansion of the specifics of the story. Likewise, the Gospels of Matthew and Luke report many of the accounts derived from Mark and serve to expound upon these stories. Another example of this parallelism is that Jeremiah is credited as the author of 1 Kings, whereas, Ezra is credited to being the Chronicler. In both cases, different composers write the history of Israel; yet, it is the documented history of the nation.

The celebration depicted here lasted 15 days: seven days for dedicating the altar, followed by the seven days of the Festival of Booths and climaxed by a one-day solemn assembly. The events conclude on the twenty-third day of the seventh month, which indicates that the celebration began on the eighth of October and lasted until the twenty-third of the same month. Additionally, this was the 9th Jubilee Year.

## EXPOSITION

### I. THE SHEKINAH GLORY (2 CHRONICLES 7:1-3)

A sure indication of God's acceptance is the power of fire emanating from heaven to consume the burnt offering and the sacrifices placed on the altar. This formidable symbol of God's satisfaction is found in several accounts, as described by Moses and Aaron at the inauguration of the Tabernacle, when fire came out from before the Lord and consumed the burnt offering and the portions of fat on the altar; and when all the people saw it, they shouted and fell on their faces (Leviticus 9:23-24). Fire was an important part of the worship of the Tabernacle and the temple, where the altars of incense and burnt offerings constantly required it. In the accounts of Leviticus and 2 Chronicles, God started the fire; whereas, in Abraham's case, he brought the fire to the altar to sacrifice Isaac (Genesis 22:1-3, 6-14).

The glory of the Lord is special and presents a powerful image. The term *kabod*, meaning glory, can also symbolize honor and reverence. If we were to envision their experiences, it would be similar to the prohibiting of firefighters from entering a burning building because of the intense power of the fire and subsequent smoke. In this biblical scenario, the smoke is not hazardous or poisonous; the fire is simply too large for the priests to occupy the same space, and most importantly, the priests are not worthy to occupy the same space with God. Recall that Moses himself was not able to enter the tent of meeting at its dedication because of the cloud and the glory of Yahweh that filled the Tabernacle (Exodus 40:35). This passage (vv. 1-3) is often referred to as a revelation of God's Shekinah Glory. The term *shekinah* is not found in the pages of Scripture; however, the Hebrew word *šekînâ* "dwelling" is a derivative of the Hebrew term *šākan*, which means to sit or to dwell. This is a rabbinic euphemism for God as present among mankind. A precedent for God dwelling with the people that serves as a historical background for the correlation of Shekinah with God's presence can be found where God says, "Let them construct a sanctuary for Me, that I may dwell among them" (Exodus 25:8).

This aspect of glory is a living glory, which will be permanent if the people wish to follow the desires of the Lord. It is also a physical glory that can be seen and felt among the people who are willing to serve the Lord. As for now, the people are attuned to the spirit of the events and the presence of God. They witness the fire coming from heaven; they are caught in the emotional throes of religious ecstasy; they bask in the power and relational closeness of Yahweh; but it will not last. History will reveal that the departure of the Shekinah Glory will later be evident when the people break their promises to God and abandon Him. After being "caught up" in this spectacle, how could they deny the lovingkindness of the Lord? How could the power and majesty of this fire cool in their hearts? At this moment, all is well, and it is surely a time for celebration of and with the Lord; however, their chants of "truly, He is good, truly His lovingkindness is everlasting" are sadly, temporary.

## II. Sacrifices and Feast (2 Chronicles 7:4-7, 11)

Now that the people were assured that God was in their midst, it was time to offer the sacrifices. This was a huge production and because of its enormity, everything was performed on a large and grand scale. Think of a spectacle such as the Olympics where the nation is focused on the athletes as well as the competition and crowds. Similarly, the sacrifices and subsequent feasts in this story were a sizzling display. During these ceremonies, it is doubtless that anyone would object or have a sense of overkill because the pride of the nation was on display for their God. Solomon offered the sacrifice of peace offerings to the Lord, which were 22,000 oxen and 120,000 sheep. So, the king and all the sons of Israel dedicated the house of the Lord (1 Kings 8:63).

Notice the vast number of animals sacrificed: 22,000 oxen and 120,000 sheep!

These animals were not being sacrificed with any other residual usage in mind. According to 1 Kings 8:63, these were peace offerings that provided food for the people during the two weeks of celebration (vv. 9-10). Therefore, by implication, nothing was wasted. Again, the number of animals sacrificed was large, especially during the time period of the actual slaughter; the precise amount of time it took to kill the animals is not documented. By today's standards, a typical slaughterhouse can process very large amounts of meats, due to modern technology and demand. For example, Tyson Foods slaughters 35,000,000 chickens, 128,000 cows (beef), and 401,000 pigs per week. When compared to the activities for this biblical feast and celebration, that which was offered to God was nothing short of magnificent! The large volume of sacrifices was certainly appropriate for this magnificent occasion and was easily financed from Solomon's great wealth. There was a spirit of cooperation in the air; the people were receptive to the festivities, and the masses pledged their undying loyalty to the Lord because together, King Solomon and all the people dedicated the house to the Lord!

As with any festival, the ceremonies would not be complete without a program of music, prayers, and other litanies. In preparation for the ceremonies, note the reference to David, who is credited for either making or purchasing the musical instruments that were used in the large orchestra of the temple. When we typically think of the talents and the role of the Levites, we think of the priests as semi-prophets, preachers of that era, or those who were assigned to minister to the needs of the people in each respective tribe. However, we often miss the large group of Levites who were musicians and composers and were dedicated to the musical portion of the worship.

The earliest account of people designated as music leaders is found in Genesis 4:21, which identifies Jubal as the "father of all those who play the lyre and the pipe." One can follow this designation through Aaron. The Jubal "School of Music" obviously became an important aspect in the life of early Israel. At face value, Psalm 150 clearly seems to refute the common claim that the use of instruments such as drums and saxophones were not a part of the biblical tradition. First Samuel 10:5 reflects the prophets of the Temple using instruments, such as the pipe, harp, psaltery, and tabret in a processional prior to offering prayers and prophesying. The prophets were keen observers of rituals; therefore, their music must have been definitive and familiar to the worship rituals if this music procession proceeded the period of divine prognostication. David is credited with composing the majority of the Psalms; according to Dilliard and Longman, David's name occurs some seventy-three times in the superscriptions that attribute the particular Psalm to its author. The hymns of praise, such as Psalm 113, usually consist of a call to praise (1-3), reasons for praising God (4-9a), and a concluding praise (9b). Temple worship was highly developed and strictly disciplined, and it represented the pinnacle of the Psalms in corporate worship.

The training for priestly musicians was extensive and rigorous, in which young men served as apprentices until it was their opportunity to formally serve as priests in their own right. The musicians, who were probably Levites and singers of the temple, followed a parallel direction in their structure and apprenticeship. First Chronicles 15:16 shows David requesting the chiefs of the Levites, or priests, to appoint their relatives to be singers; and instruments played by the latter included (but were not limited to) harps, lyres, and loud sounding cymbals to raise sounds of joy. Moreover, 1 Chronicles 25:1, describes David setting apart and assigning some of the sons of Asaph, Herman, and Jeduthun to prophesy with lyres, harps, and cymbals. In addition, verses six and seven state that all, including his daughters, were under the direction of their father, Herman, to sing in the house of the Lord. The number of these trained in singing to the Lord, along with their relatives, all who were skillful, was 288. The growth and practice of music as a component of temple worship continues to flourish during the reign of Solomon; and although the rites would suffer neglect, the skill and practices of the musicians would continue.

Solomon consecrated or dedicated an area that was considered to be the middle of the court that was before the house of the Lord. The Hebrew term *paniym* means to face, presence, or sight, thus, indicating that this area faced the main building that held the Holy of Holies or was in the presence or sight of this edifice. It was in this area that Solomon sacrificed his burnt, peace, and grain offerings, providing the best of animals (and most likely, wheat) that were set aside for the offering to Yahweh. However, Solomon faced a problem because the bronze altar that was before the Lord was too small to receive the burnt offerings, the grain offerings, and the fat of the peace offerings (1 Kings 8:64).

The original altar was constructed by Bazalel, a skilled artisan, who was chosen to fabricate the Tabernacle and its furnishings as well as the Arc of the Covenant (Exodus 37:1). The dimensions of the original altar were that five cubits was its length and five cubits its width—it was square—and its height was three cubits (Exodus 38:1-2); however, the altar that Solomon constructed was much larger: twenty cubits was its length, twenty cubits, its width, and ten cubits, its height (2 Chronicles 4:1). Yet, even this replacement altar was inadequate because the bronze altar that was before the LORD was too small to receive the burnt offerings, the grain offerings, and the fat of the peace offerings (1 Kings 8:64). Because of the fantastic number of sacrifices, even the very large altar was not able to hold all the sacrificial animals. The Chronicler may have felt that the altar itself was not to be criticized; it was just the extraordinary circumstances of this festival that made the altar inadequate. The sacrifice revealed that Solomon was giving back to Yahweh from an overabundance and exuberance that reflected his love for Yahweh.

Solomon successfully finished the house of the LORD and the king's palace, although the writer does not focus on the palace, preferring to emphasize the work on the temple. The Chronicler observes that Yahweh was pleased with all of Solomon's efforts, both physically and spiritually. As a coda or an epilogue to the occasion, the Chronicler allows the reader to sense the excitement and spectacle of these sacrifices, as well as the presence of the Lord. The people would return to their homes (tents), happily rejoicing that they had not only participated in the feast and festival but had experienced the presence of the Lord, creating an account that has a "and they lived happily ever after" atmosphere. As for Solomon, he was able to see the fruition of his work, in not only the feast and the festival but in the completion and dedication of the house of the Lord.

## THE LESSON APPLIED

God blessed Solomon through his father David in both wealth and in His promise of an eternal kingship. For example, so numerous were the sacrifices that Solomon instructed that they be made in a specially constructed and dedicated area in the courtyard before the temple. This account of the completion and subsequent dedication of the temple speaks to God's presence among His people. If the spectacle seems overdone, it is not; this was an initial occurrence, and the thought was that the temple would last forever. Therefore, the event should be spectacular for a God who is also spectacular!

## LET'S TALK ABOUT IT

Christian adults understand the importance of celebrating sacred spaces. Depending upon the success or failure of a large social gathering such as a music festival, the mood of the people is usually joyous. In this case, the festival and celebration seemed to be a success; therefore, the feeling of the people probably reflected this sense of excitement. As the people returned to their homes, they were probably tired from the fifteen-day celebration. Think of the large festivals of celebration held at our respective churches; do we tire, even when we experience a sense of joy from the events? Have you ever heard committee members complain, "We're not doing this next year"? We generally ignore these sentiments because our love for the church and our Lord outweighs the effort and the costs. That's exactly how the Israelites were feeling after this triumphant celebration!

## GET SOCIAL

Share your views and tag us @rhboydco. Use #rhboydco.

@rhboydco

## HOME DAILY DEVOTIONAL READINGS
### MAY 12–18, 2025

| MONDAY | TUESDAY | WEDNESDAY | THURSDAY | FRIDAY | SATURDAY | SUNDAY |
| --- | --- | --- | --- | --- | --- | --- |
| Joy Comes with the Morning | Songs of Gratitude | Blessed Be the Merciful, Consoling God | Enter God's Presence with Thanksgiving | Worship in the Spirit of God | The Exiles Return | Building a New Foundation |
| Psalm 30 | Colossians 3:12-17 | 2 Corinthians 1:2-14 | Psalm 95 | Philippians 3:1-14 | Ezra 1 | Ezra 3:1-6, 10-13 |

LESSON XII                                                                    MAY 18, 2025

# WORSHIP IS RESTORED AFTER EXILES RETURN

ADULT TOPIC:                                        BACKGROUND SCRIPTURE: EZRA 3:1–13
MOURNING THE PAST OR CELEBRATING THE FUTURE?  LESSON PASSAGE: EZRA 3:1–6, 10–13

## EZRA 3:1–6, 10–13

### KJV

AND when the seventh month was come, and the children of Israel were in the cities, the people gathered themselves together as one man to Jerusalem.

2 Then stood up Jeshua the son of Jozadak, and his brethren the priests, and Zerubbabel the son of Shealtiel, and his brethren, and builded the altar of the God of Israel, to offer burnt offerings thereon, as it is written in the law of Moses the man of God.

3 And they set the altar upon his bases; for fear was upon them because of the people of those countries: and they offered burnt offerings thereon unto the Lord, even burnt offerings morning and evening.

4 They kept also the feast of tabernacles, as it is written, and offered the daily burnt offerings by number, according to the custom, as the duty of every day required;

5 And afterward offered the continual burnt offering, both of the new moons, and of all the set feasts of the Lord that were consecrated, and of every one that willingly offered a freewill offering unto the Lord.

6 From the first day of the seventh month began they to offer burnt offerings unto the Lord. But the foundation of the temple of the Lord was not yet laid.

• • • • • •

10 And when the builders laid the foundation of the temple of the Lord, they set the priests in their apparel with trumpets, and the Levites the sons of Asaph with cymbals, to praise the

### NRSVueue

WHEN the seventh month came and the Israelites were in their towns, the people gathered together as one in Jerusalem.

2 Then Jeshua son of Jozadak with his fellow priests and Zerubbabel son of Shealtiel with his kin set out to build the altar of the God of Israel, to offer burnt offerings on it, as prescribed in the law of Moses the man of God.

3 They set up the altar on its foundation because they were in dread of the people of the lands, and they offered burnt offerings upon it to the Lord, morning and evening.

4 And they kept the Festival of Booths, as prescribed, and offered the daily burnt offerings by number according to the ordinance, as required for each day,

5 and after that the regular burnt offerings, the offerings at the new moon and at all the sacred festivals of the Lord, and the offerings of everyone who made a freewill offering to the Lord.

6 From the first day of the seventh month they began to offer burnt offerings to the Lord. But the foundation of the temple of the Lord was not yet laid.

• • • • • •

10 When the builders laid the foundation of the temple of the Lord, the priests in their vestments were stationed to praise the Lord with trumpets, and the Levites, the sons of Asaph,

**MAIN THOUGHT:** All the people responded with a great shout when they praised the LORD, because the foundation of the house of the LORD was laid. (Ezra 3:11, KJV)

## Ezra 3:1–6, 10–13

### KJV

Lord, after the ordinance of David king of Israel.

11 And they sang together by course in praising and giving thanks unto the Lord; because he is good, for his mercy endureth for ever toward Israel. And all the people shouted with a great shout, when they praised the Lord, because the foundation of the house of the Lord was laid.

12 But many of the priests and Levites and chief of the fathers, who were ancient men, that had seen the first house, when the foundation of this house was laid before their eyes, wept with a loud voice; and many shouted aloud for joy:

13 So that the people could not discern the noise of the shout of joy from the noise of the weeping of the people: for the people shouted with a loud shout, and the noise was heard afar off.

### NRSVueue

with cymbals, according to the directions of King David of Israel;

11 and they sang responsively, praising and giving thanks to the Lord, "For he is good, for his steadfast love endures forever toward Israel." And all the people responded with a great shout when they praised the Lord because the foundation of the house of the Lord had been laid.

12 But many of the priests and Levites and heads of families, old people who had seen the first house on its foundations, wept with a loud voice when they saw this house, though many shouted aloud for joy,

13 so that the people could not distinguish the sound of the joyful shout from the sound of the people's weeping, for the people shouted so loudly that the sound was heard far away.

## LESSON SETTING

**Time:** Circa 536 BCE
**Place:** Jerusalem

## LESSON OUTLINE

I. Israel Assembles to Build the Altar (Ezra 3:1-3)
II. Celebration of the Feast of Booths (Ezra 3:4-6)
III. Building the Foundation of the Temple (Ezra 3:10-13)

## UNIFYING PRINCIPLE

When magnificent buildings are destroyed, it can be difficult to restore them to their original glory. How do we celebrate the new while we are still grieving the loss of the former? When the exiled Israelites returned and laid the foundation for a reconstruction of the temple, the priests and Levites sang praises. Still, others wept because the second temple was not as magnificent as the original.

## INTRODUCTION

The Jewish exiles have returned to Israel and now, they are tasked with worshiping Yahweh through sacrifices and offerings. However, they must first build the sacred altar while celebrating one of the annual festivals, the Feast of Booths. Additionally, the men of the nation will be called upon to build the foundation of the Second Temple, which will cause some consternation and anxiety. The cry is so great that Josephus emphasizes the irrevocable loss of the First Temple by interpreting the verse to mean that the sound of the elders' and priests' wailing was louder than the sound of joy and the trumpets (Ant. 11:4.2). In their return to the land, however, Israel will invoke her traditional worship practices and rituals, and what will occur is that the glory and splendor of Solomon's Temple will be continually remembered. After their return, the new building begins under the governorship of Sheshbazzar (1:8-14; 5:14-16), then, after an interruption, will resume under the governorship of Zerubbabel and the priestly instruction of Jeshua. Some scholars identify Zerubbabel with Sheshbazzar because both are credited with the building of the Second Temple. However, it seems most likely that Sheshbazzar initiated the rebuilding and Zerubbabel completed it.

## EXPOSITION

### I. ISRAEL ASSEMBLES TO BUILD THE ALTAR (EZRA 3:1-3)

At the beginning of this account, we find that many people of the nation, identified in verse one as the "sons of Israel," were living in "cities," which probably meant that they were living in other towns and enclaves. In fact, the New Jerusalem Bible indicates that the sons of Israel resettled in these unidentified towns (v. 1), meaning that they were in other places (other than Jerusalem). When Israel returned from Babylonia, they chose to move into various other areas of the country. Their journey from Babylon to Israel, which was a distance of approximately 530 miles, probably took at least four months. Ezra would write that he later made this same journey. Starting on the first day of the first month, he began his journey from Babylon, and on the first day of the fifth month, he came to or arrived in Jerusalem (Ezra 7:9).

Now, however, there was an urgent need for the people to assemble or come together at Jerusalem. The phrase "they gathered as one man" indicates that they were united together as a community bound for a common purpose. In verse 2, Jeshua, the priestly son of Jozadak (also known as Jehozadak), returned to Jerusalem with Zerubbabel to rebuild the temple. During the temple restoration, Jeshua (a descendant of Aaron) was overshadowed by Zerubbabel (a descendant of David), though he is mentioned ahead of Zerubbabel in connection with the restoration of the altar. With the reestablishment of the temple and the priesthood, and in the absence of a king, Jeshua rose to prominence. The combination of Jeshua, the priest, and Zerubbabel, a governor of Davidic descent, establishes an authoritative link to pre-exilic times or the period before Israel's deportation to Babylon. In their return to Jerusalem, Judah remains under Persian dominance and rule. Moreover, they arose and built the altar of the God of Israel for the purposes of offering sacrifices, as commanded by the Law of Moses. It was imperative that the returnees would find themselves returning to the Mosaic Covenant, and because their forefathers had abandoned the covenant, the nation had been driven into captivity. Therefore, the emancipated and former exiles did not want to make that same mistake.

As the people came together, they set up the altar, such as what Joshua had done when Israel first entered the land: he built an altar to the Lord, the God of Israel, in Mount Ebal (Joshua 8:30). The erection of the altar of Ezra's day was just as important because of the need to perform the offerings and sacrifices to Yahweh; however, building the altar was also a necessary symbol to serve notice that Israel was back in the land and (although under Persian sovereignty) the land continued to belong to Yahweh. Remember, the local people, who were pagan, also had altars and high places set up to honor their pagan deities, but it would seem as if the reception Israel received was hostile and unwelcoming. The returnees are intimidated by the hostile behavior of the local peoples and are offering sacrifices to Yahweh to appeal for divine protection. This conflict was between the returnees and the local people, many of whom were likely Judahites who were not exiled to Babylonia. Upon the completion of the altar, the priests sacrificed according to the Law of Moses, both in the morning and culminating in the evening.

## II. CELEBRATION OF THE FEAST OF BOOTHS (EZRA 3:4-6)

Under Ezra, Israel celebrated the Feast or Festival of Booths which had lapsed during the period of Babylonian captivity. Beginning on the fifteenth day of the seventh month (Tishri), this festival, also known as tabernacles, was the third great occasion, following Passover and Pentecost, that all Hebrew males were required to observe annually. The Feast of Booths lasted for one week and involved pilgrimage. It was associated initially with the end of the year when the agricultural work had been completed. As part of the rituals, Israel was to live in booths for seven days: "All the native-born in Israel shall live in booths, so that your generations may know that I had the sons of Israel live in booths when I brought them out from the land of Egypt" (Leviticus 23:42-43), the Scripture also providing details of how the festival was to be celebrated. Moreover, Numbers 29:12-32 offers a detailed description of the daily prescribed sacrifices that were required.

Although the people continued to fear the locals – which also included some foreigners who had been deported by the Assyrians into the land that remained during Israel's Babylonian captivity – God's people built the altar and offered the proper sacrifices, as these were the first sacrifices to Yahweh in this place since the deportation in 586 BCE when the temple was torn down. The excitement and actions of the people were driven by their desire to please Yahweh. However, there existed a problem amid all of the festivities: Israel had neglected to prepare the foundation of what would be the Second Temple. In what was considered a "slight," a contrast here is made between the giving of offerings and the rebuilding of the Temple. It was not considered right that the altar should be used when nothing had been done to restore the temple. Recall that Cyrus, king of Persia, had freely donated funds for the rebuilding of the Jewish Temple, even though he may have felt his gifts to the project were borne out of some sort of guilt (or his belief that Yahweh had blessed him with his position and power). Nonetheless, Israel seemed to be complacent and satisfied, although needed, with just the building of the altar and the accompanying festival.

## III. BUILDING THE FOUNDATION OF THE TEMPLE (EZRA 3:10-13)

As the feast was progressing, it may have been possible that the laying of the foundation of the temple was occurring while Jerusalem was filled with pilgrims who were in the city celebrating the Festival of Booths, in addition to the aforementioned documentary of the building of the sacred altar. It would be seemingly feasible that while the workmen were dedicated to a building project, Ezra would have encouraged the transition from the altar to the foundation of the temple. Moreover, the work on the foundation of the temple would be of high significance, as the temple served as the heart and soul of Israel, the pride of the nation, and a symbol that God was with them. Therefore, as Israel followed the national and religious protocol, the priests would be present and arrayed in the splendor of their official apparel. Although this was only the building of the foundation, it was extremely important, which is reflected by the participation of the orchestra, or components thereof. Ezra notes that although there may seem to be an emphasis on the work, there existed a dedicatory worship in praise to Yahweh. The ceremonies and worship were done according to the instructions that were instituted by David at the height of the nation's power and prestige and were now in a position to be observed by the people.

The order of worship followed the same pattern as when David brought the ark to Jerusalem. At that time, the priests blew trumpets and Asaph sounded cymbals (1 Chronicles 16:5-6). Here, the priests blew trumpets and the sons (descendants) of Asaph played the cymbals. The people were thrilled and ecstatic, singing and shouting with great joy; however, there was a segment of the Israelite returnees who were either old enough to remember the appearance and splendor of Solomon's Temple, or they were those who had heard stories of the grandeur and majesty of God's house. Upon noticing the dimensions of the foundation, this segment realized that Israel would not be replicating Solomon's Temple.

Verses 12-13 reveal a dichotomy that permeated the celebration of the feast, the worship, and the construction of the foundation of the temple. Many of the people abandoned the euphoria of the building process to lament over what they perceived as the "smallness" of their situation. The weeping was not limited to the general-aged populace but included some of the priests and Levites who were familiar with what they had had in the "old days." It is possible that the youth were singing praises because they did not have any references from the past, whereas, some of the elders may have felt that although they were witnessing the building of the foundation, they would not live to see the completion of the Temple. As a result, there existed a clashing of sounds, of weeping and shouts of joy, that served to cancel-out the celebrations that should have been evident from the blessings of the Lord.

## The Lesson Applied

God has made it possible for Israel to be emancipated from Babylon and returned to the Promised Land. When they returned, they realized that there were problems in that the sacred places, such as the temple and much of Jerusalem, are either destroyed or in disrepair. There is a celebratory sensation in the air because of the nature of God's blessings in the rebuilding and restoration of Israel. However, today, there exists a sinister building movement among a segment of supposed Christians who are planning to build small towns and enclaves that are to be occupied by invitation only. These towns are designed to be rural in location and nature as part of the theory that their isolation will guarantee the "American way of life." This particular movement is supposedly inspired and buoyed as a response to sanctuary cities that are usually urban in demographics and nature. Situations such as this can be a result of gerrymandering impatience, the revised laws not moving fast enough, or the belief that there should be purposeful segregation. However, the results of this movement will serve as a division among peoples, including Christians, and could return society to a time of sundown towns and areas. What these pseudo-Christians may not realize is that all building in the name of the Lord will not be recognized by the Lord, as Christians who do wrong in the name of God are simply that – wrong! In the end, God will have the final say.

## Let's Talk About It

Christians are encouraged to adapt a worship celebration during which all generations in the community celebrate God together. Recall when churches were neighborhood churches, and there would be large celebrations, such as the church anniversary or homecoming, where the entire neighborhood felt as if the celebrations were a neighborhood affair. In this scenario, the neighborhood was always invited to the church during the normal course of the year, and these special days were just that – special – because it invoked a sense of unity, and of the church belonging to the neighborhood and its citizens, regardless of how dedicated or committed they were in their actual attendance. All generations felt that they were a part of these celebratory days, and the youth admired the spirit of the adults, from their preparation to their service, knowing that one day, they would continue the tradition of a worship service that was inclusive of the entire neighborhood and community. Alas, most churches are not "neighborhood" churches, and unless there is a deliberate movement to return to these roots, many generations will never share in these experiences.

## Get Social

Share your views and tag us @rhboydco. Use #rhboydco.

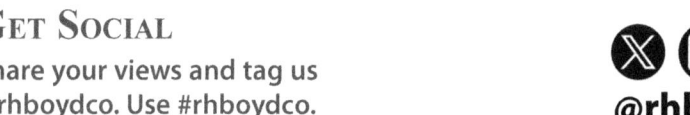

@rhboydco

### Home Daily Devotional Readings
### May 19–25, 2025

| Monday | Tuesday | Wednesday | Thursday | Friday | Saturday | Sunday |
| --- | --- | --- | --- | --- | --- | --- |
| A New Covenant | Saved by Grace | A New Covenant | Hear the Word of the Lord | Remember God's Salvation | A Better Covenant | Revitalized Worship |
| Jeremiah 31:27-34 | Ephesians 2:1-10 | Luke 22:7-20 | Nehemiah 8:1-3, 5-6, 8-12 | Nehemiah 9:2-3, 6-17, 32 | Hebrews 8 | Nehemiah 10:28-39 |

LESSON XIII                                        MAY 25, 2025

# A Covenant Renewal

**ADULT TOPIC:**
HERE WE GO AGAIN!

**BACKGROUND SCRIPTURE:** NEHEMIAH 8:1–10:39
**LESSON PASSAGE:** NEHEMIAH 10:28–39

## NEHEMIAH 10:28–39

### KJV

AND the rest of the people, the priests, the Levites, the porters, the singers, the Nethinims, and all they that had separated themselves from the people of the lands unto the law of God, their wives, their sons, and their daughters, every one having knowledge, and having understanding;
29 They clave to their brethren, their nobles, and entered into a curse, and into an oath, to walk in God's law, which was given by Moses the servant of God, and to observe and do all the commandments of the Lord our Lord, and his judgments and his statutes;
30 And that we would not give our daughters unto the people of the land, not take their daughters for our sons:
31 And if the people of the land bring ware or any victuals on the sabbath day to sell, that we would not buy it of them on the sabbath, or on the holy day: and that we would leave the seventh year, and the exaction of every debt.

32 Also we made ordinances for us, to charge ourselves yearly with the third part of a shekel for the service of the house of our God;
33 For the shewbread, and for the continual meat offering, and for the continual burnt offering, of the sabbaths, of the new moons, for the set feasts, and for the holy things, and for the sin offerings to make an atonement for Israel, and for all the work of the house of our God.
34 And we cast the lots among the priests, the Levites, and the people, for the wood offering,

### NRSVueue

THE rest of the people, the priests, the Levites, the gatekeepers, the singers, the temple servants, and all who have separated themselves from the peoples of the lands to adhere to the law of God, their wives, their sons, their daughters, all who have knowledge and understanding,
29 join with their kin, their nobles, and enter into a curse and an oath to walk in God's law, which was given by Moses the servant of God, and to observe and do all the commandments of the Lord our Lord and his ordinances and his statutes.
30 We will not give our daughters to the peoples of the land or take their daughters for our sons,
31 and if the peoples of the land bring in merchandise or any grain on the Sabbath day to sell, we will not buy it from them on the Sabbath or on a holy day, and we will forego the crops of the seventh year and the exaction of every debt.

32 We also lay on ourselves the obligation to charge ourselves yearly one-third of a shekel for the service of the house of our God:
33 for the rows of bread, the regular grain offering, the regular burnt offering, the Sabbaths, the new moons, the appointed festivals, the sacred donations, and the sin offerings to make atonement for Israel, and for all the work of the house of our God.
34 We have also cast lots among the priests, the Levites, and the people for the wood offering,

**MAIN THOUGHT:** We will not neglect the house of our God. (Nehemiah 10:39, KJV)

## Nehemiah 10:28–39

### KJV

to bring it into the house of our God, after the houses of our fathers, at times appointed year by year, to burn upon the altar of the Lord our God, as it is written in the law:
35 And to bring the firstfruits of our ground, and the firstfruits of all fruit of all trees, year by year, unto the house of the Lord:

36 Also the firstborn of our sons, and of our cattle, as it is written in the law, and the firstlings of our herds and of our flocks, to bring to the house of our God, unto the priests that minister in the house of our God:
37 And that we should bring the firstfruits of our dough, and our offerings, and the fruit of all manner of trees, of wine and of oil, unto the priests, to the chambers of the house of our God; and the tithes of our ground unto the Levites, that the same Levites might have the tithes in all the cities of our tillage.
38 And the priest the son of Aaron shall be with the Levites, when the Levites take tithes: and the Levites shall bring up the tithe of the tithes unto the house of our God, to the chambers, into the treasure house.
39 For the children of Israel and the children of Levi shall bring the offering of the corn, of the new wine, and the oil, unto the chambers, where are the vessels of the sanctuary, and the priests that minister, and the porters, and the singers: and we will not forsake the house of our God.

### NRSVueue

to bring it into the house of our God, by ancestral houses, at appointed times, year by year, to burn on the altar of the Lord our God, as it is written in the law.
35 We obligate ourselves to bring the first fruits of our soil and the first fruits of all fruit of every tree, year by year, to the house of the Lord;
36 also to bring to the house of our God, to the priests who minister in the house of our God, the firstborn of our sons and of our livestock, as it is written in the law, and the firstlings of our herds and of our flocks;
37 and to bring the first of our dough, and our contributions, the fruit of every tree, the wine and the oil, to the priests, to the chambers of the house of our God; and to bring to the Levites the tithes from our soil, for it is the Levites who collect the tithes in all our rural towns.

38 And the priest, the descendant of Aaron, shall be with the Levites when the Levites receive the tithes, and the Levites shall bring up a tithe of the tithes to the house of our God, to the chambers of the storehouse.
39 For the Israelites and the sons of Levi shall bring the contribution of grain, wine, and oil to the storerooms where the vessels of the sanctuary are and where the priests who minister and the gatekeepers and the singers are. We will not neglect the house of our God.

## LESSON SETTING
Time: Circa 444 BCE
Place: Jerusalem

## LESSON OUTLINE
I. The People Swear an Oath (Nehemiah 10:28–30)
II. Maintenance for the Temple (Nehemiah 10:31–33)
III. Obligation of Provisions (Nehemiah 10:34–36)
IV. Pledges to the House of God (Nehemiah 10:37–39)

## UNIFYING PRINCIPLE

People appreciate efforts to restore time–honored practices and institutions. How can we match external efforts at restoration with internal ones? At the renewal of the Mosaic covenant, the people pledge to observe the commands of the Torah and reject the abuse and neglect of the temple.

## INTRODUCTION

The people of Israel have been presented with a document of obligations that will ensure their dedication to an agreement with Yahweh and also place them under covenantal protection and blessings from Yahweh. The obligations are to return to the Lord a portion of what He has provided. These gifts were given to the people, as well as the land. Obviously, all people would benefit from God's provisions, but the land was also to be blessed, as the induction of a sabbatical year would rejuvenate the land and people, as well as restore a sense of freshness to their society. However, the emphasis will be placed on their faithfulness to Yahweh during the reemergence of a new emancipation and return to Israel.

## EXPOSITION

### I. THE PEOPLE SWEAR AN OATH (NEHEMIAH 10:28–30)

The account begins with a focus on the "rest of the people" who are not part of the list that is found at the beginning of chapter 10 (Nehemiah 10:1–27). This list consists of civil and religious leaders, Levites and priests, and others from the heads of prominent families who affixed the seals or signatures to a written agreement or covenant, that they would abide by the Law of Moses and thereby, honor Yahweh. Notably, the list (and probably, the first signature) is that of Nehemiah (although Ezra is omitted), who as a leader, sets an excellent example for the people.

One of the more important aspects of verse 28 is the attention given to all of those who had separated themselves from the peoples of the lands to the law of God. Ezra identifies that this group came with the sons of Israel who returned from exile, and all of those who had separated themselves from the impurity of the nations of the land to join them, to seek the Lord God of Israel, ate the Passover (Ezra 6:21). This group that joined with Israel were former pagans that had been converted to Judaism through a prescribed process, which also included circumcision. Additionally, these were family units, i.e., wives, sons, and daughters, who are now part of the community of the Lord.

Israel promised to follow the Law of Moses in her return to the land, which included following a series of promises that would place them in a position to honor their dedication and faithfulness to Yahweh. The people agreed to take on a curse and swear an oath to be faithful in their walk with God. The people agreed (1) not to marry heathens, (2) to keep the Sabbath and holy days free of commercial activity, (3) to observe the sabbatical year, and (4) to support the temple. In this case, the curse is not described, but the people realize that there will be severe punishment and retribution if the oath, which is a verbal form of a covenant, is broken.

### II. MAINTENANCE FOR THE TEMPLE (NEHEMIAH 10:31–33)

Although Israel was newly emancipated from Babylonian exile, as part of their oath, the people were reminded to "remember the Sabbath day, to keep it holy. Six days you shall labor and do all your work, but the seventh day is the Sabbath of the LORD your God. In it you shall do no work: you, nor your son, nor your daughter, nor your male servant, nor your female servant, nor your cattle, nor your stranger who is within your gates. For in six days the Lord made the heavens and the earth, the sea, and all that is in them, and rested the seventh day. Therefore, the Lord blessed the Sabbath day and hallowed it" (Exodus 20:8–11). Recall that God commanded Moses that Israel was to faithfully observe His sabbaths as a covenantal sign between the two parties. As a connection to Yahweh's creation in six days and His resting on the seventh, Israel was to follow the pattern, which included prohibition from labor on the sabbath; and death was the punishment for anyone who broke the commandment (Exodus 31:12–17). In addition, this allowed a period of rest and refurbishment for all entities involved, such as the people, the animals, and the land (in that which would later be known as crop rotation, see Exodus 23:12). Again, this principle is then extended into the whole seventh year, to be set apart for rest from labor, providing food to the poor, cancellation of debt, and reading the law. The cancellation of debt is later connected with forgiveness of sins in the Dead Sea Scrolls. Freeing slaves is also mandated on a seven–year cycle, but in the seventh year after the indenture of a given individual rather than in a universal release. In their adherence to these commandments, the people who brought wares or grain to sell on the Sabbath day should not have had any buyers because of their faithfulness to the Law. Moreover, Yahweh promised Israel that He would bless them to such an extent that they did not have to plant crops during the sixth year because the yield of the seventh year would be so bountiful.

Additionally, Israel was obligated to contribute an annual contribution of one–half shekel for the support of the temple. The shekel was a standard silver coin that was valued for its weight, which was approximately a half of an ounce. Therefore, the gift of each man would be one–third (or 0.166) of an ounce. However, the command in Exodus 30:11–16 is that every male 20 years old was to provide a half–shekel, as being numbered among God's people. This is related to Torah law, which requires every Israelite to pay half a shekel, where payment is required for repair of the temple. The indication of the reduced rate of one–third may suggest relief for those who may have been in poverty at the time. Moreover, these funds served to support the temple and the annual festivals that were part of the worship and dedicatory ceremonies offered to the Lord. Additionally, the funds would maintain the Temple and be used for other needs that may occur.

### III. OBLIGATION OF PROVISIONS (NEHEMIAH 10:34–36)

As part of their obligations to the temple, the people cast lots to determine who was responsible to furnish wood for the fire on the altar that had to be kept burning continuously for sacrifices in the sanctuary. The Scriptures contain several references of people casting lots to determine who would be chosen for a purpose. In Nehemiah, the actual objects used for casting lots are not known, as they could have been small pieces of wood or small stones or perhaps something with writing on it. Nonetheless, it is explicit that this was the method used, and the wording of the *Good News Translation* makes explicit that the purpose of casting lots was to decide whose turn it was to bring the firewood each year.

Verses 35 and 36 focus on the giving of the first fruits of the nation. These include (but are not limited to) the first fruits of the ground and to "every tree," meaning each plant of every farm, indicating in the command that "you shall bring the choice first fruits of your soil into the house of the LORD your God" (Exodus 23:19). Additionally, the first fruits of the animals were to be brought to the temple as a dedication to the Lord in the offertory sacrifices, as the priests would administer the ceremonies. The first fruits were then extended to the individual families proper, noting that the people are to bring to the house of our God the firstborn of our sons (v. 36).

## IV. Pledges to the House of God (Nehemiah 10:37–39)

The people joined in the pledge to bring in the first of all of their belongings to give to the priests in the House of their God. Israel was not to make the mistake that befell Cain in his giving God his secondary crops while withholding his finest. They pledged to God and gave to the priests "all the best of the fresh oil and all the best of the fresh wine and of the grain, the first fruits of those which they give to the LORD, I give them to you" (Numbers 18:12). These gifts were to be stored in the inner chambers of the temple, which were specially designated for these purposes. Moreover, the obligation was not limited to the people in the towns and cities but was to include all of the rural areas and villages.

The Levites were commanded to collect tithes from people in these areas. It was determined that these "sons of Aaron" would be responsible for bringing the gifts to Jerusalem to the Temple and placing the commodities into the storehouse of the Lord. In order to ensure the gathering of the produce from the areas away from Jerusalem, the Levites, ironically, become tax collectors who will also benefit from what they collect. The Levites are to be accompanied by the priest, the son of Aaron, when they receive the tithes. Additionally, as part of their support, the priests would receive a tenth of the tenth that they gathered.

Israel had an obligation to maintain the House of God, the Levites, priests, porters, singers, and ancillary personnel who were part of the temple service. Here is a premium on not neglecting the House of God, of which in Nehemiah, the neglect was obvious. Although the people could not maintain the sanctuary while they were in Babylonian exile, the results of the estrangement or separation became evident when the people returned to the land. These promises were not lost on the people; they viewed the ruins of the walls of Jerusalem and the destruction of the sanctuary and were saddened, just as those who remembered the splendor of Solomon's Temple and vowed that it would never occur again.

One of the controversies of the lesson was centered around the prohibition of mixed marriages. These prohibitions were against marriages to people of different religions and faiths because Yahweh realized that the weakness of His people would almost inevitably result in their worshiping the heathen's gods. Even Solomon would dabble in recognizing some of the idols of his period. In this case, Solomon would abandon the good precedent set by his father by building high places for his many wives, worshiping at these high places, and worshiping other gods (1 Kings 11:1–8). Solomon's misdeeds infuriate Yahweh, who ends Solomon's peace by raising up a series of foreign adversaries against him (1 Kings 11:14–25). The lesson of this prohibition does not escape Nehemiah, and he becomes quite protective of this commandment.

## The Lesson Applied

There are constant needs that arise in the churches and sanctuaries of our present period. Being public buildings (to an extent), church buildings require a greater degree of maintenance and support than do single–family dwellings. It has been documented that only 15–20 percent of the membership tithes in their financial support of the church. However, as the membership ages (while at the same time, the number of members declines), a realistic question should be, "What will the state of church offerings be in the future?" Although our vision of the future is not precise, we must continue to give as God has given to us and encourage others to embrace their returning to the Lord what is His for the care of our churches.

## Let's Talk About It

Christians must understand the significance of the people's commitment to God and God's house. As with any building or thing made by human hands, churches will decay as they age; however, are new edifices being constructed at the same rate as in prior periods? Vacant church buildings do not offer the same financial attractiveness or need in the real estate market as do normal family dwellings. Yet, in many places today buildings erected to accommodate churches are being bought by secular groups and being converted into establishments such as theaters, community centers, and restaurants.

**Therefore, a pertinent question could be asked: "Will the future result in more vacant churches because of the decline in giving and the loss of members?"**

The significance of the church remains a powerful symbol, even in a godless world, and that importance is a continual reminder of the sanctuaries and worship centers that reflect the Christian's commitment to the Lord.

## Get Social

Share your views and tag us @rhboydco. Use #rhboydco.

@rhboydco

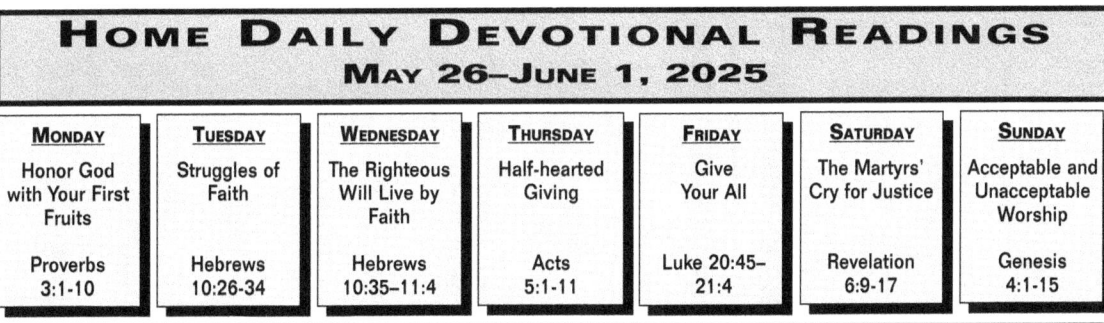

# Fourth Quarter

*September*

*October*

*November*

**LESSON I**  JUNE 1, 2025

# CAIN AND ABEL OFFER SACRIFICES

ADULT TOPIC:
GIFT–GIVING THAT MATTERS

BACKGROUND SCRIPTURE: GENESIS 4:1–25
LESSON PASSAGE: GENESIS 4:1–15

## GENESIS 4:1–15

### KJV

AND Adam knew Eve his wife; and she conceived, and bare Cain, and said, I have gotten a man from the Lord.
2 And she again bare his brother Abel. And Abel was a keeper of sheep, but Cain was a tiller of the ground.
3 And in process of time it came to pass, that Cain brought of the fruit of the ground an offering unto the Lord.
4 And Abel, he also brought of the firstlings of his flock and of the fat thereof. And the Lord had respect unto Abel and to his offering:
5 But unto Cain and to his offering he had not respect. And Cain was very wroth, and his countenance fell.
6 And the Lord said unto Cain, Why art thou wroth? and why is thy countenance fallen?
7 If thou doest well, shalt thou not be accepted? and if thou doest not well, sin lieth at the door. And unto thee shall be his desire, and thou shalt rule over him.
8 And Cain talked with Abel his brother: and it came to pass, when they were in the field, that Cain rose up against Abel his brother, and slew him.
9 And the Lord said unto Cain, Where is Abel thy brother? And he said, I know not: Am I my brother's keeper?
10 And he said, What hast thou done? the voice of thy brother's blood crieth unto me from the ground.
11 And now art thou cursed from the earth, which hath opened her mouth to receive thy brother's blood from thy hand;

### NRSVue

NOW the man knew his wife Eve, and she conceived and bore Cain, saying, "I have produced a man with the help of the Lord."
2 Next she bore his brother Abel. Now Abel was a keeper of sheep, and Cain a tiller of the ground.
3 In the course of time Cain brought to the Lord an offering of the fruit of the ground,
4 and Abel for his part brought of the firstlings of his flock, their fat portions. And the Lord had regard for Abel and his offering,
5 but for Cain and his offering he had no regard. So Cain was very angry, and his countenance fell.
6 The Lord said to Cain, "Why are you angry, and why has your countenance fallen?
7 If you do well, will you not be accepted? And if you do not do well, sin is lurking at the door; its desire is for you, but you must master it."
8 Cain said to his brother Abel, "Let us go out to the field." And when they were in the field, Cain rose up against his brother Abel and killed him.
9 Then the Lord said to Cain, "Where is your brother Abel?" He said, "I do not know; am I my brother's keeper?"
10 And the Lord said, "What have you done? Listen, your brother's blood is crying out to me from the ground!
11 And now you are cursed from the ground, which has opened its mouth to receive your brother's blood from your hand.

**MAIN THOUGHT:** The LORD said to Cain, "Why are you angry, and why has your countenance fallen? If you do well, will you not be accepted?"
(Genesis 4:6–7, NRSVue)

# Genesis 4:1–15

## KJV

12 When thou tillest the ground, it shall not henceforth yield unto thee her strength; a fugitive and a vagabond shalt thou be in the earth.
13 And Cain said unto the Lord, My punishment is greater than I can bear.
14 Behold, thou hast driven me out this day from the face of the earth; and from thy face shall I be hid; and I shall be a fugitive and a vagabond in the earth; and it shall come to pass, that every one that findeth me shall slay me.
15 And the Lord said unto him, Therefore whosoever slayeth Cain, vengeance shall be taken on him sevenfold. And the Lord set a mark upon Cain, lest any finding him should kill him.

## NRSVue

12 When you till the ground, it will no longer yield to you its strength; you will be a fugitive and a wanderer on the earth."
13 Cain said to the Lord, "My punishment is greater than I can bear!
14 Today you have driven me away from the soil, and I shall be hidden from your face; I shall be a fugitive and a wanderer on the earth, and anyone who meets me may kill me."

15 Then the Lord said to him, "Not so! Whoever kills Cain will suffer a sevenfold vengeance." And the Lord put a mark on Cain, so that no one who came upon him would kill him.

## LESSON SETTING
**Time:** Post Creation period over 6000 BCE
**Place:** Ancient Near East near Eden

## LESSON OUTLINE
I. Two Sons Give Offerings (Genesis 4:1–5)
II. The Wrong Heart (Genesis 4:6–10)
III. God's Punishment (Genesis 4:11–15)

## UNIFYING PRINCIPLE

Giving gifts to show appreciation and honor is a common practice. How do we expect our gifts to be received? From their very livelihood, Cain and Abel offer gifts to God, but Cain grew angry because Abel's gift was more pleasing to God.

## INTRODUCTION

In just about every service, the church receives an offering. Each church has their own traditions of how to conduct a collection. It does not take one long to learn the giving tradition in church. But what about the gift that cannot be seen with the naked eye? People can see if one drops in the basket a dollar or whatever the amount. But this lesson points to the fact that God considers more than the amount and traditions of offerings. He looks at the heart.

Eve, the wife of Adam, bore two sons named Cain and Abel. In some way, they had been taught the importance of making sacrifices to God. The Law of Moses had not been created yet, but a natural law was instilled within their minds that required them to make sacrifices. The elder son named Cain broke the standard of proper sacrifice resulting in him and his offering being rejected. As the lesson is revealed, take note that God rejected Cain before He rejected his sacrifice. This act can generate an interesting discussion of why Cain was reprimanded before the rejection of his sacrifice. Yet at the same time, the Lord respected Abel and his sacrifice. One should engage in self-examination when giving to the Lord and realize that God wants more than money. He wants the individual.

## EXPOSITION

### I. TWO SONS GIVE OFFERINGS (GENESIS 4:1–5)

Once Adam and Eve were driven from the Garden of Eden, they had to continue with life. It was now a life infected with the sin represented by the actions of their son. Although the Bible does not delineate exactly the location of the scene of this lesson, the Scripture does give a clue in Genesis 3:24 that Adam and Eve may have lived east of the Garden of Eden. Wherever their exact location, the first couple procreated and had two sons named Cain and Abel. Despite their punishment, God still blessed them to produce children. The blessing of reproduction shows that God had mercy upon Adam and Eve when He could have easily cut off their lineage and allowed the human family to cease.

Eve recognized this blessing by declaring Cain's birth as a gift from the Lord. One can see the character of God in this blessing. Adam and Eve's sins did not stop the Lord's benevolence. Verse 2 indicated that Eve bore her second child named Abel. In both instances, the sons are given from God with specific purposes for their lives. The Lord showed Himself to be consistent in the birth of these sons showing no partiality toward either. The text revealed both sons came with help from the Creator, and both had a purpose from God. Cain was assigned to be a tiller of the ground while Abel was a keeper of flock. It is important to note the consistency of God in His blessings, for that same fairness is shown in His judgments. No one can say that God is unfair because everyone starts with a clean slate, just like Cain and Abel, to make good or bad decisions in their lives.

At the time of sacrifice, both sons brought offerings from what God had given to them. These offerings were an important part of worship in ancient biblical times. They did not have an organ or choir, nor even a church building to worship during the Adamic age. But God instinctively put within the first family that sacrifices were a way of showing reverence. In Genesis 3:21, an animal was likely sacrificed to clothe Adam and Eve from their nakedness after they had sinned. This act may have put in the ancestors' minds that sacrifice was necessary to pay for sin.

Cain brought an offering from the harvest and Abel brought an offering from the flock. As one compares the offerings, the text reveals some differences. The Bible does not indicate that Cain's offering was his first fruit, but Abel's offering was his first. Moreover, Abel also gave the fat of his flock which showed that he took time to take the fat from one of his animals and give that to the Lord. Abel's offering reveals a sacrifice of both priority and time which is very important in the worship of God. Many people say that they are worshipping God, but He is not priority. God and His work can quickly be relegated to secondary.

As a result, God had respect for Abel's offering but not Cain's. The word respect in Hebrew indicates to gaze or to draw one's attention. Verse 4 is a powerful affirmation of Abel's heart for he did something that made God stop and pay attention. This act provides insight on how the Heavenly Father deals with sacrifices. It is not just what one gives, but also who and how one gives that makes the difference. When the righteous Judge rejected Cain's offering, his true heart came to the fore. He became angry with the Lord and more so with his brother. God requires the best gift, which is a gift of one's total self. When Abel made his offering, it represented the best from his heart. When Cain gave, it was only his excess but not his best, and brought to light his angry heart.

## II. THE WRONG HEART (GENESIS 4:6–10)

Although God rejected Cain's offering, verse 6 reveals that the Creator did not reject Cain, for the Lord asked him why he was so angry. The act of God taking time to talk with His children shows mercy. It was an opportunity for Cain to repent. The angry brother was given a spiritual mirror where he could see himself. He could have easily corrected the error and submitted his heart to God, for the door of reconciliation was still open. But verse 7 conveyed that if Cain refused the Lord, the consequences of sin would meet him at the door of judgment. In this text, sin was personified as an animal waiting to pounce upon its prey. Genesis 4:7 is the first time the word "sin" was used in the Bible. Cain's life was in danger, but it did not have to be if he repented. The phrase "thou shalt rule over him" highlights that at the very introduction of sin in the Scriptures, God made a way to conquer it through repentance.

Tragically, Cain rejected that opportunity. Instead, he approached Abel in the field and killed him. Sin had pounced and devoured its prey, which revealed a deeper reason of why God rejected Cain's offering. Even if Cain were to have given the first fruits of his crops, the gift still would have been lacking. For the elder brother had the wrong heart. God knew it from the start, which angered the unrepentant man. It was not what Cain gave that caused the Lord's rejection. It was who gave it and the type of heart from which the gift came from.

The Lord asked Cain, "Where is thy brother?" This question was not because God did not know the answer; it was to bring to the murderer's attention what he had done. Still in denial, Cain told God that he did not know of Abel's location. This shows the result of a heart hardened by sin. For Cain had no contrition and his heart felt no remorse, even to the point of lying to God. When one has been overtaken by sin, the heart becomes deceitful above all things and desperately wicked. Verse 10 confirms that one never gets away with sin. Although Cain would not admit his wrong, Abel's blood from the ground cried out the truth. The author brings to life the blood as a witness to the crime. This personification of the blood reminds readers of its power. Blood can save one from sin, but it also can condemn. In verse 10, like a judge in the courtroom, God listened to the testimony of the blood which convicted Cain as the murderer.

## III. GOD'S PUNISHMENT (GENESIS 4:11–15)

With the trial of Cain complete, God moved to the sentencing phase in verse 11. The sinful brother had a chance to correct his offering but rejected it. He had a chance to admit his crime but also turned that down. Therefore, God had no other alternative but to place judgment upon Cain. The Lord cursed him through the earth. Instead of the earth being the source of his food and strength, the earth would be his enemy. This point shed light on a method of God's judgment. He turned what was originally designed as a means of support into a curse of destruction. The reference to Cain being a fugitive and vagabond indicates how God put the murderer on the run from himself. Wherever he went, the earth would meet him there and punish Cain some more. When Cain realized his punishment, he complained about the harshness of it. How could one endlessly wander? Moreover, his wandering was away from the presence of the Lord. The punishment included the turning away of three faces.

The faces of the earth, the people, and God were turned from Cain. It is the first example of total excommunication. Adam and Eve were driven from the Garden of Eden but Cain's punishment was worse in that he was driven from everything and everybody. God even marked him where no one could kill him as he went from the presence of the Lord in the land of Nod.

## THE LESSON APPLIED

Cain's punishment highlights God's original judgment for murder. It was a life sentence; Cain had to live with himself while abandoned, though God still protected him. Some might question what is the best punishment for crimes such as murder? Verse 15 shows that vengeance belongs to the Lord. Throughout the ebbs and flows of this lesson, from Eve's joy in childbirth to Cain's tragic judgment, the righteous Lord had the last say.

## LET'S TALK ABOUT IT

**How can we be certain that God is pleased with our offerings?**

The key centers on searching one's heart. People must sincerely assess the ways and motives of their service to God. The lesson indicated that God considered the giver before He considered the offering. If the gift comes from a pure heart, then the Lord will be satisfied with the offering.

## GET SOCIAL

Share your views and tag us @rhboydco. Use #rhboydco.

@rhboydco

# HOME DAILY DEVOTIONAL READINGS
## JUNE 2–9, 2025

| MONDAY | TUESDAY | WEDNESDAY | THURSDAY | FRIDAY | SATURDAY | SUNDAY |
|---|---|---|---|---|---|---|
| Obedience to God's Command | Jesus Joins Us in the Storm | Peace through the Word | God Protects | A Herald of Righteousness | A Cry for Deliverance | A Covenant of Peace |
| Genesis 6:11-22 | John 6:15-20 | John 14:18-27 | Genesis 7:11-24 | 2 Peter 2:1-9 | Psalm 77:1-2, 7-19 | Genesis 8:13-22; 9:11-13 |

LESSON II  JUNE 8, 2025

# NOAH BUILDS AN ALTAR

**ADULT TOPIC:**
THE RAINBOW PROMISE

**BACKGROUND SCRIPTURE:** GENESIS 6:1–9:17
**LESSON PASSAGE:** GENESIS 8:13–22; 9:11–13

## GENESIS 8:13–22; 9:11–13

### KJV

AND it came to pass in the six hundredth and first year, in the first month, the first day of the month, the waters were dried up from off the earth: and Noah removed the covering of the ark, and looked, and, behold, the face of the ground was dry.

14 And in the second month, on the seven and twentieth day of the month, was the earth dried.

15 And God spake unto Noah, saying,

16 Go forth of the ark, thou, and thy wife, and thy sons, and thy sons' wives with thee.

17 Bring forth with thee every living thing that is with thee, of all flesh, both of fowl, and of cattle, and of every creeping thing that creepeth upon the earth; that they may breed abundantly in the earth, and be fruitful, and multiply upon the earth.

18 And Noah went forth, and his sons, and his wife, and his sons' wives with him:

19 Every beast, every creeping thing, and every fowl, and whatsoever creepeth upon the earth, after their kinds, went forth out of the ark.

20 And Noah builded an altar unto the Lord; and took of every clean beast, and of every clean fowl, and offered burnt offerings on the altar.

21 And the Lord smelled a sweet savour; and the Lord said in his heart, I will not again curse the ground any more for man's sake; for the imagination of man's heart is evil from his youth; neither will I again smite any more every thing living, as I have done.

22 While the earth remaineth, seedtime and

### NRSVue

IN the six hundred first year, in the first month, on the first day of the month, the waters were dried up from the earth, and Noah removed the covering of the ark and looked and saw that the face of the ground was drying.

14 In the second month, on the twenty-seventh day of the month, the earth was dry.

15 Then God said to Noah,

16 "Go out of the ark, you and your wife and your sons and your sons' wives with you.

17 Bring out with you every living thing that is with you of all flesh—birds and animals and every creeping thing that creeps on the earth—so that they may abound on the earth and be fruitful and multiply on the earth."

18 So Noah went out with his sons and his wife and his sons' wives.

19 And every animal, every creeping thing, and every bird, everything that moves on the earth, went out of the ark by families.

20 Then Noah built an altar to the Lord and took of every clean animal and of every clean bird and offered burnt offerings on the altar.

21 And when the Lord smelled the pleasing odor, the Lord said in his heart, "I will never again curse the ground because of humans, for the inclination of the human heart is evil from youth; nor will I ever again destroy every living creature as I have done.

22 As long as the earth endures, seedtime and

**MAIN THOUGHT:** [God said,] "I have set my bow in the clouds, and it shall be a sign of the covenant between me and the earth." (Genesis 9:13, NRSVue)

## Genesis 8:13–22; 9:11–13

### KJV

harvest, and cold and heat, and summer and winter, and day and night shall not cease.

••• 9:11-13 •••

11 And I will establish my covenant with you, neither shall all flesh be cut off any more by the waters of a flood; neither shall there any more be a flood to destroy the earth.
12 And God said, This is the token of the covenant which I make between me and you and every living creature that is with you, for perpetual generations:
13 I do set my bow in the cloud, and it shall be for a token of a covenant between me and the earth.

### NRSVue

harvest, cold and heat, summer and winter, day and night shall not cease."

••• 9:11-13 •••

11 I establish my covenant with you, that never again shall all flesh be cut off by the waters of a flood, and never again shall there be a flood to destroy the earth."
12 God said, "This is the sign of the covenant that I make between me and you and every living creature that is with you, for all future generations:
13 I have set my bow in the clouds, and it shall be a sign of the covenant between me and the earth.

---

**LESSON SETTING**
  **Time:** Post Flood over 4000 BCE
  **Place:** Mountains of Ararat, Modern Turkey

**LESSON OUTLINE**
  I. A New Start (Genesis 8:13–19)
  II. A New Covenant (Genesis 8:20–22; 9:11–13)

## UNIFYING PRINCIPLE

When people come through harrowing events, they feel grateful. How do people express these feelings? After the Great Flood, Noah built an altar on dry land and offered burnt offerings that so pleased the Lord that God promised never again to destroy the earth with a flood.

## INTRODUCTION

Many people, particularly those who live in coastal areas, can relate to the dangers of floods. Water can rush in without warning, inundating the land and destroying all within its path. With the world consisting of more than 70 percent water, there is no way humans can escape a worldwide flood. This lesson comes out of that context where the world had been overwhelmed with a catastrophic flood destroying every breathing creature. Some key principles in this lesson are God does not tolerate sin, but He still gave humanity plenty of time to repent before sending the flood. Scripture revealed Noah preached to the people at least 100 years prior to judgment. Another principle is that the righteous God's wrath does not last forever. Eventually, the flood ended, and they were delivered. Noah properly responds to God's mercy by building an altar of sacrifice. A concluding takeaway is God responds with a covenant. As one studies this lesson, tease out the important points of how to worship the Lord. The world begins and ends with God.

## EXPOSITION

### I. A NEW START (GENESIS 8:13–19)

In Genesis 7:6, the Bible indicated that Noah was 600 years old when he entered the ark, and the flood began. He and his family remained in the ark for about one year. The period prior to the flood is called the "antediluvian age" which was a time when humans lived unusually long lives compared to modern lifespans of 70–80 years. During Noah's time, their lifespans would range from 700–900 years. After the flood, lifespans declined to about 120–500 years. These years reveal a glimpse of God's eternal nature. He originally wanted creation to live forever, but humans marred that plan due to sin. The drowning of the wicked found in the background verses of this lesson certainly reveals God's wrath, but it also reveals God's grace. Genesis 8:13 conveys how it was a part of God's plan to move the world back to its original eternal design. The Lord disposed of the wicked people of the world to bring forth new lives who would serve him. This process made way for eternal life. As a righteous line of people emerged from Noah's family, it would be his descendants who would eventually bring forth Jesus Christ.

Genesis 8:13b indicated that the waters dried up from the earth after about 150 days. By the twenty-seventh day of the second month, the earth was dry enough for everything to leave the ark. The author of Genesis, who was likely Moses, carefully detailed the days leading up to the exit. This chronology shows that through the process of time, God moves His people toward deliverance. Noah had preached for 120 years and finally the door of the ark was opened where the people could start anew. The Lord's timing is not the same as humans, for He uses time to reconcile the world back to Him. As His children, believers should embrace the value of time in the same way.

In verses 15–17, God instructed Noah to bring everything and his family out of the ark and charged them to be fruitful and multiply. The term *fruitful* in verse 17 entailed a command to grow. The word *multiply* was a directive to reproduce or bear many. He wanted the new progenitors to reproduce a growing creation that worshipped Him and declared His glory. As Noah led the exodus from the ark, every saved creature had a job. It was to prepare a new order that would submit to the lordship of God. Of course, the new starters did not perfectly fulfill that role, but at least they initiated the world on a path back toward paradise.

## II. A NEW COVENANT (GENESIS 8:20–22, 9:11–13)

As Noah left the ark, he intuitively built an altar to sacrifice unto the Lord. The biblical laws of using altars for worship had not been established, yet Noah's inner conscience moved him to sacrifice. This act serves as foreshadowing of God's ultimate plan for humanity which is to have the law of righteousness written upon their hearts. Genesis 7:2 indicated that Noah knew the difference between clean and unclean animals prior to the Law of Moses. God led him to take seven each of every clean animal on the ark compared to two each of unclean creatures. When Noah sacrificed, it was likely a sheep, goat, or turtledove but neither a dog, cat, nor hog. This act of sacrifice conveyed how God instills within humanity a sense of right and wrong, whether they hear a sermon or read the Bible. No one has an excuse to sin, for everyone starts with a moral conscience. Noah displayed one of many benefits of sacrifice, showing gratitude to God. The sacrifice was worship. It was Noah's acknowledgement that those sacrificed animals could have been him and his family were it not for the mercy of the Lord.

When God smelled the aroma of the burned offering, it moved the Creator to promise never again destroy the world with a flood. The aroma of Noah's sacrifice represented devotion to God. It was Noah's way of putting on cologne for God. He wanted Jehovah to smell something good from him. A takeaway from Noah's altar sacrifice is to do things that soothe God rather than self. The words "sweet savour" in verse 21 conveyed that it had a calming or quieting effect upon God. The world had become so wicked that it enraged the Creator to destroy the people in the flood. But Noah had found a way to calm the Supreme's anger. It was through a sincere and devoted burnt offering.

Verses 21–22 show the positive results of making a sincere offering. Instead of the offering having a diminishing effect on the giver, it provided a replenishing impact. God promised to never again break the earth's cycle of seedtime and harvest nor the complementary cycle of seasons. When the faithful consistently give themselves to God without reservation, they never have to worry about running out of resources. This blessing to Noah was the opposite of the curse of Cain explored in last week's lesson. For Noah, the earth would work in his favor. The earth would provide food and the seasons would aid in his survival. With Cain, the earth would be his enemy. The benefits of genuine worship can never be minimized for it is the difference between life and death.

Genesis 9:11 highlights the Noahic Covenant. The Lord made a two–fold promise with Noah. The covenant stated that all flesh would not be destroyed by water, nor the entire world destroyed. This agreement marked the second covenant made between humanity and God. The first one was called the Adamic Covenant found in Genesis 1:26–30, 2:16–17. Adam and Eve were given dominion in the Garden of Eden, but instructed not to eat from the Tree of Knowledge of Good and Evil. With Noah's covenant, he was given a similar command to be fruitful and multiply. But this one guaranteed that all humanity would not be destroyed. God declared an everlasting love for His creation despite its sinful nature. Instead of cutting flesh off due to sin, the Lord will give humanity a built–in package to eternal life through Jesus Christ. The Noahic Covenant serves as typology of Jesus who declared that He came to save the world and not destroy it.

God placed a bow in the sky after the rain to remind both humanity and creatures that the promise to not totally eradicate them still holds. The author of Genesis specifically used the pronoun "my bow" in verse 13. It serves as a sign of life. Because of Noah's obedience, God promised him that humanity will live.

## THE LESSON APPLIED

One of the many problems in the world is murder and war. People can become so enraged that wars and senseless killings plague society. The natural response is to retaliate, which often deteriorates into an endless cycle of death. This lesson makes clear that unending death cannot not solve the problem of sin. At some point, the killing must stop, and a new covenant must be implemented. God displayed that process in this story. The wickedness in the world had become so bad that a time for death was inevitable. Something had to be done, for without a new start, man would have permanently been separated from God. The judgment of the flood lasted for forty days and nights and some things likely continued to die for years following the flood. However, the beautiful thing about God's way is life was birthed out of death. God made a new covenant with Noah which indicated that one day, there would be no more death. This promise would be achieved when people turned to real worship. People must be willing to offer their lives to God on the altar of sacrifice. Noah revealed through his altar sacrifice that the Spirit moved on his heart.

## Let's Talk About It

**What should be taking place when Christians respond to an altar call?**
Many churches have a period during the worship service when members and visitors in the congregation are invited to the altar for prayer. Noah performed the first altar call in the Bible when he sacrificed unto the Lord. Noah's actions provide insight on the importance of altar calls in the modern church. First, the call to the altar should not be self-centered. Noah's sacrifice was to the Lord. He could have easily said, "I am so glad to get out of that ark, Lord, help me find my way home." But his agenda was secondary to doing something that pleased the Lord. Second, one should put forth a sacrificial effort during the altar call. Noah sacrificed clean animals and birds. Christians should search their hearts to determine something worthy to surrender to the Heavenly Father. Finally, the altar call should be a time to hear God's instructions and promises. Often, people are so caught up in praying about their own needs that they do not hear nor obey God's commandments. When one comes to the altar, he or she should leave with the plan of God. Noah built an ark and an altar. As result of this lesson, what will you build?

## Get Social
Share your views and tag us @rhboydco. Use #rhboydco.

@rhboydco

## Home Daily Devotional Readings
### June 9–15, 2025

| Monday | Tuesday | Wednesday | Thursday | Friday | Saturday | Sunday |
|---|---|---|---|---|---|---|
| God Promises a Son | Abraham's Righteous Faith | Life Out of Death | A Blessing to the Nations | Joy for Weeping | Abraham's Courageous Faith | God Will Provide a Lamb |
| Genesis 17:15–22 | Romans 4:1–15 | Romans 4:16–25 | Genesis 12:1–7 | Psalms 125–126 | Hebrews 11:8–12 | Genesis 22:1–14 |

LESSON III                                         JUNE 15, 2025

# ABRAHAM MAKES AN OFFERING

ADULT TOPIC:                           BACKGROUND SCRIPTURE: GENESIS 22:1–19
THE VALUE OF A LIFE                              LESSON PASSAGE: GENESIS 22:1–14

## GENESIS 22:1–14

### KJV

AND it came to pass after these things, that God did tempt Abraham, and said unto him, Abraham: and he said, Behold, here I am.

2 And he said, Take now thy son, thine only son Isaac, whom thou lovest, and get thee into the land of Moriah; and offer him there for a burnt offering upon one of the mountains which I will tell thee of.

3 And Abraham rose up early in the morning, and saddled his ass, and took two of his young men with him, and Isaac his son, and clave the wood for the burnt offering, and rose up, and went unto the place of which God had told him.

4 Then on the third day Abraham lifted up his eyes, and saw the place afar off.

5 And Abraham said unto his young men, Abide ye here with the ass; and I and the lad will go yonder and worship, and come again to you.

6 And Abraham took the wood of the burnt offering, and laid it upon Isaac his son; and he took the fire in his hand, and a knife; and they went both of them together.

7 And Isaac spake unto Abraham his father, and said, My father: and he said, Here am I, my son. And he said, Behold the fire and the wood: but where is the lamb for a burnt offering?

8 And Abraham said, My son, God will provide himself a lamb for a burnt offering: so they went both of them together.

9 And they came to the place which God had told him of; and Abraham built an altar there, and laid the wood in order, and bound Isaac his

### NRSVue

AFTER these things God tested Abraham. He said to him, "Abraham!" And he said, "Here I am."

2 He said, "Take your son, your only son Isaac, whom you love, and go to the land of Moriah and offer him there as a burnt offering on one of the mountains that I shall show you."

3 So Abraham rose early in the morning, saddled his donkey, and took two of his young men with him and his son Isaac; he cut the wood for the burnt offering and set out and went to the place in the distance that God had shown him.

4 On the third day Abraham looked up and saw the place far away.

5 Then Abraham said to his young men, "Stay here with the donkey; the boy and I will go over there; we will worship, and then we will come back to you."

6 Abraham took the wood of the burnt offering and laid it on his son Isaac, and he himself carried the fire and the knife. And the two of them walked on together.

7 Isaac said to his father Abraham, "Father!" And he said, "Here I am, my son." He said, "The fire and the wood are here, but where is the lamb for a burnt offering?"

8 Abraham said, "God himself will provide the lamb for a burnt offering, my son." And the two of them walked on together.

9 When they came to the place that God had shown him, Abraham built an altar there and laid the wood in order. He bound his son Isaac

**MAIN THOUGHT:** Abraham called that place "The LORD will provide," as it is said to this day, "On the mount of the LORD it shall be provided." (Genesis 22:14, NRSVue)

## Genesis 22:1–14

### KJV

son, and laid him on the altar upon the wood.

10 And Abraham stretched forth his hand, and took the knife to slay his son.

11 And the angel of the Lord called unto him out of heaven, and said, Abraham, Abraham: and he said, Here am I.

12 And he said, Lay not thine hand upon the lad, neither do thou any thing unto him: for now I know that thou fearest God, seeing thou hast not withheld thy son, thine only son from me.

13 And Abraham lifted up his eyes, and looked, and behold behind him a ram caught in a thicket by his horns: and Abraham went and took the ram, and offered him up for a burnt offering in the stead of his son.

14 And Abraham called the name of that place Jehovahjireh: as it is said to this day, In the mount of the Lord it shall be seen.

### NRSVue

and laid him on the altar on top of the wood.

10 Then Abraham reached out his hand and took the knife to kill his son.

11 But the angel of the Lord called to him from heaven and said, "Abraham, Abraham!" And he said, "Here I am."

12 He said, "Do not lay your hand on the boy or do anything to him, for now I know that you fear God, since you have not withheld your son, your only son, from me."

13 And Abraham looked up and saw a ram, caught in a thicket by its horns. Abraham went and took the ram and offered it up as a burnt offering instead of his son.

14 So Abraham called that place "The Lord will provide," as it is said to this day, "On the mount of the Lord it shall be provided."

**LESSON SETTING**
   Time: 2054 BCE
   Place: Land of Moriah in
         Mt. Gerizim

**LESSON OUTLINE**
   I. Presented with a Test
      (Genesis 22:1–5)
   II. Taking the Test
      (Genesis 22:6–9)
   III. Passing the Test
      (Genesis 22:10–14)

## UNIFYING PRINCIPLE

Obedience and trust are marks of commitment to one another. What do we offer to demonstrate ultimate allegiance and commitment? Abraham passes the test of faithfulness to God in his willingness to sacrifice his own son, Isaac, on the altar.

## INTRODUCTION

This lesson emerges out of the context of God keeping a covenant with Abraham. Starting in Genesis 12, Jehovah promised Abram that his lineage would be made into a great nation. His descendants would be as numerous as the stars, and through them the world would be blessed. At that time, Abram and Sarai already past typical childbearing age and were childless, but Abram believed the Lord and took faithful action based on God's promise. Abram received the fulfillment of that promise at age 75.

More than twenty–five years later, God continued to affirm that covenant. But the Lord did it in the unique way of calling upon Abraham to sacrifice his beloved son, Isaac. Some people might view a command to sacrifice a child as being too harsh for a loving God and creator of life; however, the deeper principles of this lesson convey the eternal grace of God. Abram's story is also a reminder to believers to remain faithful to God and trust in Him and His promises.

# EXPOSITION

## I. PRESENTED WITH A TEST (GENESIS 22:1–5)

Abraham's experiences can be described as a journey. In Genesis 12, he was instructed to leave his home of Ur and go into the land of Canaan seeking the plan of God. At every stage of his journey, the Lord spoke, giving him assurance of the promised covenant. In verse, 1, the Scripture gives another example of God speaking. This time, the voice of the Lord tested Abraham to go into the Land of Moriah and sacrifice Isaac as a burnt offering. Abraham's initial response to the Lord's call was "here I am." This willing response provides a good example of how believers should react. Abraham models that one can never fully come to know Elohim by turning a deaf ear. Bible readers have the advantage of knowing the end of this story at the beginning. In the end, Isaac will not be sacrificed, and Abraham will know more assuredly that the Lord provides. But this more mature understanding would have never been realized had Abraham not started by saying, "Here I am."

After the Lord told Abraham to sacrifice his son, verse 3 revealed he rose early in the morning and moved out to do it. Abraham does not delay the test, which proved to be wise. He did not give the devil or doubters time to dissuade him. Not only must one admire his faith, but also Isaac and Sarah, the mother. The text does not indicate that he shared with them God's command, but they also had to trust. He, Isaac and two servants traveled a three-day journey from Beersheba to the region of Moriah. Abraham followed God. Isaac followed his father. The servants followed their master and even the donkey had to comply.

Verse 5 revealed the steadfast faith of Abraham for he told the servants that he and Isaac were going further to worship, and they would return. In some way, Abraham's worship convinced him that things would be all right. When being tested by God, draw on that inner assurance. Abraham believed that although he did not know the outcome, somehow both he and Isaac would return from their encounter with God. When presented with a very difficult task, Abraham was ready. Are you ready for your test?

## II. TAKING THE TEST (GENESIS 22:6–9)

In biblical times, offerings were used by various religions to appease their god. Abraham came from Ur in the region of Mesopotamia and they were known for human sacrifices to their kings and gods. Therefore, the thought of human sacrifice was not foreign to Abraham. But he was now learning the ways of a new God named Elohim who was vastly different from his old Chaldean god, Nanna. The need for believers to set aside their idols is still relevant, for the methods of worship in the past do not apply with the God of Abraham, Isaac, and Jacob. Nevertheless, in verse 6, Abraham continued toward Mount Moriah, equipped with wood, fire, and his son in preparation for a burnt offering sacrifice to the Lord.

Isaac asked his father where the sacrifice would come from. It is important to note that Isaac was a very young man while Abraham was more than 100 years old. Isaac could have easily escaped from his father had he feared for his life. The fact that Isaac remained by his father's side is indicative of the son's deep level of trust in his father. It is likely Isaac had to help his father as they travelled the arduous journey to Moriah. Therefore, the son displayed just as much faith as Abraham. One can see the parallels in this story to that of the Heavenly Father sacrificing His Son, Jesus, on the cross.

Abraham responded to Isaac's question with a statement of faith that "the Lord will provide." Some will consider this term to mean that the Lord will make a way or give something to meet the need. However, a deeper meaning refers to God being there with Abraham and Isaac. This proved true. In verse 9, God was there, identifying the place for the altar while Abraham complied as he prepared Isaac for sacrifice. Isaac also complied, for the text does not show him resisting. Abraham was successfully taking his test and his teacher was there facilitating the process. The lesson highlights what appears to be an impossible expectation can be achieved, if one will trust that the Lord will provide.

## III. Passing the Test (Genesis 22:10–14)

As Abraham stretched out his hand to kill his son, the angel of the Lord called his name. This act revealed that Abraham intended to follow through with the sacrifice. For a burnt offering to be acceptable, the sacrifice must be killed and then consumed by fire. A partial offering would not suffice. Abraham could not simply wound or maim Isaac; he had to summarily slit his throat and sprinkle his blood on the altar. It would be excruciating to even think of such an act, but it reinforces the intense way that God dealt with sin.

As in Genesis 22:1, when the angel of the Lord called in verse 11, the man of faith answered by saying, "Here I am." In both instances, the text reveals the importance of staying in tune with God. Abraham passed his test and proved that he feared God. The angel commanded him not to harm Isaac in any way. His willingness not to withhold anything from God spoke volumes about the meaning of genuine faith. Just at the appropriate time, the man of God saw behind him a ram caught in a thicket. One might wonder whether the ram had always been there or did God miraculously put it there at the right time. Faith causes one to recognize the Lord's provisions. Some trials can be so consuming that it is hard to see the handiwork of God. This lesson conveys that if one will sincerely worship, the Lord will reveal the answers to life's challenges. When Abram offered the ram instead of Isaac, it served as typology for the substitutionary atonement of Jesus Christ. Jesus died in place of humanity to pay for the sins of the world in similar fashion as the ram in the place of Isaac. Students should also note the unselfishness of Abraham's worship. He could have killed the ram for himself, but the ram belonged to God and Abraham was careful not to hold anything back.

## The Lesson Applied

During the offertory period, many churches sing "You Can't Beat God Giving." The words emphasize that no matter how hard we try, we can never out give God. Abraham's charge to give up his son reinforces the truth of that song. Whatever God expects His children to give, the Lord will do more. This principle is important to remember when being tested. A person's natural inclination is to assume that God's requirement is unreasonable. One can point to the test of tithing or a commitment to mission. People tend to say that God expects too much. Yet, Abraham revealed that if a person has unwavering faith, God shows His presence and brings forth an increase. When asked to do something on behalf of the Lord, Christians should look for what will be gained from the experience rather than what may be lost.

Abraham gained in faith. As he grew in years, Abraham never wavered from the Lord's covenant. Abraham also gained in prosperity (Genesis 24:1). And he gained in posterity for his future generations continued their relationship with the true God. When the Lord speaks, ask the question, what is God wanting to do in my life? Even though one may not always understand God's ways, the promise of the Scriptures is in the end, believers come out blessed.

This lesson underscores the importance of unconditional worship. Abraham and his household extended themselves beyond the norm, and they did it through faith. Often, churches try to make worship too convenient. Technology has advanced so a person can comfortably watch a worship service at home or even at a coffee shop on Sunday morning. Abraham's example was different. He had to go out of his way to really encounter God. Christians must be careful of making worship so commonplace that they can claim they are experiencing God while simultaneously watching a football game on a split screen TV. Authentic worship entails sacrifice—time, effort, and sometimes even life. But for those who are willing to hold nothing back, God withholds nothing from them in return.

## LET'S TALK ABOUT IT
**Do you have the faith of Abraham?**

It is a mistake to assume that one cannot have faith like Abraham. Some people may read about his extraordinary faith and sigh indicating that will never be their faith. But with God all things are possible. All believers have the potential of great faith through the power of the Holy Spirit. As a result of this lesson, each person should declare they have faith like Father Abraham.

@rhboydco

## GET SOCIAL
Share your views and tag us @rhboydco. Use #rhboydco.

# HOME DAILY DEVOTIONAL READINGS
## JUNE 16–22, 2025

| MONDAY | TUESDAY | WEDNESDAY | THURSDAY | FRIDAY | SATURDAY | SUNDAY |
|---|---|---|---|---|---|---|
| Love the Alien as Yourself | Isaac's Prayer for Rebekah | Living as an Alien | God Will Supply Every Need | God Blesses and Provides | Live in Harmony; Welcome One Another | 15:1–13 Making Peace with Others |
| Leviticus 19:30–37 | Genesis 25:19–28 | Genesis 26:1–11 | Philippians 4:10–19 | Genesis 26:12–23 | Romans | Genesis 26:24–33 |

**LESSON IV**                                **JUNE 22, 2025**

# ISAAC CALLS ON THE NAME OF THE LORD

**ADULT TOPIC:**                          **BACKGROUND SCRIPTURE:** GENESIS 26:1–33
DIGGING YOUR OWN WELL                  **LESSON PASSAGE:** GENESIS 26:24–33

## GENESIS 26:24–33

### KJV

AND the Lord appeared unto him the same night, and said, I am the God of Abraham thy father: fear not, for I am with thee, and will bless thee, and multiply thy seed for my servant Abraham's sake.
25 And he builded an altar there, and called upon the name of the Lord, and pitched his tent there: and there Isaac's servants digged a well.
26 Then Abimelech went to him from Gerar, and Ahuzzath one of his friends, and Phichol the chief captain of his army.
27 And Isaac said unto them, Wherefore come ye to me, seeing ye hate me, and have sent me away from you?
28 And they said, We saw certainly that the Lord was with thee: and we said, Let there be now an oath betwixt us, even betwixt us and thee, and let us make a covenant with thee;
29 That thou wilt do us no hurt, as we have not touched thee, and as we have done unto thee nothing but good, and have sent thee away in peace: thou art now the blessed of the Lord.
30 And he made them a feast, and they did eat and drink.
31 And they rose up betimes in the morning, and sware one to another: and Isaac sent them away, and they departed from him in peace.
32 And it came to pass the same day, that Isaac's servants came, and told him concerning the well which they had digged, and said unto him, We have found water.
33 And he called it Shebah: therefore the name of the city is Beersheba unto this day.

### NRSVue

AND that very night the Lord appeared to him and said, "I am the God of your father Abraham; do not be afraid, for I am with you and will bless you and make your offspring numerous for my servant Abraham's sake."
25 So he built an altar there, called on the name of the Lord, and pitched his tent there. And there Isaac's servants dug a well.
26 Then Abimelech went to him from Gerar, with Ahuzzath his adviser and Phicol the commander of his army.
27 Isaac said to them, "Why have you come to me, seeing that you hate me and have sent me away from you?"
28 They said, "We see plainly that the Lord has been with you, so we say, let there be an oath between you and us, and let us make a covenant with you
29 so that you will do us no harm, just as we have not touched you and have done to you nothing but good and have sent you away in peace. You are now the blessed of the Lord."
30 So he made them a feast, and they ate and drank.
31 In the morning they rose early and exchanged oaths, and Isaac set them on their way, and they departed from him in peace.
32 That same day Isaac's servants came and told him about the well that they had dug and said to him, "We have found water!"
33 He called it Shibah; therefore the name of the city is Beer-sheba to this day.

**MAIN THOUGHT:** [Isaac] built an altar there, called on the name of the LORD, and pitched his tent there. And there Isaac's servants dug a well.
(Genesis 26:25, NRSVue)

**LESSON SETTING**
  Time: 1977 BCE
  Place: Beersheba

**LESSON OUTLINE**
  I. Blessed by God
     (Genesis 26:24–29)
  II. The Blessings of Peace
      (Genesis 26:30–33)

## UNIFYING PRINCIPLE

As children grow to adulthood, they step into their own lives. What do we take with us from our family of origin? Isaac receives the blessing and promises that God made to his father, Abraham. In response, Isaac builds an altar and calls on the name of the Lord.

## INTRODUCTION

This lesson opens in the context of Isaac trying to survive during a time of famine. Isaac was moving throughout the land of Canaan trying to find food and particularly water to supply his household. The Lord instructed him not to go into Egypt, but rather to remain in Gerar where he would be blessed. This command was concerning because the Philistines occupied the region. These people had little interest in the welfare of Isaac and did not serve the Lord. Nevertheless, Isaac obeyed God and benefited from the Lord's watchful eye. When Abimelech saw how God was with Isaac, it moved him to form a partnership. Isaac's reverence for God showed how faithfulness can turn an enemy into an ally. Jehovah was there at every juncture of Isaac's sojourn, no matter how bleak the circumstances looked, keeping His covenant promise with Abraham. Isaac acknowledged this reality by building an altar and making sacrifices unto the Lord.

## EXPOSITION

### I. BLESSED BY GOD (GENESIS 26:24–29)

A consistent aspect of God's relationship with both Abraham and Isaac is the Lord remained present in their lives. Verse 24 indicated that the Lord appeared unto Isaac in Beersheba. In the Hebrew, the word appeared is "raah" meaning "to see." It reaffirmed to Isaac that the Lord was continuously seeing him and had not changed the covenant promise. In the same way Yahweh was with Abraham, Isaac received that equal assurance. When Isaac received this confirmation, he was struggling during a famine to find wells of water to survive. Yet, one can learn from this text that during challenging times, the Lord will reaffirm His word. It is important to prayerfully look and listen for the Lord's appearance. With Isaac, God showed up at night in a type of audible voice. But there are many ways how God manifests His presence. It may be through a sermon, a song, or often through the confirming words of another Christian. The key is to be spiritually awake to hear the voice of God.

Isaac was awake that night and heard the voice of God. Yahweh's message included five parts: God identifying Himself; the command not to fear; the declaration of the Lord's presence; a promise to bless; and the multiplication of Isaac's future generations. The name used in the text to identify God was Elohim, which points to His supremacy or dominion over everything. Because of that supremacy, Isaac had no need to fear. This encounter was God's check–up call to declare blessings. Isaac realized that the blessings which reached back to his father applied with him as he searched for water, but also extended forward into the future.

As a result of this amazing experience, Isaac worshipped through building an altar and prayer. Verse 25 gives insight on a worship style that pleases God. It's a style where one must sacrifice something and call on God. It certainly required sacrifice to build, but the work was a labor of love. When one takes themselves out of the equation and places the focus on the supreme, it moves the heart of the Lord. Isaac's actions show that God-centered worship is not about personal preferences. True worship simply requires one to give something and do it for the Lord. When Isaac properly gave to God, the Lord turned around and gave back to him. First, Isaac found another water source so he dug a well. With water being a valuable resource, particularly in a famine and more so with them living in a desert, God gave to Isaac a very valuable blessing. This reality conveys how God operates with those who trust him. When one truly worships, the faithful always receive in return whatever they need.

Abimelech was king of the Philistines, and they envied Isaac. Every time Isaac and his herdsmen dug a well, the Philistines quarreled with them and took the well. With Isaac's entourage being small, they could not fight Abimelech and the Philistines, so they had to continuously move to find places of water to survive. But Jehovah–Jireh was there, and he touched the heart of Abimelech to make an oath of peace with Isaac. God turned Isaac's haters into rejuvenators, and He did it through keeping the covenant promise. When Abimelech saw how this man found sources of water seemingly everywhere, the king acknowledged the handiwork of God. The results of a divine covenant between Abraham and Isaac led to a human covenant between Abimelech and Isaac. The peace between these two men shows the ultimate purpose of being blessed: one is blessed to produce additional blessings with people in the world.

## II. THE BLESSING OF PEACE (GENESIS 26:30–33)

The ceremonial feast in verse 30 foreshadowed the Jewish fellowship meals associated with the peace offering in Leviticus chapters 3 and 7. In ancient times, eating together was symbolic of unity and considered a sacred activity. Those partaking in the festivities would wash their hands and sometime their whole bodies to emphasize cleanliness before God. Abimelech's willingness to eat with Isaac also showed a respect for his faith. The king of Gerar was primarily a polytheistic king (Benamozegh, Israel and humanity). Yet, Abimelech takes food provided by the God of Isaac which indicated his respect for a monotheistic faith. Moreover, the sharing of food required both parties to trust each other. In ancient times, poisoning food and or drinks was a means to eliminate an enemy. This celebration revealed that the fear of poisoning was not an issue. Peace was at hand and Isaac's commitment to his father's covenant made it a reality.

Verse 31 highlighted how this meal was not done in isolation. Abimelech had Ahuzzath and Phichol with him while Isaac included his household. These witnesses could carry the news to others that the principal leaders had made an oath of peace. Their presence was important in keeping the peace because sometimes the leaders have come together but the rest of the group remains at odds. For example, during the War of 1812, there was a conflict that did need to be fought called the Battle of New Orleans. The fallout from the fighting left nearly 2500 people dead simply because the soldiers had not received word that a peace treaty had already been signed. This principle applies to one's spiritual life for some individuals are still at war with themselves trying to overcome sin. But Christ has already signed an oath of peace with humanity through His sacrifice at Calvary.

This consummation of the oath between Isaac and Abimelech took place early the next morning. There are numerous examples in the Bible where significant events were initialized early. Abraham made the journey to Mt. Moriah early in the morning and Jesus was resurrected early on the third day. The timing of the oath seemed to indicate the urgency of the act. Isaac and Abimelech saw peace between themselves as something that could not be delayed. If they would have delayed, Satan could have changed their minds. Therefore, God's work should not be set to the side but prioritized. Their actions were part of the Lord's plan to save lives.

When Abimelech departed, the text revealed that he left in peace. The Hebrew word for peace in verse 31 is *shalom*. It not only means the end of conflict, but it also means completeness. The results of worshipping God and calling on His name led to both Isaac and Abimelech being in a state of completeness. Had they not achieved peace, everyone involved would have remained in conflict. This act indicates the importance of genuine peace. It promotes a sense of wholeness where parties become compatible. Abimelech and Isaac understood that they were each other's keepers. They needed each other to eliminate the brokenness within their own lives.

Once the brokenness was mended, God rewarded them with a well of water. When Isaac found peace, his servants found water. The Lord's provision was not a coincidence. Peace and prosperity dovetail together. When people stop fighting with each other, God shows them how everyone can prosper. As long as conflict continued, both Isaac and the Philistines quarreled over the shortage of water. It was clear that water was always available underground, but the constant turmoil made it difficult for all parties to find it. The takeaway from this lesson is when people find the covenant God of Abraham and Isaac, they find peace. When they find peace, they find everything else that they need.

## THE LESSON APPLIED

The lesson revealed that Isaac built an altar, then he called upon the Lord. It does not indicate that Abimelech did the same thing. However, the king of Gerar's actions inferred that he must have also had some type of divine encounter. The king's response to the divine emphasizes why it is so important to consistently live a godly life. Some people's encounter with God will be through observing a believer. Isaac was the lens in which Abimelech saw the Lord. The lesson also teaches the importance of maintaining proper conduct when faced with life challenges. Isaac was faced with survival issues as he searched for water in a famine. He must have been under constant stress and could have easily forsaken his convictions and resorted to ungodly activities to survive. Isaac may have had a choice to worship the Philistine god thinking that might make life better for him. He certainly could have become polytheistic and tried to blend in with the culture. But he did not; Isaac continued to trust in his father's God during the hard times which must have impressed Abimelech. The king realized that Isaac's faith was not just during prosperity but also during the hard times. A consistent faith proves to be a powerful witness of God. People are watching how you respond during the days of famine.

## LET'S TALK ABOUT IT

Could Isaac's digging of wells be like making investments?

The Scripture reveals how Isaac and his herdsmen dug four wells and named each. These wells were located where Abraham had dug them. Isaac seemed to remember his father's activities and used that as a plan for himself. His father even made an oath to Abimelech in Genesis 21:22–34. These wells were business investments. Isaac was an agriculturalist, and having water for his flock and his crops was essential. The man of God showed wisdom by building upon what his father had started, which helped him to prosper. Christians should follow suit and make investments to better themselves. One cannot sit on their hands and hope their personal lives improve. Instead, the Bible teaches to use the blueprints given by the ancestors and build on it to increase.

Isaac took risks to dig those wells, but they were calculated risks guided by God. The same principle applies in one's personal affairs. Sometimes the digging of a well may turn up dry, but do not stop digging because God has promised water. As you study this lesson, put yourself in it and ask the Lord to reveal places where you can invest. As those investments produce returns, use them to be a blessing to others.

## GET SOCIAL

Share your views and tag us @rhboydco. Use #rhboydco.

@rhboydco

| HOME DAILY DEVOTIONAL READINGS JUNE 23–29, 2025 | | | | | | |
|---|---|---|---|---|---|---|
| **MONDAY** Purify Yourself before God Genesis 35:1–7 | **TUESDAY** Abide in Christ, the True Vine John 15:1–8 | **WEDNESDAY** Seek God with All Your Heart Jeremiah 29:8–14 | **THURSDAY** Christ Is among His Gathered People Matthew 18:15–20 | **FRIDAY** Christ Is with Us Always Matthew 28:16–20 | **SATURDAY** Fullness of Joy in God's Presence Psalm 16 | **SUNDAY** The Lord Is in This Place Genesis 28:10–22 |

LESSON V     JUNE 29, 2025

# JACOB SETS UP A SACRED PILLAR

ADULT TOPIC:
JACOB MARKS GOD'S FAITHFULNESS

BACKGROUND SCRIPTURE: GENESIS 28:1–22; 33:17–20; 35:1–7
LESSON PASSAGE: GENESIS 28:10–22

## GENESIS 28:10–22

### KJV

AND Jacob went out from Beersheba, and went toward Haran.
11 And he lighted upon a certain place, and tarried there all night, because the sun was set; and he took of the stones of that place, and put them for his pillows, and lay down in that place to sleep.
12 And he dreamed, and behold a ladder set up on the earth, and the top of it reached to heaven: and behold the angels of God ascending and descending on it.
13 And, behold, the Lord stood above it, and said, I am the Lord God of Abraham thy father, and the God of Isaac: the land whereon thou liest, to thee will I give it, and to thy seed;
14 And thy seed shall be as the dust of the earth, and thou shalt spread abroad to the west, and to the east, and to the north, and to the south: and in thee and in thy seed shall all the families of the earth be blessed.
15 And, behold, I am with thee, and will keep thee in all places whither thou goest, and will bring thee again into this land; for I will not leave thee, until I have done that which I have spoken to thee of.
16 And Jacob awaked out of his sleep, and he said, Surely the Lord is in this place; and I knew it not.
17 And he was afraid, and said, How dreadful is this place! this is none other but the house of God, and this is the gate of heaven.
18 And Jacob rose up early in the morning, and took the stone that he had put for his pillows,

### NRSVue

JACOB left Beer-sheba and went toward Haran.
11 He came to a certain place and stayed there for the night, because the sun had set. Taking one of the stones of the place, he put it under his head and lay down in that place.

12 And he dreamed that there was a stairway set up on the earth, the top of it reaching to heaven, and the angels of God were ascending and descending on it.
13 And the Lord stood beside him and said, "I am the Lord, the God of Abraham your father and the God of Isaac; the land on which you lie I will give to you and to your offspring,
14 and your offspring shall be like the dust of the earth, and you shall spread abroad to the west and to the east and to the north and to the south, and all the families of the earth shall be blessed in you and in your offspring.
15 Know that I am with you and will keep you wherever you go and will bring you back to this land, for I will not leave you until I have done what I have promised you."

16 Then Jacob woke from his sleep and said, "Surely the Lord is in this place—and I did not know it!"
17 And he was afraid and said, "How awesome is this place! This is none other than the house of God, and this is the gate of heaven."
18 So Jacob rose early in the morning, and he took the stone that he had put under his head

**MAIN THOUGHT:** Jacob rose early in the morning, and he took the stone that he had put under his head and set it up for a pillar and poured oil on the top of it. He called that place Bethel. (Genesis 28:18–19, NRSVue)

## Genesis 28:10–22

### KJV

and set it up for a pillar, and poured oil upon the top of it.
19 And he called the name of that place Bethel: but the name of that city was called Luz at the first.
20 And Jacob vowed a vow, saying, If God will be with me, and will keep me in this way that I go, and will give me bread to eat, and raiment to put on,
21 So that I come again to my father's house in peace; then shall the Lord be my God:
22 And this stone, which I have set for a pillar, shall be God's house: and of all that thou shalt give me I will surely give the tenth unto thee.

### NRSVue

and set it up for a pillar and poured oil on the top of it.
19 He called that place Bethel, but the name of the city was Luz at the first.
20 Then Jacob made a vow, saying, "If God will be with me and will keep me in this way that I go and will give me bread to eat and clothing to wear,
21 so that I come again to my father's house in peace, then the Lord shall be my God,
22 and this stone, which I have set up for a pillar, shall be God's house, and of all that you give me I will surely give one-tenth to you."

## LESSON SETTING
**Time:** 1928 BCE
**Place:** Bethel

## LESSON OUTLINE
I. Jacob's Dream
(Genesis 28:10-15)
II. Jacob Wakes Up
(Genesis 28:16-22)

## UNIFYING PRINCIPLE

Meaningful events and places can hold a lasting impression. How do we mark important events in life? Jacob marks his important encounters with altars, offerings, and signs of worship.

## INTRODUCTION

Believers should cleanse their minds of any false gods to recognize the true God. Jacob had the correct spiritual frequency which allowed Jehovah to encounter his subconscious mind. From his experience, Christians should consider what occupies their minds. Paul taught in Philippians 4:8 to think on the things true, honest, just, pure, lovely, and of good report. When one keeps his or her mind on these things, it opens the door for God's manifestations. Once Jacob saw the dream, he responded with worship. This principle proves very valuable. It is not enough to experience a supernatural event and continue as if nothing has happened. The faithful should use their godly dreams as a springboard to help others develop a relationship with the God of Abraham, Isaac, and Jacob.

When Jacob received this dream, he was on a journey toward Haran. He was running from his brother Esau because he had deceptively stolen his sibling's blessing. The man was a professional cheater which caused his relationships with others to always be suspicious. So, this dream could be described as the first step of God molding Jacob into a person of integrity. It is important to note that one cannot properly change his or her behavior without a relationship with God. The adage that a leopard cannot change his spots is true. Jacob's leopard-like tendency was to deceive. But while on the run, the supplanter runs into God. And this experience proved beneficial, for Jacob gained assurance that the Lord had not broken the covenant promise. Just like his father and grandfather, despite their sins, Jehovah kept His word with Jacob.

This lesson stimulates students to embrace the value of having a covenant with God. Some people may feel as if their sins separate them from the love of God. Some say, "I have done too much wrong to be saved or go to church." Yet, this lesson shows that God's promises are not based on one earning them. The Lord keeps His word despite one's sins. The Heavenly Father blesses His children based on His goodness. Even when one feels unworthy, pay attention to the spiritual manifestations for they are means in which the Lord reconciles His people.

## EXPOSITION

### I. JACOB'S DREAM (GENESIS 28:10-15)

Due to Jacob taking Esau's blessing, he had to escape his brother's wrath. Verse 10 described the escape stating that he went out from Beersheba toward Haran, and he stopped to rest at a place called Luz. Jacob was tired because he had traveled about 450 miles, which was about a month's journey. During this time, the supplanter must have thought about his sins. He had plenty of time to pray and ask for repentance. This journeying period reveals how God works with His children. He may not immediately correct or punish them but gives sinners time to reflect on their transgressions. It is important not to waste this time because time can run out. The hope is this space of time results in sinners opening their hearts to an encounter with the Living God. The lesson makes clear that no one can escape the presence of the Lord. While on the run, Jacob was unknowingly getting ready to meet His master.

As he prepared to sleep, Jacob used stones for a pillar. Stones have often been used to prepare a foundation for structures. Both Abraham and Isaac used stones to build their altars unto the Lord. Jacob did not know that his makeshift headrest would be a type of altar. But God knew it because these stones ultimately foreshadowed the foundation of the church in the New Testament. In the Bible, stones also served as an element to help people remember what happened at a sacred place. Jacob's experience proved to be holy as he fell asleep and dreamed of a ladder that reached heaven.

The ladder was a point of connection showing how heaven and earth did not operate in isolation. What happened on earth was impacted by divine plans in heaven. This point is important because some believe that God is either disconnected from all activities on earth or nonexistent. A theological term called *transcendence* relates to this idea of a distant or disconnected God. Theologians who espouse total transcendence might question whether the divine has any involvement on earth. Yet, the ladder in Genesis 28:12 revealed that Jehovah set up a system where heaven and earth would interact.

The ascending and descending of the angels convey a communication system between the Lord and humanity. The order of the angels' movement on the ladder was ascension then descent. The messengers heard the prayers of humans and carried them up to God. Then, they received Jehovah's directives, which were carried back to earth. God received the message of Jacob's anguish. He had been banished to Haran thousands of miles from home. Yet, the Holy One stood above the ladder and reaffirmed His covenant promise. Jehovah standing above the ladder rather than on it was significant. Although the ladder touched earth and reached heaven, neither entity impacted the stability of God. With Jehovah above it all, the dream revealed that nothing on earth nor in heaven could disturb His promises.

The covenant ensured Jacob that God was with him. The land belonged to his descendants and through his seed, the earth would be blessed. This message was so unequivocal that God spoke it Himself. Wherever the man of God went, the Lord promised to be with him and bless his seed. The concern that Jacob had about being permanently exiled from his home was calmed. Eventually, he would return to Canaan. This dream gave blessed assurance that everything promised to Abraham and Isaac also applied to him.

## II. Jacob Wakes Up (Genesis 28:16-22)

When Jacob awoke from his dream, he immediately realized the presence of God. His first response was to declare the Lord's presence. The Bible teaches that there is power in what one says. Despite his limitations, the dreamer did not doubt. God regularly speaks to His children, but it takes faith to acknowledge it. A person may ask how can one encounter an invisible God? Jacob reveals that a key centers on accepting what the Lord does reveal. Abraham saw and heard God through a ram caught in a thicket. Isaac knew He was present through wells flowing with water. Jacob experienced a dream. Each patriarch was afraid when they encountered the divine, but they did not let fear keep them from receiving and responding to the message.

The supplanter's actions show that believers should not be paralyzed by fear. The presence of God is overwhelming to any creature. Scriptures such as Exodus 33:20 and John 1:18 point to the inability of humans to see all the glory of God and live. However, the Lord reveals enough to get a person's attention but not so much of Himself to kill that person. This holy manifestation revealed the mercy of God and Jacob responded by acknowledging such an awesome event. What made the event awesome was that the dreamer envisioned God dwelling with him on earth. The patriarch possessed a natural reverence for the true God and any close encounter with Him was an amazing experience. Jacob was not casual with God. Some people today will come to worship and spend more time on their cell phone than in prayer. But Jacob had a sense of holy awe about the divine. So, he responded by erecting a type of altar to express reverent worship.

Abraham, Isaac, and Jacob responded to their spiritual experience in a similar fashion. They built something. The pillars of stone that Jacob built can be likened to various monuments in the Old Testament. Moses used pillars to affirm the Sinai Covenant in Exodus 24:4. Joshua erected 12 stones to remember the crossing of the Jordan in Joshua 4:19-20. Samuel used a set up stones called Ebenezer to commemorate God helping Israel to defeat the Philistines in 1 Samuel 7:12.

The Hebrew word for erected pillars is *massebot,* which means 'standing stones.' Stones to Jehovah were plain, with no inscriptions upon them, which distinguished them from stones built to other deities. Moreover, the Hebrews' pillars served to memorialize an event—remember the occurrence, affirm a covenant, and declare a place sacred. The pouring of oil on top of the pillar indicated that the marker was to be holy, for it was the place where God had made Himself known on earth.

When Jacob named the place where he dreamed Bethel, the word means "house of God." Of course, God is too big to be confined to one location, even less so a house. But the ceremony was Jacob's way of saying, "this is where I met God." One should always cherish the place where he or she first encountered God. It should be a type of mental revival to relive what happened when the Lord intervened in one's life and brought salvation. Jacob was not saved in Genesis 28, but he was reassured of the presence and keeping power of the Lord. If an individual feels burned out, a good inspiration is to return physically or mentally to that place where God was unquestionably apparent.

Jacob's experience is one of many reasons why believers should go to a physical church building. For being in an environment that has been dedicated as the house of God can help one focus on the divine. Deuteronomy 16:16 conveys the command to worship at the place that the Lord chooses. It is an act of aligning with the same spot that God picked on earth to manifest Himself. By going to that place, the worshippers acknowledge that if the spot was good enough for the Lord to show up, it is good enough for them to show up.

As Jacob worshipped, he made a vow to follow the Lord and give a tenth of his possessions. This vow shows the participatory nature of worship. God made a vow and Jacob responds with his own commitment. Often it is said, "that you can never meet the Lord and leave the same way." Verses 21 and 22 confirm that reality. Worship requires an ongoing commitment every time one enters the house of the Lord. However, Jacob's commitment was conditional for he promised to tithe only if God kept His promise. Jacob wanting God to do everything first revealed that the supplanter still had ulterior motives. When one truly gives themselves to God, all conditions must be removed. The trickster still had some growing to do but at least he was moving in the right direction.

## THE LESSON APPLIED

Dreams can be very intriguing in many ways. People of faith may wonder if their dreams have meaningful messages or was it the result of eating a bad late-night meal? An application from this lesson is to recognize dreams that come from God and positively respond to them. Jacob immediately recognized his dream being from the Lord. The following are some ways of discerning dreams. A dreamer may talk to a trusted Christian about their experience and listen to their perspective. Another believer may confirm the activity of the Holy Spirit in the revelation. Dreamers should also look for affirmations or dis-affirmations in the teachings of Scripture. God's word never contradicts a godly vision, so whatever one dreams, the Bible will provide insight. If one is convinced they have received a divine encounter, the believer must act on it and trust in God's support and presence.

Jacob received assurance that the Lord was with him, and every dreamer has that same guarantee. When discerning dreams, one must remember that God's timing transcends human understanding. Just because an individual has dreamed something, it does not mean that all of it will take place within their lifetime. The faithful must keep an open mind when experiencing God. The Lord is sovereign, and humans are a part of a much larger plan. By allowing God to set the terms of the dream rather than interpreting the experience with pre-conceived notions, it relieves the dreamer from trying to figure everything out. Through divine providence, the dream and the dreamer will come to know that God is in this place.

## LET'S TALK ABOUT IT
**Does one have to give a tithe?**
The lesson revealed that after encountering God, Jacob promised to tithe. Therefore, yes, giving a tithe is required. The Scripture revealed in verse 22 that Jacob would offer a tenth of all that God gave to him. Moreover, tithing is far more than giving money to pay the church bills or the pastor's salary. Tithing is an act of joining in an everlasting cycle with God. The cycle consists of God always giving 100 percent of everything and the worshipper giving back 10 percent. It is a way of ensuring that the faithful will always have everything they need from God. A failure to tithe results in the giver receiving less than the best from God. For example, one who fails to tithe is due 100 percent from God but the person is not picking up the full benefits of the check. Who would work a job and intentionally take less than the salary? God has made a covenant promise to bless Abraham, Isaac, Jacob, and their seed. Those who place their trust in their God have that same promise. In order to join the cycle of blessings, one must also participate in the cycle of giving back.

## GET SOCIAL
Share your views and tag us @rhboydco. Use #rhboydco.

@rhboydco

## HOME DAILY DEVOTIONAL READINGS
### JUNE 30–JULY 6, 2025

| MONDAY | TUESDAY | WEDNESDAY | THURSDAY | FRIDAY | SATURDAY | SUNDAY |
|---|---|---|---|---|---|---|
| Living in God's Presence | Anointed by the Holy One | Remember Israel's Redemption | Rejoice before the Lord | Judah Has Become God's Sanctuary | The Father and I Are One | Jesus Learns in His Father's House |
| Psalm 27 | 1 John 2:20–28 | Deuteronomy 16:1–10 | Deuteronomy 16:11–17 | Psalm 114 | John 10:22-30, 34–38 | Luke 2:41–52 |

LESSON VI — JULY 6, 2025

# THE BOY JESUS IN THE TEMPLE

ADULT TOPIC: HOME ALONE

BACKGROUND SCRIPTURE: LUKE 2:41–52
LESSON PASSAGE: LUKE 2:41–52

## LUKE 2:41–52

### KJV

NOW his parents went to Jerusalem every year at the feast of the passover.

42 And when he was twelve years old, they went up to Jerusalem after the custom of the feast.

43 And when they had fulfilled the days, as they returned, the child Jesus tarried behind in Jerusalem; and Joseph and his mother knew not of it.

44 But they, supposing him to have been in the company, went a day's journey; and they sought him among their kinsfolk and acquaintance.

45 And when they found him not, they turned back again to Jerusalem, seeking him.

46 And it came to pass, that after three days they found him in the temple, sitting in the midst of the doctors, both hearing them, and asking them questions.

47 And all that heard him were astonished at his understanding and answers.

48 And when they saw him, they were amazed: and his mother said unto him, Son, why hast thou thus dealt with us? behold, thy father and I have sought thee sorrowing.

49 And he said unto them, How is it that ye sought me? wist ye not that I must be about my Father's business?

50 And they understood not the saying which he spake unto them.

51 And he went down with them, and came to Nazareth, and was subject unto them: but his mother kept all these sayings in her heart.

### NRSVue

NOW every year his parents went to Jerusalem for the festival of the Passover.

42 And when he was twelve years old, they went up as usual for the festival.

43 When the festival was ended and they started to return, the boy Jesus stayed behind in Jerusalem, but his parents were unaware of this.

44 Assuming that he was in the group of travelers, they went a day's journey. Then they started to look for him among their relatives and friends.

45 When they did not find him, they returned to Jerusalem to search for him.

46 After three days they found him in the temple, sitting among the teachers, listening to them and asking them questions.

47 And all who heard him were amazed at his understanding and his answers.

48 When his parents saw him they were astonished, and his mother said to him, "Child, why have you treated us like this? Your father and I have been anxiously looking for you."

49 He said to them, "Why were you searching for me? Did you not know that I must be in my Father's house?"

50 But they did not understand what he said to them.

51 Then he went down with them and came to Nazareth and was obedient to them, and his mother treasured all these things in her heart.

**MAIN THOUGHT:** [Jesus] said to them, "Why were you searching for me? Did you not know that I must be in my Father's house?" (Luke 2:49, NRSVue)

## Luke 2:41-52

| KJV | NRSVue |
|---|---|
| 52 And Jesus increased in wisdom and stature, and in favour with God and man. | 52 And Jesus increased in wisdom and in years and in divine and human favor. |

**LESSON SETTING**
  Time: 8 CE
  Place: Jerusalem

**LESSON OUTLINE**
  I. Looking for Jesus
     (Luke 2:41-45)
  II. Finding Jesus
     (Luke 2:46-52)

## Unifying Principle

Some children are wise beyond their years. How do we respond when we encounter such wisdom? At the age of twelve, Jesus already understands more about his relationship to the temple than his parents can comprehend, and they are astonished by his wisdom.

## Introduction

This lesson gives one of the few snapshots of Jesus' life as a boy. Scholars have debated about what happened to Jesus during his youth. This period was known as the silent years. Matthew 2:13-23 reveals that Jesus' family fled to Egypt and later returned to Nazareth after King Herod died. Scripture does not detail His activities from that time till age 12, nor from adolescence until age 30. However, this lesson shows Jesus' transition from being under the oversight of His earthly parents to the guidance of His Heavenly Father. God had a mission for the Lad beyond carpentry in Nazareth. The ministry transition took place in the Temple at Jerusalem. One could say that Jesus was moving from being under Joseph's roof in Nazareth to God's house in the world. When Christ told Mary that He must be about His Father's business, it was as though He was announcing His call to the ministry. This lesson should inspire readers to examine their own spiritual journey to determine whether they are ready to do the Father's business.

## Exposition

### I. Looking for Jesus
   (Luke 2:41-45)

Jews who were observant of the Mosaic Law celebrated three annual spring festivals which were Passover, the Feast of Weeks, and the Feast of Booths. Passover was particularly important for it reminded Israel of God miraculously delivering them out of Egypt. Jesus' parents had a custom of coming to Jerusalem for this activity. They likely arrived on the evening before the feast. When verse 41 revealed His parents going to Jerusalem every year, it affirmed their preparation of young Jesus to do His Heavenly Father's work. As parents study this lesson, they should examine themselves to see if they are properly training their children for the Lord's service. If Jesus needed godly parents, surely everyone needs righteous mothers and fathers in their upbringing.

Jesus and His parents participated in the Passover for seven days. Then verse 43 indicated that the activities were completed, and it was time to return home. Jesus' entourage must have been large for as they made their way back to Nazareth, the Lord, unbeknown to the family, remained behind in Jerusalem. It should be noted that Jesus was not trying to be disobedient by separating Himself from the company. He simply had a greater calling than hanging out with His earthly family.

Mary's natural motherly instincts became apparent when she discovered that her child was not in the group. Can you imagine the anguish that she felt? Her child was missing! But Jesus was not absent without leave. He was missing in action, meaning that the Lord was in action following the Father's will. Unable to find her child, Mary probably demanded that they symbolically turn the car around. In desperation, they had to go back to Jerusalem and find their child. During Passover, the city may have contained millions of people. Jerusalem's normal population ranged between 30,00–80,000 but when people throughout the region came for the festival the numbers grew substantially. How would they find a child among the millions? Yet, God reveals in this text that if one wants to find Jesus, He is accessible.

## II. Finding Jesus (Luke 2:46–52)

Mary and Joseph found the lad sitting among the teachers, likely in the outer court of the temple. One might ask what was Jesus doing among the teachers at the age of twelve? The Jewish education of children was organized with three levels. *Bet Sefer* was homeschooling from ages 6–10. Jewish boy and girls would memorize the Torah during this period. *Bet Talmud* was a more advanced study for children ages 10–14. This level was shown by what Jesus was doing in verse 46 where Jewish teachers quizzed the students with questions. Then, students responded with questions to show their knowledge of the Scriptures. *Bet Midrash* was the highest level of study where only the best students connected with a scholar to become his disciple. When Jesus was found in the temple, he was in a type of high school, learning with the Hebrew teachers. The young Lord was not being disrespectful in His questioning of the scholars. He simply conveyed the effectiveness of His parents' home training and His readiness to grow into a rabbi.

As Jesus gave answers, it amazed the crowd at His scholarship. Of course, they did not know that He was the omniscient God, but His answers conveyed a higher level of the traditional teachings of the law. Jesus' responses must have caused people to think about how the law impacts one's heart. Jesus also displayed unique understanding. His explanations put things together in a different way. One can imagine that since they had just finished Passover, Jesus may have raised the question of who can permanently end the need for animal sacrifices for sins. The scholars would know that only the Messiah could completely end the need for sacrifices. The Lord probably made them think about the need for an ultimate sacrifice and, of course, He would be that person.

As Mary watched these activities, her natural instincts cast aside Jesus' intellectual superiority and wanted to know why He had brought such emotional stress upon the family. His parents had been feverishly searching for Him and here He was in a debate with scholars. Jesus' answer highlights His ultimate reason for being on this earth. It was to do God's assignment. Gradually, Jesus was turning His parents' Passover ritual into more than a celebratory trip to Jerusalem; Christ was beginning to convey Himself to be that sacrificial lamb. Luke used the term "must" (v. 49) to emphasize what Jesus had to do. The calling of God is not optional for believers; it is a requirement. Sometimes it may be emotionally hard to totally give over to the Lord's business, but remember His business makes all other business better.

Mary and Joseph did not fully understand Jesus' actions, but seeds were being planted in their hearts about the importance of the work God had ordained Him to do. Throughout the entire scenario, the young Lord never disrespected His parents. He was only 12 years old, and despite the great charge upon His life, Jesus remained subject to His earthly parents. This point is valuable for all children to take note, but particularly for gifted and talented ones. Many children are literally smarter than their parents. They have been exposed to more information at an earlier age, and in most cases they are more savvy when it comes to navigating technology. Yet, they still must show respect for wisdom, and great intellect includes an understanding of how to use it. Verse 52 tells us that as Jesus grew in stature, He also increased in wisdom. He exchange in the temple courts confirms His depth of knowledge. Jesus knew when to use His knowledge and His wisdom. Knowledge is accumulating facts, while wisdom is applying those facts in meaningful ways. Jesus portrayed wisdom by returning to Nazareth at the direction of His parents, though He probably possessed greater knowledge.

These three building blocks lay the groundwork for doing the Father's business. One must have wisdom, which is divine knowledge and understanding. Stature constitutes a full level of maturity, for often a person can have gifted ability, but lack the maturity to use those skills in a constructive way. Then, favor refers to a grace given by both God and people. As Jesus grew up, an argument could be made that people embraced Him because of His wisdom, stature, and favor. Jesus was anointed in His early years to minister but the people in His environment and the favor of the Lord prepared Him.

## THE LESSON APPLIED

This Passover experience proved to be one Mary would never forget. Luke records that Mary kept these events in her heart. Richard Foster wrote a classic titled, *Celebration of Discipline: The Path to Spiritual Grow,* which laid out twelve disciplines to help a person grow spiritually. The first was meditation, as Mary did regarding Jesus. Mary did not have an answer for all that she experienced but she stored her thoughts to ruminate at a later time them. A takeaway from this lesson is to think about the information. One might even ask silent questions during meditation to understand the message from God. The following are some meditation thoughts from this lesson: Does God have some business for me to complete? Am I willing to break away from my family for a time to seek God's will? Does God have a calling on my life as Jesus did at a young age?

As one considers the Word of the Lord, the goal is for everyone to submit to the will of God. One must be mindful that the pathway to increase is doing the Lord's business. Sometimes individuals claim that their secular work is so important that they have no time for Kingdom work. The lesson shows that one's work becomes successful and will gain the favor of both God and people when the Lord is put first. At age 12, Jesus provided the perfect example of how to mature from a child to an adult. He submitted to His parents. He learned from and taught His teachers. He accepted His Heavenly Father's business and all who followed Him were blessed.

## LET'S TALK ABOUT IT

**What is the proper age of accountability?** A church was in the process of voting for a new pastor. They were clarifying the rules of who was eligible to cast a vote. One suggested that the youth t needed to be at least twelve years old. This arbitrary age raised questions from the young people about why they could not participate in the voting. These kinds of issues raise concerns regarding the proper age is for one to be spiritually accountable for one's soul. Based on Jesus' example, age twelve has been established in some churches as an age of accountability to participate in significant matters of the church. However, the Bible does not identify an age of accountability. Instead, it gives characteristics a person should exhibit to demonstrate accountability.

Jesus showed a desire to participate in His faith. The Lord readily joined His family in the trip to Jerusalem. The text does not indicate any resistance or disinterest by the Lord concerning Passover. Christ clearly displayed an understanding of the faith as He answered and provided questions to the Jewish scholars. He also revealed a sincere commitment to serving the Lord as He acknowledged His Heavenly Father's business. Finally, Jesus always showed respect as a lad towards His parents and others. If one has a question about a child's age of accountability, these markers can help in the decision. The most important thing to remember is that God always looks at the heart instead of the outside (age) of a person.

### GET SOCIAL
Share your views and tag us @rhboydco. Use #rhboydco.

@rhboydco

## HOME DAILY DEVOTIONAL READINGS
### JULY 7–13, 2025

| MONDAY | TUESDAY | WEDNESDAY | THURSDAY | FRIDAY | SATURDAY | SUNDAY |
|---|---|---|---|---|---|---|
| Honor the Sabbath Day | Strive to Enter God's Rest | Who Defines the Sabbath? | Give Thanks and Sing God's Praises | Jesus Sets Us Free from Satan | Holy Bread for the Journey | Christ Is Greater than the Temple |
| Deuteronomy 5:1–7, 12–15 | Hebrews 4:1–10 | John 7:14–24 | Psalm 92 | Luke 13:10–17 | 1 Samuel 21:1–6 | Matthew 12:1-8 |

**LESSON VII**       **JULY 13, 2025**

# LORD OF THE SABBATH

**ADULT TOPIC:**  
A QUESTION OF AUTHORITY

**BACKGROUND SCRIPTURE:** MATTHEW 12:1–14  
**LESSON PASSAGE:** MATTHEW 12:1–8

## MATTHEW 12:1–8

### KJV

AT that time Jesus went on the sabbath day through the corn; and his disciples were an hungred, and began to pluck the ears of corn and to eat.
2 But when the Pharisees saw it, they said unto him, Behold, thy disciples do that which is not lawful to do upon the sabbath day.
3 But he said unto them, Have ye not read what David did, when he was an hungred, and they that were with him;
4 How he entered into the house of God, and did eat the shewbread, which was not lawful for him to eat, neither for them which were with him, but only for the priests?
5 Or have ye not read in the law, how that on the sabbath days the priests in the temple profane the sabbath, and are blameless?
6 But I say unto you, That in this place is one greater than the temple.
7 But if ye had known what this meaneth, I will have mercy, and not sacrifice, ye would not have condemned the guiltless.
8 For the Son of man is Lord even of the sabbath day.

### NRSVue

AT that time Jesus went through the grain fields on the Sabbath; his disciples were hungry, and they began to pluck heads of grain and to eat.
2 When the Pharisees saw it, they said to him, "Look, your disciples are doing what is not lawful to do on the Sabbath."
3 He said to them, "Have you not read what David did when he and his companions were hungry?
4 How he entered the house of God, and they ate the bread of the Presence, which it was not lawful for him or his companions to eat, but only for the priests?
5 Or have you not read in the law that on the Sabbath the priests in the temple break the Sabbath and yet are guiltless?
6 I tell you, something greater than the temple is here.
7 But if you had known what this means, 'I desire mercy and not sacrifice,' you would not have condemned the guiltless.
8 For the Son of Man is lord of the Sabbath."

**LESSON SETTING**
    Time: 28 CE
    Place: Galilee
**LESSON OUTLINE**
    I. The Pharisees' Sabbath
      (Matthew 12:1–3)
   II. The Lord's Sabbath
      (Matthew 12:4–8)

## UNIFYING PRINCIPLE

People legitimize the authority of institutions. When is it appropriate to question this authority? During the discourse of plucking grain on the Sabbath, Jesus declares that His authority supersedes that of the temple.

**MAIN THOUGHT:** "I tell you, something greater than the temple is here." (Matthew 12:6, NRSVue)

## INTRODUCTION

Some hotels in Israel have what are known as Shabbat elevators. These elevators are in mechanisms for observant Jews who are careful to keep the Sabbath day from sunset Friday until the end of night on Saturday. The guests ride these elevators during the sacred time because they go to each floor without having to press the buttons. It is one of the ways that the Jews are observing the Sabbath prohibition of working on that day.

As the Jews keep the Sabbath, the question arises of whether they are reverencing the Mosaic Law or reverencing God. An important takeaway from this lesson is for Christians to worship the Lord of the Sabbath more than the rules of the Sabbath. Believers should examine traditions within their churches to determine where their allegiance lies. Sometimes those lines can become unknowingly blurred. One can have a sincere desire to worship God but below those efforts is a homage to self–centeredness and ego. This problem is evident in the lesson. The Pharisees claimed to worship God but really it was a worship of their interpretations of the Sabbath Law, which they arrogantly refused to change.

During the process of the creation of the world, the Bible says God rested on the seventh day. The law of resting on the seventh day was based on God's act of ceasing from work. For six days, work is permitted but the Sabbath is set aside for the Lord. Today's lesson revolves around the doctrine of Sabbath. The question is how one should observe this law of God. Does the term "rest" mean that one should absolutely cease from all work? Does Sabbath mean to engage in essential activities but not the non–essential? How can one distinguish between them? These dilemmas and more were debated among the religious leaders of Jesus' time. One can imagine that trying to keep any of the 613 laws of Moses was difficult because of so many interpretations. Therefore, Israel needed legal referees and the Pharisees filled that role.

The Pharisees interpreted the oral traditions of the law. These teachings are found in what the Jews called the Mishnah, which contained thirty-nine rules concerning Sabbath. One of those rules regulated reaping and harvesting. On the Sabbath, Israel was not to cut or bind any crops. The Pharisaic interpretation taught that if one gleaned crops, it disrespected God's superiority over nature. The Pharisees knew these nuances of the law and tried to use them to discredit Jesus. Yet, they failed to recognize that Christ was the law and that there was more to holiness than examining who plucked grain from a stalk.

## EXPOSITION

### I. THE PHARISEES' SABBATH (MATTHEW 12:1–3)

Verse 1 opens with three words: "at that time." This phrase is important because it sets the context for Jesus teaching important principles about the Sabbath law. Sometimes, a tradition can continue for so long that it becomes ingrained into the mindset of the people. The Sabbath teachings had been established for more than 1400 years. The time had come to correct the wrong interpretations. Matthew's reference to timing showed that Jesus understood the principle of timing in His ministry. The Lord knew that the Pharisees had misused the laws from day one of His ministry. But it was not until this time that Jesus capitalized on the opportunity to set the record straight.

Christian leaders can gain wisdom from Jesus' timing. Often leaders see something wrong in ministries and aggressively charge forward to correct it. Usually, this method does not work as people generally do not quickly change established norms. The right people must be in place to change hardened beliefs and the right conditions must be in place to change things. This lesson shows that the time had come when both of those stipulations were met. The people who initiated a revisiting of the Sabbath law were Jesus' disciples. Except for Judas, the disciples had a commitment to follow Jesus. This heart to follow was important because they knew that the law prohibited them from reaping on Sabbath. Nevertheless, their allegiance to Jesus was greater so they pressed forward anyway collecting grain from the field. The condition was also conducive as the disciples were hungry. Jesus knew that their hunger would outweigh their concern about oral traditions. In essence, the Lord knew His disciples, making the conditions right for them to break tradition, which created a perfect time to teach God's meaning and motive of Sabbath.

As the Lord and the disciples went into the grainfields on the Sabbath, the crop was available to glean. Leviticus 23:22 gave a command for farmers to leave the corners of their field unharvested so the poor or foreigners might gather food. This act points to the true purpose of the laws of God, which is to encourage love and compassion. The Pharisees could not embrace the idea of unconditional love for all people, but Jesus could, and He begins to reveal how to display that behavior. Verse 1 indicated that the disciples were hungry, which took priority over the tradition of not reaping on the Sabbath.

The Lord allowed His disciples to pluck the grain and eat despite it being Saturday afternoon because meeting a person's physical need of hunger was more important than oral traditions. Some Bible translations may render the word "grain" as "corn." However, this was not the corn that people eat today. Instead, it was likely barely or wheat. The disciples were so hungry that they were probably eating raw wheat or barely. The conjunction "and" in verse 1 between plucking grain and eating indicated their immediate transition from hand to mouth. As soon as they plucked the grain, they ate it. They did not wait to turn the wheat into bread or roast the barley into a better taste.

When the Pharisees saw this, they immediately began to criticize Jesus. An interesting note was the text does not say that Jesus ate, yet He still received the condemnation. The Pharisees' actions show that they were not concerned about adhering to the law. Their primary goal was to find fault and discredit the Lord. Their behavior uncovered the ulterior motives of these religious leaders. It was all about self-glorification and the condemnation of anyone who threatened their false sense of authority. Jesus made the Pharisees look bad because they were not practicing sincere holiness. So, their goal was to use the law to prove that Jesus was a false prophet. Yet, every believer knows that you cannot discredit the source of the law with the law.

In verse 3, Jesus referred the Pharisees to David going into the synagogue and eating the shewbread, which was supposed to only be for the priests. The Lord made the point that meeting the need of hunger took precedence over legalistic traditions. Jesus permitting His disciples to eat conveyed why God gave the law in the first place. It was designed to teach the followers to care for one another. The Pharisees' view of Sabbath centered on criticism while the Lord's Sabbath centered on compassion.

## II. THE LORD'S SABBATH (MATTHEW 12:4–8)

In response to the criticism, Jesus pointed out that David ate shewbread designed for the priests according to Leviticus 24:5–9. The shewbread offering consisted of twelve loaves which represented the tribes of Israel. The priests ate the bread that had been left over from the previous week every Sabbath in reverence to the Lord. The shewbread was one of Israel's ways of honoring God's priestly system. And it emphasized that Israel must show gratitude for the abundant blessings received from above. The ritual called for the bread to be placed in a row of six cakes on a gold table. Frankincense would be in each row and the priest would consume an offering with fire. The fire symbolized that God is light.

Jesus knew the entire traditional activities of the shewbread memorial and declared in verse 4 that David had not broken the law. This statement stymied the Pharisees' attacks as the legacy of King David was highly respected. They dared not claim that his actions were wrong for that might undermine their own religious authority. So, the Pharisees had to remain quiet as the Lord continued to convey the true purpose of Sabbath. Jesus asked them in verse 5 whether the priests were breaking the law by conducting their work in the temple during Sabbath.

The Lord was causing His audience to consider what constituted a real Sabbath rest. Did the law of Sabbath mean to stop all work? Did the law mean to simply commune with God while still doing various approved tasks? Jesus' Sabbath meant to do both. Whatever mundane activities that hindered a person from encountering God needed to stop. Therefore, a proper observance of Sabbath requires the leadership of the Holy Spirit. The Spirit helps to distinguish between activities that brought one closer to God as opposed to those things that distracted from the Lord. When the priests made the fire or cut the wood to prepare for the Sabbath offerings, they were not breaking the law. These things, when practiced properly, ushered them into the presence of God.

In verse 6, Jesus did not condemn the priestly activities of preparing the temple for Sabbath worship. But He revealed that God transcended temple rituals and was the ultimate focus of Sabbath worship. Jesus' perspective centered on the Lord of the Sabbath rather than mindlessly adhering to the rituals of the Sabbath. Sometimes it can be hard to follow the Lord of the Sabbath because it requires one to make judgment calls about something being right or wrong. In David's situation of being on the run from King Saul and needing food, Abiathar, the high priest, had to make a judgment call of whether to feed him. Jesus had to make a similar decision about feeding His disciples on the Sabbath. These dilemmas require believers to commune with God to gain revelation on the proper actions. For these reasons, one must not neglect the importance spending time with God on Sabbath and every day. The Lord will reveal what is right.

Jesus stated in verse 7 how to arrive at the right conduct for God. He wants the faithful to show mercy and not just heartless sacrifices. If one is trying to determine how to respond when a need arises on Sabbath, make the decision based on mercy and love toward the needy. The Sabbath was never designed to be a burden upon humanity. Its purpose was to bring believers closer to each other and to the Lord. Jesus concluded His response to the Pharisees by identifying Himself as the "Son of Man" in verse 8. The Pharisees knew this term referred to divinity, which offended them even more. Christ displayed that His authority to overrule their interpretations came from Him being God in human flesh.

Jesus' authority makes clear why His teachings supersede Jewish legalistic traditions. If one is to understand proper Sabbath worship, he or she must come into a relationship with the Lord. One must study the words and actions of Jesus and use that as the basis of how to worship. John 4:24 says, "God is a Spirit: and they that worship him must worship in spirit and truth." The act of learning the rules of Sabbath is not enough to be a Christian. One must also learn the ways of Jesus. It is a way of love, compassion, and mercy. When believers follow in that way, true Sabbath worship will be achieved. This is an important lesson to remember today, as too easily we forget the true meaning of Sunday. It's another box to check off for the week: attended church, sang the songs, gave my offering. That kind of attitude isn't honoring to God and it cheapens the incredible gift we have to commune with the Living God on a regular basis! Please don't take it for granted.

## THE LESSON APPLIED

This lesson addressed the question of whether it is right to break the law. Jesus strategically revealed that allowing His disciples to eat from the field on Sabbath did not really break the Law of Moses. Instead, His teachings clarified a poor understanding of oral traditions. It is important to note that the law was not wrong in prohibiting mundane labor. But the Pharisees' interpretation was off because they omitted the weightier matters of the law which were being just, showing mercy, and practicing faithfulness. These keys provide an excellent filter in determining proper conduct regarding the Sabbath and all matters of the Mosaic Law. Jesus' actions were never designed to declare the law as sin. His actions always focused on maturing the sinner into a state of godly behavior.

## LET'S TALK ABOUT IT

**What is the proper day to observe the Sabbath?**

The Christian Sabbath is different from Jewish practice. Christians focus on Sunday as their Sabbath. The Bible teaches that the resurrection of Jesus took place upon the first day of the week. Therefore, Sundays became a holy day of worship. Also, the church began to gather for fellowship and worship on the first day of the week according to Acts 20:7. Moreover, the Scriptures urge believers to not be carried away with specific days of worship for what is most important is a continuous fellowship with God. Paul gave a warning in Galatians 4:9–10 not to become preoccupied with observing days of worship. It can become a type of enslavement where the day becomes more important than the Lord.

A man was very distressed about not being able to come to church on Sundays. He expressed to his pastor that every Sunday he was required to work. The pastor explained that a day in the week did not constitute true reverence. Instead, one must have a heart to encounter God every day. Moreover, Christians must remember that each person constitutes the church. A person going to a building on Sundays does not necessarily mean that he or she is in worship. Believers must focus more on the spirit of worship, which can take place anywhere. When considering Jesus' teachings in this lesson, should one completely stop going to church and simply claim to worship at home? This question can be addressed through the lens of justice, mercy, and faithfulness.

The complete abandonment of church causes one to fall short in the above areas. Assembling with the saints provides opportunities to show justice, mercy, and faithfulness towards other believers. It allows one to share their faith with like–minded people. When one comes to church, it says to others that the individual's faith is active and ready to connect in the corporate body. Church attendance also provides a chance to exercise mercy. One might encounter another member who needs help, which provides an opportunity to show compassion. Then, church attendance offers the chance to display justice. One's presence expresses to the rest of the church a desire to live righteously. Therefore, Jesus did not come to eliminate Sabbath observance. He came to put it in proper perspective of loving God and neighbor, which is the greatest commandment of the law.

## GET SOCIAL

Share your views and tag us @rhboydco. Use #rhboydco.

@rhboydco

## HOME DAILY DEVOTIONAL READINGS
### JULY 7–13, 2025

| MONDAY | TUESDAY | WEDNESDAY | THURSDAY | FRIDAY | SATURDAY | SUNDAY |
|---|---|---|---|---|---|---|
| God Gathers Outcasts to the Temple | Unalloyed Worship | Guard Your Steps in God's House | God Doesn't Live in Human Shrines | The False Security of Religious Posturing | The Lord Appears in the Temple | Zeal for God's House |
| Isaiah 56 | 1 Timothy 2:1–8 | Ecclesiastes 5:1–7 | Acts 17:22–34 | Jeremiah 7:1–15 | Malachi 3:1–6 | John 2:13–25 |

# Lesson VIII

July 20, 2025

# Cleansing the Temple

**Adult Topic:**
Bake Sales Gone Bad!

**Background Scripture:** John 2:13–25
**Lesson Passage:** John 2:13–25

## John 2:13–25

### KJV

AND the Jews' passover was at hand, and Jesus went up to Jerusalem.
14 And found in the temple those that sold oxen and sheep and doves, and the changers of money sitting:
15 And when he had made a scourge of small cords, he drove them all out of the temple, and the sheep, and the oxen; and poured out the changers' money, and overthrew the tables;
16 And said unto them that sold doves, Take these things hence; make not my Father's house an house of merchandise.
17 And his disciples remembered that it was written, The zeal of thine house hath eaten me up.
18 Then answered the Jews and said unto him, What sign shewest thou unto us, seeing that thou doest these things?
19 Jesus answered and said unto them, Destroy this temple, and in three days I will raise it up.
20 Then said the Jews, Forty and six years was this temple in building, and wilt thou rear it up in three days?
21 But he spake of the temple of his body.

22 When therefore he was risen from the dead, his disciples remembered that he had said this unto them; and they believed the scripture, and the word which Jesus had said.
23 Now when he was in Jerusalem at the passover, in the feast day, many believed in his name, when they saw the miracles which he did.

### NRSVue

The Passover of the Jews was near, and Jesus went up to Jerusalem.
14 In the temple he found people selling cattle, sheep, and doves and the money changers seated at their tables.
15 Making a whip of cords, he drove all of them out of the temple, with the sheep and the cattle. He also poured out the coins of the money changers and overturned their tables.
16 He told those who were selling the doves, "Take these things out of here! Stop making my Father's house a marketplace!"
17 His disciples remembered that it was written, "Zeal for your house will consume me."
18 The Jews then said to him, "What sign can you show us for doing this?"

19 Jesus answered them, "Destroy this temple, and in three days I will raise it up."
20 The Jews then said, "This temple has been under construction for forty-six years, and will you raise it up in three days?"
21 But he was speaking of the temple of his body.
22 After he was raised from the dead, his disciples remembered that he had said this, and they believed the scripture and the word that Jesus had spoken.
23 When he was in Jerusalem during the Passover festival, many believed in his name because they saw the signs that he was doing.

**MAIN THOUGHT:** [Jesus] told those who were selling the doves, "Take these things out of here! Stop making my Father's house a marketplace!"
(John 2:16, NRSVue)

## John 2:13–25

| KJV | NRSVue |
|---|---|
| 24 But Jesus did not commit himself unto them, because he knew all men, | 24 But Jesus on his part would not entrust himself to them, because he knew all people |
| 25 And needed not that any should testify of man: for he knew what was in man. | 25 and needed no one to testify about anyone, for he himself knew what was in everyone. |

### LESSON SETTING
Time: 27 CE
Place: Jerusalem Temple

### LESSON OUTLINE
I. Wrong Use of the Temple (John 2:13–17)
II. Right Use of the Temple (John 2:18–25)

## UNIFYING PRINCIPLE

People sometimes lack awareness of building protocols and may enter a space with little regard for the business that transpires there. What does it mean to honor a building and the purpose for which it was constructed? Jesus shows proper reverence for the temple when He zealously clears out the merchants.

## INTRODUCTION

Passover was one of Israel's sacred celebrations. It took place yearly and Jesus had a custom of attending the feast in Jerusalem since He was a child. In this text, Jesus has reached adulthood and is beginning His early ministry. He had recently worked a miracle in Cana by turning water into wine. After spending a few days in Capernaum, Jesus made the 85-mile journey to Jerusalem. Every aspect of the Passover celebration was to be done with piety. Even the journey to Jerusalem was to be sacred. The pilgrims recited Scriptures and sang songs as they went up to Jerusalem. One can imagine that Jesus was expectantly looked forward to a holy environment when He arrived at the temple. Unfortunately, Jesus encountered the opposite. He entered the Lord's house and found moneychangers and sellers taking advantage of people.

This sight enraged the Lord for thieves were using Passover as an opportunity for self–aggrandizement. What was supposed to be a reverent time had become a money–making time. The lesson will show the way in which the thieves took advantage of the worshippers. Their actions constituted highway robbery. Jesus' response conveyed that the Lord would execute wrath upon sinners. Often, the Lord is depicted as kind and gentle but not in all cases. The Lord has a special concern about taking advantage of the poor and powerless. Moreover, the lesson made clear Who owned the Temple; for the house belonged to God and not human beings. This point must always be emphasized in the church. Individuals can easily forget that the church does not belong to any one person. The church is the body of Christ which means no one has a right to use the church for self benefit.

## EXPOSITION

### I. WRONG USE OF THE TEMPLE (JOHN 2:13–17)

The temple was divided into various sections and along the east side was Solomon's porch. This area, known as the outer court, contained the moneychangers' tables. When worshippers came to make sacrifices during Passover, they were required to pay a half-shekel tax in support of the temple and to atone for sin. This tax was levied annually and was often paid during Passover feast. Matthew 17:24 identified these tax collectors when they questioned the Lord about His bill. Of course, the Lord stayed current and paid the tax according to the law. These temple tax collectors would travel throughout Israel getting money. Then, in the month of Adar before Passover, they would be stationed in the temple to exchange currency to pay the assessment.

In this lesson, the moneychangers exchanged the pilgrims' money into the only acceptable coin for payment which was the Jewish half-shekel. The high priest demanded the half-shekel because it contained the highest percentage of silver. So, the money changer's role was very important and lucrative. They could charge as much as 4 to 8 percent interest on their exchanges. They also served as depositories where they acted as bankers. If one needed a loan, the moneychangers, also known as *shulhani*, would issue money with interest. When Jesus told the unprofitable servant in Matthew 25:27 that he should have deposited his money with the bankers, the Lord was referencing a role of the moneychangers.

The sellers of animals in the temple also made money off the captive Passover congregants. Travelers to Jerusalem could not bring a lot of animals with them as they went through desert and mountainous regions to reach the holy city. So, they bought their animal sacrifices at the temple upon arrival. Like the cost of a hotel room at a Super Bowl game, the cost of the sacrificial animals skyrocketed. A poor woman may have had to pay as much as forty dollars in today's money to make a dove sacrifice. Moreover, the animals sold may not have met the standard of being unblemished. So, inspectors would be paid to examine the animals to declare them clean and likely extracted bribes for their examinations. The temple became such as a marketplace that everyone got a cut of the money while the pilgrims suffered as pawns in the claws of thieves.

As Jesus observed these scandalous activities, He made a whip out of chords and chased the charlatans out of His Father's house. Can you imagine the mayhem of running from the wrath of God? Yet, it was justified because the temple belonged to the Son of God. Jesus was a zealot for wanting things done right in the House of the Lord. David in Psalm 69:9 expressed a similar zeal. So, as the disciples observed the Lord's actions, they remembered the Scriptures and how God was very particular about conduct in sacred spaces. The people used the Temple for the wrong reasons and the Man of the house was determined to make it right.

## II. Right Use of the Temple (John 2:18-25)

When the Jews saw Jesus' actions, they demanded a sign of His authority to drive them from the temple. The Lord claimed that the house belonged to His Father, which was a huge statement. Was Jesus declaring himself to be the Son of God? The religious leaders considered that assertion to be blasphemy. The high priest during this scene who likely challenged Jesus was Caiaphas. According to Luke 3:2, he succeeded Annas and was in charge during this cleansing of the Temple episode. Caiaphas, along with all the priests during Jesus' era, loved money and were in cahoots with the Roman government. They took bribes, hoarded the temple treasury, beat those who would not pay tithes, and withheld money from elderly priests who needed support. The opponents of Jesus had little concern about His Messianic statements. Sure, it was wrong to claim lordship over the temple, but that did not matter to them. They had heard many before making outlandish divinity claims, but what really raised their ire was the Lord's threat to their financial enterprise. So, the demand for a sign was used by the Jewish leaders to attack Jesus' authority.

In verse 19, the Lord gave His proof using the symbolism of the temple. He said, "Destroy this temple and in three days I will raise it up." The Jews thought that He spoke about the physical building, but the Lord spoke about Himself. He conveys that the right use of the temple requires one to move into the spiritual realm. For hundreds of years, the Jews placed too much emphasis on physically satisfying the use of the temple. They brought physical animals to the building. They burned physical incense and exchanged physical money. However, Christ wanted the people to consider the state of their spiritual heart as they worshipped.

Jesus did not drive the people from the temple because they were engaged in business endeavors. The real problem was their greedy and self–centered hearts. What was going on in the Temple angered the Lord because the people did it with the wrong motives. They loved money more than God. So, the Lord called the people's attention to His ultimate mission on earth. He came to sacrifice His life on the cross as the final payment for the penalty of sin and resurrect in people a heart that loved God and one another.

The Jewish clergy could not imagine something of that nature, so they assumed Jesus spoke about the physical building. The Jews had been physically restoring the building since the time of Herod the Great around 20 BCE, which consisted of a 46-year effort. One could suggest that since the rebuilding of the second temple around 516 BCE, some types of refurbishing activities were continuously being done. In the Jews' minds, they were never going to finish working on the building. But Christ spoke of His bodily sacrifice on the cross. He would do in three days what human efforts could never achieve. The Lord would usher in the proper use of the temple. God established the temple building as a tool to bring Israel into a right relationship with Him.

Throughout Israel's history, the temple represented the presence of God. Before the temple, it was the tabernacle that highlighted God with His people. When the Hebrew children traveled in the wilderness, they set up camp in a formation with the tabernacle in the center and everything else facing it (Numbers 2:2). When they established their nation, Kings David and Solomon had the desire to build the house of the Lord. Once they came out of exile, the rebuilding of Zerubbabel's temple took place, later known as Herod's temple. In each instance, Israel thought they could find God by turning to His house. In verse

20, Jesus expanded their spiritual perception to declare that His life and ministry meant God was with them. Of course, the religious leaders would not believe that assertion, but the disciples took note of the Lord's words.

Verse 22 revealed Jesus' effectiveness in planting spiritual seeds in one's heart. At the beginning of His ministry, no one could fully grasp the depth of Jesus' words and the Lord knew it. But He used the technique of strategically planting seeds of faith at opportune times to progressively move His followers to understand His mission. Although they did not realize it, Jesus gave them signs of His divinity and work all along the journey toward the cross. For the unbelievers, signs were meaningless but for the believers, they became building blocks of faith. As they listened and observed the Lord, many started to believe, but it was a progressive activity. Jesus did not tell them everything about His work nor overload them with heavy expectations.

Verse 24 indicated that He was careful not to commit too much of Himself to them at one time. Leaders can learn from Jesus' early days of ministry. Some leaders can expect too much of their followers and load on them too much of the vision at one time. The natural response of being gagged is to choke and to spit it out. The work of God must be done incrementally, particularly at the beginning of one's ministry. Before they can carry out the vision, they must first gain confidence in the visionary. Verse 25 can be explained that Jesus did not need to read man's resume. He already knew their hearts. The Lord knew He was dealing with indecisive people who needed a lot of growth before they could fully embrace His work and ministry. Yet, His efforts were not in vain. People like His disciple Peter and even a Pharisee named Nicodemus watched Him and were discovering that no man could do what Jesus did without God being with Him.

## THE LESSON APPLIED

A question could be raised concerning whether Jesus' actions of cleansing the temple were sinful. The text clearly shows that the Lord was angry and violent as He chased people with a whip. One might wonder, did He hit anyone? His actions can be explained by looking at His motive. The Lord possessed a heart of love so the cleansing was not sin but could be described as tough love. Sometimes, Christians must use tough love where they do not allow just anything to take place in God's house. Others may not understand why the standard may seem hard, but the goal should always be to act in a way that moves people toward a right relationship with God. Jesus understood that if He did not stop the exploitations, souls would go to hell even within God's house. This principle applies in the church. Leaders must act when they see things that jeopardize the souls of humanity. The key centers on acting out of righteous zeal rather than unrighteous wrath.

## LET'S TALK ABOUT IT

**Should Christians sell things in the church?**

This question is best answered by the local church's guidelines. Some congregations have a strict prohibition against selling and use Bible verses in this lesson as justification. Other congregations have very profitable business ventures under the umbrella of the church—from bookstores to residential properties and investment enterprises. Whatever the decisions regarding business dealings, the key centers on the heart. Jesus spoke about the heart many times during His ministry. He said during the Sermon on the Mount, "where your treasure is there will your heart be also" (Matthew 6:21). He made the point that one's heart and money were connected. If a person is to have fair business dealings, they must have a Christ–centered heart. Moreover, even the prohibition of selling in the church does not guarantee that a person's heart is righteous as some may forbid selling to ensure that the church gets all the money for a particular person.

Therefore, the cleansing of the Temple is a call to examine one's own spiritual temple. In the same manner that Jesus declared Himself to be the temple, Christians are also temples. First Corinthians 6:19 states, "your body is the temple of the Holy Spirit who is in you, whom you have from God, and you are not your own" (NKJV). People of faith must zealously search their hearts to make sure what they are doing is right since the Holy Ghost lives inside of their sanctuaries. Before engaging in any activity, whether it is business transactions or personal relations, saints must remember that their house belongs to the Heavenly Father.

A person received the wrong change from a cashier. Instead of getting a few dollars back, he received an extra hundred–dollar bill mixed in with the other money. He had a dilemma—walk out of the store with a $100 bonus, or return the cash that did not belong to him. The man chose to keep the money, only to be arrested later for trying to pass what turned out to be a counterfeit $100 bill. Without Christ, the human heart is deceitfully wicked and causes a person to lose not only money, but also the soul. What always matters most to Jesus is the state of our hearts, above everything else.

## GET SOCIAL

Share your views and tag us @rhboydco. Use #rhboydco.

@rhboydco

## HOME DAILY DEVOTIONAL READINGS
### JULY 21–27, 2025

| MONDAY | TUESDAY | WEDNESDAY | THURSDAY | FRIDAY | SATURDAY | SUNDAY |
| --- | --- | --- | --- | --- | --- | --- |
| God Preserves | Victory through the Lamb's Blood | David's Lineage Is Cut Down | The Temple Is Destroyed | The Willfulness of Evil Rulers | Lament for the Wicked City | Don't Be Led Astray |
| Revelation 11:1–13 | Revelation 12:1–11 | 2 Kings 25:1–7 | 2 Kings 25:8–21 | Daniel 11:21–35 | Matthew 23:1–12, 37–39 | Matthew 24:1–8 |

# LESSON IX — JULY 27, 2025
# JESUS PREDICTS THE TEMPLE'S DESTRUCTION

**ADULT TOPIC:**
THE HARDER THEY FALL

**BACKGROUND SCRIPTURE:** MATTHEW 23:37–24:35
**LESSON PASSAGE:** MATTHEW 24:1–14

## MATTHEW 24:1–14

### KJV

AND Jesus went out, and departed from the temple: and his disciples came to him for to shew him the buildings of the temple.
2 And Jesus said unto them, See ye not all these things? verily I say unto you, There shall not be left here one stone upon another, that shall not be thrown down.
3 And as he sat upon the mount of Olives, the disciples came unto him privately, saying, Tell us, when shall these things be? and what shall be the sign of thy coming, and of the end of the world?
4 And Jesus answered and said unto them, Take heed that no man deceive you.
5 For many shall come in my name, saying, I am Christ; and shall deceive many.

6 And ye shall hear of wars and rumours of wars: see that ye be not troubled: for all these things must come to pass, but the end is not yet.
7 For nation shall rise against nation, and kingdom against kingdom: and there shall be famines, and pestilences, and earthquakes, in divers places.
8 All these are the beginning of sorrows.
9 Then shall they deliver you up to be afflicted, and shall kill you: and ye shall be hated of all nations for my name's sake.
10 And then shall many be offended, and shall betray one another, and shall hate one another.
11 And many false prophets shall rise, and shall deceive many.

### NRSVue

AS Jesus came out of the temple and was going away, his disciples came to point out to him the buildings of the temple.
2 Then he asked them, "You see all these, do you not? Truly I tell you, not one stone will be left here upon another; all will be thrown down."
3 When he was sitting on the Mount of Olives, the disciples came to him privately, saying, "Tell us, when will this be, and what will be the sign of your coming and of the end of the age?"
4 Jesus answered them, "Beware that no one leads you astray.
5 For many will come in my name, saying, 'I am the Messiah!' and they will lead many astray.

6 And you will hear of wars and rumors of wars; see that you are not alarmed, for this must take place, but the end is not yet.
7 For nation will rise against nation and kingdom against kingdom, and there will be famines and earthquakes in various places:

8 all this is but the beginning of the birth pangs.
9 "Then they will hand you over to be tortured and will put you to death, and you will be hated by all nations because of my name.
10 Then many will fall away, and they will betray one another and hate one another.
11 And many false prophets will arise and lead many astray.

**MAIN THOUGHT:** Jesus asked [the disciples], "You see all these, do you not? Truly I tell you, not one stone will be left here upon another; all will be thrown down." (Matthew 24:2, NRSVue)

## MATTHEW 24:1–14

### KJV

12 And because iniquity shall abound, the love of many shall wax cold.
13 But he that shall endure unto the end, the same shall be saved.
14 And this gospel of the kingdom shall be preached in all the world for a witness unto all nations; and then shall the end come.

### NRSVue

12 And because of the increase of lawlessness, the love of many will grow cold.
13 But the one who endures to the end will be saved.
14 And this good news of the kingdom will be proclaimed throughout the world, as a testimony to all the nations, and then the end will come.

---

**LESSON SETTING**
　　Time: 30 CE
　　Place: Jerusalem

**LESSON OUTLINE**
　I. Signs of the Times
　　(Matthew 24:1–8)
　II. Endure to the End
　　(Matthew 24:9–14)

## UNIFYING PRINCIPLE

Grand structures appear to be indestructible. What might cause even the sturdiest buildings to deteriorate? Jesus warns that the magnificent Temple will be destroyed as a sign of His coming and of the end of the age.

## INTRODUCTION

In this lesson, Jesus is preparing His disciples for the end of His ministry, but also His second return to earth. He was soon to give His life on the cross, so His discourse progressed to move His disciples from a present-day focus to an eternal view. The Lord used the temple as a tool to orient His followers' minds toward future things. In theological studies, the term *eschatology* is used to focus on what will come during the end of time. Most observant Jews held a high regard for the temple. The structure itself was considered the House of God. So, it served as a foundation of Israel's faith and hope for the future. They believed that if the temple stood, then God was with them. Yet, Jesus challenged their ingrained security by telling His disciples that the building would be destroyed.

These statements shook their faith. How would they survive without the temple? They wanted to know when such a tragedy would take place, and what would be a sign of the Lord's return. In answering their questions, the Lord did not give specific dates, but He did give scenarios. As these things came to pass, they would point to the Lord's imminent return and establishment of His kingdom on earth. The important point to remember regarding the Lord's teaching about the future is to be prepared for it. It is not necessary for Christians to try and figure out when the Lord will return as only the Heavenly Father has that answer. This lesson simply serves as a wake-up call to be ready whenever the end of time does take place.

## EXPOSITION

### I. SIGNS OF THE TIMES (MATTHEW 24:1–8)

When Jesus departed from the Temple, according to verse 1, He likely exited the complex through the East Gate. Today, that gate is not visible as it is underground. But during Jesus' time, the gate was significant because it was where Jesus entered Jerusalem during His triumphant procession recorded in Matthew 21. According to Ezekiel 10, the East Gate was where the glory cloud of the LORD exited the Temple, and it was permanently shut, according to Ezekiel 44:2. This gate gained notoriety because it was deemed the entry point reserved for the Messiah when He returned to earth. As the disciples and Jesus proceeded through the East Gate, the Lord's followers showed Him the architecture. One could imagine it was a scenario much like that of a child coming home from school to teach his or her mother the alphabet. Jesus probably graciously listened, but the Lord had more important things to share with them.

Jesus declared to His disciples that every stone of the temple would be torn down. This statement must have disturbed the disciples' train of thought. They were touting the greatness of the structure while Christ told them it was all going to be destroyed. The walk from the Temple to the Mount of Olives took about twenty minutes. While they made the trek up the mountain, what Jesus said simmered in the disciples' minds. Once they reached their destination, Jesus sat down in the typical teaching position of a rabbi. They asked the master three questions. When will the Temple be destroyed? What is a sign of the Messiah's return? And what would be indicators of the end of time?

Jesus began His response with a warning that they were not to be deceived by people claiming to be the Messiah. Acts 5:36 mentions a Messianic figure known as Theudas and his 400 followers. The Bible revealed he claimed to be somebody, but in the end, he was killed. Simon of Perea, Athronges the Shepherd, and Judas the Galilean were other false prophets who lived during the first century that led many astray. Jesus made clear that the pervasiveness of false prophets signaled the approach of the last days.

Another sign would be unending conflict between nations and kingdoms. During the disciples' lifetime, conflict was all over the world. In Africa, the Aksum empire conquered the Himyarite kingdom. In China, the Han Dynasty fought with the Wang Mang warriors. And throughout Europe and Asia, the Romans conquered their enemies. War would be the norm throughout the world. Jesus taught His disciples to pay attention to that sign of the times.

In conjunction with war, the by–products of famine, disease and earthquakes would destabilize the world. Everything that made the world secure would be unhinged as the return of the Lord approached. The Lord explained that these events would be like the beginning of birth pains. The signs would be like a mother struggling to have a child. Every event was like a contraction moving toward a certain delivery. Bible students who now look back in history know that the Romans destroyed the temple in 70 CE, but the disciples were on the front–side of history. They had to believe the Lord's words and watch the signs of the times. The signs are still being made revealed today, which calls on believers to be ready for the Lord's second return at any time.

## II. Endure to the End (Matthew 24:9–14)

After identifying signs of the end of the age, Jesus turned His attention to what His disciples would face. These words applied to them at that time but also to succeeding Christians. Jesus' followers would face persecution for their faith. Verse 9 raises the question of who are the people that will bring such intense oppression upon the disciples? The Scripture brings to light that many of these people would be Jewish religious leaders who felt threatened by the teachings of Jesus. Among the disciples, James would be the first martyr of the faith. He and his brother John were known as "the Sons of Thunder." James boldly declared his faith in the Gospel of Jesus Christ, which angered the Jewish leaders in Jerusalem. When Herod Agrippa became king of Judea, he carried out an onslaught against the Christians, resulting in James being delivered up to tribulation, according to Jesus' prophecy. Herod beheaded James to gain favor with the Jews. But an ironic by–product of James' death was his accuser repented and accepted Christ. Fox's *Book of Martyrs* revealed that when the accuser of James witnessed his courage in the face of death, it inspired his faith. King Herod then beheaded both of them.

In verse 10, the Lord spoke about the offensive nature of the Gospel. Salvation in Christ should have been welcoming news to the world, but as the end approached, people rejected it. Even other believers abandoned the faith because of its challenging doctrine. The Bible described this desertion as a great falling away (2 Thessalonians 2:3). The offensive nature of the Gospel was already becoming evident during Jesus' ministry. John 6:66 pointed out that many no longer followed the Lord after He told them the high demands of discipleship. They began to turn on each other. Judas Iscariot would be the first to betray the Lord. The Bible identified other betrayers such as Peter, John Mark, Saul of Tarsus in his persecution of the church, and Demas when he abandoned Paul. It was clear that Jesus' words were being fulfilled as He delivered them.

Paul's missionary journeys illustrated how disciples would be rejected and hated by all nations. While in Athens, the intelligentsia ignored his appeals for Christ. Governor Festus at Caesarea mocked him as a crazy man and ultimately Nero executed him in Rome. As one considers the modern era, many Christians in places such as China practice their faith at their own peril. A *Christianity Today* article identified North Korea, Somalia, and Yemen as the top three countries where its hardest to be a Christian (*Christianity Today* editor's, "The 50 Hardest Countries to Follow Jesus").

Jesus continued to teach in verse 11 that those who did not believe the faith perverted the faith. False prophets then and now twist the Gospel for their own benefits. These deceivers would be tricky with their appeals. As the Gospel was spread, fakers came behind the disciples' ministries and undermined their work. The Pharisees, Sadducees, Judaizers, Gnostics and those who propagate the Gospel for power and money are examples of the false leaders warned against by Jesus. The word "deceive" used in the text means to lead from the truth. As the end of time approached, the concept of truth would become relative. Today, philosophers call this era the postmodern age where there is no absolute truth. Some people believe that Jesus is not the final say on truth, resulting in humanity developing their own sense of righteousness. Because truth has been disfigured, it became easy for false prophets to mislead people. Paul's words in 2 Timothy 4:3 about people not enduring sound doctrine and having itching ears proved to be another sign of Jesus' prophecy.

Verse 12 conveyed an indifference toward the Gospel. The imminent return of the Lord would be in the context of apathy. Even those believers who should care about Jesus and his work will not care. The statement about the love of many waxing cold highlights the lack of concern that people will have for God and ministry. The word "wax" means to breathe cold. People will become more and more disinterested in the things of God as the world blows tribulation, apostasy, perversion, and indifference over their hearts. Jesus is describing a gradual freezing of one's love. It is like an estranged couple on the verge of divorce sleeping on the edge of both sides of the bed. Neither can explain why they are so far apart, but the gradual freezing of their love created the separation.

The good news of Jesus' discourse is He gives the disciples advanced knowledge about the future. A hope found in these difficult days is the certainty about the imminent return. The Lord encouraged His disciples to endure to the end (v. 13). When the Romans destroyed the temple in 70 CE, about a million Jews died. This event must have been heart-wrenching for the faithful. Many likely asked, "where is God in the midst of such atrocities?" Yet, Jesus urged His disciples to keep the faith because hope was not lost. When Jesus told them to endure to the end, He taught that salvation emerged out of one's faith. Does this statement mean salvation comes because of persistence rather than the gift of God? Not completely, salvation is always a gift, but real disciples will prove they are saved through their faithfulness. When Christians face tribulation, it can be like a mother pushing as she delivers her baby. The pain can be excruciating but if she can press forward eventually, she receives the gift of a baby. Amid everything that the believers will face, the Word will be preached, and the newborn baby of the Gospel will be birthed throughout the world. Whatever struggles we may face, we can trust that God is with us and has a plan to rectify it all. We must simply remain steadfast in Him, and trust that He's in control.

## THE LESSON APPLIED

When one thinks about the end times, it is not a cheery subject to many because of the bad things that will occur in the world. Yet, Jesus teaches that the faithful should not avoid studying prophesies about the future. It helps saints keep their focus on what is most important in life, which is to be prepared for the Lord's return.

The lesson sends the message to receive Jesus as Lord and Savior, for without Christ the end of the world leads to eternity in hell. Once saved, believers should focus on developing their faith. The Lord made clear that saints will be persecuted. Therefore, individuals must remain strong in their convictions even to the point of death. Christians should recognize that many who initially claimed the faith will turn on them. Others will come with enticing words and attractive lifestyles. They will say, "Follow my way to the best life." However, believers must hold to the words of Jesus and endure unto the end. Although the end times will bring about great tribulation, the positive aspect is that the Gospel will spread and souls will be saved. When people see the faithful trusting in Jesus, it can be an inspiration to them to make Jesus their Lord also.

## LET'S TALK ABOUT IT

**Will Jesus literally return on a white horse coming out of the clouds?**

The scene of Jesus' second return has often been depicted with Him riding a horse coming out of the clouds. This imagery comes from Revelations 19:11–16. The Bible says, "Now I saw heaven opened, and behold, a white horse. And He who sat on him was called Faithful and True, and in righteousness He judges and makes war (Revelations 19:11). It is a powerful scene and this writer believes it to be true. However, the most important thing to remember about the second coming is its certainty. Whether one sees Jesus on a white horse or a bright light in death, whatever the method, the world as one knows it now will end.

Even Jesus did not give specific dates regarding His prophecies. He used general statements about events, such as wars, famines, pestilence. The lack of details allows readers to apply His words to every generation. Whether it is the first century or the 21st century, the second coming of the Lord is certain. Instead of trying to watch the news and make questionable interpretations about with every prophetic word, the faithful should examine themselves and make sure they have Christ as their Lord.

The takeaways from Jesus' message are for believers to receive Christ, salvation, and the importance of being witnesses to the world. No man knows the day nor hour when the Son of Man shall return, for that knowledge belongs to the Father. Disciples are charged to share the knowledge that they do know, so the world will be ready when Jesus comes back.

## GET SOCIAL
Share your views and tag us @rhboydco. Use #rhboydco.

**@rhboydco**

**Lesson X**  
**August 3, 2025**

# Believers (the Church) as God's Temple

**Adult Topic:** Construction Zone

**Background Scripture:** 1 Corinthians 3:1–23
**Lesson Passage:** 1 Corinthians 3:10–23

## 1 Corinthians 3:10–23

### KJV

ACCORDING to the grace of God which is given unto me, as a wise masterbuilder, I have laid the foundation, and another buildeth thereon. But let every man take heed how he buildeth thereupon.
11 For other foundation can no man lay than that is laid, which is Jesus Christ.
12 Now if any man build upon this foundation gold, silver, precious stones, wood, hay, stubble;
13 Every man's work shall be made manifest: for the day shall declare it, because it shall be revealed by fire; and the fire shall try every man's work of what sort it is.
14 If any man's work abide which he hath built thereupon, he shall receive a reward.
15 If any man's work shall be burned, he shall suffer loss: but he himself shall be saved; yet so as by fire.
16 Know ye not that ye are the temple of God, and that the Spirit of God dwelleth in you?
17 If any man defile the temple of God, him shall God destroy; for the temple of God is holy, which temple ye are.
18 Let no man deceive himself. If any man among you seemeth to be wise in this world, let him become a fool, that he may be wise.
19 For the wisdom of this world is foolishness with God. For it is written, He taketh the wise in their own craftiness.
20 And again, The Lord knoweth the thoughts of the wise, that they are vain.
21 Therefore let no man glory in men. For all things are your's;

### NRSVue

ACCORDING to the grace of God given to me, like a wise master builder I laid a foundation, and someone else is building on it. Let each builder choose with care how to build on it.
11 For no one can lay any foundation other than the one that has been laid; that foundation is Jesus Christ.
12 Now if anyone builds on the foundation with gold, silver, precious stones, wood, hay, straw—
13 the work of each builder will become visible, for the day will disclose it, because it will be revealed with fire, and the fire will test what sort of work each has done.
14 If the work that someone has built on the foundation survives, the builder will receive a wage.
15 If the work is burned up, the builder will suffer loss; the builder will be saved, but only as through fire.
16 Do you not know that you are God's temple and that God's Spirit dwells in you?
17 If anyone destroys God's temple, God will destroy that person. For God's temple is holy, and you are that temple.
18 Do not deceive yourselves. If you think that you are wise in this age, you should become fools so that you may become wise.
19 For the wisdom of this world is foolishness with God. For it is written, "He catches the wise in their craftiness,"
20 and again, "The Lord knows the thoughts of the wise, that they are futile."
21 So let no one boast about people. For all things are yours,

**MAIN THOUGHT:** No one can lay any foundation other than the one that has been laid; that foundation is Jesus Christ. (1 Corinthians 3:11, NRSVue)

## 1 CORINTHIANS 3:10–23

### KJV

22 Whether Paul, or Apollos, or Cephas, or the world, or life, or death, or things present, or things to come; all are your's;
23 And ye are Christ's; and Christ is God's.

### NRSVue

22 whether Paul or Apollos or Cephas or the world or life or death or the present or the future—all are yours,
23 and you are Christ's, and Christ is God's.

## LESSON SETTING
**Time:** 54 CE
**Place:** Corinth

## LESSON OUTLINE
I. A Wise Builder
(1 Corinthians 3:10–15)
II. A Christ-like Building
(1 Corinthians 3:16–23)

## UNIFYING PRINCIPLE

People yearn for a sense of belonging within a community that shares a common set of values. How do splinter groups threaten the community? Paul says disputes among believers are destructive and that unity emerges only when the church's foundation is built on Jesus Christ.

## INTRODUCTION

The apostle Paul planted the church of Corinth during his second missionary journey described in Acts 18:1–18. As he continued to other places in his travels, he received word that the church was struggling with cliques and pride. So, he responded to these problems in this letter. Paul made it clear that no member in the church could boast of their superiority over another. Instead, each member was to work together and build on the foundation of Jesus Christ. Instead of being divided by nepotism and personal interests, the Corinthians were urged to learn the ways of Jesus. They were to see themselves as a part of His master plan. Through His death and resurrection, Jesus laid the foundation of a building ordained by God.

Paul used the analogy of a building to convey that the Corinthians had no time for division because Jesus wanted to use them in promoting the kingdom of God. Some of the most noticeable buildings in Corinth were the temples to idols such as Aphrodite. The Corinthians probably saw that impressive construction on a regular basis. Yet, Paul explained that the building of Christ was far more significant than temples for idols. Those constructions consisted of earthly elements that would not last. If the church joined in the construction of the spiritual temple of God, then it would last and serve as an eternal refuge for believers. The temple of God was not erected upon an earthly foundation. It started within the hearts of every person who placed their trust in Christ.

## EXPOSITION

### I. A WISE BUILDER (1 CORINTHIANS 3:10–15)

As the Corinthians got bogged down in sectarianism, Paul strove to unravel their separatism by explaining his role in planting the church. In verse 10, Paul emphasized that he only served as an architect of the church under the Lord Jesus Christ. His role in the church was never to dominate but represent the Lord. This principle should be the reason for all Christian service. Members in the church serve by the grace of God. Therefore, no member can claim supremacy over another. Christianity is a journey of submitting to the blueprints of the master builder, Jesus Christ.

As Paul followed God's blueprint, his role was to lay the foundation of Christianity in Corinth. He taught them that salvation only came through faith in the birth, life, burial, resurrection and second coming of Jesus. These foundational principles were essential for the Corinthians to be saved. They had been indoctrinated with a culture of sin permeated by carnal immorality. These people were so far from God that their lifestyle was labeled "corinthianized" which meant to practice sexual immorality. Their context was driven by self–centeredness and satisfying the flesh. So, they needed to learn how to work together and complement each other. Instead of being competitors, they were to build upon each other's spiritual gifts. Paul charged each member to examine their part in building the kingdom of God. Whatever they did, it must stand upon the foundation of Jesus Christ.

When the Scripture referred to building with gold, silver, precious stones, wood, hay, or straw in verse 12, Paul explained that these elements will be tested by God. Therefore, the Corinthians had to examine their motives of what they did in the body of Christ. If their actions originated from elements of the world, then when God judged them, their works would be destroyed. One might think that using gold, silver, or stone would withstand fire. However, the fire in verse 13 was designed to enlighten and consume. When God judged the works of members in the church, it will bring to light the true intents of their hearts. If the intents are pure, then fire will reveal the goodness of those actions resulting in rewards. There is no greater reward than to hear God say, "well done thou good and faithful servant." If one's works are sinful, then fire of judgment will consume those activities and lead to punishment. Paul emphasized to the church that their behavior was being recorded and measured against the standards of God to ensure that everything was right.

Verse 15 made clear that the works which did not meet the righteousness of God would be lost. People who have participated in construction activities can relate to this consequence. After so much work is done, an inspector comes to the site to examine whether everything meets blueprint specifications and city codes. If something is not right, the completed work might be a loss and the workers start over. Paul was encouraging the Corinthians to be wise builders as they served the Lord. The church had no place for divisiveness. Their work would follow them resulting in rewards or penalties.

## II. A Christ–like Building (1 Corinthians 3:16–23)

The Corinthians had some predispositions that hindered them from being a Christ–like building of God. Paul addressed them hoping that it would mold the believers into a church without spot nor wrinkle. For one, they struggled with using their bodies for self–gratification. These activities were likely influenced by idol worship that took place at the Temple of Aphrodite. Therefore, Paul implored the

Christians to remember that their bodies were the temple of God. He effectively contextualized the believers' bodies with being a temple. Paul conveyed that every believer was a part of the corporate temple of God with the Holy Spirit as the deity that lived in them. The apostle warns his audience not to defile their personal sanctuaries of God as the consequence was the Lord would destroy that person.

The Corinthians also had a predisposition toward prideful wisdom. The city of Corinth was very diverse. It was a sea coastal city consisting of mariners and others from throughout the ancient Grecian world. They brought with them all types of religious beliefs, such as emphasizing self–knowledge. The apostle warned the church against following those lifted in pride and carried away with the world's wisdom. They were to be marked as fools because they were dead to salvation in Christ. True wisdom came from God and not the doctrines of idols.

The last predisposition that Paul warned the Corinthians against was the danger of following human leaders rather than Christ. This tendency proved evident in the Corinthian forming spiritual alliances with Paul, Apollos, Cephas, the world, or futurism. In each case, the danger of turning these human entities into idols was real. When Paul received the report of their tendencies for sectarianism, it angered the apostle to where he was glad to have not baptized any of those members except Crispus and Gaius (1 Corinthians 1:14). Human leaders cannot save anyone. Therefore verse 21 emphasized to remember that everyone belonged to God.

An arrogant mindset can lead to a great downfall as leadership is a privilege given by God to serve others and not to exploit the opportunity. Verses 22 and 23 made clear that every person and thing belonged to God. When one follows and leads with that view, it results in liberty and success. The liberation comes because one is free to stand back and allow the wisdom of God to take precedence. Since God is omniscient, the obvious result will be success. If the Corinthians and even believers today avoid the tendencies of self–gratification, prideful wisdom, and humanism, then they would become a part of that Christ–like building that will stand for eternity.

## THE LESSON APPLIED

It is important to have flexibility as the Lord constructs a person's life. A Christian must be open to the progressive movement of God in his or her life and in the life of the Church. Just because something was done one way in church last year, does not mean it should continue indefinitely. Sometimes the Lord expects members to change and evolve, to move forward with new plans. However, flexibility must be balanced with unmovable truths within one's foundational core. Truths such as salvation in Christ and the certainty of God's word should never change.

The Christian foundation must also include stress tests to determine whether it can withstand storms. Pressure can strengthen faith. When believers are stress tested, the hope is that they will become an even more established building that can withstand the storms of life. Members of Christ should examine themselves according to the blueprint of God. Then, they should join the corporate body of Christ to fulfill the ultimate plan in God's Kingdom.

## LET'S TALK ABOUT IT
### Can a Christian's building fall?

This question addresses the humanity of a believer. Psalm 103:14 says, "For he knoweth our frame; he remembereth that we are dust." A Christian can develop a view that he or she must always be perfect. This unnecessary pressure causes people to fear doing things in church because they might make a mistake and be embarrassed. God knows His children's limitations. The Lord wants sincere hearts available to Him for service. When earnestly one tries to carry out the Lord's assignments, it provides an opportunity to experience the power of God. Jesus uses human limitations to display His glory.

This lesson urges believers to join in the construction process. People will never do everything perfectly and sometimes their efforts will fail. When one falls, the key is to get back up again. Every time one continues to exercise their faith, it is a witness to the reality of Jesus Christ. The Lord did not come to save perfect people. Jesus came for sinners willing to get up from their afflictions and follow Him.

A man was engaged in building a model skyscraper. He placed each piece in the model to where it reached three feet. When the model building was almost finished, the artist took a break to make a snack. Suddenly, he heard a crash. He ran into the room to discover that his dog had knocked the entire structure down. Without saying a word, the man immediately began rebuilding the structure. His son came in the room and asked, "Why didn't you scold the dog? What are you doing?"

The faithful man responded, "Buildings may fall, but the key is how you respond after they come down." Christians will make mistakes, but the question is how we respond after the fall. The lesson does not reveal how all the Corinthians responded to Paul's teachings, but the hope is some of them continued in the faith, becoming that building of God, eternal in the heavens.

### GET SOCIAL
Share your views and tag us @rhboydco. Use #rhboydco.

@rhboydco

## HOME DAILY DEVOTIONAL READINGS
### AUGUST 4–10, 2025

| MONDAY | TUESDAY | WEDNESDAY | THURSDAY | FRIDAY | SATURDAY | SUNDAY |
|---|---|---|---|---|---|---|
| God Creates Man and Woman | Life Is Short; Live Wisely | Live Gloriously | Receive God's Gifts with Thanksgiving | No Hiding Place from God | Fearfully and Wonderfully Made | A Temple of the Holy Spirit |
| Genesis 2:4–7, 18–25 | Psalm 90:1-12 | 1 Corinthians 10:23–33 | 1 Timothy 4:1–5 | Psalm 139:1–12 | Psalm 139:13–24 | 1 Corinthians 6:12–20 |

LESSON XI  AUGUST 10, 2025

# OUR BODIES BELONG TO GOD

ADULT TOPIC:  BACKGROUND SCRIPTURE: ROMANS 12:1–21; 1 CORINTHIANS 6:12–20
HOW TO BE HAPPY  LESSON PASSAGE: 1 CORINTHIANS 6:12–20

## 1 CORINTHIANS 6:12–20

### KJV

ALL things are lawful unto me, but all things are not expedient: all things are lawful for me, but I will not be brought under the power of any.
13 Meats for the belly, and the belly for meats: but God shall destroy both it and them. Now the body is not for fornication, but for the Lord; and the Lord for the body.

14 And God hath both raised up the Lord, and will also raise up us by his own power.
15 Know ye not that your bodies are the members of Christ? shall I then take the members of Christ, and make them the members of an harlot? God forbid.
16 What? know ye not that he which is joined to an harlot is one body? for two, saith he, shall be one flesh.
17 But he that is joined unto the Lord is one spirit.
18 Flee fornication. Every sin that a man doeth is without the body; but he that committeth fornication sinneth against his own body.

19 What? know ye not that your body is the temple of the Holy Ghost which is in you, which ye have of God, and ye are not your own?

20 For ye are bought with a price: therefore glorify God in your body, and in your spirit, which are God's.

### NRSVue

"ALL things are permitted for me," but not all things are beneficial. "All things are permitted for me," but I will not be dominated by anything.
13 "Food is meant for the stomach and the stomach for food," and God will destroy both one and the other. The body is meant not for sexual immorality but for the Lord and the Lord for the body.

14 And God raised the Lord and will also raise us by his power.
15 Do you not know that your bodies are members of Christ? Should I therefore take the members of Christ and make them members of a prostitute? Never!
16 Do you not know that whoever is united to a prostitute becomes one body with her? For it is said, "The two shall be one flesh."
17 But anyone united to the Lord becomes one spirit with him.
18 Shun sexual immorality! Every sin that a person commits is outside the body, but the sexually immoral person sins against the body itself.
19 Or do you not know that your body is a temple of the Holy Spirit within you, which you have from God, and that you are not your own?
20 For you were bought with a price; therefore glorify God in your body.

**MAIN THOUGHT:** Do you not know that your body is a temple of the Holy Spirit within you, which you have from God, and that you are not your own? (1 Corinthians 6:19, NRSVue)

**LESSON SETTING**
  Time: 54 CE
  Place: Corinth

**LESSON OUTLINE**
  I. Do Not Join with Sin
     (1 Corinthians 6:12-16)
  II. Join with Christ
     (1 Corinthians 6:17-20)

## UNIFYING PRINCIPLE

We desire happy and satisfying lives that are pleasing to both ourselves and others. By what standard do we measure a good life? In his letter to the Corinthian church, Paul advocates a way of life governed by a conviction that our bodies belong to God.

## INTRODUCTION

Corinth was a port city where travelers would stop for trade and entertainment. The city was located on an isthmus that mariners would go through to reach other parts of the Greek world, such as Athens and Sparta. Because the area was dangerous to navigate, they built a four-mile paved stretch of rocks called *diolkos* where ships could be dragged across the isthmus. While the ships were being moved overland, it gave the businessmen and women opportunities to trade services. One service readily offered was prostitution. This activity proved to be a temptation for many who frequented the city including members of the church. So, Paul teaches them about sexual immorality, making it clear that liberty from the Law of Moses did not give license to sin.

## EXPOSITION

### I. DO NOT JOIN WITH SIN
   (1 CORINTHIANS 6:12-16)

The Corinthian Christians lived in a context where people justified their sins. This mindset also infected the church where they took Paul's teachings about the Law of Moses to the extreme. The apostle taught that they were not to make the law a yoke of legalism. He conveyed that trying to be justified through the law amounted to being enslaved. But some took this liberty too far by claiming that all their behaviors were lawful. Paul never intended that in his teachings. His emphasis on liberty related to observing ceremonial laws such as circumcision, consumption of foods, or adhering to holy day traditions. The Corinthians likely understood what Paul meant, but sin had a way of hardening their hearts. Sinners who are determined to rebel find ways to continue their conduct.

In verse 12, Paul responds to their behavior by telling the church that some things may be permissible, but it is still not helpful in the witness of a Christian. Paul's instruction causes every believer to engage in self-examination of their lifestyle. They should ask questions such as the difference between things doctrinally acceptable but not helpful to the cause of Christ. For example, Christian teaching may not specifically forbid listening to certain types of music, but should one listen to it in private or with others? Should Christians watch movies that are laced with profanity or sexually revealing scenes? Or is it appropriate to go into a club that promotes lewd behavior? The believer must make all types of judgment calls to determine proper conduct.

The Corinthians were faced with similar challenges for the two issues in this text were the types of acceptable foods to eat and sexual immorality. The Law of Moses was very specific on foods deemed to be clean versus unclean. As a church, the Corinthians had only been established for about four years, so Jewish food regulations were still a new subject to them. Moreover, Corinth was a city that had temples for idols and many of these temples contained rooms where idol worshippers consumed meat sacrificed to these gods. The Jewish priests had similar traditions of eating lamb or other foods used in their worship of Jehovah. The Corinthians had questions on whether these foods were appropriate to eat. They understood Paul taught them that the dietary restrictions of the law did not forbid them, but did this include meat offered to idols?

Paul answered (v. 13) by conveying that an overemphasis on food and a disregard for the Lord would lead to destruction. The Corinthians' view was if you needed to eat, go ahead and do it. They saw no need to worry about whether it had been used for idols or not. But Paul did not get bogged down in the details of which food to eat. His point was the church needed to heed the spiritual ramifications of what they did with their bodies. One's body was designed to be in union with the Lord, not for sinful activities. In the same way that God raised Jesus' body from the grave, He would raise those who believed in Christ. Therefore, the body was to be a holy vessel in union with Jesus.

Paul's reference to being in sexual union with a harlot must have been piercing for the Corinthian church members. Obviously, some in the church had participated in that activity. First Corinthians 5:3 spoke about a man engaged in sexual intercourse with his father-in-law's wife. This incestuous conduct was one example of sexual immorality being practiced in the church. So, the apostle made clear that one could not expect to be raised from the dead and go to heaven practicing this type of behavior. Paul's reference to "one flesh" reminded the believers of Jesus' description of marriage in Matthew 19:5, where a marriage union constitutes two people becoming one. If members are becoming one with harlots, then it will be impossible for a Christian to go to heaven carrying a prostitute along as baggage. The details of what to eat or with whom to engage in relations paled in comparison to the most important law—to have a right relationship with Jesus Christ.

## II. JOIN WITH CHRIST (1 CORINTHIANS 6:17–20)

Theologians describe the unity of God the Father and the Son as *homoousias,* meaning they are the same substance. A similar connection can be made with humanity and Christ. Verse 17 reveals that whoever is joined with Christ has the same Spirit. The reference to "spirit" is very important as it relates to salvation. The Holy Spirit is who raises one from the dead into eternal life. Paul's analogy of joining with the right spirit sheds light on why one must be very conscientious of their sexual partner. If that person does not have the Holy Spirit, one could be united with a spirit that puts his or her soul in jeopardy. This reality explains why verse 18 warns to flee from sexual immorality.

These sinful activities bring destruction upon one's own body. And the behavior sheds a negative light upon the body of Christ. Sometimes a person may say that what he or she is doing does not hurt anyone else. But this statement is false.

When people find out about the sexual sins of Christians, especially leaders, other believers are discouraged. A leader must remember that people are always watching, and sin can become a very difficult stumbling block for many to overcome.

Moreover, the sexual immorality of the Corinthians was a direct rejection of God. Not only were they rejecting the Spirit of Christ, but the union also indicated that they were giving their allegiance to an idol god. The idol god Aphrodite was known for offering temple prostitutes who worked in that shrine. Part of what drew people to the idol was sex offered by the prostitutes. When the potential worshippers had sex with the prostitutes, it was a type of entry into the cult. Therefore, opportunities for sexual intercourse became an effective tool to lure people into idol worship. This method was called sacred prostitution and had been used throughout the Bible. One reason why God forbade the Hebrew children from marrying the Canaanites and other foreign women is because of the influence that sex had upon them. Even Solomon, despite his great wisdom, fell victim to the influence of sex.

Because God knows the human body, He understands the power that sexual relations can have upon a person. When those relations are ungodly, one's commitment is not totally to Christ, and most dangerously, one's mind is divided to the extent that the person loses singular focus on the Lord. Paul reminds the Corinthians that all these things are an insult to the true God. He made human bodies to be the temple of the Holy Spirit. Yet, the individual has taken something that does not belong to him or her and given it to an idol resident. The insult to God can be likened to someone renting your house and then they allow a squatter to come in and live. As an owner, you would be angry about the renter housing a trespasser.

This principle was being driven home by Paul. The Corinthians then and Christians today have no right to allow a trespasser to live in a temple created for the Holy Spirit. The point is further confirmed as Paul declares that believers are bought for a price. When Jesus died on the cross and shed His blood for sinners, He paid the ultimate price for the souls of humanity.

No Christian can claim, "my body and my choice." The body has been fearfully and wonderfully made by God. Therefore, it is designed to glorify God. Verse 20 provides a good filter of how to determine the proper use of the body. It should be used to glorify God and not self.

## The Lesson Applied

A person may study this lesson and become discouraged about the prohibition against sexual sins. One may say, "I may as well forget about living to this standard for I have committed these sins too many times." But sexual sins are no different than any other shortcoming in the sense that God offers forgiveness. If one has fallen, the proper response is to repent and stop the improper behavior. The Corinthians tried to justify their activities, but Christians should repent.

The lesson gives some powerful reasons to stop sexual immorality. One of the most important reasons is a person could lose their soul over improper sex. A few moments of pleasure cannot compare to an eternity in hell. Paul concluded his teaching with a better activity than sexual sin which was to glorify God. If believers focus on God rather than flesh, then one can overcome the temptation. God created sex for His glory. Sexual activity, along with everything else, should lead to a union with the Holy Spirit.

## Let's Talk About It
**Can a person commit sexual sin without physically engaging in the act?**

Jesus taught (Matthew 5:28) that if one looks upon another person with lust, that person has committed adultery. His point was that sin begins in the heart long before a sinful deed takes place. But this is true with all sin—sinful behavior begins when sinful thoughts fo unchecked. A person cannot claim to be righteous because he or she has not engaged in the act. The key to overcoming sexual sin is to keep focused on Christ. A woman could not understand why her husband no longer desired her. Her counselor explained, "He left you in his mind long before he left you physically." This same principle applies to sin. A person decides to sin because of a broken relationship in their heart with God.

James 1:14–15 describes how person can be drawn way by lust, and that brings in sin, which ultimately leads to death. Therefore, to avoid sexual mishaps, one must continuously guard the heart. Instead of thinking about things that satisfy the flesh, focus on things that are positive, virtuous, and give praise to God. The key to repairing hearts that have fallen to sexual promiscuity is to find joy in other things. Often people devolve into deviant behavior because of a lack of joy. They look for ways to escape the pains and the depressions of life. Jesus has made a way to escape by yielding to the Holy Spirit. Paul strategically made clear that the body is a temple of the Holy Spirit. Therefore, in the same way that one prepares to live in a house, the faithful must dutifully prepare a place within for the Holy Spirit. The next time you are tempted to sin, create more space for the Holy Spirit. If one spends time making their temple fit for the Holy Ghost, it will leave no room for the devil.

## Get Social
Share your views and tag us @rhboydco. Use #rhboydco.

@rhboydco

## Home Daily Devotional Readings
### August 11–17, 2025

| Monday | Tuesday | Wednesday | Thursday | Friday | Saturday | Sunday |
|---|---|---|---|---|---|---|
| A Light to the Nations | God's Mercy Reaches All | Salvation Is for All | Privilege with Humility | God Will Dwell in Our Midst | Seek God Together | Built into a Holy Temple |
| Isaiah 49:1–6 | Romans 9:14–24 | Romans 10:1–15 | Romans 11:16–29 | Zechariah 8:1–12 | Zechariah 8:13–23 | Ephesians 2:11–22 |

LESSON XII                                                                    AUGUST 17, 2025

# JEWS AND GENTILES FORM ONE TEMPLE

ADULT TOPIC:                                   BACKGROUND SCRIPTURE: EPHESIANS 2:11–22
FINDING PEACE IN A CONFLICTED WORLD                    LESSON PASSAGE: EPHESIANS 2:11–22

## EPHESIANS 2:11–22

### KJV

WHEREFORE remember, that ye being in time past Gentiles in the flesh, who are called Uncircumcision by that which is called the Circumcision in the flesh made by hands;
12 That at that time ye were without Christ, being aliens from the commonwealth of Israel, and strangers from the covenants of promise, having no hope, and without God in the world:

13 But now in Christ Jesus ye who sometimes were far off are made nigh by the blood of Christ.
14 For he is our peace, who hath made both one, and hath broken down the middle wall of partition between us;
15 Having abolished in his flesh the enmity, even the law of commandments contained in ordinances; for to make in himself of twain one new man, so making peace;
16 And that he might reconcile both unto God in one body by the cross, having slain the enmity thereby:
17 And came and preached peace to you which were afar off, and to them that were nigh.

18 For through him we both have access by one Spirit unto the Father.
19 Now therefore ye are no more strangers and foreigners, but fellowcitizens with the saints, and of the household of God;

20 And are built upon the foundation of the apostles and prophets, Jesus Christ himself

### NRSVue

SO then, remember that at one time you gentiles by birth, called "the uncircumcision" by those who are called "the circumcision"—a circumcision made in the flesh by human hands—
12 remember that you were at that time without Christ, being aliens from the commonwealth of Israel and strangers to the covenants of promise, having no hope and without God in the world.
13 But now in Christ Jesus you who once were far off have been brought near by the blood of Christ.
14 For he is our peace; in his flesh he has made both into one and has broken down the dividing wall, that is, the hostility between us,
15 abolishing the law with its commandments and ordinances, that he might create in himself one new humanity in place of the two, thus making peace,
16 and might reconcile both to God in one body through the cross, thus putting to death that hostility through it.
17 So he came and proclaimed peace to you who were far off and peace to those who were near,
18 for through him both of us have access in one Spirit to the Father.
19 So then, you are no longer strangers and aliens, but you are fellow citizens with the saints and also members of the household of God,
20 built upon the foundation of the apostles and prophets, with Christ Jesus himself as the

**MAIN THOUGHT:** In [Jesus Christ] the whole structure is joined together and grows into a holy temple in the Lord; in whom you also are built together spiritually into a dwelling place for God. (Ephesians 2:21–22, NRSVue)

## EPHESIANS 2:11–22

### KJV

being the chief corner stone;
21 In whom all the building fitly framed together groweth unto an holy temple in the Lord:
22 In whom ye also are builded together for an habitation of God through the Spirit.

### NRSVue

cornerstone;
21 in him the whole structure is joined together and grows into a holy temple in the Lord,
22 in whom you also are built together spiritually into a dwelling place for God.

## LESSON SETTING
Time: 62 CE
Place: Ephesus

## LESSON OUTLINE
I. One in the Blood
(Ephesians 2:11-13)
II. One in Christ
(Ephesians 2:14-18)
III. One in the Building
(Ephesians 2:19-22)

## UNIFYING PRINCIPLE

Differing cultural and religious backgrounds can stir up conflict. How do we find a sense of peace that will enable us to thrive in the world today? Ephesians declares that Jews and Gentiles, who were once alienated from each other, were brought together in Christ, who has broken down the dividing wall and made them one—joined together and growing into a dwelling place for God.

## INTRODUCTION

The Ephesian church was planted by Paul during his second missionary journey. In Act 19, Paul returned to Ephesus and ministered in the area for over three years. Ephesus was a commercial city known for trading timber, fruits, cooper, and silver. A man named Demetrius lived in the city and made a huge profit selling silver shrines of an idol goddess named Diana. Paul interfered with this business by teaching people not to serve gods made with hands.

Paul's teachings were so influential that it led to a riot, but it also revealed how many in Ephesus embraced the Gospel. As the church grew, division arose between the Jews and Gentiles. Each group belittled the other by calling one other names. The Jews were labeled as the Circumcision while the Gentiles were referred to as the Uncircumcision. This was the type of divisiveness that the apostle wanted to end.

He explained in this letter to the church that their common faith in Christ brought them together. Without Christ, one could understand why Jews and Gentiles remained at odds as they lacked a common bond to hold them. But Christ brings about peace. The division should end because the entire church transitions from separatism to being a part of the building of God. Paul wrote these words to the Ephesians while imprisoned in Rome. Yet, he did not allow his confinement to stop his advocacy for unity. One may ask, how can there be peace amid so much conflict? This lesson reveals that when everyone focuses on joining the kingdom of God, the Lord brings about peace. Christ removes the points that make members different and transforms them into being one with the Lord.

# Exposition

## I. One in the Blood (Ephesians 2:11–13)

As Paul called for unity in the church, he reminded the Ephesians of their status without Jesus Christ. It was a condition of labels. The Gentiles were called the Uncircumcised and ridiculed for their failure to adhere to the Mosaic Law. Those identified as Circumcised glorified themselves as being faithful to the law. One of the problems of labels is they make it easier to discriminate because he or she is seen as different. Yet, the text shows that highlighting differences is a characteristic of the world but not the church.

Verse 12 reveals reasons why those without Christ cannot achieve unity. They lack the unifying ingredients of being part of the commonwealth of Israel, a participant in the covenant, and the hope of Christ. The word *commonwealth* refers to citizenship. Paul was not saying that citizenship in the nation of Israel brings people together. The attacks that the Jewish leaders made against Jesus and the way other Israelites treated Paul underscored that mere citizenship did not constitute unity. Instead, Paul was referring to being a part of the symbolic Israel, those who placed their faith in Christ. Galatians 6:16 identified these people as the Israel of God. Without that citizenship, unity cannot be accomplished. The reference to the covenant reminded the church of the promise God made with Abraham. Whoever had the faith of Abraham participated in a promise of eternal life through Jesus Christ. But without Christ, unity with God is unachievable. However, those in Christ are brought into fellowship with God through faith in the blood shed by Jesus.

When the Lord died on the cross, His blood atoned for the sins of the world. The blood is the most powerful unifying agent of the church for all who profess faith have redemption, forgiveness, and grace. Paul's call for unity affirmed that the Ephesians were once distanced from God, even to the point of being a stranger. But a common reliance upon the blood brought the church together with each other and with Christ.

## II. One in Christ (Ephesians 2:14–18)

Paul placed such an emphasis upon Christ that he identified Him as the peace that made the church whole. The word *peace* in verse 14 means to cause something or someone to fit together. The Bible revealed that if the church focused on Christ, then He would bring everyone together. When Jesus died on the cross, He tore down the separation that God had with humanity. People tried to be in relationship with God by attempting to keep the Laws of Moses. But those efforts were futile, for all it did was maintain hostility. Christ removed that separation and reconciled God with His creation. No longer were they separate entities, but God and humanity became one. Verse 15 described this reconciled relationship between God and humanity as the "new man." Through Jesus, humanity has access to the Father.

This transformation is achieved by the supernatural work of the Holy Spirit. For this reason, humanity can never overcome differences without the Lordship of Jesus Christ. The biblical teaching about unity is humbling for a believer as it rejects principles of humanism that claim that peace is achieved through the works of man. The Scriptures convey that unity is only reached when individuals surrender themselves to the nature and character of Jesus. Verses 17 and 18 declare that this message of peace with God was preached to both Gentiles and Jews. The text identified Gentiles as being afar off and Jews as being nearby. The Lord does not discriminate for salvation is available to anyone who wants to be in the fellowship.

## III. ONE IN THE BUILDING (EPHESIANS 2:19–22)

Paul was an amazing writer who effectively used analogies that his audience could relate to in order to relay important spiritual points. In this section, the apostle referenced the relationship between God and humanity as being a part of a building. In verse 19, the Ephesian Christians are informed that they are not longer aliens from God. The world's critiques of pitting folks against one another had no place in the church. Paul affirmed that the members are joined in the household of God. In ancient Ephesus, they did not have many provisions for orphans or even widows. If one was not in a family, they faced a hard life of poverty and abandonment. Yet, Paul provided good news because in Christ believers enjoy all the privileges of being in the family of God. It was like being a part of a house.

Verse 20 revealed that Christ was the cornerstone, the doctrine of the apostle served as the foundation, and every member of the church made up the rest of the house. This house illustration made clear the importance of each member. If a house is missing a roof, the family will be flooded with rain. If the house does not have a wall, the structure is weak. And if the house lacks a cornerstone, the entire edifice will fall. Therefore, every member must be connected to Christ to survive. As members join the building of God, this structure is not stagnated. It must continue to grow into a holy temple.

Verse 21 emphasizes that it is not enough to join a church and go home. Christianity is a lifestyle of maturation. One must stay connected to the building to develop into holiness. Most people understand that if a house or building does not receive ongoing maintenance, it will deteriorate. The same principle applies with members of the church. They must be continuously fed the Word of God. They must pray. They must practice their faith through love, witness, and fellowship. These activities fall in the category of the Holy Spirit carrying out maintenance in the life of a believer.

The text also reveals that spiritual maintenance is not optional, because a saint's life does not belong to him or her. It belongs to God. The goal of being a member of the building of God is to make one's life conducive for the operation of the Holy Spirit. When one thinks about the need for shelter, the inclination centers on making that place comfortable for that individual.

When one is a part of God's building, the objective is to make it comfortable for the Holy Spirit. How does one make their life comfortable for the dwelling of the Holy Ghost? The key centers on aligning with the Word of God. Jesus said, "If you abide in me and my words abide in you, you will ask what you will, and it shall be done for you" (John 15:7, NKJV). Members of the Ephesian church were to operate as a dwelling place of the Holy Spirit. They had to grow out of selfish agendas and see themselves as part of a much larger plan of God.

## THE LESSON APPLIED

This lesson offers valuable principles to guard against unfairness in the church. Members must be careful about using labels to categorize people, for they highlight differences more than similarities. Sometimes, church folks may not recognize how they are making differences within the congregation, such as the tradition of publicly broadcasting the amounts of money given by individuals. This practice can be viewed as discriminatory behavior. Obviously, those who have nice sums are affirmed in their generosity.

But what about those who may feel insecure because they cannot meet a specific standard of giving? Another difference local churches might examine is how individuals are chosen for positions. Sometimes, these decisions are made based upon perks and relationships rather than spiritual gifts and practical qualifications. We see division everywhere—among races, religions, political parties, and even within families and communities. This lesson should inspire continued examination to ensure that believers are growing toward that holy standard set by God so when Christ makes His final judgment upon the church, He will not find a spot nor wrinkle.

## LET'S TALK ABOUT IT

**Have you ever faced discrimination?**
Many people know the pain of being unfairly excluded or mistreated. In the ancient world, the discrimination took place between the Jews and Gentiles within the church. Then, on a different level, the church faced discrimination between the Greco–Roman world and the Christians. The destructive nature of discrimination can sometimes work in that way. People who are discriminated against practice the same unfair treatment among themselves. Therefore, Paul spent a lot of time discouraging this type of behavior particularly within the church.

### GET SOCIAL
Share your views and tag us @rhboydco. Use #rhboydco.

@rhboydco

## HOME DAILY DEVOTIONAL READINGS
### AUGUST 18–24, 2025

| MONDAY | TUESDAY | WEDNESDAY | THURSDAY | FRIDAY | SATURDAY | SUNDAY |
|---|---|---|---|---|---|---|
| Return to the Lord | Faith without Works Is Dead | Everlasting Reign | A New Song | Teach Us to Pray | Practice Deeds of Mutual Love | Offer Sacrifices of Praise |
| Joel 2:12–17 | James 2:14–26 | Psalm 146 | Psalms 149–150 | Luke 11:1–13 | Hebrews 13:1–8 | Hebrews 13:9–21 |

LESSON XIII　　　　　　　　　　　　　　　　　　　　　　　　　　AUGUST 24, 2025

# SACRIFICES OF PRAISE AND GOOD WORKS

ADULT TOPIC:　　　　　　　　　　　　BACKGROUND SCRIPTURE: HEBREWS 13:1–21
ALL WE NEED IS LOVE　　　　　　　　　　　　　LESSON PASSAGE: HEBREWS 13:9–21

## HEBREWS 13:9–21

### KJV

BE not carried about with divers and strange doctrines. For it is a good thing that the heart be established with grace; not with meats, which have not profited them that have been occupied therein.
10 We have an altar, whereof they have no right to eat which serve the tabernacle.
11 For the bodies of those beasts, whose blood is brought into the sanctuary by the high priest for sin, are burned without the camp.
12 Wherefore Jesus also, that he might sanctify the people with his own blood, suffered without the gate.
13 Let us go forth therefore unto him without the camp, bearing his reproach.
14 For here have we no continuing city, but we seek one to come.
15 By him therefore let us offer the sacrifice of praise to God continually, that is, the fruit of our lips giving thanks to his name.
16 But to do good and to communicate forget not: for with such sacrifices God is well pleased.
17 Obey them that have the rule over you, and submit yourselves: for they watch for your souls, as they that must give account, that they may do it with joy, and not with grief: for that is unprofitable for you.
18 Pray for us: for we trust we have a good conscience, in all things willing to live honestly.
19 But I beseech you the rather to do this, that I may be restored to you the sooner.

### NRSVue

DO not be carried away by all kinds of strange teachings, for it is good for the heart to be strengthened by grace, not by regulations about food, which have not benefited those who observe them.
10 We have an altar from which those who officiate in the tent have no right to eat.
11 For the bodies of those animals whose blood is brought into the sanctuary by the high priest as a sacrifice for sin are burned outside the camp.
12 Therefore Jesus also suffered outside the city gate in order to sanctify the people by his own blood.
13 Let us then go to him outside the camp and bear the abuse he endured.
14 For here we have no lasting city, but we are looking for the city that is to come.
15 Through him, then, let us continually offer a sacrifice of praise to God, that is, the fruit of lips that confess his name.
16 Do not neglect to do good and to share what you have, for such sacrifices are pleasing to God.
17 Obey your leaders and submit to them, for they are keeping watch over your souls as those who will give an account. Let them do this with joy and not with sighing, for that would be harmful to you.
18 Pray for us; we are sure that we have a good conscience, desiring to act honorably in all things.
19 I urge you all the more to do this, so that I may be restored to you very soon.

**MAIN THOUGHT:** Through [Christ] . . . let us continually offer a sacrifice of praise to God, that is, the fruit of lips that confess his name. (Hebrews 13:15, NRSVue)

## Hebrews 13:9–21

### KJV

20 Now the God of peace, that brought again from the dead our Lord Jesus, that great shepherd of the sheep, through the blood of the everlasting covenant,
21 Make you perfect in every good work to do his will, working in you that which is wellpleasing in his sight, through Jesus Christ; to whom be glory for ever and ever. Amen.

### NRSVue

20 Now may the God of peace, who brought back from the dead our Lord Jesus, the great shepherd of the sheep, by the blood of the eternal covenant,
21 make you complete in everything good so that you may do his will, as he works among us that which is pleasing in his sight, through Jesus Christ, to whom be the glory forever. Amen.

### LESSON SETTING
Time: 68 C.E.
Place: Rome, Italy

### LESSON OUTLINE
I. A Different Altar
(Hebrews 13:9–14)
II. A Different Sacrifice
(Hebrews 13:15–21)

## UNIFYING PRINCIPLE

We struggle with loving others and doing good toward family, friends, and neighbors. What lasting examples do we have to guide our actions toward others? The writer of Hebrews urges Christians to look to Jesus, who suffered outside the city gate in order to sanctify the people by His own blood, and through Him, continually share what we have as sacrifices pleasing to God.

## INTRODUCTION

In the lesson text, the Hebrews were being influenced by other religions. The author expressed why these false religions were not the way to a relationship with Christ. The doctrines of the false teachers were wrong for placing too much emphasis on the physical aspects of religious worship and not enough on a person's heart. Following the way of Christ was different from the other religions in Rome. Therefore, the faithful had to learn what Jesus did in His atoning sacrifice for the world. When one follows the patterns of Christ, it pleases God.

## EXPOSITION

### I. A DIFFERENT ALTAR (HEBREWS 13:9–14)

The Hebrew writer begins in verse 9 warning against being misled by strange doctrine. Since the early days of Jewish religious history, God continuously cautioned them about serving idols. The first of the ten commandments forbad the worship of another god. These idol belief systems contained all type of teachings that conflicted with Christianity. If the Hebrews audience was living in Rome, they certainly encountered a plethora of idols such as Jupiter, Apollo, and Mars. On top of that pile of strange teachings, the people in the Roman empire had to give allegiance to Caesar as a god. So, these teachings must have been a challenge for the recipients of Hebrews.

These idols also had rules regarding sacrificial feasts. The Christians in the Graeco–Roman world had to decipher questions about proper foods to eat. If they came from Jewish ancestry, these budding Hebraic believers struggled with whether certain foods were considered clean or unclean. Today, most Christians do not have a religious problem about foods, but these people were new to the faith. Most of their religious background came out of a Jewish context, so the question of eating proper foods was a big deal to them. Verse 9 explained that an over-emphasis on dietary rules would not save them. The Hebrew Christians had to learn that salvation was the result of giving one's heart to Christ.

The Hebrews must have noticed how people worshipped using sacrifices upon altars. Verses 10–12 reveal that Christians sacrifice on the altar of Jesus Christ. The writer is taking something that the readers know and transferring that to the saving work of Jesus Christ. The Jews understood that on the Day of Atonement, the high priest made an animal sacrifice for the sins of Israel. They believed that when that blood was sprinkled on the mercy seat, God would see the blood and forgive the congregation of their sins.

Of course, the rituals of the Day of Atonement had to be done yearly according to the law. So, the writer conveyed that Jesus became that permanent sacrifice upon the altar of the cross. His sacrifice also took place outside the gates of Jerusalem. As the Lord hung on the cross, the people viewed Him as a curse. But verse 13 shows that believers who have the correct understanding of the Lord's sacrifice are to follow Him spiritually outside the camp of the world's powerless belief systems. As the faithful look to Christ, they understand that this earth is not their final home. Verse 14 affirms that Christians look for a city beyond this world which has foundations whose builder and maker is God.

## II. A DIFFERENT SACRIFICE (HEBREWS 13:15–21)

Within the ancient world, altar sacrifices required something to die whether it was an animal, crops, or even a human. Verse 15 indicates that a Christian sacrifice allows something to live. The text calls it the sacrifice of praise to God. This sacrifice should be done continuously as saints thank the Lord for saving their souls. The word *sacrifice* means to make an offering or give up something in response to what has been received. When Jesus died on the cross, His act ended the need for blood atonements for sin. Now, the offering is designed as a witness to the Lord. When saints praise God, it says to themselves that God is worthy to be magnified.

In Jewish teaching, congregants were to sacrifice the fruit of their labor as thanksgiving to God. They practiced this in the three festivals of Passover, Tabernacles and Weeks. Verse 15 highlights an offering to God from one's lips. Christians are to hail the greatness of God verbally and physically. While at the same time, they must not neglect sharing with others. One can see this balance in verse 16 where praise to God is good but it must also include physical deeds of caring for those in need. The beauty of the Christian faith is the practice never totally rejects the Mosaic laws but places them in a context of love for God and for neighbor.

God's infinite wisdom knows that Christian doctrines can be difficult to follow, particularly for those who have been engrained in a different religious context. Therefore, God gives the church pastors who feed the people with knowledge and understanding. These leaders have a God-ordained assignment to equip the people for proper ministry. Verse 17 explains that these leaders have two functions of watching for souls and giving an account to God. This verse raises the question of whether pastors have the authority to be a type of advocate for their congregants before God.

If so, obeying those in spiritual authority is an important part of entering heaven. The pastor may be the one to stand at the judgment bar to talk with Christ about the faithfulness of their members. Moreover, the pastor must take his or her assignment very serious as God assigns them to care for their members' souls. The spiritual leader must learn the ways of Christ and model it before the congregation. They must teach, train, correct, rebuke, and inspire members to stay on the path to eternal life. Verse 18 emphasizes the need to pray for spiritual leaders that they stay true to their calling and live lives worthy of respect.

The devil targets spiritual leaders since if they can be discredited, then it stains the witness of the body of Christ. So, the church should pray for their pastor to live a holy life. That way, no one can point the finger at them and say, "I told you it wasn't anything to Christian faith." In verse 19, the Hebrew writer urged the audience to pray for their leaders because the witness of the church was dependent upon it. Some folks love to see pastors fall to sin. Other members of the church may do almost anything and be excused.

Like a good Christian shepherd, the author of Hebrews longed to be in the physical presence of the recipients. Paul in his letters to the church expressed that desire in Romans 1:15 where he was ready to preach the Gospel to the Romans. Jesus in John 16:16 made a similar statement when He told the disciples that in a little while, He would come back to them. The nature of Christian fellowship is saints always looking forward to coming together and engaging under their unifying faith in Christ Jesus.

The discourse of this epistle closes with a blessing between the writer and readers while they remain apart. In church, this blessing is called a benediction. Because the Christian offers a different sacrifice, they also offer a different way of parting. Verses 20–21 reveal a benediction that prays for the God of peace to remain active in everyone's lives. The God of peace is affirmed to have raised Jesus from the dead and is the great Shepherd of the flock. He saved the members through the blood of Jesus and completes every good work in them. He makes one whole and brings about what is pleasing in the sight of God. This benediction declares who God is and what He has done and what He will continue to do forever.

## The Lesson Applied

The lesson text called on the Jewish Christians to offer the sacrifice of praise. The focused was on praising God with the lips rather than ritual sacrifices. A takeaway from this lesson should be use service to others as a sacrifice of praise. The Lord does not bless simply to enjoy the fruits of God's abundance.

In this modern era, volunteerism is becoming less of a characteristic of the church. Seemingly, members must be paid for practically every activity. Local congregations used to enjoy bringing potluck dinners to the church and everyone sharing in a meal. Now, the meals are catered as it is difficult to get people to volunteer. This lesson should encourage people to sacrifice some of their time and skills to promote the work of Christ. Jesus provided the perfect example of sacrifice. He gave Himself to the world and did not charge one cent. A sacrifice of praise entails more than lip service, it requires love of service where others experience Christ through actions of the church.

## LET'S TALK ABOUT IT
**Should members in a church remain for the benediction?**

The structure of the church service today is heavily regulated by time constraints. Studies have been done to show that people's attention spans are limited, so information must be disseminated quickly and effectively. Often people will sit through a sermon, but after the invitation is given, they swiftly exit. This lesson Scripture closes with a powerful benediction. It was a blessing upon the people that they be made whole through their relationship with Jesus Christ. Prior to the benediction passage in verse 20–21, a request was given to pray for the spiritual leaders in Hebrews 13:19. This call to pray for one another makes clear that people should remain in the worship service to receive the benediction. The description of God in the benediction confirms that whatever one feels is so urgent can be done through the intervention and continued presence of God.

If God has the power to give one perfect peace and even raise Jesus from the dead, whatever an individual needs to do can be achieved through the Lord. The benediction is the last sacrifice of praise in the order of service. It is one that urges the church to give the Lord just a few more minutes to be prayed for, then watch God address whatever issues that must be dealt with after the benediction.

### GET SOCIAL
Share your views and tag us @rhboydco. Use #rhboydco.

@rhboydco

## HOME DAILY DEVOTIONAL READINGS
### AUGUST 25–31, 2025

| MONDAY | TUESDAY | WEDNESDAY | THURSDAY | FRIDAY | SATURDAY | SUNDAY |
| --- | --- | --- | --- | --- | --- | --- |
| A Sure Foundation | Let Us Enter the Lord's House | Offer a Sacrifice of Thanksgiving | One in Christ Jesus | One Lord, One Faith, One Baptism | Everlasting Joy of the Ransomed | Rejected by Mortals, Chosen by God |
| Isaiah 28:14–22 | Psalm 122 | Psalm 50:1–15 | Galatians 3:23–29 | Ephesians 4:4–16 | Isaiah 51:9–16 | 1 Peter 2:1–12 |

LESSON XIV  AUGUST 31, 2025

# LIVING STONES IN A SPIRITUAL TEMPLE

ADULT TOPIC:
BUILDING FROM THE GROUND UP

BACKGROUND SCRIPTURE: 1 PETER 2:1–17
LESSON PASSAGE: 1 PETER 2:1–12

## 1 PETER 2:1–12

### KJV

WHEREFORE laying aside all malice, and all guile, and hypocrisies, and envies, and all evil speakings,

2 As newborn babes, desire the sincere milk of the word, that ye may grow thereby:

3 If so be ye have tasted that the Lord is gracious.

4 To whom coming, as unto a living stone, disallowed indeed of men, but chosen of God, and precious,

5 Ye also, as lively stones, are built up a spiritual house, an holy priesthood, to offer up spiritual sacrifices, acceptable to God by Jesus Christ.

6 Wherefore also it is contained in the scripture, Behold, I lay in Sion a chief corner stone, elect, precious: and he that believeth on him shall not be confounded.

7 Unto you therefore which believe he is precious: but unto them which be disobedient, the stone which the builders disallowed, the same is made the head of the corner,

8 And a stone of stumbling, and a rock of offence, even to them which stumble at the word, being disobedient: whereunto also they were appointed.

9 But ye are a chosen generation, a royal priesthood, an holy nation, a peculiar people; that ye should shew forth the praises of him who hath called you out of darkness into his marvellous light;

### NRSVue

RID yourselves, therefore, of all malice and all guile, insincerity, envy, and all slander.

2 Like newborn infants, long for the pure, spiritual milk, so that by it you may grow into salvation—

3 if indeed you have tasted that the Lord is good.

4 Come to him, a living stone, though rejected by mortals yet chosen and precious in God's sight, and

5 like living stones let yourselves be built into a spiritual house, to be a holy priesthood, to offer spiritual sacrifices acceptable to God through Jesus Christ.

6 For it stands in scripture: "See, I am laying in Zion a stone, a cornerstone chosen and precious, and whoever believes in him will not be put to shame."

7 This honor, then, is for you who believe, but for those who do not believe, "The stone that the builders rejected has become the very head of the corner,"

8 and "A stone that makes them stumble and a rock that makes them fall." They stumble because they disobey the word, as they were destined to do.

9 But you are a chosen people, a royal priesthood, a holy nation, God's own people, in order that you may proclaim the excellence of him who called you out of darkness into his marvelous light.

**MAIN THOUGHT:** Like living stones, let yourselves be built into a spiritual house, to be a holy priesthood, to offer spiritual sacrifices acceptable to God through Jesus Christ. (1 Peter 2:5 NRSVue)

# 1 Peter 2:1–12

## KJV

10 Which in time past were not a people, but are now the people of God: which had not obtained mercy, but now have obtained mercy.
11 Dearly beloved, I beseech you as strangers and pilgrims, abstain from fleshly lusts, which war against the soul;
12 Having your conversation honest among the Gentiles: that, whereas they speak against you as evildoers, they may by your good works, which they shall behold, glorify God in the day of visitation.

## NRSVue

10 Once you were not a people, but now you are God's people; once you had not received mercy, but now you have received mercy.
11 Beloved, I urge you as aliens and exiles to abstain from the desires of the flesh that wage war against the soul.
12 Conduct yourselves honorably among the gentiles, so that, though they malign you as evildoers, they may see your honorable deeds and glorify God when he comes to judge.

## LESSON SETTING
**Time:** 64 CE
**Place:** Asia Minor

## LESSON OUTLINE
I. A Chosen Assignment
(1 Peter 2:1–6)
II. A Chosen People
(1 Peter 2:7–12)

## UNIFYING PRINCIPLE

People desire a solid foundation on which to build their lives. What examples from history provide a pattern for such a foundation? First Peter reminds Christians that we, like living stones built on the spiritual foundation of Christ, are called to live sacrificially.

## INTRODUCTION

By the time Peter wrote this letter, he understood what it meant to endure persecution. He was likely in Rome and would soon be executed by the wicked King Nero. Yet, Peter did not let his circumstances deter the ministry. He focused on encouraging the Christian community in Asia Minor by urging them to trust the Word of God and remain faithful to Christ. One can only imagine how difficult it must have been for him to encourage others while facing certain death. Nevertheless, he understood something more important was at stake. He reminded the church that they were a holy people chosen by God to display a spiritual temple in the world. The people during Peter's time understood the significance of religious temples. They knew that worshippers built these houses in honor of the deities they believed would sustain their lives. Peter took that context and applied it to the church.

He declared that the church was a type of building who represented the true God. Therefore, followers of Christ were expected to live holy amid a dark world. They had no time for division and turning upon themselves. Peter expressed how Christians had a charge from God to set the example for society to get out of spiritual darkness into the marvelous light of Jesus Christ. This calling to bring the world to the light would not be easy for many were offended by Christians. This lesson urges believers to live out their God-ordained assignment.

## EXPOSITION

### I. A CHOSEN ASSIGNMENT (1 PETER 2:1–6)

When people are under pressure, it is easy for them to forget their purpose and identity. Peter's readers had lost focus on who they were called to be as Christians. They believed in the Lord and were trying to live a new life in Christ. Yet, the folks were tearing each other down rather than building each other up. Peter reminded them of how they were to behave as children of God. Verse 1 showed that the people turned against themselves which led to them turning against their neighbors. The text named malice, decent and hypocrisy as the sins of them turning against themselves. Peter called on them to lay aside these vices for it led to envy and evil speaking. The connection is clear that when one does not live in their God–ordained purpose, they hurt themselves and then hurt others.

Peter explained that the way back from self–deterioration is to consume the word of God (v. 2). The apostle coached believers by telling them that they started out doing well with their faith. But this text shows that just because someone has tasted does not guarantee that they will continue. Peter urged them to keep drinking from God's word, for it developed spiritual maturity. The transforming word of God will keep the beleiver on track to becoming a living stone.

As a living stone, Peter used this earthen element to convey the purpose and work of Christian discipleship. Their assignment requires them to connect with Christ as a stone perfectly fits in the construction of a building. However, the difference between stones in a physical edifice and Christian chosen stones is they are alive. Unlike stones in a temple built for idols, Jesus is alive. When people connect with Christ, they join in the development of a spiritual house that leads to eternal salvation.

### II. A CHOSEN PEOPLE (1 PETER 2:7–12)

As the church received their assignment, Peter transitioned in verse 7 to discussing their identity. Their identity emerged out of how they viewed Jesus. The chief cornerstone referenced in the text is Jesus Christ. The faithful considered Him precious. Peter knew Jesus' teaching and expressed that believing in the Word of God was so valuable and powerful that it transformed one's identity. One moved from being disobedient to obedient. What the world rejected as being an offense, Christians embraced as a building block to eternal life.

Verse 8 informed the church that following Christ required overcoming rejection. Disciples had to be strong in their self-esteem and be confident in who they were as Christians. The Scriptures revealed a number of reasons why experiencing rejection would be an intrinsic part of following Christ. First, the Lord's focus was on a world to come while most placed their interest in the present. Second, Jesus demanded a holy lifestyle that centered on love. Society rejected that message because their interest centered on love for themselves and maybe their kin but not a general love for the world. Then, Christ was rejected because of His claim to be the only way to God. Hearers of His message hated the exclusivity of Jesus' claims.

They griped, "How could he be the only way to God for he was committing blasphemy?" For these reasons, the message of Jesus being the Messiah was what text calls a rock of offense.

Apparently, some recipients of this epistle superficially received Christ but as the pressures of the faith increased, they stumbled and became disobedient to the word. Verses 9–10 provided how one must view themselves to remain faithful to the Lord's work. Peter explained that Christians are to see themselves as a chosen generation. God called them out to be servants to the world.

The Jewish priests in the Old Testament could not serve the people in any way. They had to be spiritually clean, and so must disciples of Christ. Believers must see themselves as set apart to offer spiritual sacrifices. The church must not conform to the standards of the world. They must be special. It does not mean the servants of God are to be arrogant, but special in the sense that their lives revolve around ministering for Jesus. Some people can be very self–centered to the point of being narcissistic. Christians, however, should be overly consumed in praising the Lord. As the Lord is magnified, verse 10 reveals how they become God's people. In Christ, saints join the family of God working together in a common assignment of bringing the world out of darkness into the marvelous light.

When the people of God know their purpose and identity, it helps them abstain from hindrances such as fleshly lust. The word lust refers to a person's desires. Christ changes what a person wants. The 23rd Psalm confirms that idea by emphasizing that following the shepherd removes vain wants from an individual's perspective. The sheep learn to trust the shepherd for everything. A disciple can recognize when he or she is being transformed by the Holy Spirit when various wants are no longer desired.

Verse 12 makes lucid that unbelievers, called Gentiles in the text, are watching Christians. They reject Christians by speaking evil of them. But God's people cannot be deterred. If they display a faithful witness, people will not be able to find criticisms that stick, as the church becomes the holy temple of God described in this lesson. Peter concludes his message by speaking about the day of visitation. This phrase refers to the end of time when everyone must stand in judgment. Saints must always remember that their lives are accountable to God. The goal is for judgment to be a time of celebrating a person's good works and not a time of punishment for being a stumbling block. Even those who did not believe ought to declare that the Christian remained true to God's calling.

## THE LESSON APPLIED

If one has observed a building constructed from the ground up, the person understands the work involved to complete the project. The building starts with construction documents approved by the city that provide details about the structure. For Christians, the construction document is the Word of God. This lesson encouraged readers to measure their lives against the standards of the Word to make sure they fit into God's building. Then, important groundwork is done to make sure the foundation is properly set. Groundwork for believers consist of accepting Christ as Lord and turning from sins that hinder a good connection with Jesus Christ. Upon the foundation, the walls and everything else are built. Jesus certainly is the base from which everything stands. It is an eternal blessing to build one's life upon the nature and character of Christ. For when this world ends, only those who stand upon the solid rock of Jesus Christ will last. Jennie Wilson wrote lyrics that said, "… build your hopes on things eternal. Hold to God's unchanging hand…." This lesson should encourage God's people to hold on for heaven is in view.

## LET'S TALK ABOUT IT
**Do you handle rejection well?**

The Christian faith sometimes entails being alone and not a part of the majority. The recipients of Peter's letter certainly experienced that reality. They had to keep the faith and deal with being outcasts. Society may consider Christians as misfits because they will not engage in certain behaviors. They are criticized as being weak, aloof, odd, and even wicked. At times, God's people may watch others in the world and become envious of their apparent success in life. Psalm 73:3 spoke about being envious at the foolish when seeing the prosperity of the wicked. So, principles must be taught on how to press through these challenges. This lesson revealed that a laser beam focus on being a servant of God helps to overcome rejection.

People of faith must see themselves as chosen to be a light to the world. Instead of feeling as outcast in the world, the church must see themselves as being the leaders in the world. The church has what the world needs.

A man was stranded with others on a deserted island. Their ship stalled so they disembarked for their safety. Everyone was distraught because they were stuck. But the Christian on board remained calm while everyone else fretted. He was asked, "Why are you so calm?" He responded, "I tithe every Sunday so do not worry, I have what my pastor needs, he'll find me." The people of God have what the world needs so do not be discouraged by rejection, pray that the lost find Christ.

## GET SOCIAL
Share your views and tag us @rhboydco. Use #rhboydco.

@rhboydco

# *PARTIAL BIBLIOGRAPHY

## 1Q

*The New American Commentary:* Genesis 11:27–50:26.

*Interpretation Commentary: Genesis.* Walter Brueggermann

*The Daily Study Bible Series: Genesis*, Volume 2

First and Second Kings: Interpretation: A Bible Commentary for Teaching and Preaching Richard D. Nelson Westminster John Knox Press, 2012

First and Second Kings (OT Daily Study Bible Series) (The Daily Study Bible Westminster John Knox Press (January 1, 1986)

First and Second Chronicles (Cornerstone Biblical Commentary) by Mark Boda (Author), Philip W. Comfort (Editor), Tyndale House Publishers 2010

First and Second Chronicles (New American Commentary, 9) (Volume 9), J.A. Thompson, Holman Publishing, 1994

First and Second Kings (OT Daily Study Bible Series) (The Daily Study Bible Westminster John Knox Press (January 1, 1986)

Miriam the Prophetess | My Jewish Learning. https://www.myjewishlearning.com/article/miriam-the-prophetess/?utm_content=buffer7aa9a&utm_medium=social&utm_source=mjlfacebook&utm_campaign=buffer&fbclid=IwAR1yHZAEkNtvw3UcgHKf1YFZSto84k4gXk_Ew–VOwS6puJWTppt9dAS9pyg

Exodus: Interpretation: A Bible Commentary for Teaching and Preaching by Terence E. Fretheim, Westminster John Knox Press, July 15, 2010

*Psalms: Interpretation: A Bible Commentary for Teaching and Preaching* by James Luther Mays Westminster John Knox Press (August 26, 2011)

*Discovering Psalms: Content, Interpretation, Reception (Discovering Biblical Texts (DBT)* by Jerome F.D. Creach Wm. B. Eerdmans Publishing Co. (September 24, 2020)

*The New American Commentary: Isaiah 1–39*, Vol. 15A (New American Commentary) (Volume 15) by Gary Smith, Holman Reference (June 15, 2007)

Isaiah 1–39: Interpretation: A Bible Commentary for Teaching and Preaching By Christopher Seitz Westminster John Knox Press (December 15, 2011)

Isaiah 1–39 (*Westminster Bible Companion*) by Walter Brueggermann, Westminster John Knox Press; 1st edition (October 1, 1998)

## 2Q

W. Baker (2013). Hebrew–Greek Key Word Study Bible, ESV. AMG Publishers. Chattanooga, TN.

T. Evans ( 2019). *The Tony Evans Bible Commentary*. Advancing god's Kingdom Agenda. Holman. Nashville, TN.

M. Henry (1997). *Matthew Henry's Concise Commentary on the Whole Bible.* Thomas Nelson. Nashville, TN.

W. Macdonald (1995). The Believer's Bible Commentary, 2nd ed. Thomas Nelson. Nashville, TN.

Life Application Study Bible, 3rd ed. KJV (2019). Tyndale House Publishers. Carol Stream, IL.

C. F. Stanley (2009). The Charles F. Stanley Life Principles Bible, NASB. Thomas Nelson. Nashville, TN.

J. S. Duval and J.D. Hays (2020). The Baker Illustrated Bible Background Commentary. BakerBooks. Grand Rapids, MI.

W. Macdonald (1995). *The Believer's Bible Commentary*, 2nd ed. Thomas Nelson. Nashville, TN.

Youngblood, R.F., Lockyer, Sr., H., Bruce, F.F., and Harrison, R. K. 2014). *Nelson's Illustrated Bible Dictionary New and Enhanced Edition*. Thomas Nelson, Nashville, TN, p. 275–276.

W. Baker (2013). Hebrew–Greek Key Word Study Bible, ESV. AMG Publishers. Chattanooga, TN.

M. Henry (1997). *Matthew Henry's Concise Commentary on the Whole Bible.* Thomas Nelson. Nashville, TN.

Spence, H.D.M and Exell, J.S. (1980). *The Pulpit Commentary*, Vol. 16, p. 1–25. Wm. B. Eerdmans Publishing Company. Grand Rapids, MI.

Tyndale Life Application Study Bible, KJV. Tyndale House Publishers. Carol Stream, Illinois, p.2098.

Spence, H.D.M., and Exell, J. S. (1980). The Pulpit Commentary, Vol. 16. Wm. B. Eerdmans Publishing Company. Grand Rapids, MI. p. 38-39.

Life Application Study Bible, 3rd ed. KJV (2019). Tyndale House Publishers. Carol Stream, IL.

## 3Q

DeVries, C. E. (1988). Jacob. In Baker encyclopedia of the Bible (Vol. 2). Baker Book House.

Elwell, W. A., & Beitzel, B. J. (1988). Sinai, Sina. In Baker encyclopedia of the Bible (Vol. 2). Baker Book House.

Hannah, J. D. (1985). Exodus. In J. F. Walvoord & R. B. Zuck (Eds.), The Bible Knowledge Commentary: An Exposition of the Scriptures (Vol. 1). Victor Books.

Jewish Study Bible, Oxford: Oxford University Press, 2014.

Ryrie, Charles, New American Standard Study Bible, (Chicago: Moody Press, 1995).

Caldecott, W. S., Orr, J., & Whitelaw, T. (1915). Tabernacle. In J. Orr, J. L. Nuelsen, E. Y. Mullins, & M. O. Evans (Eds.), The International Standard Bible Encyclopaedia (Vol. 1–5). Chicago: The Howard–Severance Company.

Conder, C. R. (1911–1912). PALESTINE. In J. Hastings, J. A. Selbie, A. B. Davidson, S. R. Driver, & H. B. Swete (Eds.), *A Dictionary of the Bible: Dealing with Its Language, Literature, and Contents Including the Biblical Theology* (Vol. 3,). New York; Edinburgh: Charles Scribner's Sons; T. & T. Clark.

Elwell, W. A., & Beitzel, B. J. (1988). Baker Encyclopedia of the Bible (Vol. 2). Baker Book House.

Jewish Study Bible, Oxford: Oxford University Press, 2014.

Koester, C. R. (2000). Tabernacle. In D. N. Freedman, A. C. Myers, & A. B. Beck (Eds.), Eerdmans Dictionary of the Bible. W.B. Eerdmans.

Myers, A. C. (1987). In The Eerdmans Bible Dictionary. Grand Rapids, MI: Eerdmans.

Osborn, N. D., & Hatton, H. A. (1999). A Handbook on Exodus. New York: United Bible Societies.

Wead, D. W. (1988). Bread of the Presence. In Baker encyclopedia of the Bible (Vol. 1). Baker Book House.

Borowski, O. (2000). Barley. In D. N. Freedman, A. C. Myers, & A. B. Beck (Eds.), Eerdmans Dctionary of the Bible. W.B. Eerdmans.

Culver, R. D. (1988). *Baker Encyclopedia of the Bible* (Vol. 1). Baker Book House.

Lindsey, F. D. (1985). Leviticus. In J. F. Walvoord & R. B. Zuck (Eds.), The Bible Knowledge Commentary: An Exposition of the Scriptures (Vol. 1). Victor Books.

Lyon, R. W., & Toon, P. (1988). Baker Encyclopedia of the Bible (Vol. 1). Baker Book House.

Péter–Contesse, R., & Ellington, J. (1992). A Handbook on Leviticus. United Bible Societies.

Harris, J. Gordon. (1988). Incense. In Baker encyclopedia of the Bible (Vol. 1). Baker Book House

Rooker, M. F. (2000). Leviticus (Vol. 3A). Nashville: Broadman & Holman Publishers.

Spence–Jones, H. D. M. (Ed.). (1910). Leviticus. London; New York: Funk & Wagnalls Company.

Hodges, Z. C. (1985). Hebrews. In J. F. Walvoord & R. B. Zuck (Eds.), The Bible Knowledge Commentary: An Exposition of the Scriptures (Vol. 2). Victor Books.

Rensberger, D. (2000). John, Letters of. In D. N. Freedman, A. C. Myers, & A. B. Beck (Eds.), Eerdmans dictionary of the Bible. W.B. Eerdmans.

Walvoord, J. F., & Zuck, R. B., Dallas Theological Seminary. (1985). The Bible Knowledge Commentary: An Exposition of the Scriptures (Vol. 2). Victor Books.

Zodhiates, S. (2000). In The Complete Word Study Dictionary: New Testament (electronic ed.). AMG Publishers.

Barbieri, L. A., Jr. (1985). Matthew. In J. F. Walvoord & R. B. Zuck (Eds.), *The Bible Knowledge Commentary: An Exposition of the Scriptures* (Vol. 2). Victor Books.

Newman, B. M., & Stine, P. C. (1992). A Handbook on the Gospel of Matthew. United Bible Societies.

Bratcher, R. G., & Hatton, H. (1993). A handbook on the Revelation to John. United Bible Societies.

New American Standard Bible: 1995 update. (1995). The Lockman Foundation.

Osborne, Grant R. Revelation, Grand Rapids, 2002, Baker Publishing Group.

Josephus, F., & Whiston, W. (1987). The Works of Josephus: Complete and Unabridged. Hendrickson.

Klein, R. W. (2006). 1 Chronicles: A Commentary (T. Krüger, Ed.). Fortress Press.

Merrill, E. H. (1985). First Chronicles. In J. F. Walvoord & R. B. Zuck (Eds.), The Bible Knowledge Commentary: An Exposition of the Scriptures (Vol. 1). Victor Books.

*New American Standard Bible*: 1995 update. (1995). The Lockman Foundation.

Raymond B. Dillard and Tremper Longman III, An Introduction of Old Testament History (Grand Rapids: Zondervan Publishing House, 1994).

Freedman, D. N., Myers, A. C., & Beck, A. B. (2000). Bezalel. In D. N. Freedman, A. C. Myers, & A. B. Beck (Eds.), Eerdmans dictionary of the Bible. W.B. Eerdmans.

Klein, R. W. (2006). 1 Chronicles: a commentary (T. Krüger, Ed.). Fortress Press.

Klein, R. W. (2012). 2 Chronicles: A Commentary (P. D. Hanson, Ed). Fortress Press.

Merrill, E. H. (1985). 1 Chronicles. In J. F. Walvoord & R. B. Zuck (Eds.), The Bible Knowledge Commentary: An Exposition of the Scriptures (Vol. 1). Victor Books.

Merrill, E. H. (1985). 2 Chronicles. In J. F. Walvoord & R. B. Zuck (Eds.), The Bible Knowledge Commentary: An Exposition of the Scriptures (Vol. 1). Wheaton, IL: Victor Books.

# *PARTIAL BIBLIOGRAPHY

New Bible Dictionary, 3rd Edition, Downers Grove: InterVarsity Press, 1997, R. J. Forbes, Studies in Ancient Technology.

The Reese Chronological Bible: (1994). Bloomington, MN: Bethany House Publishers.

www.tyson.com/investor-relations/investor-overview/tyson-factbook

Chapman, B. C. (2000). Jesus. In D. N. Freedman, A. C. Myers, & A. B. Beck (Eds.), Eerdmans dictionary of the Bible. W.B. Eerdmans.

Freedman, D. N., Myers, A. C., & Beck, A. B. (2000). Jeshohaiah. In D. N. Freedman, A. C. Myers, & A. B. Beck (Eds.), Eerdmans dictionary of the Bible. W.B. Eerdmans.

Harrison, R. K. (1988). Feasts and Festivals of Israel. In Baker encyclopedia of the Bible (Vol. 1). Baker Book House.

Martin, J. A. (1985). Ezra. In J. F. Walvoord & R. B. Zuck (Eds.), The Bible Knowledge Commentary: An Exposition of the Scriptures (Vol. 1). Victor Books.

New American Standard Bible: 1995 update. (1995). The Lockman Foundation.

Noss, P. A., & Thomas, K. J. (2005). A Handbook on Ezra and Nehemiah (P. Clarke, S. Brown, L. Dorn, & D. Slager, Eds.). United Bible Societies.

Smith-Christopher, D. L. (2000). Zerubbabel. In D. N. Freedman, A. C. Myers, & A. B. Beck (Eds.), Eerdmans dictionary of the Bible. W.B. Eerdmans.

Dozeman, T. B. (2000). Bread of the Presence. In D. N. Freedman, A. C. Myers, & A. B. Beck (Eds.), Eerdmans dictionary of the Bible. W.B. Eerdmans.

Getz, G. A. (1985). Nehemiah. In J. F. Walvoord & R. B. Zuck (Eds.), The Bible Knowledge Commentary: An Exposition of the Scriptures (Vol. 1). Victor Books.

Knauth, R. J. D. (2000). Sabbatical Year. In D. N. Freedman, A. C. Myers, & A. B. Beck (Eds.), Eerdmans dictionary of the Bible. W.B. Eerdmans.

Knoppers, G. N. (2000). Solomon. In D. N. Freedman, A. C. Myers, & A. B. Beck (Eds.), Eerdmans dictionary of the Bible. W.B. Eerdmans.

Noss, P. A., & Thomas, K. J. (2005). A Handbook on Ezra and Nehemiah (P. Clarke, S. Brown, L. Dorn, & D. Slager, Eds.). United Bible Societies.

Ryrie, Charles, New American Standard Study Bible, (Chicago: Moody Press, 1995).

**4Q**

A Localized Flood? https://biblearchaeology.org/research/chronological-categories/flood-of-noah/4083-a-localized-flood. Accessed 22 Nov. 2023.

Attenborough, Richard. "You'll Find There's Room for All of Us Here." - Gandhi. 2022, https://clip.cafe/gandhi-1982/yo-ll-find-theres-room-us-all/.

Benamozegh, Elia. Israel and Humanity. New York : Paulist Press, 1995, http://archive.org/details/israelhumanity0000bena.

Beth Dagon - Encyclopedia of The Bible - Bible Gateway. https://www.biblegateway.com/resources/encyclopedia-of-the-bible/Beth-Dagon. Accessed 30 Nov. 2023.

Carole Cadwalladr, "Jimmy Carter: 'We never dropped a bomb. We never fired a bullet. We never went to war.'" The Guardian. Published September 10, 2012, Accessed November 29, 2023, http://www.theguardian.com/world/2011/sep/11/president-jimmy-carter-interview.

Carson, D. A. *The Gospel According to John*. Reprint edition, Eerdmans, 1990.

Celebration of Discipline, Special Anniversary Edition: The Path to Spiritual Growth: Foster, Richard J. Accessed 9 Dec. 2023.

"1 Corinthians - Read Epistle and Study Bible Verses Online." Bible Study Tools, https://www.biblestudytools.com/1-corinthians/. Accessed 12 Dec. 2023.

Carr, James. The Battle of New Orleans and the Treaty of Ghent, Diplomatic History, Volume 3, Issue 3, July 1979, Pages 273–282, https://doi.org/10.1111/j.1467-7709.1979.tb00315.x

Deming, William Edwards. "The Unity of 1 Corinthians 5-6." Journal of Biblical Literature 115 (1996): 289.

Editors, Ct. "The 50 Countries Where It's Hardest to Follow Jesus in 2023." News & Reporting, 17 Jan. 2023, https://www.christianitytoday.com/news/2023/january/christian-persecution-2023-countries-open-doors-watch-list.html.

Foxe's Book of Martyrs: Chapter I. https://sacred-texts.com/chr/martyrs/fox101.htm. Accessed 22 Dec. 2023.

Genesis, Exodus, Leviticus, Numbers (The Expositor's Bible. https://www.goodreads.com/book/show/669554.Genesis_Exodus_Leviticus_Numbers. Accessed 18 Nov. 2023.

Graesser, Carl F. "Standing Stones in Ancient Palestine." The Biblical Archaeologist, vol. 35, no. 2, 1972, pp. 34–63, https://doi.org/10.2307/3211046.

Hold to God's Unchanging Hand > Lyrics | Jennie B. Wilson. https://library.timelesstruths.org/music/Hold_to_Gods_Unchanging_Hand/. Accessed 26 Dec. 2023.

Hutchins, R.M. "Thesmophoriazusae" The Great Books of the Western World, N.Y. William Benton, pp. 6471.

Is Your All on the Altar? | Hymnary.Org. https://hymnary.org/text/you_have_longed_for_sweet_peace. Accessed 23 Nov. 2023.

"Κακος | Abarim Publications Theological Dictionary (New Testament Greek)." Abarim Publications, https://www.abarim-publications.com/DictionaryG/k/k-a-k-o-sfin.html. Accessed 26 Dec. 2023.

Long, Phillip J. "What Was the Problem with Food in 1 Corinthians 8:4–8?" Reading Acts, 30 Sept. 2017, https://readingacts.com/2017/09/30/what-was-the-problem-with-food-in-1-corinthians-84-8/.

Megillah 13b, 29a-b: Shekel Cycle mention of Money changers in the temple at Passover. http://www.aishdas.org

Money Changers. https://www.jewishvirtuallibrary.org/money-changers. Accessed 20 Dec. 2023.

National Geographic Society. (2022, June 2). "The Kingdom of Aksum." Retrieved from http://education.nationalgeographic.org/resource/kingdom-aksum.

PASSOVER SACRIFICE - JewishEncyclopedia.Com. https://www.jewishencyclopedia.com/articles/11934-passover-sacrifice. Accessed 25 Nov. 2023.

Passover. https://josephus.org/Passover.htm#events. Accessed 9 Dec. 2023.

Publishers, Thomas Nelson. The NKJV Study Bible: New KJV, Black, Study Bible. Revised edition, Thomas Nelson Inc, 1997.

Reich, Ronny. "A Note on the Population Size of Jerusalem in the Second Temple Period." Revue Biblique (1946-) 121, no. 2 (2014): 298–305. http://www.jstor.org/stable/44092497.

STEVE. "Jewish Educational System." Stevecorn.Com, 1 Nov. 2010, https://stevecorn.com/2010/11/01/jewish-educational-system/.

Strabo, Geography, Book 8, Chapter 6, Section 20. https://www.perseus.tufts.edu/hopper/text?doc=Perseus:abo:tlg,0099,001:8:6:20. Accessed 12 Dec. 2023.

Strong's Hebrew: 430. מֱהֹלִא 'ĕlōhîm (Elohim) -- God, God. https://biblehub.com/hebrew/430.htm. Accessed 29 Nov. 2023.

Strong's Greek: 1839. Ἐξίστημι (Existémi) -- to Displace, to Stand aside From. https://biblehub.com/greek/1839.htm. Accessed 9 Dec. 2023.

Strong's Greek: 5594. Ψύχω (Psuchó) -- to Breathe, Blow, to Make Cool. https://biblehub.com/greek/5594.htm. Accessed 22 Dec. 2023.

Strong's Hebrew: 7200. רָאָה (Raah) -- to See. https://biblehub.com/hebrew/7200.htm. Accessed 25 Nov. 2023.

Strong's Greek: 1784. Ἔντιμος (Entimos) -- Valued, Precious. https://biblehub.com/greek/1784.htm. Accessed 26 Dec. 2023.

Strong's Hebrew: 3290. בקעי (Yaaqob) -- a Son of Isaac, Also His Desc. https://bibleapps.com/hebrew/3290.htm. Accessed 2 Dec. 2023.

The Amish Way: Patient Faith in... by Kraybill, Donald B. https://www.amazon.com/Amish-Way-Patient-Faith-Perilous/dp/111815276X. Accessed 19 Nov. 2023.

The Antiquities of the Jews, by Flavius Josephus. https://gutenberg.org/files/2848/2848-h/2848-h.htm. Accessed 20 Dec. 2023.

"The Jewish War, Volume I." Harvard University Press, https://www.hup.harvard.edu/books/9780674995680. Accessed 21 Dec. 2023.

What Are Some Pharisee Rules for Sabbath Observance? 6 June 2017, https://bibleask.org/rules-pharisees-made-sabbath-observance/.

"What Was Happening around the Globe When Jesus Was Alive? - Explore the Bible." Bible Study Tools, 30 Sept. 2021, https://www.biblestudytools.com/bible-study/explore-the-bible/what-was-happening-around-the-globe-when-jesus-was-alive.html.

Woolley, Leonard. Ur "of the Chaldees." London : Herbert, 1982, http://archive.org/details/urofchaldees0000wool.

* See Full Bibliography online at rhboyd.com.

www.ingramcontent.com/pod-product-compliance
Lightning Source LLC
Chambersburg PA
CBHW081207170426
43198CB00018B/2878